Revolution of the Heart

Revolution of the Heart

A GENEALOGY OF LOVE
IN CHINA, 1900–1950

Haiyan Lee

STANFORD UNIVERSITY PRESS

STANFORD, CALIFORNIA

2007

Stanford University Press
Stanford, California

Printed in the United States of America on acid-free, archival-quality paper

Library of Congress Cataloging-in-Publication Data

Lee, Haiyan.
  Revolution of the heart : a genealogy of love in China, 1900-1950 / Haiyan Lee.
    p. cm.
  Includes bibliographical references and index.
  ISBN-13: 978-0-8047-7327-0 (pbk. : alk. paper)
    1. Chinese literature—History and criticism—Theory, etc. 2. Chinese literature—Philosophy. I. Title. II. Title: Genealogy of love in China, 1900-1950.

PL2261.L415 2007
895.1'09384—dc22

                                    2006009784

An earlier version of Chapter Six was published under the title "Sympathy, Hypocrisy, and the Trauma of Chineseness" in *Modern Chinese Literature and Culture* 16 (2), 2004. I thank the editor, Kirk Denton, for permitting me to revise it for inclusion in this book.

Typeset by inari in 11/14 Adobe Garamond

When we say that nobody but God can see (and, perhaps, can bear to see) the nakedness of a human heart, "nobody" includes one's own self—if only because our sense of unequivocal reality is so bound up with the presence of others that we can never be sure of anything that only we ourselves know and no one else.

— HANNAH ARENDT

Love, however, is feeling, i.e. ethical life in the form of something natural. . . . The first moment in love is that I do not wish to be a self-subsistent and independent person and that, if I were, then I would feel defective and incomplete. The second moment is that I find myself in another person, that I count for something in me. Love, therefore, is the most tremendous contradiction.

— G. W. F. HEGEL

Many people would not have fallen in love had they not heard of it.

— LA ROCHEFOUCAULD

Contents

Acknowledgments

My interest in the topic of love goes back to a graduate seminar on Victorian prose taught by Paul Sawyer at Cornell University. As I worked my way through a paper on George Eliot and the power of sympathy, repeated sensations of déjà vu made me realize that a similar project, albeit on a much larger scale, could be attempted for modern Chinese literature. For the next ten years or so, I became immersed in a subject that seemed to grow in both depth and breadth as I probed its crossroads and pushed its boundaries. Rereading the classics of Chinese literature, perusing early twentieth-century books and periodicals, consulting a broad range of scholarly works on love and related subjects, educating myself on new concepts and modes of analysis—these are the basic steps I have taken in carrying this project forward from notes to dissertation to book. But the engine of progress was crucially sped along by the guidance and support I have received from my graduate advisors, fellow students, colleague-friends, and family.

My greatest intellectual debt is owed to Prasenjit Duara, my graduate school mentor and longtime friend. Over the years, Prasenjit has continuously stimulated my intellectual curiosity and thirst for new ideas and new methods. He read the dissertation and book chapters with care and lent his analytical acuity and theoretical vision to the shaping of this project from its inception. In the revision stage, Tani Barlow, Paul Festa, John Fitzgerald, Viren Murthy, and William Schaefer also read portions of the manuscript and offered invaluable comments and suggestions. I also wish to acknowledge the input of Kirk Denton, Judith Farquhar, Peter Gries, Edward Gunn, Theodore Huters, Dominick LaCapra, Neil Saccamano, Naoki Sakai, Paul Sawyer, Timothy Weston, and Emily Yeh, as well as the organizers and participants of the Cornell Society for the Humanities seminar series, Cornell Comparative

Literature colloquium series, Berkeley Institute for East Asian Studies colloquium series, and Fairbank Center & Reischauer Institute workshop on emotion, where I presented materials drawn from this project. Last, I am most grateful to Yomi Braester and Ban Wang, who read the entire manuscript for Stanford University Press and offered me informed, incisive, and thoroughgoing feedback that was critical in pushing me to expand my dialogues, refine my ideas, and tighten my arguments.

A grant from the American Council of Learned Societies' Committee on Scholarly Communication with China funded the initial dissertation research in Beijing and Shanghai. Further research and writing were made possible by an Andrew W. Mellon postdoctoral fellowship from the Cornell Society for the Humanities and a Junior Faculty Development Award from the Council on Research and Creative Work at the University of Colorado at Boulder. Muriel Bell, Kirsten Oster, and Judith Hibbard at Stanford University Press were instrumental in assisting me to overcome the final hurdles of the revision and manuscript preparation and in bringing the project to fruition. The Eugene M. Kayden Prize Committee at the University of Colorado selected my manuscript as the 2005 winner and provided a generous subvention to help defray the publication cost. An earlier version of Chapter 6 was published under the title "Sympathy, Hypocrisy, and the Trauma of Chineseness" in *Modern Chinese Literature and Culture* 16 (2004). I thank the editor, Kirk Denton, for permitting me to revise it for inclusion in this book.

Devoting the past ten years to the study of sentiment has made me more attuned than ever to the nature and magnitude of support my families on both sides of the Pacific have given me. In particular, my parents-in-law, Paul E. and Mary Lou Festa, have given me a caring and affectionate home that has anchored my nomadic academic life in more ways than I can name. Above all, I dedicate this book, with love, humility, and gratitude, to my husband Paul Festa—companion, accomplice, and critic—for the precious life we share.

Haiyan Lee
August 2006
Boulder, Colorado

Abbreviations

ADT Zhang Jingsheng, ed. 1928. *Aiqing dingze taolun ji* (The rules of love debate). Shanghai: Mei de shudian.

CC Arthur Smith. 1894. *Chinese characteristics*. Fleming H. Revell.

DS Yuan Jing (Yuan Ching) and Kong Jue (Kung Chueh). 1958. *Daughters and sons*. Translated by Sidney Shapiro. Peking: Foreign Languages Press.

EYZ Wen Kang. 1976. *Ernü yingxiong zhuan* (Tales of heroic sons and daughters). Taipei: Sanmin shuju.

FXQ Pan Guangdan. 1993. Feng Xiaoqing: yi jian yinglian zhi yanjiu (Feng Xiaoqing: A study of narcissism. In *Pan Guangdan wenji* (Collected works of Pan Guangdan). Beijing: Beijing daxue chubanshe.

GL Hong Ruizhao. 1928. *Geming yu lian'ai* (Revolution and love). Shanghai: Minzhi shuju.

GQY Chen Quan. 1990. Geming de qian yimu (On the eve of the revolution). In *Zhongguo xiandai wenxue buyi shuxi* (A supplementary compendium of modern Chinese literature). Edited by Kong Fanjin. Jinan: Mingtian chubanshe.

IMW Ding Ling. 1989. *I myself am a woman: Selected writings of Ding Ling*. Edited by Tani E. Barlow and Gary J. Bjorge. Boston: Beacon Press.

LD Han Shaogong. 1995. The leader's demise. In *The Columbia anthology of modern Chinese literature*. Edited by Joseph S. M. Lau and Howard Goldblatt. New York: Columbia University Press.

LX Lu Xun. 1977. *Lu Hsün: Selected stories*. Translated by Yang Hsien-yi and Gladys Yang. New York: Norton.

S Feng Yuanjun. 1998. Separation. In *Writing women in modern China: An anthology of women's literature from the early twentieth century*. Edited by Amy D. Dooling and Kristina M. Torgeson. New York: Columbia University Press.

SK   Yu Dafu. 1981. Sinking. In *Modern Chinese stories and novellas, 1919–1949.* Edited by Joseph S. M. Lau, C. T. Hsia, and Leo Ou-fan Lee. New York: Columbia University Press.

SR   Wu Jianren. 1995. *The sea of regret: Two turn-of-the-century Chinese romantic novels.* Translated by Patrick Hanan. Honolulu: University of Hawaii Press.

SX   Shi Zhecun. 1991. Shi Xiu zhi lian. In *Shi Xiu zhi lian* (The love of Shi Xiu). Beijing: Renmin wenxue chubanshe.

WM   Shi Nai'an. 1993. *Outlaws of the marsh* [aka The water margin]. Translated by Sidney Shapiro. 3 vols. Beijing: Foreign Language Press.

ZFL   Wang Pingling. 1926. *Zhongguo funü de lian'ai guan* (Chinese women's view of love). Shanghai: Guanghua shuju.

Revolution of the Heart

What's Love Got to Do with It?

In the first decade of the twentieth century, Liu Tie yun (aka Liu E, 1857–1909), the author of a popular picaresque novel, *The Travels of Lao Can* (1906–1907), made the puzzling choice to expatiate on weeping in the preface to what is usually considered a novel of social criticism:

> When a baby is born, he weeps, *wa-wa*; and when a man is old and dying, his family form a circle around him and wail, *hao-tao*. Thus weeping is most certainly that with which a man starts and finishes his life. In the interval, the quality of a man is measured by his much or little weeping, for weeping is the expression of a spiritual nature. Spiritual nature is in proportion to weeping: the weeping is not dependent on the external conditions of life being favorable or unfavorable. . . .
>
> Spiritual nature gives birth to feeling; feeling gives birth to weeping. . . . We of this age have our feelings stirred about ourselves and the world, about family and nation, about society, about the various races and religions. The deeper the emotions, the more bitter the weeping. This is why the Scholar of a Hundred Temperings from Hongdu [author's penname] has made this book, *The Travels of {Lao Can}*. (Liu T'ieh-yün 1990, 1–2)

Before I comment on Liu's preface, let me turn to an article by the anthropologist Sulamith Potter on the cultural construction of emotion in rural China. In this article, Potter contrasts the privileged status of emotion in western societies to the Chinese devaluation of emotion as a social force. Speaking reflectively, Potter reminds us that one of "our" most basic assumptions about emotion is that it is the legitimizing basis of all social relationships and social actions. We believe that social relationships are formed and sustained on the basis of emotion, and that any relationship that is not founded on emotional authenticity is impoverished and doomed to dissolution. We therefore invest great amounts of time, money, and effort to initiate, maintain, and fortify emotional ties, and we place a high premium on the expression and enactment of personal feelings. One manifestation of this tendency is the therapeutic culture characterized by a continuous and pervasive attention to psychological processes that "must be defined, explained, expressed, analyzed, understood, and utilized" (1988, 184). We view the expression of feeling as the means by which social relationships are created and renewed. The cultural code of sincerity and authenticity makes it necessary for one to align one's inner life with the formal requirements of the social order or else face the charge of hypocrisy (see also Abu-Lughod 1986; Lutz and Abu-Lughod 1990; Sennett 1992).

Turning to Chinese culture, Potter believes the opposite is true—that is, the Chinese do not ground the social order in the emotional life of individuals. She concedes that the Chinese do have a rich emotional life and that emotions do bear a relationship to social experience. But the key is that in China, emotion is not thought of as a fundamental phenomenon of social life, or one that is capable of creating, perpetuating, injuring, or destroying social relationships. In other words, emotional experience has no formal social consequences. Chinese emotions, therefore, are understood at the level of the "twitch," not at the level of the "wink" (here Potter is borrowing Clifford Geertz's terms). An important corollary is that "sincerity" does not refer to inner feeling, but requires only the proper enactment of civility. Valid social action, then, hinges on a culturally shared code of expression and conduct and does not have to be consistent with inner feeling (Potter 1988).

Let us now return to *The Travels of Lao Can*. Critics have tried to make sense of the oddity of the author's choice to expatiate on weeping by suggesting that at a time of national crisis and social upheaval, a conscientious literatus had every reason to be sad. This explanation, though not entirely unjustified, glosses over the fundamental connection made by the author between weeping and human nature. What Liu Tieyun insists on is precisely what Potter believes not to be the case with the Chinese: to wit, the centrality of sentiment in defining human identity and community. Liu conceptualizes humanity in terms of our innate ability to feel and react to pain, sorrow, and suffering through the gesture of weeping. As an inborn quality, sentiment puts all of humanity on a par, however divided they may be socially and politically. It is the lowest common denominator to which human beings can always appeal to argue for ultimate parity. At the same time that sentiment levels social hierarchies and distinctions, it posits a new principle of ordering human society: the degree of intensity and authenticity of feeling. Thus the more one weeps, the greater one's humanity. And because weeping is dissociated from "the external conditions of life," a happy person living a happy life in a happy time must still weep to prove his or her possession of a "spiritual nature," that is, humanity.

Potter bases her arguments on field research conducted among villagers. One can justifiably challenge her on historical as well as ethnographic grounds. Her assertion that "there is no cultural theory [in Chinese society] that social structure rests on emotional ties" (1988, 185) erases not only the cult of *qing* (sentiment) that flourished in late imperial times, but also the epochal transformations in the twentieth century in which emotion (or love) has become a keyword of social and cultural life. Liu Tieyun's preface, situated at the crossroads between the native discourse of *qing* and the imported episteme of romanticism, offers the best counterevidence to Potter's reduction of Chinese emotional life to the order of an involuntary muscle spasm, a twitch. Liu's philosophy of sentiment constituted merely one instance of multivalent, heterogeneous, and extensive discourses of sentiment encompassing a wide array of texts devoted to the subjects of love, feeling, desire, and sympathy, which form the primary subject of this study.

I begin this introduction by juxtaposing a novelist's effusive tribute to the power of tears on the one hand, and an anthropologist's reflexive observations about the state and status of emotional life among rural Chinese on the other. My purpose is not to prove one or the other wrong but to highlight a fundamental transformation of modernity: the reconceptualization of identity and sociality in emotive terms, or the signification of emotion as the legitimizing basis for a new social order. For this reason, Potter's insights into the cultural construction of emotion among rural Chinese do not lose their potency or relevancy, for they remind us that we cannot take the question of love for granted, even if it seems familiar and natural. They also help to define the cultural context in which modern Chinese literature—and for that matter, the project of modernity—must be understood and critiqued at the most intimate level.

THE DISCOURSE OF SENTIMENT: AN OVERVIEW

From the late Qing and the early Republic (1890s–1910s) through the May Fourth and post–May Fourth periods (1920s–1940s), discourses of sentiment dominated the field of literature and popular culture. Both thematically and ideologically, sentiment figured prominently in the late Qing novels of sentiment (*xieqing xiaoshuo*), Lin Shu's (1852–1924) translations of foreign fiction, the novels of sentiment (*yanqing xiaoshuo*) of the Mandarin Duck and Butterfly School,[1] and the works of May Fourth and post–May Fourth romanticists. The idea of sentiment, a protean concept inherited from the late imperial cult of *qing*, underwent a complex process of transformation with the importation of the Romanticist ideal of free love and the Freudian theory of sexuality in the early twentieth century. This process, marked by collisions, appropriations, and repressions, was inextricably bound up with the ways in which identity and community were renegotiated and reinvented in an era of social, cultural, and political reform and revolution.

At the turn of the twentieth century, with the phenomenal rise of the popular press, sentiment for the first time became the self-conscious marker of a literary genre—the novel of sentiment. It was pioneered by Wu Jianren (aka Wu Woyao, 1866–1910), a prolific novelist and essayist best known for his exposé fiction. Wu's 1906 novella, *Henhai* (The sea of regret), and Lin Shu's classical Chinese rendition of *La dame aux camélias* (1899) became the founding texts of a popular style of romance known as Mandarin Duck and Butterfly fiction, whose influence and share of readership have only recently been seriously assessed. Xu Zhenya's (1889–1937) best-selling *Yu li hun* (Jade pear spirit, 1914) marked the high point of Butterfly romance, though sentimental novels and short stories continued to be written in both classical and vernacular prose in the following decades, cramming the space of fictional monthlies, literary supplements, entertainment magazines, and even political journals. The overwhelming presence of sentimental fiction was certainly not lost on the newly professionalized men of letters who pontificated, in the same print media, on the craft of sentimental fiction and its social utility.

The May Fourth movement (late 1910s and early 1920s) pushed the Mandarin Duck and Butterfly School and its poetics of sentiment to the margins of culture, though by no means also of the market (indeed, the latter's tenacious grip on the readership remained a source of frustration and resentment for May Fourth writers and intellectuals). In place of the Butterfly glossing of sentiment as virtue, the May Fourth generation proposed "love" (*aiqing*) as a symbol of freedom, autonomy, and equality. Hu Shi's (1891–1962) one-act play, "Zhongshen dashi" (The greatest event in life, 1919), set the basic tone for much of the May Fourth representation of "free love" as a battle between tradition and modernity, East and West, feudalism and enlightenment, hypocrisy and authenticity, old and young. Women writers such as Feng Yuanjun (1900–1974) and Ding Ling (1904–1986) rose to national prominence for their poignant portrayals of the passion, ardor, and rebellious courage of young women in love. The intensity of feeling infusing May Fourth fiction was well matched by a new form of essay known for its searing attack on the aridity and hypocrisy of traditional Chinese culture.

The early 1920s were the heyday of free love fueled by the iconoclastic spirit of the May Fourth. Countless stories and essays lashed out against the authoritarian family system, the subjugation of women, and the lack of individual freedom and autonomy. In the late 1920s and 1930s, however, free love came under attack from radical quarters for its bourgeois limitations and from conservative quarters for eroding social morality and the institution of marriage and family. At the same time, there was a veritable explosion of social discourse in the form of psychological, sociological, and historical treatises on love, marriage, and sexuality. Here, love more or less shed its moral weightiness of the previous decades and entered the phenomenological realm of the everyday. One could be tutored in the art of courtship and conjugal love with the aid of how-to books such as *Lian'ai ABC* (Love ABC). It was also in this period that sexuality came out of the shadow of romantic love and became a bona fide social topic and vehicle for radical agendas. While a small number of anarchist thinkers saw sexuality as the means to realizing universal emancipation, more and more voices emerged to condemn the baleful impact of free love/free sex on social mores and the nation-building project. Political ideologues, in particular, called for a total commitment to the nation by subordinating the romantic imperative to that of revolution.

Why was the idea of sentiment so important in an age of enlightenment, nationalism, women's liberation, and commercial culture? By examining the discourses of sentiment in literary, intellectual, and popular writings, this study seeks to understand the conceptual as well as social issues underlying the centrality of sentiment. In particular, it seeks to address the following questions: What was the significance of grounding identity in emotion or sexual desire rather than in kinship or native-place ties—as identity had traditionally been defined in China? What ideological beliefs and values were embodied by sentiment-based subjects such as "the man/woman of sentiment" (*duoqingren*), "the romantic" (*langmanpai*), and "the heroic lover" (*ernü yingxiong*)? In what sense was the changing meaning of *qing*—from asexual virtue to romantic love, sexual desire, and patriotic fervor—part and parcel of the changing conceptions of self, gender, and community in modern China?

Early twentieth-century discourses of sentiment drew linguistic, moral, and epistemological resources from both European Romanticism and the late imperial cult of *qing*. It was declared (as well as demanded) that love was the sole principle underscoring all social relationships: between parents and children, between husband and wife, and among fellow Chinese. Any social institution that was not hinged on the existence and continued articulation of love was believed to be impoverished and illegitimate. During the May Fourth period, the Confucian family and its code of conduct thus came under relentless attack as the epitome of hypocrisy. Filial piety, in particular, was denounced for its empty formality and disregard for the psychological and emotional life of the inner self. Equally vehemently targeted was the institution of arranged marriage. For the modernizing elite endeavoring to make emotion the mainstay of personal identity and social life, it was wholly unacceptable for marriage to be dissociated from the emotional experiences of the marital partners.

The transformations of modernity in China have been extensively researched and debated by scholars across the disciplines; nationalism, civil society, and revolution have been the staple subjects of modern Chinese studies, with the field led primarily by historians, political scientists, and sociologists. Scholars in literary and cultural studies have also made significant contributions by exploring the modern experience in terms of new or hybrid genres, media, ideas, ideologies, and material cultures. In particular, *identity* has come to define an increasingly interdisciplinary mode of inquiry, threading together the methods and concerns of the humanities and social sciences around questions of gender, sexuality, race, class, and nation. But the divide between a humanistic and social scientific approach to modernity persists, in large part due to the failure, on both sides, to theorize the linkages between modern subjectivity and modern political institutions, particularly the nation-state. One exception is John Fitzgerald's work on nationalism in modern China, in which he makes the seminal connection between the melancholy ruminations about the private self in May Fourth writing and the abiding discourse of national awakening. He contends that patriotism was not born in public debates about the political obligation between citizens and the state, but in the "self-awakenings chronicled in romantic fiction," and that romantic fiction helped to "craft and popularize a model of the relationship between self and community that supplied a model for love of nation, or patriotism" (1996, 92, 95). But Fitzgerald does not take up the questions of what this new model of self-society relationship is and why it is conducive to patriotism.

In foregrounding the centrality of sentiment in the transformations of modernity, I aim to offer an empirically as well as theoretically rigorous mapping of the relationship between the modern subject and the modern political community. To anticipate my argument, let me say that the connection resides in the fact that the modern subject is first and foremost a sentimental subject, and that the modern nation is first and foremost a community of sympathy. In dwelling on the brooding, melancholy lover, romantic fiction invents the individual as a self-centered, self-coherent, and ethically autonomous monad. It thus supplies the most ideal subjects for the nation that distinguishes itself from particularistic solidarities such as the family by subscribing to a universalist conception of humanity. In other words, the national community is where ascriptive differences and social hierarchies are, in theory at least, nullified. Everyone can claim the same equal relationship to the nation through citizenship, which is enacted again and again in the romantic motif of falling in love with and marrying *any* of one's fellow citizens regardless of genealogy or social station. The serendipity and impetuosity of the romantic heart thus lend the most compelling support to the ideals of democratic citizenship and primordial national belonging. Conversely, nationalism is also the strongest ally of the May Fourth iconoclasts who launch their assault on the Confucian family in the name of free love *and* patriotism.

Existing studies of the question of love in modern Chinese literature have generally failed to elucidate the dialectic of individualism and nationalism— beyond noting that the two discourses interrelate, and that the former is constrained or subsumed by the latter. In my view, this failure is the result of approaching love as a transhistorical and transcultural constant rather than as a linguistic and cultural resource mobilized and mobilizable by the project of modernity. Moreover, the tendency to regard love as the most natural and time-honored motif in literature is one of the main reasons why the existing scholarship has not dealt with the preoccupation with love either structurally or historically.

To break with this intellectual inertia, I adopt the working assumption that discourses of sentiment are not merely representations or expressions of inner emotions, but articulatory practices that participate in (re)defining the social order and (re)producing forms of self and sociality. Emotion talk is never about emotion pure and simple, but is always also about something else, namely, identity, morality, gender, authority, power, and community. I build this project on the works of many scholars who have contributed to our understanding of the problem of affect in modern Chinese literature. However, given their divergent thematic and/or methodological orientations, they have generally not problematized love as a discursive technology for constructing individual and collective identities or explored how these identities changed over time in relation to the changing meanings of love. In the following sections, I lay out an analytical framework that, I hope, will enable me both to overcome the limitations of previous scholarship and to uncover new grounds of intellectual inquiry.

THE STRUCTURES OF FEELING

I conceive of my project as a critical genealogy of sentiment informed methodologically by poststructuralism. It traces the itinerary of the signifier *qing* by identifying the different points of emergence, appropriation, and interpretation. It is not a history of the idea of sentiment gradually emerging out of the shadows of delusion, miscomprehension, and repression and triumphantly unfolding its true essence under the aegis of enlightenment. Rather, it discerns the process of transformation by capturing the episodic recurrences of *qing* in the cult of sentiment, the exaltation of passionate heroism, the pursuit of free love and gender equality, the quest for national sympathy, the discovery of libido, the dream of sexual liberation, the ideology of conjugal love and middle-class domesticity, and the uneasy alliance of romance and revolution. The genealogical method enables me to overcome the limitations of conventional literary history by first of all calling into question the periodization scheme that posits a radical break between the late Qing/early Republic and the May Fourth periods. This scheme takes May Fourth literature as the beginning of Chinese literary modernity, the moment of triumph of enlightenment thought over the "feudal" ideology of Confucianism, of individual over society, of spontaneous feeling over stultifying formalism. The genealogical method disrupts the received myth of origin by retrieving a repressed history outside of the master narrative of sentimental emancipation. Rather than the originary birthplace of everything modern, the May Fourth will be seen "in the density of the accumulation in which [it is] caught up and which [it] nevertheless never cease[s] to modify, to disturb, to overthrow, and sometimes to destroy" (Foucault 1972, 125). It is a process of appropriation, which forces earlier discourses of sentiment to participate in a different "game"—that of enlightenment, individualism, and nationalism.

The genealogical method also allows me to disentangle myself from the Chinese/western or native/foreign debates about romantic love. I take the position that love was neither wholly imported nor wholly indigenous, but was rather a hybrid signifier that came to play a significant role in the topography of emotions in early twentieth-century China. In other words, I concern myself with what Tani Barlow calls "the localization of signs" (1991). I examine the ways in which new ideas about the self and its emotions entered the local circulation of signs and meanings, clashing, negotiating, or converging with existing notions and generating new significations. I ask how the discourses of sentiment situated the individual in society, what kind of power relations they sought to undermine or reinforce, and what kind of community they endorsed and endeavored to realize.

A central thread of this study is the contradictory role that love played in the project of modernity. On the one hand, love heralded the rise of the private, the personal, and the everyday. The modern self began its career as a sentimental self, proudly parading its tears and sensibilities as the incontrovertible signs of subjectivity, perpetually looking inward, or deep down, for moral and spiritual sustenance, and forever judging and justifying social relationships and actions in reference to the heart. The modern self was also an unheroic self, prone to be suspicious of grand narratives and utopian ideals. It preferred to locate redemption and fulfillment in the quotidian world of work, commerce, and family life. It elevated the values of the everyday—affection, health, human connectedness—as hypervalues that demanded the same kind of

unconditional devotion and sacrifice and that brought the same kind of rewards as that which used to be exclusively associated with the heroic life. This
is what Charles Taylor describes in his book on the making of the modern
identity as "the affirmation of ordinary life." Taylor's moral philosophical
framework will be central to our understanding of the persistent and expansive
interest in such everyday topics as love, sex, marriage, family, and work in the
social imaginary of the Republican period. The affirmation of ordinary life was
necessarily accompanied by a repudiation of supposedly higher modes of activity such as civil service, military exploits, religious pietism, philosophical contemplation, aesthetic cultivation, or political activism (Taylor 1989, 70). Not
surprisingly, this impulse immediately ran up against the hegemonic ideology
of modern China: nationalism.

As a modern ideology, nationalism also spoke the language of love. Ideologically, the nation was organized in emotive terms, emphasizing horizontal
identification, egalitarianism, voluntarism, and patriotic sacrifice. Nationalism insisted on a higher, or heroic, mode of activity—national liberation, resistance, revolution—that transcended and subordinated the everyday, and articulated the tension between the heroic and the everyday as the conflict between
patriotic love and romantic love. In philosophical and social debates, this was
translated into the dialectic between the greater self (*dawo*) and the smaller self
(*xiaowo*). In the first half of the twentieth century, there emerged three overarching modes of response to this basic tension: the Confucian, the enlightenment, and the revolutionary. This study investigates these different modes by
employing Raymond Williams's concept of the "structure of feeling."

Williams introduces the structure of feeling as an alternative to the more
formal concept of "worldview" or "ideology," which, in his view, is limited to
codified beliefs, formations, and institutions. The structure of feeling captures social consciousness as lived experience *in process,* or *in solution,* before it
is "precipitated" and given fixed forms. Feeling here is not opposed to
thought, but "thought as felt and feeling as thought." A structure of feeling
refers to a "particular quality of social experience and relationship, historically
distinct from other particular qualities, which gives the sense of a generation
or of a period" (1977, 131). For Williams, this definition allows him to cir-
cumvent the unproductive dichotomy of base/superstructure or social/per-
sonal. It leaves open the causal relationship between the "quality of social
experience and relationships" on the one hand, and formal institutions and social and economic relations on the other.

Williams uses *feeling* loosely to refer to emergent values and meanings and lived experiences. The key point is that feeling is not opposed to thought, but rather embodies thought. In other words, feeling has structures that can be subjected to rational analysis. This is precisely what concerns anthropologists and moral philosophers of emotion. Charles Lindholm, for example, complains that the dominant epistemes for romantic love—poetry and obscenity—remove the experience from rational discourse, so that "any study of romantic love appears either to be missing the point altogether, or else to be engaging in voyeurism under the guise of research" (1998, 247). In a recent book, Martha Nussbaum extensively and convincingly argues the thesis that emotion embodies thoughts and judgments of values (2001). Other philosophers such as Charles Taylor and Alasdair MacIntyre have also advanced this line of argument, though more in the context of elucidating the origins of the modern identity. The modern identity, according to Taylor, is the ensemble of largely unarticulated understandings of "what it is to be a human agent" in the modern West. It has three major facets: (1) inwardness, or the idea that the individual has "a self" with inner depths, (2) the affirmation of ordinary life, and (3) the expressivist notion of "nature" as an inner moral source (1989, ix–x). In his monumental effort to map out the connections between identity and morality, Taylor brings a philosopher's insights to bear on the Romantic movement, which, according to him, consolidated the expressivist model of self that grounded ethical subjectivity in a human nature largely defined in affective terms. The Romantics gave such "a central and positive place to sentiment . . . [that] it is through our feelings that we get to the deepest moral and, indeed, cosmic truths" (371).

In his critique of the modern identity, MacIntyre contrasts the modern "emotivist self" (unfavorably) to the traditional self (which he sometimes calls the "heroic self"): the latter is wholly defined by one's membership in a variety of social groups such as family, lineage, local community, and political institution. Beneath one's membership in these interlocking groups, there is no hidden core, or "the real me" (1984, 33). The ideas of social "roles," "masks," or "personae" are distinctly modern inventions. In the heroic society (which resembles Potter's rural Chinese society), a man is what he does; he has no hidden depths. Moral judgments are formed on the basis of the ethics of action, not on a hermeneutics of intention. The emotivist self, on the contrary, prides itself on being an autonomous moral agent freed from the hierarchy and teleology of traditional society. Its moral authority resides squarely within itself, rather than in the external authorities of traditional morality. This newly invented interior space, or what Taylor calls "inwardness," is designated as the seat of the individual truth and the fountainhead of one's desire and action. Emotion, perceived as a quintessentially natural and private phenomenon, is thought to constitute the very essence of that interior space, the core of the self.[2]

The distinction between the modern expressivist or emotivist self and the traditional heroic self as mapped out by Taylor, MacIntyre, and other moral philosophers dovetails with what a number of anthropologists, including Potter, have said about the subject of emotion in nonwestern versus western societies. In general, these anthropologists aim to accomplish two tasks, the first of which is to treat discourses of emotion as social practices within diverse ethnographic contexts. Their second goal is to cast reflexive light on received western notions about the self and on the entrenched oppositions between emotion and reason, instinct and rationality, body and mind, nature and culture, individual freedom and social restraint, private sentiment and public morality, and inner truth and outer expression.

The two tasks are so intertwined that anthropologists devote nearly as much attention to their own "modern western" assumptions as they do to the social construction of emotion in their target cultures. Arjun Appadurai's study of praise in Hindu India, for example, begins with a reflection on the variability of the relationship between language, feeling, and what he calls "the topographies of the self" in human societies. He points out that "our" commonsense beliefs about intention and expression, about "real feelings" as opposed to "voiced sentiments," about "hypocritical" subterfuges serving to conceal actual desires and feelings, are no more than our embodied doxa misrepresented as universal truths about the relationship between affect and expression (1990, 92). Approaching praise as an "improvisatory practice," Appadurai shows that sentimental bonds can be created quite independently of the "real" feelings of the persons involved by the skillful orchestration of a shared, formulaic, and publicly understood set of codes or gestures. This conclusion casts a questioning glance at the universality of the core western topography of the "person," which, in Appadurai's gloss, features a linear narrative of progress and a spatial image of layers. The narrative (epitomized in the paradigmatic genre of bildungsroman) has it that the biologically anterior "self," through the vicissitudes of "personal development," becomes a recognizable though distinct moral unit, the "individual." The spatial image

grounds personal truth in the "affective bedrock" and holds language, particularly public expressions, suspect for its supposed distance from the somatic
side of personality (93).

Researching the Bedouin culture of poetry recitation, Lila Abu-Lughod is
drawn to the discrepancy between the amorous feelings expressed in poems
and the rigid sense of modesty that envelops daily communications. She
probes the interplay between the moral sentiment of modesty as a form of def-
erence and an index of hierarchy tied up with relations of power on the one
hand, and the poetic sentiment of love as a discourse of defiance, autonomy,
and freedom on the other (1986, 1990). But she refuses to privilege the poetic
sentiments as revealing a truer self because such a move would impose a characteristically western "hermeneutics of feeling" (or what Appadurai calls "the
topography of self") that takes feeling as the touchstone of personal reality
(1990, 24). In a more systematic and historically informed analysis of various
"western" understandings of the relationship between language, emotion,
and the self, Catherine Lutz points out that the concept of emotion is a master
category that accentuates much of the modern essentialist thinking about
self, consciousness, and society: "Emotions have always been sought in the
supposedly more permanent structures of human existence—in spleens,
souls, genes, human nature, and individual psychology, rather than in history,
culture, ideology, and temporary human purposes" (1986, 287). Even so, as
the product of a long and contested history, contemporary ideas about emotion are far from reducible to a monolith that can be facilely contrasted to
nonwestern understandings.

According to Lutz, emotion has been chiefly understood in opposition to
two notions: rational thought and estrangement. When opposed to rational
thought, emotion is evaluated either negatively as irrational or instinctual,
as biological imperatives that are precultural and potentially antisocial, or
positively as natural facts, as raw, wild, and primitive forces. In this tradition
women are designated as the gender of emotionality, which in turn proves
their weakness and further justifies their exclusion from positions of power
and responsibility. Alternatively, the Romantic tradition equates the natural
with "the uncorrupted, the pure, the honest, and the original" (296). Hence
things of the heart are "the true, real seat of the individual self," and things
of the mind are the superficial, social self (296). To a lesser extent, emotion
is also opposed to a negatively evaluated estrangement from the world, in
the same way that life is opposed to death, community and connection to

alienation, commitment and value to nihilism (290). In this sense, to say that someone is "unemotional" is to suggest that he or she is withdrawn, alienated, or even catatonic. It also suggests that "to have feelings is to be truly human, which is to say, transcendent of the purely physical" (295). Paradoxically, emotion is both human beings' closest link to nature and their salvation from the brute state of nature.

Owen Lynch also explores emotion's paradoxical relationship to nature through the Enlightenment-inspired "physicalist theory," a theory that underlies much of the western commonsensical understanding of emotion. Paying close attention to the everyday language used to describe emotional experience, Lynch points out that when the verb *to feel* is extended from organic sensations to psychosomatic "feelings," emotion is reified as things and equated with physiological states. Thus, "just as one feels the heat of fire, so too one feels the heat of rage" (1990, 5). As such, emotions are always passively experienced: "they are 'things' that happen to us, we are 'overwhelmed' by them, they 'explode' in us, they 'paralyze' us, we are 'hurt' by them, and they 'threaten to get out of control'" (5). The common hydraulic metaphor vividly conjures up the image of a reservoir of brimming psychic energy ready to swell up and break the dam of rationality. It also postulates the person as a layered entity, with emotions stored in "the lower faculties of the body" and completely separate from "the higher faculty of the mind" (5). The physicalist conception shores up the Enlightenment conviction that at bottom all human beings, regardless of race, gender, and class, share common emotional attributes, even if they share nothing else (5).

Contra the physicalist theory, Lynch promotes a social constructionist approach to emotion. For a social constructionist, emotions are "appraisals" or "judgments of situations based on cultural beliefs and values" (9). As appraisals, emotions are not a natural given but rather learned behavior and inevitably implicate agent responsibility. In western societies, emotions are no less "moral judgments about prescribed or expected responses to social situations" than they are in Indian society on which Lynch focuses most of his discussion. Moreover, as Michel Foucault puts it, "our feeling" has been "the main field of morality, the part of ourselves which is most relevant for morality" (1997, 263). Foucault's later work shows that sexuality would join feeling as the part of ourselves that is most relevant for ethical judgment (Foucault 1997, 263). However, feeling or sexuality has not been the main field of morality or the primary ethical substance at all times, nor has it been universally bound up with issues of selfhood and identity.[3] The linkage between emotion and identity, for example, is largely absent in the Confucian model of personhood. In classical Chinese narratives, as in classical western art, love as a "subjective spiritual depth of feeling"—that is, as a substance of identity—does not exist; or when it does appear, it is usually only a subordinate feature connected with "sensuous enjoyment" (Hegel 1975, 1:563). It is in this sense that I find valuable Potter's insights on the emotional life of the Chinese peasantry. At the very least, her analysis serves to alert us to those moments in the genealogy of love that disrupt the East/West binarisms (as, for instance, Liu Tieyun's preface), moments in which love is no longer mere sensuous enjoyment, but pertains to basic conceptions of human nature and basic problems of ethics.

Liu Tieyun's ode to weeping can be placed in the long lineage of the late imperial cult of *qing* that brought sentiment from the margins of the ethical field to the center and made it a foundational principle of identity. The cult enthroned the heart as an alternative moral authority, without positing a radical break between the inner self and the outer social order. It was perhaps the most radical critique of Confucian ethics on behalf of the inner self, but as I will argue in this study, it did not pit the individual against society in the manner of iconoclastic May Fourth intellectuals. The spokesmen of the cult worked within the parameters of Confucian ethics, endeavoring to reinterpret the essential Confucian virtues as homologous and substitute affective reciprocity for ritual hierarchy. For this reason, I will use the term "the Confucian structure of feeling" to characterize both the cult of *qing* and its recuperation in Butterfly sentimental fiction.

The Confucian structure of feeling is somewhat counterintuitive in that it encompasses a range of values and experiences that are critical of Confucian orthodoxy (in late imperial times) as well as modern romanticism (early 1900s). My usage is therefore intended to highlight its peculiar location in the genealogy of love as a dispersed element of modernity. The Confucian structure of feeling is an essentially modern formation in its celebration of feeling as fundamental to human existence, its rendering of ethical codes into subjectively meaningful experience, and its dramatization of what Hegel calls "love's collisions" with the interests of the state and the family (1975, 1:566). The May Fourth Movement, however, introduced "the enlightenment structure of feeling," pursuing a radical epistemic break with the Confucian structure, and rejecting Confucian values in favor of an expressivist or physicalist understanding of emotion and other universalizing norms of enlightenment humanism and nationalism. If the Confucian structure of feeling is preoccupied with "virtuous sentiments," then the enlightenment structure is obsessed with "free love." The dispute and contestation between these two modes raged on in the 1920s but were largely overcome by a more hegemonic mode, or what I call "the revolutionary structure of feeling."

Promoted primarily by intellectuals and writers aligned with the Chinese Communist Party (CCP) and the Nationalist Party (KMT), the revolutionary structure of feeling negates the radical implications of the enlightenment structure while recuperating elements of the Confucian structure. Its best-known literary articulation, "revolution plus romance," is an attempt to resolve the basic conflict of modernity between the heroic and the everyday as well as to address the paradoxical status of emotion in the modern episteme. Love now "supplements" subjectivity, but it is also sternly called upon to "efface its supplementary role" (Terada 2001, 8) so that it does not contest the hegemony of the collective project.

I deploy the structure of feeling to approach a complex process of hybridization whose inevitable clashes, compromises, convergences, and dispersals cannot be adequately dealt with through the anthropological mode of binary analysis. While my project has benefited a great deal from the anthropological critique of the prevailing western assumptions of emotion, I am critical of anthropologists' tendency to reduce emotion in nonwestern cultures to the ahistorical antithesis of western constructs. What they often neglect is the profound impact of colonialism on the moral and epistemological paradigms of the colonized. In the semicolonial context of China, the enlightenment project effected a wrenching transformation in social imaginaries, much of which was articulated in a language of feeling and debated as a problem of love. Writers and readers appropriated the Romanticist celebrations of passion and individual autonomy to critique or redact indigenous Confucian discourses of sentiment. The contentious relationship between romantic love and filial piety, for example, became an important site on which new modes of subjectivity and sociality were worked out. By using the structure of feeling to capture broad paradigmatic shifts, I aim to show that modern Chinese conceptions of love are not just a creation of the enlightenment project spearheaded by the modernizing elite, but a deeply historical product of colonial modernity marked by cross-hybridization, displacement, contestation, and repression. It is neither the enduring sign of universal humanity, nor the crystallization of an alien tradition taken by some anthropologists to be the ultimate site of alterity.[4]

The structure of feeling also allows me to distance my project from the narrow or exclusive focus on sexuality that has been the trend in the wake of Foucault's *The History of Sexuality* (1990a). Many studies that fold sexuality into more conventional modes of inquiry such as feminism, Marxism, nationalism, and racism have uncritically reproduced the modern biases that Foucault critiqued, thereby failing to situate sexuality within the larger problematics of the history of morals and the history of the subject. But Foucault cannot be blamed for the persistent bias against morality talk, the overt or covert preference for sexual frankness in historical materials, and the continued privileging of sexuality as a naturalized and unproblematic category of inquiry.[5] For this, we need to look no further than what Foucault himself has singled out for trenchant critique: the repressive hypothesis, a legacy of psychoanalysis and the sexual liberation movements of the mid-twentieth century.

We may all sometimes find it difficult completely to shed the peculiarly twentieth-century conviction that the Victorians and their counterparts in other cultures are hopelessly repressed and insufferably conceited. We are apt to detect hypocrisy (with all our twentieth-century assumptions about the distance between private feeling and public expression), and we are all too quick to dismiss talk of virtue as a mask of falsehood and to reduce talk of love to the subterfuge or sublimation of an ultimate reality—sexual desire. The historically important distinction of spiritual versus physical love is often brushed aside as the by-product of erstwhile naïveté or hypocrisy. Critics find themselves in search of open-minded attitudes toward sex in historical and literary archives, working with the presupposition that the more candid the description, the more enlightened and/or subversive the author, the text, or the period. The anachronistic projection of twentieth-century assumptions onto earlier discursive formations has in fact greatly contributed to the paucity of rigorous treatment of sentiment despite its centrality in modern Chinese culture. My decision to canvas the full spectrum of the discourses of sentiment, be they conservative or liberal, sexually frank or modest, as subjective technologies of individual and community is thus an attempt to overcome these biases.

The book is structured chronologically: I begin with the late Qing (Part 1), move through the Republican and, to a lesser extent, the socialist periods (Parts 2 and 3), and conclude with the reform era (Conclusion). Intersecting the chronology is the threefold scheme that registers the major shifts in the changing notion of love: the Confucian, the enlightenment, and the revolutionary structure of feeling. However, even the necessarily sketchy summaries provided below show that the three periods do not correlate neatly with the three structures of feeling. Not only are there overlaps and recuperations between the periods, but within each period, there is no shortage of rivalries and contestations.

In Part 1, I begin with a short "prehistory" of sentiment by rereading three representative texts of the Ming-Qing cult of *qing* movement: Feng Menglong's (1574–1646) *The Anatomy of Love*, Tang Xianzu's (1550–1616) *The Peony Pavilion*, and Cao Xueqin's (1715?–1763) *The Dream of the Red Chamber*. These texts are important not only as milestones in the history of sentiment, but also because late Qing and early Republican writers of sentimental fiction self-consciously positioned themselves as the inheritors of the cult of *qing*. I then turn to a mid-nineteenth-century novel called *A Tale of Heroic Sons and Daughters*, one of the earliest texts to combine the heroic and the sentimental romance. I seek to understand why these two separate genres were brought together and to what ideological effect. My main objective in Part 1, however, is to delineate the Confucian structure of feeling as articulated in the sentimental writings of the Mandarin Duck and Butterfly School. Beginning with Wu Jianren's *Henhai* (Sea of regret, 1906) and moving among both well-known Butterfly texts such as *Yu li hun* and run-of-the-mill sentimental short stories, I show how Butterfly fiction attempts to redact the Confucian structure of feeling for the age of enlightenment.

In Part 2, I aim to show how the ascendancy of the romantic and psychoanalytic definitions of love displaced earlier cosmic-ethical definitions, and how free love—the key trope of universal subjectivity—was bound up with the iconoclastic project of overthrowing the Confucian family order. In Chapter 3, I construct a genealogy of romance both as a literary genre and as a cultural signifier. I use Charles Taylor's moral philosophical categories to examine the genealogical recurrences of romance first as *le grand amour*, then as conjugal love, and then as a game. The texts under examination include May Fourth classics such as "Regret for the Past" and "Miss Sophia's Diary" and the works of Feng Yuanjun, Ling Shuhua (1900–1990), Shi Zhecun (1905–2003), Zhang Henshui (1895–1967), and Zhang Ailing (1920–1995).

In Chapter 4, I map the social discourse of love by focusing on a series of debates wherein educators, journalists, writers, and common readers sought to reevaluate free love in an increasingly politicized climate. These debates may revolve around a well-publicized matrimonial affair, a love murder, or a provocative opinion piece. I structure the debates both topically (by the specific agent provocateur) and ideologically (by the radical, moderate, or conservative positions taken by the participants). My primary example of topical debate is the "rules of love" debate led by Zhang Jingsheng (1888–1970) in the early 1920s. For the latter type, I outline several overlapping debates waged among conservatives, liberals, and anarchists. I link these debates to a body of texts also concerned with the nature and rules of love: self-help literature. Chapter 5 documents an important shift in the discourse of sentiment: with the introduction of Freud and the sexual sciences, sexuality acquired legitimacy apart from love and came to displace love in defining the subject. I choose three case studies to illustrate the repressive hypothesis at work in constructing the sexual subject: Pan Guangdan's psychobiography of the legendary poetess Feng Xiaoqing, Yuan Changying's Freudian feminist rewriting of the ancient ballad "Southeast Flies the Peacock," and Shi Zhecun's pathography of misogyny and perversity in his retelling of an episode from *The Water Margin*.

In Part 3, I return to a canonical moment of modern Chinese literature and focus on the nationalist definition of love that underscores literary modernity as a whole. I begin, in Chapter 6, with Lu Xun (1881–1936) and revisit some of his classic texts depicting the crowd as a countercommunity devoid of love and sympathy. Here I highlight the quest for nationhood by examining the linkage between the notion of national sympathy and the discourse of national character. I also read May Fourth polemical essays that denounce the Confucian order for its failure to achieve emotional authenticity, or its "hypocrisy." Last, I reread Yu Dafu's (1896–1945) notorious "Sinking" to expose the perverse logic of national sympathy. In Chapter 7, I examine the reformulation of the late imperial *ernü yingxiong* (love and heroism) ideal in the new genre of "revolution plus romance." I am interested in the ways in which party ideologues on both the left and right sought to discipline and appropriate this popular genre in order to reassert the priority of the collective over the individual and everyday. I read the works of Jiang Guangci (1901–1931), Ding Ling, Chen Quan (1903–1969), and others who endeavored to politicize a commercialized lifeworld preoccupied with the pleasures and anxieties of everyday life. I show that the apparently formulaic genre is in fact deconstructive in its drive to render love a supplement to revolutionary subjectivity. The variations on the formula are indeed different strategies with which the revolutionary structure of feeling attempts to conceal love's supplementarity.

The war of resistance against Japan (1937–1945) and the communist revolution dramatically reconfigured the terms and parameters of the literary and cultural fields. In the socialist period, love's many shades of meaning metamorphosed into a few bold strokes associated with radically new regimes of sanctity and exclusion. The discourse of sentiment was deployed in new games of truth to invent new subjects and communities (Chapter 7). In my concluding chapter, I attempt to draw some larger points about the trajectory of love in modern China and the role it played in the monumental reconstruction of identity and ethics.

NOTES ON TERMINOLOGY

I come to the question of terminology at the end of this introduction with considerable trepidation. If I may be allowed to speak in metaphors for a moment, I would say that the entire book is, in a sense, a sustained wrestling with an ever-shifting team of players. These players appear, disappear, and reappear; they come into the arena alone or in pairs; they form alliances, break them up, and make enemies; they wear beguiling masks and wigs, speak in borrowed tongues, and make grandiose claims. They are, of course, the family of affective terms that make up the warp of this study: *qing, ai, yu, aiqing, qingyu, xingyu, se, ganqing, qinggan, tongqing*. Their sometimes nemeses and sometimes partners—*li* (ritual), *lijiao* (Confucianism), *lizhi* (reason), *lixing* (rationality), *daode* (morality), *renge* (character), *xiao* (filiality), *yingxiong* (heroism), *geming* (revolution)—are the woof. Needless to say, translating these terms is always a work in progress, as it were. To avoid a total collapse of terminological coherence, I follow three provisional principles. First, I use "love" in both the narrow and broad senses of the English word which correlate with the Greek notions of *eros* and *agape*. When necessary, I use "romantic love" to invoke *eros*. Second, I switch to "sentiment," "feeling," or "emotion" (and their adjectival forms) when I engage relatively abstract or philosophical materials or when I need an overarching term to encompass the entire gamut of words of affect. For instance, I mostly translate *qing* as "sentiment" when it appears by itself (for example, in the late imperial cult of *qing*) or in relation to "reason" (*li, lizhi, lixing*), "ritual" (*li, lijiao*), or "virtue" (*de, daode*).

Third, in individual cases, I generally follow the conventional practice of translating *ai, lian'ai*, and *aiqing* as love or romantic love, *yu, qingyu*, and *xingyu* as sexual desire, *ganqing* and *qinggan* as passion or emotion, and *tong-qing* as sympathy or pity. These terms have complex lexicographical histories, and although my interest is not primarily philological, I do attend to their interactions with cognate Chinese (and sometimes Japanese) words and with their English translations. In translating these terms, I also bring into play the subtle differences in historical and cultural connotation among familiar emotion words in English. As Catherine Lutz notes, feeling tends to be used to refer to bodily sensations, whereas passion tends, more than emotion, to refer specifically to love or sexual desire (1986, 304–5, n2). Rei Terada makes a more rigorous set of distinctions. For her, *emotion* connotes a psychological and interpretive experience whose physiological manifestation is *affect*. *Feeling* is a more capacious term in that it encompasses both affects and emotions (2001, 4). The point in trying to distinguish these emotion words, even if it might appear to be a self-defeating task, is that they organize different lived experiences and moral visions, and are decidedly *not* a baroque collection of labels designating the same essential reality. My rule of thumb is flexible attentiveness. I try to choose English renditions most suitable for the context, taking into full consideration the ideational and ideological baggage carried over in the process. I vary my terminology according to the dictates of linguistic felicity as well as cultural sensitivity, and according to how a particular term is situated in a web of relational signs and references.

PART ONE

The Confucian Structure of Feeling

The Cult of *Qing*

Students of Ming-Qing cultural history (fourteenth to nineteenth century) have seldom failed to note the centrality of sentiment (*qing*) and desire (*yu*) in the philosophical, literary, and theatrical discourses of the time. They have generally termed the phenomenon the "cult of *qing*" movement and situated it in the context of a maturing money economy, a rising merchant middle class, and a trend toward gender equalization, particularly in the lower Yangzi region (*Jiangnan*). There has also been a tendency to characterize the cult as a countercultural movement led by disaffected literati who rejected the rigid morality of Confucian ritualism in favor of spontaneous expressions of natural human desires. This characterization, although not wholly mistaken, proceeds largely from the modern dualism of reason and emotion and offers us too thin a background against which to understand the cultural permutations of late Qing sentimentalism and May Fourth romanticism.

In this chapter, I reevaluate the "cult of *qing*" movement by way of three key texts: *The Peony Pavilion*, *The Anatomy of Love*, and *The Dream of the Red Chamber*. My primary purpose here is not so much to offer new, text-based interpretations of these well-studied works, as to assess their broader significance in mapping the topography of sentiment in late imperial China. I also reread Wen Kang's *A Tale of Heroic Sons and Daughters* in order to show that by the mid-nineteenth century, there emerged a distinctive "Confucian structure of feeling" that combined elements from orthodox Confucianism as well as the cult of *qing* and that was both repudiated and recuperated by later transformations.

THE CONFUCIAN STRUCTURE OF FEELING

Sponsored by the imperial state and embedded in social institutions (kinship and bureaucracy) and rituals (the state cult and ancestor worship), orthodox Confucianism emphasizes ritual principles and social ethics (*lijiao*), or what Kwang-ching Liu calls "the socioreligious ethic." It is tolerant of the spiritual and esoteric pursuits of other religions so long as its core tenet governing the fundamentals of social relationships and the cosmic order—the Three Bonds (*sangang*) (also the Five Relations [*wulun*] or Five Constant Virtues [*wuchang*])—is not challenged. The Three Bonds essentially make the monarch, the parent, and the husband religious symbols commanding unconditional devotion (Liu 1990, 54). As a belief system, Confucianism also acknowledges a transcendent entity—Heaven—presiding over the cosmos (the natural and social world as one) and sanctioning the moral authority of the monarch, parent, and husband. The Heavenly will is a moral one—"on the side of goodness" (55). It is also inexorable, so the moral authority of these earthly figures is binding and not subject to negotiation. In the Confucian conception, to be a moral person is to embody the cosmic order and fulfill one's destiny by aligning oneself with the socioethical injunctions codified in the classics. Liu argues that Confucian orthodoxy is more than just a set of moral codes: "the dictates of one's best self almost always included filial piety, wifely devotion, and loyalty to the monarch—virtues that could be regarded as mere conventions, but could nonetheless touch on the sublime" (55).

Liu emphasizes the religious quality of Confucianism to account for its simultaneous austerity and elasticity. Closely related to this religiosity is the little-theorized affective dimension of orthodox Confucianism, or what might be called "Confucian sentimentality." Confucian sentimentality sanctifies a hierarchical mode of cathexis centering mostly on two of the Three Bonds—the bonds between lord and subject and between parent and child. The two bonds are male-centric (pertaining only to the male child/subject) and are posited as metonymic equivalents. In other words, a filial (*xiao*) son is necessarily a loyal (*zhong*) subject and vice versa (whereas the husband-wife relation is equivalent with the two primary bonds only *metaphorically*). Within each bond, the emotional cathexis or investment is in theory reciprocal: the lord bestows benevolence (*ren* or *en*) in return for loyalty; the parent exudes kindness (*en* or *ci*) in return for filial devotion. However, reciprocity is secondary to hierarchy, and it is loyalty and filiality that constitute the foundational moral sentiments in orthodox Confucianism. This, to a considerable degree, accounts for the preponderance of filial stories over stories about parental affection.

The discursive history of Confucian sentimentality prior to the Ming is relatively sparse. Revisionist claims notwithstanding, Confucius (551?–478? BCE) was, at least on record, reticent on the matter of emotion. It has been pointed out that *qing* appears only once in the *Analects,* where it actually means "trust," not "emotion" (Wang 1999, 9). Mencius (ca. 372–289 BCE) has just a few more words to say about *qing*: "If you allow people to follow their feelings [*qing*], they will be able to do good" (quoted in Huang 1998, 154). Here *qing* is equated with one's moral nature (*xing*) which for Mencius is innately good. In poetry criticism, *qing* is given the pride of place by Lu Ji (261–303), who redefines poetry as the "expression of emotion" (*shi yan qing*) (Huang 1998, 160). This formulation invokes the more familiar maxim: "Poetry expresses the mind's intent" (*shi yan zhi*). In Marston Anderson's opinion, this does not amount to an expressive theory of art for the author is understood less as an autonomous creator than as a vessel through which the patterns or principles (*wen*) of nature and culture manifest themselves (1990, 13). Whether it is the mind's intent or emotion, poetry is the product of harmonizing the intellect with the propensity of things, of uniting the heart/mind with the cosmos, of fusing inner emotion (*qing*) with outer scene/situation (*jing*). The ubiquitous term of Chinese poetry criticism, *qingjing*, bespeaks precisely this nonmimetic orientation. In this context, the meaning of *qing* is firmly situated within the Confucian framework of moral sentiment. It connotes "communal and universally shared human emotions rather than private, antisocial passions" (19–20).[1]

Since the Han (206 BCE–220 CE), the association of poetry with moral sentiment is registered in the following expression: "Poetry inspired by emotion should arrive at ritual propriety" (*fa yu qing, zhi yu liyi*). In other words, emotion must be delimited and made meaningful by ritual, lest it turn into antisocial passion, or excessive desire (*yu*) or lust (*yin*). There is an implied sense that although *qing* may be made "good," it is somehow inherently susceptible to corruption and its nature seems to incline it toward the negative end of the moral spectrum. In Song neo-Confucianism, *xing, qing,* and *yu* are affixed in a hierarchy, as aptly illustrated by Zhu Xi's (1130–1200) water metaphor: If *xing* can be compared to still water, then *qing* is flowing water and *yu* turbulent waves threatening to overflow the dam of ritual propriety (Huang 1998, 155–57). Note that sentiment and desire are distinguished from *xing* not categorically but in terms of the distinction between the state of tranquility (*weifa*) and that of arousal (*yifa*). Indeed, sentiment and desire are only altered states of human nature, not alien or unknown forces that must be subjected to repression (as the id in Freud). It is important to bear this in mind when we speak of the better known ethico-ontological dichotomies of *tianli* (heavenly principle) and *renyu* (human desire), *li* (metaphysical principles) and *qi* (ether, material forms in the experiential realm), *li* (ritual) and *qing/yu*. We cannot easily align these dichotomies with the enlightenment binary oppositions of reason and passion, morality and desire, which presuppose a far more radical duality of mind and body.

Practical pronouncements on emotion in the Confucian classics usually concern the father-son relation (and, to a lesser extent, the mother-son relation). For example, the *Sanzi jing* (The three-character classic), a primer of Confucian ethics that first appeared in the thirteenth century, prescribes "affection" of a son for his father. The *Xiao jing* (The book of filial piety) gives instruction on how to enact filial affection: "In serving his parents, a filial son renders utmost reverence to them while at home; he supports them with joy; he gives them tender care in sickness; he grieves at their death; he sacrifices to them in solemnity" (quoted in Liu 1990, 86). Confucian sentimentality thus charts out a grid of moral sentiments that regulates behavior and reproduces normative identities as deeply felt. The relative paucity of affective terms and references in the classics is not necessarily a sign of emotional aridity. Rather, it stems from the fact that sentiments such as filial piety are moral requisites for all properly socialized persons. In other words, moral sentiments are not a matter of voluntary choice or free-willed commitment. The shift from ethical imperative to voluntary choice is precisely the transformation wrought by the cult of *qing* and given radical formulations in the twentieth century.

That Confucian sentimentality is most forthright and commendatory about hierarchical familial emotions has its correlation in the overwhelmingly familial "emotional orientation" (*ganqing dingxiang*) that Fei Xiaotong (1910–

2005) finds in rural Chinese society in the early twentieth century. The family, he observes, subordinates the conjugal relationship to vertical kin relations and discourages open expressions of emotional attachment between the couple, while ultimately subordinating all emotional life to the life of productivity (*shiye*) (Fei Xiaotong 1991, 46–52). Fei's insights about the emotional orientation of the peasantry tally with Charles Lindholm's observation that "relative stable societies with solidified extended families, age-sets and other encompassing social networks that offer alternative forms of belonging and experiences of personal transcendence through participation in group rituals are not prone to valuing romantic involvement" (1998, 257). In such societies, Lindholm maintains, romantic love is usually pursued clandestinely, or in milieu outside formal kinship structures, to wit, in brothel or courtesan establishments (250–54). It is regarded with distrust by mainstream society and is rarely a legitimate basis for marriage, which is a public institution charged with political purposes and socioeconomic functions. Nor can romance constitute the primary basis for identity. Instead, identity is forged in the hierarchical world of family and state.

Other scholars have stressed that premodern Chinese society (and contemporary peasant society to some extent) was organized along differences of power, rank, and kin more than gender (Barlow 1994; Kutcher 2000; Mann 2000; Potter 1988; Song 2004). It was a rigorously gender-segregated society, and its gender norms were enmeshed in an array of political and social configurations. The male/female dyad did not constitute a fundamental principle of identity. Susan Mann reminds us that men, especially upwardly mobile men, spent most of their social life in exclusive male company and were able to forge strong and lasting ties of patronage, protection, and friendship. Male homosociality, then, was a product of the normative family order, the examination system, and patterns of male sojourning. She points to a wealth of historical texts that testify to the "deep emotional attachment" that men formed outside the kinship system: from the legendary oath of the Peach Garden[2] to empathic personal memoirs to wistful poetry of parting and longing (2000). At the village level, affective life outside the family also revolves around horizontal homosocial ties. The rare moments of intimacy are usually found among persons of the same gender and age group—Fei Xiaotong gives the example of men, who usually have nothing to say to their wives, talking, laughing, and fraternizing with verve in teahouses, opium dens, even street corners and alleyways (1991, 46). Because homosociality offset the rigidity of hierarchies in celebrating nonascriptive associations, it was highly amenable to heterodox appropriations—by secret societies, sectarian religious groups, literary or political cliques, and to a limited extent, women. It was therefore regarded with circumspection by orthodox Confucians, who issued precepts and parables to drain its emotional force and delimit its subversive potential. Apropos of "friendship," the only non–kin- and non–state-oriented relationship in the Confucian social imaginary, Norman Kutcher makes this point: "So geared was the Confucian schema of social relations around the hierarchical needs of the state-family that equality in friendship was potentially subversive" (2000, 1616).

The notion of friendship that Kutcher examines, needless to say, pertains only to men. Although Fei Xiaotong suggests that men and women are equally able to move in same-sex sociability, it is the masculine mode of homosociality that enjoys most discursive visibility and sanctification. Emotional ebullience is positively reckoned so long as it remains a masculine affair, contrary to popular perceptions about men's disinclination to shed tears. Memorable stories are told and retold about the strength of the bond among men in their various social roles as benevolent lords, loyal ministers, matchless warriors, resourceful counselors, reckless assassins, roving bandits, upright scholar-officials, bohemian poets/artists, reclusive hermits, and, of course, fathers and sons. In the *Romance of the Three Kingdoms*, Liu Bei, the self-proclaimed heir to the Han ruling house, sheds hot tears for every worthy loyal to himself and his cause, regardless of their origin and the particular manner in which they demonstrate their devotion.[3]

Contrary to the enlightenment regime of gender and emotion, Confucianism does not conceive of women as specialists of the heart, innately endowed with rich emotions or preternaturally in touch with their feelings. Women's role in Confucian sentimentality is by and large limited to the mother—as both the dispenser of maternal affection and the recipient of filial devotion. The wife, to be sure, is expected to be devoted to her husband, but the emotional relationship between a heterosexual couple remains a discursive terra incognita. If anything, orthodox Confucianism, even more so than at the village level, proscribes overt manifestations of conjugal attachment and commends suicidal women (in defense of their chastity) in terms evocative of heroism (*lie*) rather than sentimentalism (*qing*). In this regard, Confucianism bears comparison with Platonism and Christianity. Plato famously deemed heterosexual love deficient, extolling instead the power of male homosexual friendship in facilitating the soul to transcend the material and become one with the Good and Beautiful. St. Paul exhorted Christian spouses to love each other, but it was a love that emphasized affection, sympathy, and goodwill. Or, as Irving Singer puts it, "it was a domestic virtue that enabled husband and wife to perform conjugal duties with a cheerful faith in the goodness of the divine order. . . . One's passion would be reserved for God; passion toward one's spouse could only be considered inappropriate and even sinful" (1984, 32). St. Augustine even defined "lust" as the enjoyment of oneself and one's neighbor (that is, another human being) without reference to God (24). In other words, sexual love is not a spiritual good in and of itself and carries no redeeming quality or transformative potential. Rather, it is more often than not associated with calamity and destruction and is invariably relegated to the margins of society. Lindholm sums up the anomalous location of love in highly structured, internally competitive social formations this way:

> It is evident that under the conditions of strong social constraint, well-formed primordial identities and intense rivalry for power . . . , the idealization offered by romantic love may offer a way of imagining a different and more fulfilling life. But because of the objective reality of the social world, romance can never form the base for actually constructing the family, as it has in Western society. It must instead stand against and outside the central social formation, and will in consequence be more fantastic and unrealistic in its imagery, more danger-ous in its enactment, than in the flexible, egalitarian and atomistic cultures of the modern world. (1998, 253–54)

One direct implication of the delegitimization of heterosexual love is the ritualization of the conjugal relation (in which attraction and attachment are irrelevant and immoral) and the split of the feminine gender into the good woman and the bad woman. The former is one's mother/wife with whom one fulfills one's duty of reproducing the social order; the latter is the erotic specialist —the concubine, the courtesan, or the fairy girl—who administers to men's quest for *amour passion*, or adventurous sexual experience outside the context of procreation and productivity. With few exceptions, stories about heterosexual love usually take place on the margins of society, most typically between a way-faring scholar or merchant (who is temporarily cut loose from the nexus of so-cial relationships and mechanisms of social control) and a demimondaine, a revenant ghost, or an animal spirit.[4] The shadowy, apparitional presence of the female lover serves particularly to accentuate both the illegitimate nature of male-female congress brought about entirely by sexual passions *and* the contingent nature of a relationship freely initiated and privately pursued by discrete, isolated individuals.

Both homosocial bonding and heterosexual romance can easily shade into a web of "rhizomatic" linkages that both support and subvert the vertical, "arborescent" structures of orthodoxy.[5] The rhizomatic mode of sentimentality is sustained by a heterogeneity of beliefs, fantasies, and practices that seek to redress the injustices, contradictions, and inadequacies of the dominant social order. Here sentiment is about observing the protocols for dealing with fairies and ghosts or the rules of play between dandies and courtesans in the floating world of sensual pleasures. It is also about the principle of solidarity in sworn brotherhoods and sectarian organizations. In literary and dramatic representations, it is manifested as alternative, semimythologized spaces—the "rivers and lakes" (*jianghu*), "forests and woods" (*lulin*), haunted chambers, spring gardens, and brothels (*qinglou*)—characterized by a sense of autonomy, an aspiration for the universal, and an egalitarian ethos. John Christopher Hamm defines *jianghu* as "the complex of inns, highways and waterways, deserted temples, bandits' lairs, and stretches of wilderness at the geographic and moral margins of settled society" (2005, 17). Its highest code of honor, righteousness (*yi*), is distinguished from other Confucian virtues by a universal scope. Instead of being directed toward specific persons, *yi* exhorts the extension of sympathy and assistance to all needy persons, including total strangers. The erotic world, for its part, thrives on chance encounters, love at first sight, and voluntary liaisons between humble scholars and otherworldly beauties. In their fascination with the spontaneous, the sensuous, and the personal, romantic stories articulate an aspiration for individual agency and a faith in the universality of sentiment seldom entertained by orthodox narratives.

The rhizomatic realm has little regard for vertical social distinctions such as status, family background, and gender. Although the class hierarchy has always to some extent been mitigated and made porous by the ideal, if not the practice, of meritocracy and men of humble station could always hitch their ambitions of upward mobility to the civil service examinations, women have traditionally had little latitude in circumventing the Confucian gender hierarchy. Besides religious celibacy, entering the rhizomatic realm to become a woman warrior or a courtesan seems to be the only culturally condoned, if not encouraged, avenue of transcending or escaping the Confucian prescriptions of womanhood. In leaving the vertical structure of the home, the woman warrior and the courtesan, like their hallowed counterpart in religious mythologies, have always captured the popular imagination with their mystique of autonomy and alterity. In romantic tales, we see heroines take charge of a liaison and lay claim to sexual agency—they (as courtesans) would receive penniless patrons in the teeth of the madam's objection, redeem themselves out of brothels in order to marry their lovers, or (as fairies or spirits) offer themselves to earthly men at the risk of divine punishment or exorcism by shamans.[6] In *jianghu* tales, gender-bending extravaganzas bring added piquancy to the fascination and thrill of free sociability. Martial heroines pride themselves on their valor, martial skills, spirit of righteousness (*yiqi*), and devotion to sworn brothers and sisters. And yet, like their romantic counterpart, they are also proud of their respect for the moral order and its human embodiments: the emperor and parents. They are often maddening sticklers for decorum, and not a few have become memorable moral paragons in literary and popular histories. It is in this sense that the vertical and horizontal axes of sentimentality are mutually reinforcing. However, with its hidden transcripts, meandering structures, and fluid identities, the rhizomatic realm is always in excess of orthodoxy and thus a perennial source of anxiety and an intermittent target of appropriation and co-optation.

Rather than a heterodox movement, the late imperial cult of *qing* represented a sustained effort on the part of Ming-Qing literati to reconcile the tension between upholding the cardinal relationships and reconceptualizing these relationships as fundamentally grounded in affect. Following the lead of Wang Yangming (1472–1529), Ming-Qing literati became preoccupied in questioning or even inverting the hierarchy between heavenly principle and human desire. Their efforts, at least in certain radical moments, bore some resemblance to the enlightenment valorization of passion and desire. Nonetheless, this was not accompanied by a theoretical critique of *xing* or *li*. Instead, *li* was always affirmed for its moral promise of temperance and for its role as the guarantor of basic humanity. The fundamental faith in the complementarity between *li* and *qing* was succinctly voiced by Yang Shen (1488–1559), a member of the Wang Yangming School: "What will happen if one promotes *xing* but neglects *qing*? He will become dead ashes. What will happen if one is moved by *qing* but forgets about *xing*? He will become an animal" (quoted in Huang 1998, 156–57).

While some bohemian literati may have sought shock value in trying to live out the latter option, most associates and followers of the Wang Yangming School opted to reconcile *qing* and *xing* within the institutional legitimacy of marriage. Indeed, it was the cult of *qing* that first theorized and celebrated the husband-wife bond—a bond, as we have noted, that lurked in a shadowy metaphorical corner of the Confucian ethical edifice. The renowned iconoclast Li Zhi (1527–1602), for example, eulogized the matrimonial relationship as a bond of passion, seeking to undermine the centrality of the father-son relationship. He writes: "Husband and wife comprise the beginnings of human life. Only after there has been a husband-wife relation can there be a father-son relation. . . . Should the relationship between husband and wife be proper, then all the relations among the myriad of living things and nonliving matters will also be proper. Thus it is evident that husband-wife is actually the beginning of all things" (quoted in Mowry 1983, 6). For Li Zhi as for many of his fellow thinkers and writers, the conjugal relationship is or should be characterized by emotional reciprocity, not domination and obedience. And by placing this egalitarian dyad at the foundation of the cosmic and social order, Li Zhi is essentially questioning the hierarchical order that so thoroughly structures orthodox Confucianism—without, however, denying the basic moral purpose of Heaven. This paved the way for later formulations of the parent-child relation or even the modern state-citizen relation as one essentially defined by voluntary emotional investment and mutuality. Any social bond that is not grounded in deep feelings but is instead merely soldered together by ethical injunctions is then deemed inauthentic and hypocritical. This revolutionary reconceptualization of sociality begins with the novel attempt to make the conjugal relation the foundation of cosmic and social order, though given our own high valuation of conjugality, this crucial change can easily elude our attention. Still, the cult of *qing* is not reducible to an early modern precursor to the twentieth-century sentimental revolution. Li Zhi was as concerned with the "proper" order of things as any Confucian worth his salt. What scholars have deemed countercultural rebels were also earnest defenders of the moral rectitude of sentiment and acerbic critics of the excesses of desire.

The Wang Yangming School's greatest challenge to orthodoxy is not simply the valorization of desire, but the claiming for *qing* a foundational status previously reserved for *xing* or *li*. Whereas in Zhu Xi *qing* designates a secondary state of being (*yifa*) derivative of basic human nature, in the writings of Wang and his followers, *qing is* human nature, the material basis of heavenly principle, the fount of ethical conduct, and the origin of all virtues. It is simultaneously a cosmological, epistemological, and ethical category requiring no further justification. The heavenly principle, though not discredited, is now dependent on *qing* for its very existence and possibility of knowledge. Chen Que (1604–1677) writes:

> Originally there was no heavenly principle in one's mind; heavenly principle is only perceptible through human desires [note that "desires" (*renyu*) here are closer in meaning to *qing* than to *yin*]. Human desires, when proper, become heavenly principle. Without human desires, there would be no heavenly principle to talk about. . . . When talking about desires, one can only ask whether they are excessive but one should never ask whether they are something that one should have or something that one should not have. (Quoted in Huang 1998, 159)

The ramifications of enshrining *qing* as the defining essence of humanity or human nature are far-reaching. A direct impact in the realm of letters is an unprecedented upsurge and continued growth of fiction and drama devoted to the celebration of *qing* as "a supreme human value" (Huang 1998, 161). In short story collections, full-length novels, and drama scripts, as well as in their prefaces and epilogues, we find more personalized and poeticized, at times idiosyncratic and at times polemical, elaborations of the philosophical discourse on *qing*; we also find a new breed of characters—"men/women of sentiment" (*youqingren* or *duoqingren*)—acting out the thrilling possibilities of a life dedicated to *qing* and its collision and collusion with the patriarchal family structure and gender ideology.

It is in its literary manifestations that the cult of *qing* most resembles the early Romantic movements in Europe. It challenges dominant neo-Confucianism with an alternative discourse that locates the moral source of human actions in an immanent notion of "moral nature" (*liangzhi*) rather than in the transcendent "heavenly principle." It insists that it is our innate moral sentiments, rather than ethical codes, that motivate and authorize us to be and do good. It reinvents *qing* as the site of virtue and individual expressiveness. For the first time, love between two strangers can take on an ethical and spiritual quality, irreducible to lust or even the esoteric pleasures of *ars erotica*. *Qing* empowers the man or woman of feeling to act not only passionately, but also virtuously and nobly. Their lives, even more so than those of emperors and warriors, are worthy of respect, admiration, and celebration—in the forms of poetry, drama, and fiction dedicated to the subject of *qing*.

Few scholars have adequately recognized the radical nature of the implicit claim that love between a man and woman is what makes life worth living. In many ways, the man or woman of feeling is the first modern subject insofar as he or she locates his or her moral source intrinsically rather than extrinsically. Ironically, students of Ming-Qing literature have tended to favor the cult of *qing* in an anachronistic way. They subsume the espousal of the personal and the subjective under the modern valorization of the individualist subject, without an analytically based appreciation for either the radical nature of the movement or its distinct alterity vis-à-vis the modern episteme. They tend to lionize Ming-Qing literati as cultural dissidents by highlighting their unconventional utterances and playing down their orthodox moments. To counteract this tendency, I propose "the Confucian structure of feeling" to emphasize the cult of *qing*'s location within the larger matrix of Confucian sentimentality. In brief, "the Confucian structure of feeling" encompasses the meanings and values pertaining to the individual's location in the cosmic/social order and as espoused by the key members of the cult of *qing* movement and recuperated by a group of late Qing and early Republican writers. It is a crucial marker of "the early modern" that has attracted more and more scholarly attention lately.

The work of James Hembree on the role of romantic narrative in the emergence of European modernity provides a useful comparison, despite its tendency toward teleological schematism. According to Hembree, the early modern period was a period of semiotic paradigm shift from a cosmological to a psychological conceptualization of personal identity, or from an objective symbolic order that prioritizes signification over representation, ontology over epistemology, sign over self, to a subjective one that conceives an interior psychological space as the locus of personal identity and self-representation. Drawing on the works of Thomas Kuhn and Michel Foucault, among others, Hembree argues that the shift of paradigms or epistemes was a gradual process involving at least three phases. The first phase, exemplified by Montaigne's *Essais*, began with a skeptical critique of the traditional foundations of meaning and a counterdiscourse fueled by an intensification of subjective self-awareness. The second phase anticipated the emergence of a new subject-centered epistemological model, but ultimately rejected it in favor of a "historicist" perspective (as introduced by the seventeenth-century French romantic novel *L'Astrée*—the focus of Hembree's book), which would eventually be superseded by the rise of a new model in the last phase. This new model, first systematically explicated in the writings of Descartes, posited subjective interiority not only as the locus of authentic selfhood, but also as the founding principle of intersubjective knowledge. Hembree summarizes this process in this way:

> To the extent that subjective interiority emerges as a fact of psychological and practical experience before it can be assimilated as a meaningful (i.e. representable) aspect of human self-understanding, Kuhn's theory provides a useful tool for analyzing the semiotic paradigm shift that takes place in the early modern period. Subjective self-awareness initially subsists as an "anomaly" within an object-centered paradigm of symbolic reference, before being "discovered" when a subject-centered paradigm takes its place, at the end of an extended period of "crisis" during which the two paradigms are inconclusively juxtaposed, and third alternatives explored. (1997,12)

The epochal paradigm shift, spanning the Renaissance and the Enlightenment, has a long prehistory in which romantic love functioned as an anomalous, marginalized, or occulted element contributing to the emergence of a new epistemic structure. In France, this prehistory began with the eleventh-century troubadours whose poetry celebrated courtly love as a personal experience poised against socially sanctioned alliances. Irving Singer sorts out several crucial beliefs associated with courtly love that mark its epochal significance. First, sexual love between men and women is something splendid in itself, an ideal worth striving for; second, it ennobles both the man and his mistress, making the lovers better human beings; third, as an ethical and aesthetic attainment, sexual love cannot be reduced to mere carnality; fourth, it centers on courtesy and courtship but is not necessarily related to the institution of marriage; and last, it can provide supreme joy not to be found elsewhere in life, a holy oneness that can fully satisfy and even sanctify (1984, 23–31). However, for all its radical impulses, courtly love also brought about a reconciliation with the objective order with its ethic of self-emptying, which substituted for social authority the absolute will of the exalted mistress. The chivalric lover succeeded only in self-transcendence for the sake of the metaphysical ideals of goodness and beauty embodied by the mistress, not in self-affirmation or establishing the individual self as the determining center of meaning. For this, we have to wait till the Enlightenment when Descartes proclaimed the *cogito*, or the transcendental knowing self (Hembree 1997, 1–42).

To what extent one can speak of a paradigm shift in late imperial China prior to the onslaught of western culture is a question the answer to which in part depends on the length of the historical perspective one adopts. For some scholars, the changes are such that the late imperial period merits the label of "early modern." But it is also important to be cognizant of its distance from the western-inspired May Fourth transformations. Hence my using "the Confucian structure of feeling" to encompass discourses of *qing* from the fifteenth to early twentieth century. The cult of *qing* movement and the Confucian structure of feeling it exemplifies have challenged the traditional foundations of meaning through a counterdiscourse that valorizes the personal and the subjective. Given its countercultural tendencies, it is perhaps counterintuitive to call it "Confucian." My reason for doing this is to stress that the cult of *qing* does not effect an epistemic break with neo-Confucian orthodoxy. For all its effort to legitimize the affective and the individual, it is still committed to patrilineal continuity, ritual propriety, and the social order. The supremacy of ritual is rarely questioned and sexuality is rarely affirmed on the ground of the pleasure principle. All social relationships are made transubstantial through *qing* and yet are still regulated by *li*. With few exceptions, the texts produced in the movement do not antagonize the cardinal relationships, or pit the horizontal axis of sentimentality against the vertical axis. Conjugality seldom stands alone without filiality and sexual passions are laudable only if they also validate, if not actually strengthen, the parent-child bond.

For this reason, the cult of *qing* and its late Qing inheritors struck many May Fourth iconoclasts as smacking of orthodox values. In their all-out assault on "tradition," the May Fourth generation habitually used terms like *Confucian* or *feudal* to designate everything that did not fit into its vision of modernity. Whatever was labeled Confucian was also backward and antimodern, doomed to be overrun by the inexorable wheels of modernity. In coining the Confucian structure of feeling and lumping together a number of texts and ideas spanning the several hundred years of late imperial history under an umbrella category, I wish to call attention to the persistent concern with virtue and its relationship to sentiment that informs most of these texts, as well as their marginal or repressed status in the historiographies of the May Fourth tradition. But for stylistic concerns, there should be quotation marks on each use of the word *Confucian*. In short, by Confucian I do not refer to anything historically specific, ideologically fixed, or demographically distinct. If anything, it is a catchall for the dimensions of the early modern experience that remain unassimilated to the master narrative of modernity and therefore appear archaic, quaint, or incomprehensible to us. Strictly, the "Confucian structure of feeling" should always be in the plural, especially because I use the term to mark both latency and marginality.

QING: FROM SINCERITY TO AUTHENTICITY

Although literary and dramatic works devoted to *qing* abound in the late Ming, Feng Menglong's *Qingshi* (Anatomy of love) stands apart for its professed object of propagating "a religion of *qing*" (*qingjiao*, as opposed to *lijiao*) and its encyclopedic scope. It is a collection of some 850 tales and anecdotes of uneven lengths in classical Chinese, compiled in the final years of the Ming dynasty. The majority of these tales and anecdotes deal with the male-female relationship, while a minority feature same-sex affairs, liaisons between humans and fairies or inanimate objects, and mating stories of beasts and insects. The entries are grouped into twenty-four chapters that are subdivided into several sections, every chapter and section bearing a distinctive title. Hua-yuan Li Mowry notes how difficult it is for a modern reader to make sense of Feng's scheme of categorization, which is at times "contrived" and at times "chaotic and confusing" (1983, 8, 10). Indeed, one is reminded of the putative "Chinese encyclopaedia," which, in his wonderment of its bizarre taxonomy, so confounded Foucault's familiar landmarks of thought that it launched him into a profound reflection on the origins of the "human sciences" (1994). Likewise, Feng's scheme of classification makes us wonder not only how he devised such a scheme, but also whence the impulse to do so at all. For this we turn to the two prefaces announcing the intentions and purposes of his taxonomic endeavor.

The first preface dwells much on Feng himself as a man of sentiment and his vision of a world made infinitely for the better by the magical powers of *qing*. It is worthwhile to quote him at some length:

> It has always been one of my ambitions to compile a history of *qing*, and even since I was a young man, I have been known to be *qing*-crazy. Amongst my friends and equals I always pour out all my heart, sharing with them in both good times and bad. Whenever I hear about a person who is in unusual distress or is suffering a great wrong, even though I may not know him, I always render my help to him if he seeks it; should it be beyond my ability to help him then I sigh for days, and at night I toss about, unable to get to sleep. And whenever I see a person rich in emotion, I always desire to prostrate myself before him. (Feng Menglong 1986, n.p.; Mowry 1983, 12)

The self-portrait Feng gives us is the likeness of a new personality type commonly and earnestly affected by many late Ming literati—the man of sentiment characterized by emotional sincerity, ebullience, and ecumenicalism. He practically decrees that the only criterion for judging a man's worth is his richness of emotion, not, as convention would have it, his rank, status, or wealth. Also highly unconventional is the extravagant manner in which emotion is demonstrated. Although Confucianism certainly encourages compassion and charitable deeds, to lose sleep over one's inability to help out a stranger would certainly make any Confucian raise his eyebrow, as would to prostrate oneself before a person "rich in emotion" but who may well be one's inferior in age, gender, or social station. Striking as it may sound, Feng's conception of a *qing*-based personality does not quite evolve into a new theory of subjectivity, one that posits an interior psychological space as the locus of personal identity. Rather, he is eminently concerned with human relationships, with how *qing* binds people together in different configurations of sociality. In the same preface, he articulates the tremendous hope he invests in *qing*, in its transformative power for man as a social being and for society as an intimate community bound together by affective ties:

> My intention has been to choose the best from among the stories concerning *qing*, both ancient and contemporary, and to write up a brief account for each, so that I might make known to men the abiding nature of *qing*, and thereby turn the unfeeling into men of sensitivity, and transform private feeling into public concern. Thus, in villages, counties, even throughout the world, men will deal amiably with one another, in the spirit of *qing*. I have always hoped that my efforts might help bring about a change in the negative customs and conventions of society. . . . I intend to establish a school of *qing* [*qingjiao*] to teach all who are living, so that a son will face his father with *qing* and vassal will face his lord with *qing*. One can, then, deduce the relations of all the various phenomena from this single point of view. . . . To observe the bursting forth of *qing* will be like seeing the budding of spring flowers, which brings joy and happiness to all. At that time, robberies and thefts will cease to happen, and evil and treason never arise; the Buddha will have no further use for his mercifulness and forgiveness, and the sage no further use for his teaching of benevolence and righteousness. (Mowry 1983, 12–13)

In a word, Feng's goal in founding the school or religion of *qing* is to forge a utopian world where evil will vanish and goodness prevail. With the blessings of *qing* as a secular religion, people will have no more need for Buddhas or sages, for each will be one's own savior—by simply exercising one's moral nature and injecting *qing* into words and actions. Here we hear echoes of Wang

Yangming whose democratizing doctrine of "innate knowledge" (*liangzhi*) recognizes the potential sagehood in every person.

In the second preface, Feng adopts the high ground of Confucian secularism and pits his "religion of *qing*" against organized religions: "The teachings of the heterodox schools [*yiduan*] advocate celibacy, supposedly with an end to attaining a quiet life. But in the extreme they lead one instead to the point of not knowing one's own lord and father" (quoted in Mowry 1983, 14). Feng's objection to religions stems not only from their hostility to human emotionality or sensuality, which directly challenges the central tenet of the "religion of *qing*," but also from their depreciation of the cardinal institution of Confucianism: the family. By aligning his project of sentiment with the ultimate orthodox concerns—to know one's lord and father—Feng underscores the conciliatory dimension of the cult of *qing*.

The staunchly secularist bent in the writings of Feng and other prominent figures of the cult of *qing* movement again invites comparisons with European Romantics. One important difference is that Feng is not pursuing personal autonomy and freedom through a theory of the intrinsic worth of the individual. Even though the stories in his anthology deal mostly with male-female relations, the constant invocation of *qing*'s indispensability to father-son, lord-subject, and brotherly relationships is clue enough that the gravitas in *Qingshi* is not the monadic individual as the center of all meanings, but *qing* as the best means of consolidating human bondings that also recognize the validity of individuality and individual experience. The goal, therefore, is not to overhaul the social order, but to make it subjectively meaningful and personally operable. Toward this end, Feng holds out the ideals of sincerity and fidelity, which, as Mowry rightly points out, constitute the two most significant and basic concerns of *Qingshi* (1983, 17).

Not surprisingly, the first chapter of *Qingshi* is entitled "chastity" or "fidelity in love" (*qingzhen*) and features a series of female suicides who use death to demonstrate sincere love and resolute loyalty. At the end of the chapter, Feng offers the following commentary:

> The Master of *Qing* says: With regard to all matters of loyalty, filial piety, chastity or heroism, if one tries to act solely from principle, then one's actions will certainly be forced; if, however, one tries to act on the basis of genuine *qing*, then his actions will certainly be sincere [*zhenqie*]. . . . The relation between a husband and his wife is of all relations the most intimate. He who is feelingless

to his wife can never be a faithful husband; she who is feelingless to her husband can never be a virtuous wife. A Confucian only knows that reason re-
strains *qing* but does not know that *qing* maintains reason. (Mowry 1983, 38)

To Feng, it makes a world of difference whether one is faithful merely for the
sake of the principle or in order to give expression to the *qing* within oneself.
Virtue has to be heartfelt, sincere (*cheng*). In other words, virtue and sincerity
validate each other.

Sincerity, or the "congruence between feeling and avowal" (Trilling 1971,
7), is different from the more modern notion of authenticity in that being sincere is not an end, but a means to being true to others. One is sincere in order
to maintain a more truthful and more congenial relationship with others. In
contrast to authenticity, sincerity requires no excruciating soul-searching and
is resolutely this-worldly, intersubjective, and public-minded—hence Feng's
goal to "transform private feeling into public concern" by turning "the unfeeling into men of sensitivity." For him, *qing* is about building a particular
kind of community, one that is based on affect, intimacy, and spontaneity
rather than on austere principles and imposed obligations. *Qing* strings together the "scattered coins" of the world and binds those "at opposite ends of
the world into one family." It enlightens people to their essential sameness:
"Those who inflict injury or hurt upon others are actually doing harm to their
own *qing*" (quoted in Mowry 1983, 13). Feng's championing of sincerity and
fidelity leads him to reappraise historical and fictional personages by asking
whether a particular figure is an insincere or unfaithful lover. He feels justified
to ridicule such revered authority figures as Zhu Xi for their hypocritical (*jia
daoxue*, false moralist) attitude in regard to *qing,* while at the same time praising the humble and the ordinary for their acts of sincerity and fidelity. Indeed,
the principle of sincerity can even justify illicit sex, elopement, adultery, or
prostitution for women as well as for men, so long as it is in the name of *qing*
and does not lead to the destruction of families and careers.

The foregoing discussion adduces only the metatexts in *Qingshi* to illustrate Feng's philosophy of sentiment. What I do not have the space to do is examine the interplay of Feng's editorial voice with the tales and anecdotes in
the collection. A careful study along this line will almost certainly reveal that
the copious materials collected here are not necessarily amenable to the goals
he lays out in the prefaces. For our purpose here, suffice it to observe that Feng
undertakes this taxonomic project both to validate an alternative cultural

ideal, *qing*, and to enlist its service to reinvent the Confucian order. Feng is essentially suggesting that society has been operating in bad faith under the misguidance of the "false moralists" and has failed to live up to the ideals of the ancients, who, after all, believed in *qing* all along.

Ming-Qing writers have found *Qingshi* a rich sourcebook for weaving more elaborate tales in the convention of the "scholar-beauty" (*caizi jiaren*) romance. The scholar-beauty romance rose to popularity during the Tang (618–907) as a more secular variant of the fantastic tale (*zhiguai*) of fairies and ghosts in the Six Dynasties period (the third to sixth centuries) (though the fantastic genre retained its popularity throughout late imperial history). A typical story tells of a talented young scholar's amorous encounter with a ravishing beauty on his way to a metropolis to sit for the civil service examination. Not only is such a story usually told from the male perspective, but the sexual liaison is almost always redeemed through the happy ending of marriage and officialdom on the heels of examination success. The Ming playwright Tang Xianzu's *Mudan ting* (The peony pavilion) best exemplifies this convention while also taking a significant step of departure by shifting the narrative focus to the female character. In the play, sixteen-year-old Du Liniang, the cloistered daughter of a high-level state official, takes a stroll and falls asleep in a blooming spring garden, encounters a young scholar named Liu Mengmei in her dream, dies of yearnings for him soon afterward, visits the wayfaring Mengmei in his room as a ghost, comes back to life three years later with Mengmei's assistance, and weds him. Mengmei then goes on to become the prize candidate of the palace examination. The play is most celebrated for its first half, which centers on Liniang's discovery of love in a dream and her extraordinary experience of traversing the boundary of life and death in quest of love. Though not without precedence, the theme of death and resurrection by dint of love's invincible power is widely recognized as highly original in Chinese literary history, whereas the latter half of the play chronicling Liu Mengmei's tribulations in seeking rank and fame follows fairly closely the conventions of the scholar-beauty romance.

Critics have been prone to heap praises on this play, reading it as a magnificent ode to love and individuality and regarding its oneiric and numinous elements as an audacious protest against the repressiveness of the wakeful world of orthodoxy where parents, tutor, and the "words of the ancients" collude to smother youthful sexuality and vitality. The play's power and originality are attributed to its dramatization of the universal contradictions between subjectivity and objectivity, ideals and reality, individual freedom and "feudal" Confucian ethic, *qing* and *li* (Yu Qiuyu 1985). Wai-yee Li, for example, reads Liniang's courageous pursuit of love as an affirmation of her subjectivity. But Li also sees in the conventional turn in Liniang's character an important clue to the "reconciliation" of *qing* and the moral order. In her view, the personal quest for love shades effortlessly into the affirmation of worldly bliss, and the fantastic world of erotic pleasure "complements rather than contravenes mundane reality" (1993, 50–64).

Although "love" and "worldly bliss" may blend effortlessly, the play introduces a new trope—passionate love—that must be distinguished from the familiar centerpiece of scholar-beauty romance: sensuous love. According to Singer, whereas sensuous love relies upon superficial but genuine pleasures of the senses, passionate love entails intense yearning and emotion upheaval—strong enough, indeed, to enable the protagonist to traverse the boundary of life and death. Although the former could accommodate its own kind of love—some of the scholar-beauty romances are delightfully memorable—but true love, it is believed, only shows itself in extreme emotionality (whence the topoi of "love-sickness" whereby disappointed lovers would pine away, suffer psychosomatic disorders, or die of broken hearts) and in the ability to forgo sensual pleasure if objective circumstances demand any such sacrifice (Singer 1984, 26, 33).

In celebrating passionate love, Tang's magnum opus is an adroit attempt to carve out a subjective space within the larger objective social structure without questioning its fundamental legitimacy. Liniang's discovery of love in the pages of a venerated Confucian classic, *The Book of Songs*, challenges the exegetical tradition bent on allegorizing eros as political loyalty, while also turning the cult of *qing* into a renaissance movement proclaiming that the subjective has always had an undeniable but forgotten place within the objective symbolic order. Moreover, that the first half of the lengthy play is largely devoted to the emotional and erotic adventures of a young woman is a significant departure from the scholar-beauty convention. Already an anomalous being as an unbetrothed daughter, Liniang has literally to enter the realm of phantasmagoria to find both herself and the object of her desire. Her new identity as a woman of sentiment (*youqingren*) sets her worlds apart from those whose desire is harmonized with the external conditions of existence and whose self-representation is a function of his (or her) participation in the social order (her father Du Bao, an upright, conscientious official, clearly belongs to the latter category). With the birth of love, Liniang enters into a period of isolated inwardness which, in the words of James Hembree, engenders "an awareness of interior

distance or estrangement from the traditional means of self-representation"
(1997, 44). The dream in the spring garden and the union in the shadowy
realm are of course supreme figurations of this awareness.

Liu Mengmei, by contrast, is more or less a conventional character—the
talented and ambitious young scholar—who does not find the sentimental existence at odds with the social world. In fact, the classical texts in which he is
immersed have always taught him that erotic gratification is part and parcel
of the reward for one's participation in the orthodox social order: "In books,
one is bound to encounter a beauty with jade-smooth cheeks" (*shu zhong zi you
yan ru yu*). The quest for love and the quest for rank and fame are therefore
never separate for Mengmei. And because he is primarily the object of Liniang's love, the distinction between the sensuous and the passionate is less
clear. Although his involvement in Liniang's journey through life and death
entails a temporary setback (he is refused recognition and even jailed and tortured by his father-in-law Du Bao), he does not perceive the setback as the result of a conflict between two distinctive modes of being. Like Du Bao, he is
able to harmonize his desire with the objective order and realize his sense of
self by submitting to the Confucian prescription of manhood.

By projecting the two lovers' basic modes of being in different directions
and yet dovetailing their trajectories of self-fashioning, the play brings about
a comic reconciliation between the subjective realm of *qing* and the objective
realm of patriarchy, bureaucracy, and war. Unlike earlier *zhiguai* stories in
which the ghostly heroine always vanishes at dawn and her palatial abode always dissolves into a desolate graveyard, *The Peony Pavilion* brings Liniang
back into the midstream of life so that the inward-turning, solitary self can be
reintegrated into the social order. But the hierarchy of *xing*, *qing*, and *yu* is already undermined. As Wai-yee Li puts it, "both moral nature and desire are
presented as being potential in and continuous with *qing*" (1993, 61).

But it is the mid-eighteenth-century novel *Dream of the Red Chamber* (aka
the *Story of the Stone*) by Cao Xueqin that fully articulates the radical potential
of the Confucian structure of feeling. For the first time, the male-female dyad
is placed not on a continuum with, but in opposition to, the parent-child one.
In particular, parental figures become, much as they would in the May Fourth
era, identified as the agents of an oppressive social order and the cruel persecutors of romantic love. We are probably justified in speaking of a paradigm shift
whereby the discourse of *qing* plays a role rather akin to what scholars have attributed to romantic narratives in early modern Europe—of disrupting the

infinite web of resemblances and affinities of the traditional symbolic order and introducing the modern episteme of difference and identity. It is true that at a superficial level, Cao Xueqin shares with Feng Menglong and Tang Xianzu a concern with sincerity and a desire to expose the hypocrisy of Confucian morality. But at a deeper level, he is rather preoccupied with the question of authenticity. Trilling argues that authenticity is essentially a modern problematic:

> "Authenticity" suggests . . . a less acceptant and genial view of the social circumstances of life. At the behest of the criterion of authenticity, much that was once thought to make up the very fabric of culture has come to seem of little account, mere fantasy or ritual, or downright falsification. Conversely, much that culture traditionally condemned and sought to exclude is accorded a considerable moral authority by reason of the authenticity claimed for, for example, disorder, violence, unreason. (1971, 11)

The male protagonist Jia Baoyu's aversion to what makes up the very fabric of Confucian culture—the classics, civil service examinations, officialdom, filial piety, and loyalty—is legendary. In stark contrast to Liu Mengmei, Baoyu's self-conscious pursuit of a sentimental existence among girl cousins and maidservants is accompanied by a resolute rejection of the dual career of public service (with its obligatory wheeling and dealing) and private lordship (ruling over an extended, polygamous household). *Qing* is quite unambiguously held up as a countercultural banner, something that cannot be reconciled with orthodoxy; and its subversive potential invariably brings upon itself a crushing suppression. The celebration of *qing* thus becomes a radical project. Unlike earlier cult of *qing* thinkers and writers, Cao Xueqin seeks to justify the writing of *qing* as much on an experiential ground as on a cosmological one. In other words, *qing* is a worthy subject not only because it is the foundation of all relations and all virtues, but also because it is *autobiographical*, moored in personal experience unmediated or unsullied by artificial conventions. In the opening passages of the novel, the author speaks through the autobiographical figure of the Stone, who urges the wondering monk Vanitas to transmit his story to the world:

> [Vanitas speaking:] "Brother Stone, according to what you yourself seem to imply in these verses, this story of yours contains matter of sufficient interest to merit publication. . . . But as far as I can see (a) it has no discoverable dynastic period, and (b) it contains no examples of moral grandeur among its characters—no statesmanship, no social message of any kind. All I can find in

it, in fact, are a number of females, conspicuous, if at all, only for their passion or folly or for some trifling talent or insignificant virtue. Even if I were to copy all this out, I cannot see that it would make a very remarkable book."

"Come, your reverence," said the Stone, "must you be so obtuse? All the romances ever written have an artificial period setting . . . In refusing to make use of that stale old convention and telling my *Story of the Stone exactly as it occurred*, it seems to me that, far from depriving it of anything, I have given it a freshness these other books do not have. . . . Surely my 'number of females,' whom I spent half a lifetime studying *with my own eyes and ears*, are preferable to this of kind of stuff [historical and boudoir romances]?. . . . All that my story narrates, the meetings and partings, the joys and sorrows, the ups and downs of fortune, are *recorded exactly as they happened. I have not dared to add the tiniest bit of touching-up, for fear of losing the true picture.*"

. . . [Vanitas] then subject[ed] the *Story of the Stone* to a careful second reading. He could see that its main theme was love; that it consisted quite *simply of a true record of real events*; and that it was entirely free from any tendency to deprave and corrupt. He therefore copied it all out from beginning to end. (Cao Xueqin 1973, 49–51, emphases added)

C. T. Hsia considers *Dream* the first Chinese novel systematically to utilize autobiographical experience: "it is precisely this autobiographical compulsion to tell the private truth, to recapture a more intimate reality that makes [Cao Xueqin] so much more of a revolutionary against the impersonal tradition of Chinese fiction" (1968, 247). The Chinese narrative tradition (both historiographical and fictional) appears impersonal because ethical concerns—that is, the imperative to transmit the Way (*dao*) and to allocate praise and blame— have always trumped the mimetic impulse (Anderson 1990, 22). With *Dream*, the mimetic impulse receives the strongest endorsement, so much so that it threatens to eclipse the ethical or even to stand traditional morals on their head. The repeated appeal to personal experience, the elevation of eyewitness accounts above grandiose histories and fantastic tales, the belief in the importance of painting a "true picture" of "real events" without "touching up," the assumption that the life experience of an ordinary person, simply because it is faithfully told, should be of interest to others—all of this points to a new epistemic paradigm, one that is best encapsulated in the concept of "authenticity" (*zhen*).

The inversion of the moral order is indeed startling: What has been culturally valued—statesmanship, didacticism, dynastic fortunes—is dismissed for pomposity and want of subjective, personal truths; what has been culturally devalued—the experience of ordinary individuals, particularly that of women ("their passion or folly or . . . some trifling talent or insignificant virtue")—is now given aesthetic value and moral authority for its simplicity, spontaneity, and experiential authenticity. Thus, on the one hand, Baoyu refuses to heed advice about preparing for the civil service examinations, socializing with officials, and making advantageous connections in the world. On the other hand, he blithely indulges in his fondness for such feminine trifles as incense, perfume, and rouge; he takes special pleasure in waiting on his maidservants and volunteers to do a maid's chore; he saves delicacies for a favorite maid and grieves over her premature death; he paints, composes verses, takes a hand at embroidery, plays chess or musical instruments with his girl cousins, and assists the young ladies in their morning toilet; he reads *Record of the Western Chamber* with Daiyu, helps her bury fallen flower petals, and alternately quarrels and reconciles with her; he laments his sisters' exit from his garden world in marriage and looks forward to his own death as an occasion for enjoying others' grieving affection. All this is recounted in the novel with loving care and a dignified sense that this is a record of life itself, life with its cornucopia of sensory perceptions and subtle feelings. The novel is confident that "a true record of real events" will not, by definition, deprave or corrupt the reader, for the authentic is inherently edifying. What is corrupting, instead, is artifice—the "dreary stereotypes" that populate the scholar-beauty romance as well as the "bombastic language" employed therein.[7]

The autobiographical self is a quintessentially modern self in that it is born of the conviction that one may be of interest to others not because one has achieved extraordinary distinctions or witnessed great events, but simply because as an individual one is of consequence. Moreover, as Trilling puts it, "the subject of an autobiography is . . . a self bent on revealing himself in all his truth" (1971, 23–25). The individual truth in *Dream* centers on *qing* which can only be revealed through representation of the affects, sensations, and intimacies of everyday life. *Qing* indexes what is intrinsic in a person as a discrete entity. Hence the express purpose of writing a love story and the extensive discourse on the unique personality of "the men/women of sentiment" as a special breed (*qingzhong*), an order of beings sui generis.

What has most puzzled commentators and critics is the odd incongruity between the novel's manifest devotion to the ordinary and the everyday and its mythological narrative frame in which the all-too-human Baoyu is given a celestial existence. I have argued elsewhere that the mythic component lends cosmological validation to a new mode of subjectivity—the sentimental self (Lee 1997). A parallel yoking together of the divine and the mundane can also be found in early modern European thought in what Charles Taylor calls "the affirmation of ordinary life," or "the notion that there is a certain dignity and worth in . . . the life of production and reproduction . . . [and] that the higher is to be found not outside of but as a manner of living ordinary life" (1989, 23). The affirmation of ordinary life has a theological phase in Christianity, which introduced a positive vision of ordinary life as hallowed by God— hence the religious sanctity of monogamy and the calling. The blessings of God once furnished the crucial moral motive for the affirmation of ordinary life—in its rivalry with traditionally venerated modes of higher life—even though we now no longer need a theological argument to believe in, and to take for granted, the intrinsic worth of the life of family and work.

In inventing the sentimental subject, Cao Xueqin faces a similar need to establish the moral worth of a mode of existence that is diametrically opposed to what has traditionally been valued as an honorable life for men: a life of public service and familial prosperity—apparently just the kind of ordinary life that Taylor speaks of. Indeed, Confucianism is on the whole chary of a life dedicated solely and fervently to the honor ethic and the pursuit of fame and glory. It scarcely endorses the demonstration of martial valor at the expense of civic and domestic virtues, a motif quite common in the European chivalric tradition. Cao's disillusionment with the Confucian way of life—elevated to a sacred ideal—aligns him closer to the European Romantics who envision yet another mode of being that is nobler than either the life of glory or the life of family and work. That alternative mode is, of course, the passionate life, a life dedicated to the pursuit of sublime emotions, a life that is fully prepared to sacrifice all the desiderata of ordinary life, including life itself, in order to attain its ideals. In a sense, what we have in *Dream* is the early Christian and the Romantic ideals rolled together, and the product is a romantic hero attempting to live out, in mundane temporality, a utopian vision of sentimentality. Through the notion of *qing*, Cao advances a natural theory of emotion that nonetheless leans on the notion of divine gift. Baoyu, therefore, is both profoundly human and ethereally godlike. But ultimately, it is his secular-sentimental existence that holds the greatest fascination for generations of readers. The novel, after all, is more an autobiography than a hagiography.

Dream also pushes the distinction between passionate love and sensuous love to a level at which they can no longer be easily reconciled (within the existing social order) and the comic ending of *The Peony Pavilion* is no longer a possibility. The novel introduces an abstract concept, "lust of the mind" (*yiyin*), to crystallize the idea of love not reducible to lust. Lust of the mind, or passionate love, is precisely what orthodox Confucianism does not entertain and refuses to dignify with a proper name. Although the clan elders condone (and practice) sexual permissiveness in their households, they react with horror and alarm over Baoyu and Daiyu's chase love and waste no time in short-circuiting it with a matrimonial conspiracy. Thus, it is not so much sex as the attempt, on the part of the young lovers, to pursue an alternative mode of existence that directly contests the vertical structure of feeling in Confucian sentimentality. Although Baoyu is by no means ready to deprive himself of the uncloyed pleasures of the senses, he fashions his life principally as a moral project, one that would allow him and his sentimental companions (male and female) to lead a life in which passion and sensuality are harmonized (as embodied in the figure of Jianmei) and in which, to borrow two terms from Greek philosophy, agape ennobles eros and eros enriches agape. When it appears to him that this project is under threat, as, for instance, when he hears of the (rumored) departure of his chief accomplice Daiyu, Baoyu loses his élan and goes into an extended state of stupor, mechanically going through the motions of daily life like a soulless robot. Or, once the news of Daiyu's tragic death reaches him at long last, Baoyu hastily discharges his obligations to the Jia family (thus repaying the favor of birth and nurturance) and promptly takes leave of the Red Dust. Unlike the other male characters in the novel whose private enjoyment of sensuous love is always subordinate to their other life projects (career, family continuity, friendship, even connoisseurship of objets d'art)—Xue Pan is an exception that proves the rule—Baoyu subordinates all else to passion without which life itself is not worth living.

Dream therefore occupies a unique place in the literary history of late imperial China in its refusal to bring about a comic resolution with orthodoxy, its reluctance to embrace the Confucian structure of feeling, and its prefiguring of a new epistemic paradigm which will be given a more definitive shape in the May Fourth generation's "discovery" of the psychological individual and universal humanity. As a result, the May Fourth generation will also have a more ambivalent relationship to the novel than to the other classics of the vernacular tradition.

THE *ERNÜ YINGXIONG* AS CONFUCIAN ROMANTIC

If *Dream* articulates, with a poignancy that has brought it literary immortality, the radical potential of the cult of *qing*, then Wen Kang's *Ernü yingxiong zhuan* (A tale of heroic sons and daughters, ca. 1870), written a century later, swings the ideological pendulum of the cult toward the conservative end. In terms of literary history, Wen's novel is said to be among the first to unite two distinct genres—chivalric fiction and scholar-beauty romance—into a new hybrid genre.[8] When read as a signpost of the Confucian structure of feeling, the novel is highly original not only for its innovation of genre but also for its effort to incorporate the moral and aesethetic insights of the cult of *qing* into orthodox Confucianism. In doing so, it gives a full-colored portrait of the Confucian romantic who is wholly respectable in orthodox eyes and who is nonetheless sympathetically attuned to the rhizomatic configurations of sentiment that the cult of *qing* has done so much to render visible and legitimate.

Wen Kang opens up *Ernü yingxiong zhuan* with the following remarks:

> Most people nowadays regard *ernü* and *yingxiong* as two different kinds of people. . . . They mistakenly think that those who indulge in force and like fighting are "*yingxiong*," while those who toy with rouge and powder or have a weakness for catamites are "*ernü*." . . . What they don't realize is that only when one has the pure nature of a hero can one fully possess a loving heart, and only when one is a truly filial child can one perform heroic deeds (1976, 3).[9]

Before the eighteenth century, chivalric fiction, or what Andrew Plaks terms "quasi-historical hero-cycles" (1977, 319), and scholar-beauty romance had rarely crossed paths. It is commonly observed that in contrast to the knight in shining armor in medieval European court romance, the *xia* (or *xiake, haohan*) in traditional Chinese chivalric fiction is a stoic hero little interested in women: he "waste[s] no time in amorous dalliance, but conserve[s] [his] energies for feats of valor."[10] Song Geng, concurring with Kam Louie and a number of other scholars, makes the emphatic point that the homosocial world of chivalric fiction "adopts a hostile attitude toward women and heterosexuality" (2004, 175). Female sexuality is feared and repulsed as a corrosive and corrupting agent by men who stop at nothing to defend their masculine honor and bonds. At times, the prerequisite for becoming a hero is to have slain a morally "lax" woman, with the assumption that heroism and eros are fundamentally incompatible.[11]

By the end of the nineteenth century, however, the figure of the swash-buckling and murderously puritanical swordsman has begun to fade in popu-larity. Instead, sentimental heroes and heroines become commonplace in popular fiction. They are likely to accomplish feats of valor only after bouts of passionate longing, heartrending disappointment, and melancholy regret. Shedding hot tears and chanting love poems are their signature gestures. The trend toward the sentimentalizing of heroes and the lionizing of lovers is ex-plicitly registered in Wen Kang's goal of disabusing his contemporaries of "misconceptions" about *ernü* and *yingxiong*. The question is: why must *ernü* and *yingxiong* be made compatible, and why must the two personae be united in a single personality? In other words, what does Wen find lacking in the hero and the lover as separate personalities? Traditional heroes may be puri-tanical, but there is no lack of brimming emotions and torrential tears in the pages of chivalric novels like the *Romance of the Three Kingdoms* and *The Water Margin*. What does it mean, then, to "sentimentalize" these hearty heroes of yore? Also, why does Wen Kang insist on a literal understanding of *ernü* as "sons and daughters" instead of the more common young men and women? I submit that the answer lies in the mission that Wen takes upon himself to reaffirm the value and dignity of the Confucian family out of the concern that the hero and the lover invariably introduce contingency into the ritual stabil-ity of the family and expose it to the adventitious, the uncertain, and the ca-pricious. On the one hand, fighting and campaigning invariably take the hero away from his domestic duties and constitute a serious disruption of the min-istration of familial affairs. The spirit of camaraderie and the code of righ-teousness on the battlefield or in the *jianghu* threaten to undermine the vertical structure of Confucian sentimentality. On the other hand, lovers, in-sofar as they are on a Fausian quest for personal fulfillment, are also a potential threat to the primacy of the collective will of the family. Moreover, in the horizontal realms of adventure and love, trust cannot be assumed on the basis of blood ties or predefined social obligations but must be established with full cognizance of risk—the basic element of sociality. Naoki Sakai has this to say about the problem of trust:

> Normally, we do not ascribe sociality to a person who can only operate within prearranged social relations such as parent-child and teacher-student. Sociality is understood to mean the ability to leave behind the sort of trust warranted by the already existing relations, to "go out in the world" and to establish new

relations with strangers. . . . By the same token, it should be evident that one's relation to the other must of necessity contain the possibility of betrayal and contingency without which trust would be empty. Only within the element of uncertainty does trust make sense. Trust . . . is a decision to expose oneself to the possibility of being betrayed. (1997, 96–97)

Precisely because uncertainty is inherent in every nonascriptive relationship and the chasm between self and other can never be reduced to "a transparent mutuality of intersubjectivity," "the repression of uncertainty in the relationality of subjective positions amounts to a refusal of the otherness of the other, of respect for the other, and after all, of sociality itself" (97). Sakai engages the problem of trust in the context of the Japanese philosopher Watsuji Tetsurō's theory of *aidagara* (in-between-ness, or the relationality of subject positions), a theory that aims to construct a national self fundamentally insulated from the uncertainty of sociality.

At a philosophical level, Wen Kang's formulation of the *ernü yingxiong* is also an attempt to repress the uncertainty of sociality. John Christopher Hamm is right in saying that the novel "harbors designs other than the simple celebration of a heroine's martial deeds" (1998, 336). In holding up filiality as the very antithesis of sociality, Wen aims to bring the contingent discourses of heroism and romance into the fold of familial stability. He does this by ridding *ernü* of its association with eros and fixing it to its literal referent of filial piety, and then by valorizing filial piety, a preeminently domestic virtue, as heroic, thus emptying heroism of its out-in-the-world and consorting-with-strangers connotations. In other words, filiality is his magic wand that transmutes heroism and love into virtues infinitely serviceable to Confucianism. For him, *ernü* and *yingxiong* are two sides of the same Virtue: *yingxiong* is its outward manifestation and *ernü* its inward motive force. The interconnection is so watertight that his pronouncements in this regard are positively tautological: "To be loyal is to have a heroic heart . . . but only if one has a filial heart of loving the monarch; . . . to be filial is also to have a heroic heart . . . but only if one has a filial heart of loving one's parents" (EYZ, 3).

Significantly, Wen Kang theorizes filiality not as a matter of ritual formality, but as a matter of feeling—captured in the idea of the "filial heart." This is where the impact of the cult of *qing* is clearly evident. For Wen, as for Feng Menglong and company, a true romantic hero/heroine cannot be unfilial, ungrateful, or disrespectful—that is, a delinquent in the other vital provinces of social life. And in transubstantiating ritual and feeling, Wen ventures into the subjective world of the Confucian structure of feeling. It is my contention that the novel represents an ambitious attempt to reappropriate the Confucian structure of feeling in an orthodox idiom. It tries to show that heroism need not be the preserve of the bandit who roams the liminal space of *jianghu*, and that everyone has a chance to be heroic within the sphere of ordinary domesticity. The novel spins a riveting tale of romance and heroism, only to have the hero and heroine submit voluntarily to a properly ordered life of career and family. In uniting heroism and romance in an all-encompassing vision, Wen Kang repudiates the more subversive elements of the two genres: violence, fortuity, sensuality, and the dereliction of duty. Hence, although he may be said to have brought heroism and love together, he does so by subordinating both to a third, at once foundational and teleological, category: filial piety. In other words, he is interested in vindicating neither bandit heroism nor defiant romanticism. His objective is rather to set his contemporaries straight of their false notions that threaten to vitiate the commitment to the family.

The first half of Wen Kang's novel tells the story of a woman warrior, He Yufeng, also known as Shisanmei or Thirteenth Sister, who becomes a *jianghu* warrior upon taking a vow to avenge her father's wrongful death. The novel relates how she rescues An Ji, the filial son of a persecuted official, from a band of cannibalistic monks, brokers a marriage for him with a virtuous girl (also her protégé), and then allows herself to be "coerced" into assuming the position of a co-wife. The rest of the novel dwells on An Ji's successful career as an official. Hamm sees the two halves mutually reinforcing: "The tale's overall narrative movement from the elderly scholar An Xuehai's vicissitudes to his son An Ji's successes represents the triumph of . . . the socio-political order. And the transformation of the dauntless Shisanmei into the devoted wife, efficient housekeeper, and proud mother He Yufeng constitutes this character's participation in the triumph of orthodoxy" (1998, 344). Thirteenth Sister's domestication has disappointed many modern readers who take a fancy to her vivacity, pluck, and swordsmanship. However, she is only too true to her role as the selfless heroine who plunges headlong into the *jianghu* in search of justice for a parent, then makes a clean break with it once the goal is accomplished. Because the family is the anchor of the novel's conception of a properly maintained social order, Thirteenth Sister's journey from the *jianghu* to the home is only a matter of course.

The plot structure of the first half of the novel conforms to the archetypal story of the woman warrior. In his genealogy of the Mulan myth, Joseph R.

Allen argues that homecoming has remained the central topoi in all of the myth's numerous guises: "a woman might temporarily accept the male role (especially to protect her father) and her performance in that role might be equal to or better than that of a man, but in the end she must return to her gender" (1996, 377, n20). Louise Edwards also detects a similar trajectory in her comparative study of women warrior characters in traditional vernacular fiction: The Amazonian women assume male garb and role in response to a loss of virtue and order in society of which their own transgression of gender roles is also a symptom; once the order is restored, they invariably retrieve to the domestic sphere, both because their mission has been accomplished and because their domestication is itself an important token of order (2001, chapter 6). If the woman warrior is a disruptive figure that promises a narrative, then her homecoming is the requisite narrative resolution.

True to its didactic nature, the novel holds up to its readers Thirteenth Sister as a new moral exemplar. She is the fictional equivalent of what Alasdair MacIntyre calls a "character" in real life. A character is someone who merges what is usually thought to belong to the individual person and what is thought to belong to social roles (1984, 28–29). In living out a culture's highest values, a character furnishes its members a cultural and moral ideal and is therefore an object of popular regard. His or her actions are highly legible to all. As a fictional "character," Thirteenth Sister launches a new mode of social existence: the *ernü yingxiong*. An *ernü yingxiong* is a "character" who has harmonized public virtue with private sentiment, and who acts virtuously not because she is obliged to do so by external rules, but because she is moved by sentiments arising out of a loving/filial heart. Driven by the moral sentiment of filial piety, she exhibits heroism in the arena of *jianghu* for the sake of justice (because justice has become inoperative in society proper) but ultimately finds her destiny in the home and hearth. This basic definition will stay with all subsequent variations of the theme, even though what constitutes "virtue," "sentiment," and "heroism" will change considerably.

Thirteenth Sister is first introduced as a doughty heroine whose filial sentiment runs deep. Harboring a "sky-high" private grievance, she lives up to the cultural and moral expectations of a righteous warrior who strikes down the mighty, conquers the brutal, and lends a helping hand to the weak. While eking out a living as a bandit, Thirteenth Sister dutifully looks after her aging mother and refuses to take any action that might jeopardize her mother's well-being. She also detests the idea of infringing upon the affairs of the state (*guojia dashi*) by taking the life of a high-ranking mandarin (who happens to be her father's enemy) out of private animosity (*sichou*). In addition, as a woman warrior, she unites the demand of chastity with the dual pursuit of filiality and heroism. For instance, after she has valiantly wiped out a dozen monks who are about to feast on An Ji, she would only go so far as to extend her bow to help the faint-hearted An Ji to his feet, mindful of the interdiction against physical contact between a man and woman. Speaking through An's father, the author opines: "'Ordinariness' is opposed to 'greatness.' Great heroes uphold the principles of loyalty, filial piety, chastity, and righteousness. An unfilial daughter is an 'ordinary woman'" (EYZ, 199). Paradoxically, greatness requires no extraordinary deeds; it resides, rather, in the actions expected of every ordinary man and woman. The novel goes to considerable lengths to show that Thirteenth Sister is no ordinary woman by way of her filial and wifely devotion, whereas her martial prowess is only showcased in a few scenes, memorable as they are.

A particularly important detail is the fact that even though Thirteenth Sister enters the world of banditry to avenge her father, she is not given a chance to do so. The novel preempts the necessity to prove her heroism in an act of violence by contriving to have her enemy executed by the emperor for some unrelated offense. For Wen Kang, it is enough to have entertained the intention of revenge, but to carry it all the way through would be to take "heroism" literally, to equate it with "force" and "fighting," and to fixate on the superficial trappings of a deeper virtue. Moreover, a showdown between Thirteenth Sister and an imperial official (however corrupt) would also antagonize filiality and loyalty (to the state) in a way that disrupts the consubstantiality of all virtues that is so central in the Confucian structure of feeling. A private revenge killing would throw into question not only the emperor's moral rulership (and hence legitimacy), but also the idea of Heavenly justice. That her foe is timely eliminated by the emperor serves to restore faith in the social and moral order wisely regulated by the son of Heaven.

As for individual heroism, Wen Kang drives home the point that there are better, less disruptive ways of proving one's possession of a filial heart—ways that do not deviate from the ritually prescribed course of action (such as filial servicing, mourning, self-immolation), or question the emperor's ability to mete out rewards and punishments, or take one on a self-asserting, self-fulfilling, and self-aggrandizing journey to the margins of society. (The massacre of the monks, taking place without premeditation, is excusable because it aids virtue in distress and destroys savagery.) Hence, upon learning of the death of her enemy, Thirteenth Sister's only wish is to bury the remains of her parents together and spend the rest of her life keeping vigil at the side of their joint grave. A fellow bandit is moved to comment: "She is only a womankind, and yet she has kept her father's memory while caring for her mother. . . . *She is a true hero.* . . . We, to the contrary, have never obeyed our parents' teachings. In the past we were wayward children, and now we are lawless bandits. I myself have a mother, but have I ever comforted her for a single day? . . . I'm quitting this confounded business and I'm going back home to work the land again. I've got to make my old mother happy for a few days at least!" Other bandits concur: "We all have parents. Let's turn back and get out of the woods before it's too late!" (EYZ, 252–53, emphasis added).

In response, An Ji's father harangues them on the comparative merits of tiller and robber, and on the affinity between heroism and filiality: "The wise choice you have made today proves beyond doubt that you are all true heroes of the world and worthy children of your parents. You shall from now on become law-abiding commoners. Go trade your steeds for oxen and throw down your arms and take up hoes. . . . If unrest breaks out on the frontiers, you can still go fighting and win glorious titles for your parents" (EYZ, 254). Aside from the familiar agrarianist message, these passages make it abundantly clear that *jianghu* heroism in "peaceful" times is not an honorable (even if glamorous and sporadically lucrative) way of life, nor a viable mode of social existence. Rather, it is only a liminal phase, a rite of passage that would be utterly meaningless without the world of honest labor and orthodox virtues awaiting at both ends. The novel thus presents its basic ideological message as the affirmation of ordinary life. The hero must come full circle to the domain of everyday ethicality that he or she has left behind temporarily, for the way to true nobility, as Trilling puts it, is through "duty acknowledged and discharged, through a selfhood whose entelechy is bound up with the conditions of its present existence, through singleness of mind" (1971, 77–78).

Readers and critics alike gravitate toward the first half of the novel wherein Thirteenth Sister is a *jianghu* heroine at large. But for the reasons outlined above, the novel's ideological gravitas is not knight-errantry heroism, much less the more commonly known meaning of "*erniiqing*"—romantic love. The *ernii* in this novel are filial sons and daughters who enter and leave the liminal world of *jianghu*, only to affirm the orthodox order and its moral ideal of filiality as heroism. Although matches are made toward the end of the first part, it is not the culmination of romance, but the reward for "courage, consistency, unity of purpose, and sacrifice" (Featherstone 1995, 62) and for "duty acknowledged and discharged."

• • •

Wen Kang was not the only Qing writer to have experimented with hybridizing the romantic and the chivalric genres. About a decade before *Ernü yingxiong zhuan*, Wei Zi'an published an equally popular novel entitled *Huayue hen* (Traces of the moon and flowers, 1858), which narrates the contrasting fortunes of two pairs of lovers against the backdrop of the Taiping Rebellion. Rather than melding the two genres in a threesome marriage, as does Wen Kang, Wei Zi'an keeps them parallel by modeling the main pair on Jia Baoyu and Lin Daiyu and giving their tragic story the greatest emotional and narrative investment while treating the minor pair's rise to fame and fortune more in the heroic story-cycle vein. David Wang believes that Wei's novel represents an important stage in Chinese literary history in rethinking "the literary and the historical figures of romantic subjectivity" (1997, 81). But ultimately, Wang considers the novel a failure, for it merely advances "a derivative aesthetics." The central love affair, in his view, is plagued with "a sense of belatedness," a sense that the lovers have missed the grand narratives of love (such as *Dream*) and can only experience the traces of *le grand amour*. Wang uses this notion of belatedness to explain the "gothic pall" that enshrouds the novel—it is as if the novel has gotten the cause-effect backward and has made its most poignant moment the "aftereffect" of romance. Its conspicuously "decadent" indulgence in melancholy and fatalism and scrupulous avoidance of "physical consummation" give the impression that the lovers are not pursuing happiness but are rather deliberately courting tragedy. This, for Wang, is the result of a failed attempt to imitate "grand conventions and remarkable emotions" (73–81).

But when placed in the *longue durée* history of the Confucian structure of feeling, *Huayue hen* carries on the mantle of the alternative tradition exemplified by *Dream*.[12] It greatly extends the sentimental vocabulary and ideology of *Dream* and further codifies the representation of passionate love as a supreme but unattainable ideal (see Luhmann 1986). In the lonely deaths of the principal lovers, the novel reaffirms *Dream*'s conviction that the existing social order cannot accommodate the ethical and aesthetic ideals of *qing*. Like *Dream*, it questions the sanguine belief in the harmony of virtue and passion as espoused by the most eloquent spokesmen for the cult of *qing*. This is perhaps how we can situate Wen Kang's intervention. Recognizing the countercultural tendency of this alternative tradition, Wen set out to mitigate its erosion by creatively articulating the orthodox implications of the main tenets of the Confucian structure of feeling. But his optimism, in historical retrospect, carries the echoes of a swan song rather than of a marching hymn. With the breakdown of the Confucian moral edifice and the onset of (semi)colonial modernity in the late nineteenth and early twentieth centuries, writers found it increasingly difficult to maintain faith in the orthodox reformulation of the Confucian structure of feeling. More and more were drawn to the alternative tradition. Consequently, *Dream* became the uncontestable masterpiece of traditional Chinese literature and the source of inspiration for the twentieth-century genre of *yanqing xiaoshuo* (sentimental fiction). *Huayue hen* too became a model for many Butterfly novels of sentiment, the best known among which were Xu Zhenya'a *Yu li hun* (Jade pear spirit, 1914) and Wu Jianren's *Henhai* (Sea of regret, 1906). It is to these two novels and similar texts that I turn in the next chapter.

Virtuous Sentiments

In his pioneering study of late Qing fiction, Qian Xingcun (aka A Ying, 1900–1977) notes approvingly that toward the latter half of the nineteenth century, publishers were increasingly reluctant to print fiction dealing with the relationship between the sexes and that this did not change until Wu Jian-ren published his highly successful novella *The Sea of Regret* in 1906 (1996, 6). Indeed, the late Qing is mostly remembered in literary histories for its many devastating political satires or what Lu Xun has called "exposé fiction" (*qianze xiaoshuo*) (1964). Scholars have explained the predominance of political themes in the so-called New Fiction (*xin xiaoshuo*) in terms of its perceived utility in addressing the internal and external plights of the Qing empire (Chen Pingyuan 1989; Doleželová-Velingerová 1980; Huters 2005; Link 1981; Qian Xingcun 1996; Tang 2000; Tsau 1980; D. Wang 1997; Yuan Jin 1992).

Nonetheless, the last decade of the Qing witnessed an unprecedented growth of sentimental fiction that came to be designated as the Mandarin Duck and Butterfly School of fiction.[1] Born in the exponential boom of the popular press and appearing (often in serialized form) mostly in entertainment magazines and newspaper supplements, Butterfly fiction became the standard cultural fare for a fast-growing, moderately educated urban population. Though it was named pejoratively for its frequent invocations of the traditional symbols of romantic fidelity—mandarin ducks and butterflies—Butterfly fiction became the blanket label for all genres of pulp fiction, including crime detection, knight-errantry, humor and satire, and science fantasy. But above all, it is the sentimental genre of thwarted love that is most successful—and the most despised by May Fourth writers. Why, despite the earlier indifference on the part of publishers, did love become the all-consuming subject at the turn of the century? How did Butterfly fiction recuperate and transform the Confucian structure of feeling, and where did it stand vis-à-vis May Fourth romanticism? In this chapter, I begin with Wu Jianren's novel *The Sea of Regret*, widely recognized as the founding text of Butterfly sentimental fiction, and ask why it constitutes a turning point in the cultural history of love. I then examine a number of fiction commentaries from the same period that seek to define a role for the novel of sentiment in the larger social and political enterprise of nation-building. Finally, I read a selection of Butterfly stories that reinvent the genre of *ernü yingxiong* to tackle the new and imposing categories of modernity: gender, race, society, and nation.

VIRTUE AS CONSTANCY

It is difficult to overemphasize how the astounding rise of New Fiction cannot be separated from the immense hope invested in that newfangled idea called progress. It is perhaps no surprise that political exposés, the genre most privileged by historians of late Qing fiction, are little more than thinly fictionalized political tracts advocating constitutional reform, racial nationalism, antisuperstition, and women's emancipation—indeed, these are the categories with which Qian Xingcun organizes his literary-historical narrative. On the other hand, the phenomenal growth of the print media provided fertile soil for new fictional genres and subgenres to proliferate. Political exposés also blended with courtesan fiction, chivalric fiction, court case/detective fiction, and science fiction, popular genres that claimed a lion's share of the readership and the market. Nonetheless, given the scale and urgency of the mission entrusted to fiction, for several decades at least, it seems that both the intellectual elite and the reading public could ill afford the luxury of reveling in stories about "boy meets girl." Even a novel bearing the title of *Ziyou jiehun* (Freedom of marriage, by Zhendan Nüshi, 1903) is only ostensibly about romantic relationship—the male and female protagonists are attracted to each other and become engaged because of their shared revolutionary zeal. The narrative makes no attempt to portray private feelings or domestic life. It is unapologetically impersonal and utopian in its chronicle of a conjugal pair single-mindedly pursuing the political project of anti-Manchu and anti-imperialist nationalism.

The very few female authors who wrote fiction did not take to writing sentimental love stories; this genre remained a nearly exclusively male territory till the May Fourth era. The best-known late Qing woman writer and revolutionary activist Qiu Jin (1875–1907), for example, wrote only classical verse and *tanci* (rhymed prose or narrative ballad) on mostly political subjects. In fact, according to Qian Xingcun, the only genre for which female authorship became noticeable was novels agitating for racial nationalism, not, as one might presume, those advocating women's liberation or gender equality. The woman question in nineteenth-century China, it should be noted, was first and foremost a political and nationalist question, and it is this historical specificity that should frame our understanding of the dearth of domestic novels, and the absence of a virtual female monopoly of this genre which was the case in European and American literary histories (see Armstrong 1987; DeJean 1991). However, with the rise of the treaty-port merchant class, the exposure to western thought, and especially the massive importation of foreign romantic novels (often dubbed as foreign *Dreams of the Red Chamber*), an emergent group of professional writers, who later came to be collectively known as the Mandarin Duck and Butterfly writers, did begin, in the first decade of the twentieth century, to explore new gender relations wrought by modern ideas and capitalism. In their hands, the novel of sentiment exploded into a mass culture industry. Many of them wrote in reaction to the libertinism glorified in courtesan novels (what Lu Xun has called *xiaxie xiaoshuo*, which David Wang translates as "novels of depravity") by resorting to the Ming-Qing discourse of moral sentiments that they updated with an infusion of contemporary sensibilities.

Late Qing and early Republican novels of sentiment are often assigned subgeneric labels informing the reader of the plot type and the general ethos: *aiqing* (tragic love), *kuqing* (bitter love), *canqing* (miserable love), *yuanqing* (wronged love), *lieqing* (chaste love), and so on. Rarely does one encounter a *huanqing* (joyous love) novel, for "it is tragic love stories [*ai iqing xiaoshuo*] that are most welcome by the public," as one writer puts it matter-of-factly (Chen Pingyuan 1989, 321). A commentator notes, with apt hyperbole, that in *Ku shehui* (A bitter world, 1905)—a novel about Chinese coolie laborers in the United States—every word is soaked in tears. Wu Jianren, before launching his career as a fiction writer, published a collection of anecdotes and pithy political commentaries entitled *Wu Jianren ku* (Wu Jianren laments, 1902). All fifty-two entries end with the phrase, "Wu Jianren laments." Also legendary are Lin Shu and his collaborator's passionate outbursts while translating *La dame aux camélias*. It is said that that the two men wailed so loudly over Marguerite Gautier's misfortune that neighbors down the street could hear them (Lee 1973, 44–45).

Lin Shu is also known for his ebullient essays of reminiscences about his family members, all of whom seem to have "such an emotional hold on him as to exceed the ritualistic expectations in the Confucian framework of social relations. Especially towards his mother during her illness and after her death, his 'emotionalism' went to such extremes (prostrating in the rain in prayer, weeping nightly and having fainting spells while in mourning) that his fellow townsmen derided him as a 'wild scholar'" (Lee 1973, 42–44). In view of the Confucian council against emotional demonstrativeness, Lin Shu's excessive sentimentality can only be read as a deliberate and self-conscious mode of self-fashioning. Public display of emotion has for Lin become a marker of aesthetic sensibility and moral superiority. It is not enough that he weeps so excessively; he must also make the act of weeping known to the wide world, turning weeping into a collective aesthetic experience. It is telling that Lin chose to record one of his eleven pilgrimages to the tomb of the Qing emperor Guangxu (r. 1875–1908) not as a political act (affirming his monarchist stance) but as a wrenchingly emotional and intensely personal experience. According to Leo Ou-fan Lee, "in one moving essay, [Lin] recounted how he arrived at the grave in the midst of heavy snow, how he could no longer restrain his tears even before prostrating himself, how he wept so hard after nine prostrations that he lost his voice" (1973, 56–57).

Surely there is more involved here than "emotional nostalgia," or the releasing of "pent-up frustrations as a Confucianist . . . in an age of increasing anti-Confucianism" (57). At the same time Lin mourns for a fallen dynasty and a lost way of life, he is also hastening the birth of a new mode of being. It is said that he had wanted his tombstone epitaph to read: "Here lies Lin Shu, a subject of the late Qing empire, *no rank*" (Hu 1995, 73, emphasis added). Lin's loyalty to the emperor may appear to be retrograde, but there is something startlingly modern about the manner of his devotion. By emphasizing his status as a *mere* subject of the late empire, with no rank or distinction, he is retroactively and anachronistically recasting the relationship between the individual and the state as unmediated and universalistic, much as the way nationalism conceives of the relationship between the citizen and the nation-state. In this new configuration, everyone, regardless of rank or gender, relates directly to the abstract State, be it the empire or the republic. The Qing empire, because it is no longer a concrete political reality, lends itself well to Lin's symbolic, if a bit histrionic, enactment of modern citizenship. Through the acts of solitary, delirious pilgrimage and the process of narrating the tear-drenched experience, Lin appropriates the legitimacy of political loyalty to elaborate a new sense of self, one that is founded on a notion of abstract, universal sentiment and the interiorization of the self.

Other writers too joined in the discursive rehearsals of private emotional experiences, recounting their weeping bouts with great relish and enshrining tears as the unique and universal sign of their newfound interiority. A year after Wu Jianren published *The Sea of Regret*, he revealed that the story had taken him only ten days to compose, and when he read it for the first time in published form, he was so moved by it that he wept uncontrollably (Qian Xingcun 1996, 227). With three novels of sentiment to his credit, Wu Jianren is frequently hailed as the forefather of the Butterfly School. *The Sea of Regret*, in particular, is considered by many to be the prototype of the Butterfly novel of sentiment. It was reprinted many times and adapted for film, drama, and regional opera. Wu begins the novel with a series of remarks that sound rather like a pastiche of the famous pronouncements on sentiment in the cult of *qing* movement:

> The story which I'm going to tell may be called a novel of sentiment. When I tell a tale it's usually about sentiment, because from birth onwards, there's not an aspect of human affairs that does not concern sentiment. The squawking of little babies is an expression of sentiment, though the vulgar would rather call that sound the bubbling of little cesspools. What the vulgar call sentiment is merely sex between man and woman. But I mean the innate feeling that Heaven has sown in our hearts and which, as we grow older, manifests itself everywhere, under various forms according to its object. Toward one's lord and country, it is loyalty; towards one's parents, it is filial

piety; toward one's children, it is parental love; toward friends, it is generosity. We can thus see that this feeling is what all great principles stem from. Love between the sexes may be called infatuation; it need not and should not appropriate the term sentiment. If one recklessly dissipates one's love, that's a case of bewitchment.

A final word. Our predecessors said of widows that they are like withered wood and ashes, or dry wells, cut off from passion. To be cut off from sentiment means that one grows old in the memory of a first love. The vulgar recognize only love between the sexes as love; they can't discriminate between sentiment and the merely frivolous. Moreover, much fiction has been written, not about sentiment, but about sex. It pretends to be about sentiment, but is really about sin and transgression.

Now I'll tell my little story, but first of all I want it understood that in writing about sentiment I'm not advocating carnality and indecency. With wisdom and discernment the reader will be able to see just what it is that I'm preaching. (Quoted in Egan 1980, 166)

Qian Xingcun, whose view is echoed by later critics, regards this passage as disingenuous, because the story apparently does revolve around love between the sexes, or "infatuation" (1996, 226). In his introduction to the English translation, Patrick Hanan gives little weight to Wu's strenuously drawn distinction between chaste sentiment and "indecent" infatuation/carnality, considering it the babble of a Confucian conservative who harbors "suspicion of any innovation derived from foreign practice" (1995, 6). And despite its popularity among contemporary readers, Hanan deems Wu's novel inferior to a contemporaneous but "obscure" novel that "does not deserve its obscurity" because of its merits in "structural perfection" and "frank sensuality" (8–9).[2] David Wang finds Wu's hostility toward sex so unappealing that he cannot find a place for it in his against-the-grain literary history aiming to recover the "repressed modernities" of late Qing fiction.[3] The irony, then, is that *The Sea of Regret* ill fits in both canonical history and revisionist history because of its seemingly antimodern insistence on virtue's incorruptibility, which irritates historians who are committed to a rather narrow vision of modernity— at least insofar as sexuality is concerned. What we need to do is to lay aside our post-Freudian/post-1960s conviction in the liberatory potential of sexuality and read the novel's distinction of sentiment and lust, much as Lin Shu's sentimental monarchism, as one kind of modern discursive strategy rather than as the remnant of an obsolete (Confucian) ideology. This, I believe, will allow us to engage more adequately not only with Wu's own moral agenda, but also with the enormous attraction the novel held for the late Qing and early Republican readership.

At the opening of the story set in Beijing, Zhang Dihua, daughter of a sojourning southern merchant, is engaged to Chen Bohe, the sprightly young son of an official family who rent a section of their residence to Dihua's family. Although we are told that Dihua and Bohe grow up together and are very fond of each other, we are not made privy to an evolving romance. In fact, as soon as Dihua reaches puberty and begins to behave coyly in the presence of Bohe, her family betake themselves to another residence to avoid impropriety. When the Boxer Uprising breaks out, Bohe is charged with the task of escorting Dihua and her mother (referred to in Hanan's translation as "Miss Bai") to Shanghai, where her father is at the moment on a business trip. On the southbound journey, Bohe becomes separated from Dihua and Miss Bai by a band of marauding Boxers. The narrative at this point breaks up into two strands. One strand, which takes up much less space, follows Bohe as he seeks refuge in a house abandoned by its wealthy owner, manages to take all the movable property with him to Shanghai, becomes corrupted by his ill-gotten wealth and the vices of the metropolis, and ends up a penniless beggar and opium addict. The main strand follows Dihua as she cares for her invalid mother, searches for Bohe, and endures the miseries of self-reproach, anxiety, and longing. In Shanghai, she and her father find Bohe, put him up in their house, and try to rid him of opium addiction. Bohe fails their expectations, returns to the street, and finally dies in a hospital, with Dihua by his side. Stricken by grief, Dihua leaves home for a nunnery.

Critics have generally identified the novel's chief merit as its representation of Dihua's emotional vicissitudes. For Michael Egan, the "novel is really the story of how Dihua is devastated by Bohe's downfall. Without her reaction the tale of Bohe's trials would be meaningless" (1980, 169). With Bohe mostly absent from the scenes and his degeneration cryptically hinted at rather than depicted, it behooves us to resist the impulse to read the novel as a familiar tragic love story. Some critics have commented in passing that Dihua seems to be more in love with the "idea of her fiancé" (that is, Bohe) than with the actual man, "who has done little to deserve it" (Hanan 1995, 13), or that her "passion is less for her fiancé than for her sense of her own virtue," which "is closer to bigotry than chastity and proves disastrous for everyone around her" (D. Wang 1997, 48). On the diegetic level, Dihua's bashfulness and discomfiture at sharing the same wagon seat with Bohe force the latter to walk by the wagon, thus directly causing their separation during the mob scene. The most gripping parts of the narration dwell on Dihua's inner struggles with her sense of modesty when it is put to the test of practical exigency, and also on her self-doubt and self-reproach when she anxiously speculates about Bohe's fate:

> At this thought [of the possibility of Bohe being trampled to death in the stampede] her heart broke, and tears trickled down her cheeks. . . . Then it occurred to her that it was all her fault, for being so concerned about proper behavior that she had refused even to speak to Bohe. . . . If only I'd been willing to talk to him, he'd have been happy to join me, and none of this would have occurred. Oh, Cousin Bohe, I'm the one who harmed you![4]

When Bohe finally collapses in the hospital, Dihua bravely overcomes all inhibitions to be his nurse. Because Bohe is too weak to swallow medicine fed to him by spoon, she feeds it to him mouth to mouth, ignoring the consternation of onlookers. Shedding her former prudery, she calls him "husband," touches his body, and confesses her feeling for him. The volte-face in Dihua's manner is remarkable, so much so that Bohe indeed appears no more than a "stage prop" in Dihua's "arduous course of female melancholy and moral development" (Chow 1991, 57).

One could also argue that the novel is much less a dramatization of psychic development than a celebration of constancy. *Constancy* is the term used by Alasdair MacIntyre in connection with the Aristotelian notion of the unity of virtues. The unity of virtues, according to MacIntyre, is intelligible only as part of a unitary life, a life that can be conceived and evaluated as a whole, or grasped within the unity of a narrative quest "whose episodes and incidents are provided through encountering and coping with the various harms, dangers, temptations, and distractions" (1984, 205, 219). The idea of a unitary life is most often crystallized in the ur-virtue of constancy and dramatized in narratives of danger and temptation. MacIntyre gives the example of Jane Austen's *Mansfield Park* in which the unflappable heroine Fanny Price affirms in her actions and choices the narrative unity central to the life of the virtues. Her constancy is pointedly contrasted to the Crawfords, whose charm proves to be pointless, even perilous, for want of constancy. Moreover, constancy presupposes the "recognition of a particular kind of threat to the integrity of the personality in the peculiarly modern social world," which for Austen is the threat of a self dissolving into the "presentation of self" (241–42).

In *The Sea of Regret*, Dihua's virtue of constancy is established beyond doubt. If there is any "moral development" to speak of, it is the steeliness of her virtue as it is put to increasingly harrowing test. For this reason, it would miss the point to say that "Dihua's love for Bohe is the only constant of her personality" (Egan 1980, 169), because Dihua's love for Bohe is founded less on a ruling passion tied to his charms and merits than on an unswerving allegiance to her sense of self. She duly falls in love with the young man chosen for her by her parents and remains in love with him in spite of (or because of) his absence and the fatal flaws in his character. Indeed, her feeling for Bohe grows stronger as the hope of marrying him grows dimmer. She invokes duty as much as passion to justify her defiance of ritual propriety in caring for the moribund Bohe. The eyebrow-raising change in her behavior is only the logical result of a personality consecrated to the virtue of constancy and determined to act out of its deepest convictions. Hence it is misleading to speak of Dihua as having been transformed from a stiff and rigid Confucian woman to an ardent romantic heroine, as if Wu Jianren had ended up writing a tale of passion/infatuation despite himself. The moral development that is charted out here does not go from repression to liberation, but from uncertainty to conviction. The hesitations and anxieties are what necessarily attend the quest for the principle that underscores a unitary life: constancy.

Constancy, moreover, is not defined procedurally as it is for European romantics. One does not automatically win admiration and approbation for remaining loyal to a cause, whatever it is, to the bitter end, to the state of martyrdom (see Berlin 1999). Rather, constancy for Wu Jianren is defined in the substantive terms of the Confucian structure of feeling. In other words, one's virtue and worth are directly hinged on one's allegiance to *qing*, the moral sentiment par excellence. A true Confucian romantic must not only abide by the demands of *qing* at all times and under all conditions, but also reconcile it to the demands of tradition and customs. Dihua's psychological torments in the middle section of the novel, therefore, are only a sign of her incomplete state of self-realization. Rather than mastering the situation through the exercise of *qing*, she allows the apparent conflict between propriety and feeling to clamp herself in a straightjacket that proves disastrous for everyone around her. In the end, however, she heroically rises to the occasion and performs the ultimate act of *qing*: after "giving" herself to Bohe at his deathbed, she symbolically follows him to the grave by renouncing the world and consecrating the rest of her life to his memory. In the climactic enactment of what Charles Taylor calls "the heroism of renunciation," Dihua affirms the central conviction of the Confucian structure of feeling, as aptly captured by Taylor in a different context: "Love transmuted by renunciation and suffering seems to offer the way to the highest in life, to an exaltation of sentiment which ordinary happiness cannot bring" (1989, 295).

Like Rousseau's programmatic novel *La Nouvelle Héloïse,* in connection to which Taylor makes the above observation, *The Sea of Regret* seeks to locate the transcendent within the moral space of secular modernity. I therefore question Xiaobing Tang's characterization of the novel as a staging ground for the conflict between culture and desire, or between meaning and experience. For Tang, the novel constitutes an "ambiguous beginning" of modern Chinese literature because it vacillates between a hagiographical intention, or ideological message as presented in the preamble, on the one hand, and a pathographical narrative centering on libidinal desire and votive attachment on the other. The upshot is a discourse of passion that "shares the psychic structure of obsessional neurosis" (2000, 2). The limits of the psychoanalytic approach are evident in the way in which it must leave out important details that cannot be explained libidinally without turning literary analysis into a quasi–case study à la Freud. With regard to Dihua's filial sentimentality, for example, Tang has little to say, for it clearly confounds the dichotomy of virtue and desire. Yet in my view, Dihua's role as a filial daughter is as central to the novel's moral vision as her gradually unfolding identity as a romantic.

Crucially, when taking her final leave of the mundane world, Dihua is able to convince her father of the propriety of her choice (reasoning that as a virtual widow she no longer has a place in her father's house) and thereby reconcile the potentially opposing requirements of wifely devotion and filial piety. Because constancy is predicated on the unity of virtues, the novel is at pains to portray Dihua as a filial daughter as well as a faithful betrothed. Filial piety here serves to solidify the idea of a unitary life, "a life that can be conceived and evaluated as a whole," instead of introducing any fundamental conflict of obligations or incongruity of personality (as it would in the May Fourth paradigm). As the bedrock of all virtues, *qing* cannot inform only one kind of relationship while failing to ground others. But this is not to suggest that there is a complete denial of conflict in the fulfillment of duty, because if this were true, there would be no virtue to speak of, much less a tale to tell. Dihua's virtue of constancy is always dramatized as a triumph over "harms, dangers, temptations, and distractions." Even the classic act of filial sacrifice—feeding

an ailing parent with one's flesh—is scrutinized in her mind for potential implications of unfiliality not just to heighten the drama, but also to present her
ethical actions as arising out of genuine conviction. Or in Kantian terms, she
refuses to let the ethical fall victim to the heteronomy of desire, to what is
merely given. Instead, she reasons with herself until whatever she does in the
end is a deliberate choice and always strongly felt. For example, when her
mother's illness takes a drastic turn for the worse, Dihua sits up all night tormented by worries and apprehensions:

> At the back of her mind she couldn't help thinking of those cases in which
> the ancients cured their parents with the aid of pieces of flesh cut from their
> own thighs. I wonder if it would work, she asked herself, because if it would,
> I'd never begrudge a tiny scrap of my own flesh . . . I know, I shan't worry
> about whether it works or not, I'll simply try it out and see. She waited until
> the middle of the night, then lit a stick of incense and said a prayer for her
> mother's speedy recovery. She also swore a secret vow: "Although we are
> taught that we inherit our bodies from our parents and must never let them
> come to any harm, I have no choice but to do this unfilial thing in the hope
> of curing my mother's illness. If it makes her better, I'll willingly atone for
> my sin." She bared her left arm, bit into a piece of flesh and drew it up, then
> with her right hand took a pair of sharp Bingzhou scissors and sheared the
> piece right off. Still feeling no pain, she quickly bound up the would with a
> piece of cloth . . . [Having prepared the concoction,] Dihua . . . offered it to
> her [mother], then stayed by her side until dawn, when her condition showed
> no sign of improvement. Dihua became even more nervous, and for the first
> time her wound began to ache. (SR, 177)

Dihua's reaction to her mother's death, consisting of swooning, weeping,
and attempted suicide, is almost identical to her reaction to Bohe's death.
The vows of loyalty Dihua gives her mother as the latter breathes her last are
as moving as any vow exchanged between romantic lovers: "Mother, we've
faced all kinds of trials together and come through them safe and sound, and
I was hoping to remain at your side forever. Now that you're so ill, it must
be my fault for not nursing you properly. If the worst should happen, I'm
ready and willing to go with you!" (SR, 178). The dying Bohe and the dying
mother occupy the structurally similar position of the needy and helpless—
the quintessential object of pity and receptacle of personal sacrifice. Dihua's
act of feeding Bohe medicine mouth to mouth has as little erotic charge as
her act of feeding her mother with her own flesh. The hospital scene is

merely an emphatic iteration of the scene at the inn, a climactic point in the unfolding of a virtuous subject.

Xiaobing Tang argues that through the figure of Dihua, Wu Jianren mobilizes from native cultural resources such virtues as "sincerity" and "devotion" both to preserve an inner realm of authenticity and to cope with a comprehensive danger situation: "In this sense, the creation of Dihua in the novel reflects a general anxiety over the continuity as much as the purity of a threatened native culture" (2000, 42–44). Similarly, Prasenjit Duara discusses the nationalist "regime of authenticity" that constructs woman as a symbol of national cultural essence and continuity, as the figure of tradition within modernity (1998). Both Tang and Duara's arguments shed considerable light on Wu's insistent evocation of virtue—what Tang glosses as Wu's self-conscious preference for hagiography over pathography. Because sentiment is the occasion for hagiography, it has to be virtuous. Wu cannot allow it to be reduced to sexual passion, which is associated, within Confucian sentimentality, with the anarchic pleasures of the private body. But like Wen Kang, Wu locates the heroic decisively within the quotidian. Above all, Wu is celebrating *qing*—"the innate feeling that Heaven has sown in our hearts"—as the linchpin of an alternative master narrative, the narrative of timelessness, of a unitary life founded on a principle that is both transcendental and immanent, abstract and concrete. Dihua's journey from Beijing to Shanghai is symbolic of the native culture's timeless core of authenticity traversing the space from tradition to modernity and stoically keeping at bay the corrosive forces of time, violence, and desire.

It would be a mistake to see Wu as an obscurantist bent upon stemming the tide of modernity, any less than it would be to read the novel as a drama of the eternal conflict between passion and morality. Dihua's subjectivity is formed not in fear or neurotic obsession. Rather, she secures her sense of self in the unity of virtues and in her ability to triumph over adverse circumstances. In presenting the master narrative of constancy, Wu is keenly attuned to new threats to the integrity of personality and the unitary life that he so values. Bohe's fate, for example, allegorizes the baleful consequences of the failure to withstand the dangers peculiar to the late Qing social world—rebellion, war, illegitimate wealth, and the treaty-port as the den of iniquities. Without the firmness of will that Dihua possesses, Bohe's degradation is set in motion as soon as the first temptation perchance presents itself and not even the promise of love can halt the downward spiral.

One can reasonably assert that *The Sea of Regret* is not a love story in the same way that *Mansfield Park* is, for love here carries none of the redemptive power that it does in the English novel. Austen rewards the constant Fanny Price with a Cinderella's happily-ever-after. Wu, however, sees no such redemptive power in romantic love. To drive home this point, he devises a mirroring subplot in which Bohe's brother Zhong'ai, who is the male counterpart of Dihua in terms of fidelity, filiality, and courage, is betrayed by his fiancée, Wang Juanjuan, who becomes a courtesan in Shanghai after losing contact with Zhong'ai. In a negative way, Juanjuan's fate disproves the facile reading of the novel as a critique of Confucian ritualism that stifles the natural expression of feeling and harms the happiness of the young lovers. If anything, the novel suggests that Juanjuan's moral handicap is a product of having had too much education (for a girl) and too much freedom in exercising her feelings. Whereas the adolescent Dihua discontinues her lessons and devotes all her time to needlework when she becomes engaged to Bohe, Juanjuan continues attending classes with the boys (including her fiancé Zhong'ai). Unlike Dihua's judicious parents, who relocate the family when Dihua reaches puberty, Juanjuan's parents let her grow up with Zhong'ai in the same residential compound.

Curiously, the same experience (of having grown up with one's betrothed) has had no adverse effect on Zhong'ai's moral development. Before he reencounters Juanjuan in Shanghai, Zhong'ai secures an official post in procurement in Shaanxi and finds himself in the company of fawning merchants and dissolute colleagues who are "addicted" to the pleasure quarters. Zhong'ai remains austerely indifferent and in fact scoffs at his colleagues for their clumsy imitation of a false idol: Jia Baoyu, the protagonist of the *Dream of the Red Chamber*. In his view, the dandies of the pleasure quarters delude themselves in imagining themselves as Baoyus and the singsong girls as their Daiyus and Baochais (Baoyu's girl cousins and love interests): if the men shuffle in and out of the brothels like in a lantern show and the women have to service one patron after another, how can one speak of the sweet joy and bitter torment of love? In one of the clearest statements in favor of the (polygamous) companionate marriage, Zhong'ai avows that "the only right place for passion is with your wife or concubine" (SR, 176).

Although it is totally unremarkable, to our ears, to suggest that one ought to love one's spouse (if we may bracket the question of polygamy for now), it is a firm repudiation of the Confucian injunction against conjugal intimacy as well as a plea for the unity of body and soul *avant la lettre*. Zhong'ai's statement affirms the central tenet of the Confucian structure of feeling that the male-female bond is the foundation of all social bonds. Involuntarily separated from his fiancé, Zhong'ai refuses to seek emotional fulfillment in the traditional venue of the brothel, where money and lust cobble together exhilarating but flimsy and fleeting sociability. Hence, as soon as he learns of Juanjuan's downfall, Zhong'ai, now an orphan, distributes all his wealth and property and disappears into the mountains. The eremitic solution is a familiar one since the *Peach Blossom Fan* and *Dream of the Red Chamber*. In refusing to match up the deserving Dihua and Zhong'ai (as Austen matches up Fanny and Edmund) and reward their virtue with conjugal bliss, Wu seems to suggest that because love is merely a manifestation of virtue (*qing*, constancy), it cannot become virtue's reward, or a narrative telos. In other words, one strives to be virtuous for its own sake. When love has served it role in the test of constancy, one gives it up rather than compromise the true principle of life.

Read in this light, Wu's novel is more than a poignant exploration of the predicament of honor and passion, morality and individuality. To be sure, the story does seem to suggest that *li* can become an impediment to *qing*: Does not Dihua blame herself (her inflexible prudishness) for being the immediate cause of Bohe's undoing? It does seem that had Dihua been able to let her love for Bohe overcome her rigid sense of modesty, Bohe might have been spared the trials and their love might not have come to grief. Do we not have here a typical conflict between personal desire and social restraints? Is not the former implicitly affirmed and the latter implicitly critiqued—especially in view of Dihua's courageous flouting of the rule of avoidance to care for the dying Bohe? Although this line of reading is not unjustified, it misses the novel's central agenda of resurrecting the Confucian structure of feeling; at the very least, it renders the episode of Dihua's filial sacrifice totally extraneous and pointless. Even more incomprehensible would be her decision after Bohe's death to "leave home" (*chujia*) in honor of his memory.

To avoid assimilating *The Sea of Regret* into the framework of love story we are familiar with, we would do well to be mindful of the fact that the lovers are separated not by authoritative parents or scheming villains, but by a historical event that is so unconnected to their lives that it merely accentuates the impersonal and erratic quality of fate. History in this novel performs a function not unlike that which is attributed to the Real. Marston Anderson holds that the Real, encoded in such recognizable topoi as hunger, violence, disease, sexual desire, and death, is a demystifying and destabilizing agent. It introduces the presence of chaos and indeterminacy and "confound[s] the efforts of the imagination to reorder the world" (1990, 17). Here, history impinges on the imaginary autonomy and integrity of the self by inflicting on the body the cruel imprints of temporality (disease and death) and by assailing the virtue of constancy with the unbearable human tragedies of separation and betrayal. For this reason, the story could be set against any large-scale social convulsion that results in dislocation, separation, and corruption. Not only is there very little sense as to where the author stands on the Boxer Uprising, but the characters' lives are merely passively *disrupted* by it rather than *entwined* with it. We have noted that Bohe's fall from moral rectitude is precipitated by his being abruptly thrown into the midst of wealth and metropolitan delights, not by his encounter with either the Boxers or foreign soldiers. The latter merely create, through their violent clashes, the conditions in which Bohe is extricated from his moral community and is forced to make moral choices in a social vacuum, without the advice and supervision of kinsmen. We readily recognize these conditions as an essential element of the alienation of modernity. Also for this reason, the novel is not, strictly speaking, a bildungsroman, for virtue is outside the stream of events, warding off the corrosive effects of change. Each discrete episode in the novel is less a stage in a cumulatively progressing plot than a moment in which history is overcome by virtue and vice versa.

The parents in the novel are exceptionally loving and caring and capable of reciprocating filial devotion with exuberant parental affection. They educate their daughters and negotiate the latter's betrothals with reason and wisdom. Dihua's father complies with all of Dihua's wishes, including her lacerating decision to take vows as a nun. Parents, in other words, are facilitators of virtue rather than its destroyers. Instead, fate is the litmus test that brings out the virtue of the truly virtuous (Dihua and Zhong'ai) and reveals the moral defects (inconstancy, avarice, lust) of the not so virtuous (Bohe and Juanjuan). With no one but the lovers themselves to blame, the novel is decidedly not a story of defiance or transgression but rather a story of constancy, with Dihua as the embodiment of the fundamental oneness of all sentiment-based virtues.

If Wu Jianren and his Butterfly followers were the turn-of-the-century standard-bearers of the Confucian structure of feeling, they also resolutely broke with its convention of comic reconciliation. Instead, time and again they reenacted in their narratives the famous ending of *Dream* in which religion and death are the final destinations of broken hearts. But Wu's attempt to reinstate a regime of virtue through one woman's heroic struggle to fulfill her destiny was apparently well appreciated by his contemporaries. Figuratively speaking, Dihua is the resolution of the tension between the imperative to uphold the hierarchies of social relationships and the need to validate the emotive foundation of these relationships, as well as the tension between the desire to hold onto a moral ideal and the growing recognition of its vulnerability under the onslaught of modernity. Conceptually, she is a direct descendant of the *ernü yingxiong* lineage, finding the heroic in the exercising of immanent virtues. Still, the novel's narrative of timelessness and individual ethical heroism was quite at odds with turn-of-the-century intellectuals' overwhelming concern with the collective fate of the "Chinese" and with the nature and purpose of the social. This accounts for the embattled status of Butterfly sentimental fiction as a whole and its marginalization in May Fourth–influenced literary histories.

NEW FICTION, NEW SOCIETY

The birth of the novel in early modern Europe is commonly associated with the emergence of a bourgeois civil society/public sphere (Habermas 1991). Accounting for the sudden flourishing of novelistic forms, particularly autobiography, Lionel Trilling writes: "Historians of European culture are in substantial agreement that, in the late sixteenth and early seventeenth centuries, something like a mutation in human nature took place. One way of giving a synopsis of the whole complex psycho-historical occurrence is to say that the idea of society, much as we now conceive it, had come into being" (1971, 21). The rise of the social has been celebrated as a momentous step forward on the path of progress—from the idiocy of village life to the modern forms of voluntary and public-spirited civil society. It is accompanied by the birth of the modern individual, who defines himself (less often herself), paradoxically, in opposition to society. Trilling points out that for the first time in history, the nature of society is not continuous with the nature of the individuals who constitute it. Society is instead hypostatized as having a life of its own that is other than human and hence a corruption of human truth, and this has given rise to the desire to bring it into accord with humanity (17–19). For Rousseau and his disciples, society inaugurates the loss of innocence and the age of pride, vanity, and dissimulation, threatening to obfuscate the truth that resides exclusively within the individual. The confessional autobiography thus rises to the fore as the preeminent genre of authenticity. One needs only to avow that one has spoken sincerely to be able to critique society with moral authority. Rousseau's *Confessions*, therefore, is not a gratuitous undertaking. Rather, "it was the painstaking demonstration of the author's authority to speak plainly, to bring into question every aspect of society" (23–24).

Social criticism in the late Qing did not entirely rest on the newly minted moral authority of the plain-speaking, confessional individual, though it certainly went beyond the Confucian tradition of remonstrance. The transition from the model of "upright versus corrupt officials" to that of "the officialdom versus the people" as discussed by Chen Pingyuan (1989, 236–50) was a clear indication of the sweepingly critical perspective adopted by the intelligentsia. Xiaren's apologia for *Dream* in his contributions to the *Xin xiaoshuo* column "Xiaoshuo conghua" (Notes on fiction, no. 12, 1904) is probably one of the most radical instances of late Qing criticism. In defending the novel against accusations of salaciousness, Xiaren elaborates a naturalist theory of human nature that shows visible influence of Darwinism. He argues that human nature (*renxing*) is inherently at odds with morality, which is a social artifice. Morality teams up with the family system and social conventions to form a deep layer of psychological sediment in people. As a result, people regard morality as natural and persecute those who have gone "astray." Given that human nature is always in conflict with morality, to safeguard the integrity of morality we would have to destroy human nature. But if there is no more human nature, how can we still speak of morality? The only alternative, the author implies, is to bring down the citadel of old morality and erect a new one that respects and conforms to human nature. This is precisely why he so admires Cao Xueqin. By his reckoning, Cao was the first person in the course of two thousand years of Chinese history to challenge a morality decreed by ancients who could have in no way foreseen the changes taking place in Cao's times. Cao created the "the sentimental breed" (*qingzhong*) to showcase a new species of human beings who have come in touch with true human nature by breaking through the barriers of social morality (Chen Pingyuan and Xia Xiaohong 1997, 89–92).

What is striking about Xiaren's essay is the pitting of human nature against an abstract, hypostatized "society." Others were less radical. Still, the moral critique of society was the general tenor of the late Qing discourse of *qing*, whereby the modernity of society was marked by its availability to "critical examination by individual persons, especially by those who make it their business to scrutinize the polity, the class of men we now call intellectuals" (Trilling 1971, 26–27). Although different critics may have gravitated toward different issues, their basic assumptions as well as overall objectives were seldom at variance: Chinese society was diseased and the literary reform, particularly the newly invented genre of New Fiction (*xin xiaoshuo*), could help bring about its cure.

The story of the rise of New Fiction has been told many times, and there is little need to belabor the point made by many scholars to the effect that late Qing reformers promoted fiction for social and political, rather than aesthetic, ends. It is commonly noted that fiction modeled on nineteenth-century European realism was accorded the same transitive efficacy that Confucians had traditionally attributed to "higher" forms of letters such as the classics, official histories, and poetry. The new power accorded to fiction—it is to be "the core paladin of the nation-state" (Huters 2005, 15)—presents difficulty when it comes to evaluating traditional Chinese fiction, a lowly genre in the Confucian hierarchy of letters. Liang Qichao (1873–1929), the foremost promoter of New Fiction, readily concedes instrumentality to traditional fiction but laments the "wrong" kind of effect it engenders. It is insidious in its social consequences because it is able to hold people under the spell of irrational ideas without their knowing it. In his oft-cited essay, "Lun xiaoshuo yu qunzhi zhi guanxi" (On the relationship between fiction and the governance of the people," in *Xin xiaoshuo*, 1902), Liang lays everything he finds objectionable about Chinese society not at the door of high Confucian culture, but traditional fiction:

> How did the Chinese develop the idea of holding scholars successful in the official examinations and prime ministers in such high esteem? It stems from fiction. What is the origin of the Chinese obsession with beautiful ladies and talented scholars? It lies in fiction. Where does the Chinese sympathy for robbers and brigands hidden away in the rivers and lakes [*jianghu*] spring from? It springs from fiction. Where does the Chinese interest in witches and fox spirits come from? It comes from fiction. (Chen Pingyuan and Xia Xiaohong 1997, 53; Denton 1996, 79, translation modified)

Clearly, the issue is not so much about fiction per se as it is about the ideological and institutional underpinnings of Chinese society. Fiction is as blameworthy for tainting the common folk with orthodox values as it is promising for its power to usher in changes from abroad (Huters 2005, 111). Reformers have hoped that the commoners will absorb their enlightenment messages as effortlessly, or even eagerly, as they have ideas about fame and rank, scholars and beauties, robbers and knight-errants, and wizards and fox spirits. The vast majority of New Fiction is indeed produced with this end in view. Literary historians are therefore wont to excuse New Fiction's crudity on account of the overload of extraliterary freight, even though its very birth is catapulted by the sense of crisis in the social and political realm. The paradox of New Fiction, of being simultaneously given life and smothered by weighty political concerns, somewhat parallels the fate of "society" in relation to the nation. The conflation of society and nation in the writings of the period both helps legitimize the pursuit of civil society and places on it a bell jar. It is worth reiterating that, for the most part, Liang Qichao's social criticism is not made in the Rousseauian spirit of defining and defending the individual against a corrupt society. More accurately, it is an effort to reform the individual and society in the hopes of revitalizing the nation.

From its inception, the late Qing discourse of sentiment has taken the nation as its primary referent. Not surprisingly, a New Fiction genre, "the novel of sentiment" (*xieqing xiaoshuo* or *yanqing xiaoshuo*), is much more taken up with the role of sentiment in reforming social mores and enhancing national cohesion than in defending individual freedoms and rights. Commentators insist on evaluating novels of sentiment according to the degree to which they *go beyond* sentiment, or the adroitness with which they combine the personal with the social and political. A novel that does not attempt to speak to "larger" issues is deemed "obscene." For example, in an open correspondence, "Zai da moujun shu" (A second reply to Mr. X, in *Xiaoshuo yuebao* 7, no. 3, 1916), Shujue launches an attack on the *Romance of the Western Chamber* as representative of all unworthy novels (and plays) of sentiment. He begins by denying that eros should constitute a legitimate subject matter unto itself: Heaven endows men and women with different anatomies and sexual desire solely so that the human race may perpetuate itself (Chen Pingyuan and Xia Xiaohong 1997, 566). If sex is not a telos, for a work of fiction to "stop" at erotic fulfillment is to go against the natural order of things.

The author continues: The primary task of a novelist is to document exemplary individual characters/events for the purpose of supplementing moral-political education (*buzhu zhengjiao*). Love and desire must come next.[5] In *Dream of the Red Chamber*, sexual love is merely the surface text while the rise and fall of the Jia clan is at the core; *The Scholars* (Rulin waishi, by Wu Jingzi) focuses on society; *The Water Margin* critiques politics—all in accordance with the purpose of perpetuating mankind. The *Romance of the Western Chamber*, on the contrary, tells only of sexual liaisons (*nannü*) and thus inverts the hierarchy of significance. Its emulators all begin their novels with sexual attraction and end them with desire fulfilled. This has become an established formula, so that nowadays novels of sentiment all end with desire fulfilled and then have nothing more to say (567).

Here the author seems to be targeting a type of risqué courtesan novels popular in the late Qing (see David Wang 1997, chapter 2). He is most direct, in a way even uncannily postmodern, about why he objects to representations of sexuality: Because "words are the mother of facts" (*yanlun wei shishi zhi mu*), novel readers gradually take it for granted that once a relationship is consummated, there is no more *qing* to speak of. So they go in search of new love by taking in concubines or contracting other more depraved forms of sexual relationship. Shujue ends his essay by turning to European novels. He avers that all European novels mix love with history, science, and crime detection, and that even straightforward romantic stories abide by the rules of family, society, morality, and religion and strive to impress upon the reader the imperative of perpetuating the human race (568).

In exhorting novelists to transcend sentiment by combining it with larger and more "meaningful" themes, Shujue makes it clear that he is not about to usher in "an affirmation of ordinary life." Sentimental fiction's specialty in portraying the manners and mores of everyday life is seldom valued despite the populist call to replace heroes with the common folk as literary protagonists. Hence the very first document marking fiction's rise to prominence in the reformist project attributes the power of fiction to its deployment of the dual motif of love and heroism—here, heroism is a catchall for political and social subjects. In "Benguan fuyin shuobu yuanqi" (Announcing our policy to print a fiction supplement, *Guowen bao*, no. 16, 1897), perhaps the earliest of the "series of wildly optimistic pronouncements about the potential of fiction to bring about a brave new world" (Huters 2005, 116), Yan Fu (1853–1921) and Xia Zengyou (1863–1921) claim that fiction keeps alive a truer kind of history than what is recorded in official histories because it documents daily life in the vernacular language (Chen Pingyuan and Xia Xiaohong 1997, 26–27). Daily life is more authentic because it is driven by evolutionary, even mechanical, principles.

To conceive of life in mechanical terms is a leap of faith made possible by Yan

Fu's conversion to Darwinism. In a striking but little-noticed passage, Yan and Xia invoke the workings of electric currents to explain the principle of love and heroism: a man and woman are attracted to each other like two opposite electric charges, whereas members of the same sex are repelled by each other like two like electric charges. The former ensures the perpetuation of the human race, and the latter is indispensable to sustaining the struggle for survival (24). In the resounding cadence of a scientific language, Yan and Xia codify the pairing of love and heroism (*ernü yingxiong*) into a politically significant fiction genre, though they are by no means its inventors.[6] We have seen in Chapter 1 how Wen Kang's *A Tale of Heroic Sons and Daughters* combines the romantic and chivalric genres in order to weave an ultimate fantasy of Confucian orthodoxy. Few novels written after it could sustain his blithe faith in the perfect harmony of virtue and desire. Chivalric fiction and courtesan fiction in the late Qing continued to indulge in "force" and "fighting" and in "rouge" and "powder," making little or no attempt to unite heroism and love under a higher principle. This greatly troubled the late Qing reformers and hence the call for a complete revamping of Chinese fiction. In the afore-cited essay by Liang Qichao, he accuses the two genres of encouraging sentimentalism and libertinism on the one hand, and inspiring secret brotherhoods and banditry on the other:

> Nowadays our people are frivolous and immoral. They indulge in, and are obsessed with, sensual pleasures. Caught up in their emotions, they versify and weep over the spring flowers and the autumn moon, frittering away their youthful and lively spirits. Young men between fifteen and thirty years of age take upon themselves the pursuit of love, sorrow, and sickness with great earnest. They are amply endowed with romantic sentiment but lack heroic spirit. In some extreme cases, they even engage in immoral acts and so poison the entire society. This is all because of fiction.
>
> Now everywhere among our people there are heroes of the forests and woods [*lulin*]. The ceremony of "swearing an oath of brotherhood in the Peach Garden" and of "oath-taking on Mount Liang" is rampant . . . among the lower classes. This has gradually led to the formation of secret societies such as the Triads and the Big Swords, culminating in the Boxer Uprising which was responsible for the loss of our Capital and for bringing foreign troops into China. This is all because of fiction. (Chen Pingyuan and Xia Xiaohong 1997, 53; Denton 1996, 80, translation modified)

Although Liang seems to be referring to traditional vernacular fiction and its contemporary imitations, plenty of Butterfly fiction produced a decade later would probably also be vulnerable to these charges. However, a newer kind of *ernü yingxiong* ideal also began to emerge that shunned the representation of violence and scorned the eclipse of the heroic spirit by "love, sorrow, and sickness." Like *A Tale of Heroic Sons and Daughters*, Butterfly *ernü yingxiong* fiction seeks to bind love to heroism. But unlike the former, the principle under which love and heroism are to be united has shifted away from filial piety and become increasingly identified with patriotism. Here, the *ernü* may still be filial, but their reigning identity has become that of sentimental lovers whose heroism is defined by their courage to love and to die for the newly imagined community of nation. In the next section, I examine how, through a recuperated discourse of *ernü yingxiong*, Butterfly novelists and critics imagine the role of sentiment in constructing the social as an eminently moral space in which enchantment, heroism, and transcendence again become possible in the modern condition.

TO LOVE AND TO DIE FOR

It may be surprising to speak of Butterfly fiction in connection with weighty concepts that are usually associated with the May Fourth movement. But as a matter of fact, Butterfly writers have produced (authored and translated) a considerable oeuvre of patriotic stories. The historical oblivion to which most of these stories have been consigned owes a great deal to the fact that Butterfly nationalism is very much articulated within the terms of the Confucian structure of feeling. It is therefore a "nation-view" (Prasenjit Duara's term) that does not fit into the dominant national narrative and is therefore largely forgotten.

Many Butterfly patriotic stories retell the heroic deeds of loyal ministers, generals, warriors, and even commoners from premodern Sino-centric myths and movements. But there are almost an equal number of translated or adapted stories featuring foreign heroes and heroines. In this regard, Butterfly nationalism is unmistakably modern in acknowledging the equivalent status of the Chinese nation vis-à-vis other nations. Indeed, one of the core differences between modern nationalism and its premodern antecedents is the recognition of the formal equality of states and the endorsement of the "comity of nations" as the ideal world order. The momentous shift in the Chinese perception of their place in the world has been well documented by historians such as John K. Fairbank and Joseph Levenson. Although some scholars have challenged the supposition of a radical break between Chinese culturalism and modern nationalism,[7] it is difficult to deny the newness of writers and readers in the first decade of the twentieth century admiring, among others, Joan of Arc, a French woman far removed in both time-space and culture simply because she is the icon of French nationalist mythology. Now, patriotic sentiment is no longer an absolute value, a marker of civilization and Chineseness; instead, it has become relative, translatable, and emulatable, a kind of global currency that renders human solidarity infinitely and immediately intelligible.

It is often observed that secular modernity in Europe arose with the repudiation of the warrior virtue and the honor ethic as aristocratic pretensions, utterly defunct and ridiculous in the age of the market and the nuclear family, or the age of the affirmation of ordinary life. The representation of ordinary life as a source of value in early twentieth-century Chinese popular fiction, however, was both encouraged (because of the new, symbolic status of the people) and hemmed in by the nationalist imperative, which fueled an intense interest in heroic narratives both foreign and indigenous. For example, Lin Shu, though most remembered for his translations of foreign sentimental fiction, found a kindred spirit in H. Rider Haggard, whose stories of imperialist plunder of far-off lands held an irresistible attraction for him. In fact, the largest number of novels (twenty-five) translated by Lin from a single foreign author came from the pen of Haggard. The aggressive white man is admirable for his "bandit spirit," which has won for him vast material resources and territories, and which is therefore far superior to the Chinese ethos of "yielding" (Lee 1973, 55).

The Butterfly School, which owed its reputation of political irrelevance and frivolity to its enormous output of sentimental fiction, did much to modernize indigenous heroic narratives by injecting patriotic sentimentalism into the genre of chivalric fiction. Gong Pengcheng (1987) notes that before Butterfly writers turned to this genre, it had been mostly limited to three categories: the rebel-hero cycle, the chivalric adventure, and the court case or detective story. These stories place high value on martial skills, worldly experience, and the intricate web of favors, debts, rewards, and retributions. They feature a group of journeyman martial artists who absorb the reader's attention with their action rather than with their psyche. Butterfly authors, however, replace the merciless world of rivers and lakes with the boudoir and the sword-toting warrior with a melancholy lover. Unlike his predecessors, the lover (usually he) is more solitary than gregarious, concerned less with the protocols of collective action than with the perfection of individual skills, literary and martial. Much ink is spilled over the ebbs and flows of his passion and the ups and downs of his relationship with a woman. In short, love is no longer anathema to martial prowess; it has become a prerequisite. Misogynist heroes like Wu Song and Shi Xiu (brutish murderers of "adulterous" women in *The Water Margin*) may still be stock characters, but they are no longer heartthrobs for every reader.

The fall of the misogynist hero has everything to do with the speed with which the principle of gender equality has prevailed in social discourse. The sentimental hero/heroine, or the *ernü yingxiong,* signals not only a new notion of self based on the universalistic principle of sentiment, but also a new vision of a horizontal community beyond the *jianghu*—the community of the nation in which everyone is a citizen, no more, no less. But more importantly, nationalism requires a fundamentally inward subject and sentimental heroism furnishes the richest vocabulary and deftest grammar for delineating such a subject. The one-time best-selling Butterfly novel of sentiment, *Yu li hun* (Jade pear spirit, by Xu Zhenya [1889–1937]), provides on the diegetic level as well as in authorial voice what is essentially the first modern articulation of the relationship between *ernü* and *yingxiong*. The story tells of the frustrated love between He Mengxia, a schoolteacher, and Bai Liying (aka Liniang), a widow. Mengxia and Liniang become attracted to each other through the innocent agency of her young son, whom Mengxia is hired to tutor. Though deeply devoted to Mengxia, Liniang is reluctant to accept his love owing to the stigma of free courtship and widow remarriage. Much of the text is taken up with their surreptitious exchange of letters, poems, and anguished sobs. After Liniang's self-willed death, Mengxia joins the revolutionary army and dies a patriotic martyr in the Wuchang Uprising in 1911. The final image of Mengxia falling on the battleground while clutching a bundle of love epistles and diaries is the ultimate *tableau vivant* of sentimental heroism.

One cannot emphasize enough the sheer distance between Mengxia and the older type of martial heroes. Rather than a man of immense physical strength and imposing stature, Mengxia is described as a gentle-mannered scholar who has never wielded a weapon before. Nonetheless, he joins the army without hesitation and faces the enemies' bullets with aplomb. It is true that the battle scene in which Mengxia achieves martyrdom is given the space of merely half a page in a close to 200-page novel.[8] The rest of the book is unapologetically devoted to the *affaire de coeur*. However, the novel is emphatic about Mengxia's heroic status and seizes on every opportunity to assert that Mengxia's identity as a lover is in some fundamental way connected to his eventual martyrdom. It articulates a philosophy of sentiment that both draws on the cult of *qing* and breaks new ground in tying heroism to patriotism.

After a classic love story scene in which Mengxia writes a letter in blood protesting his undying love to Liniang, the author launches into a disquisition about the double meaning of shedding blood:

> Alas! A man's blood is never shed for nothing. Today, Mengxia sheds it for romantic love [*ernü zhi aiqing*] and it is well worth it. Heaven and earth are but one giant grotto of sentiment; and all heroes are natural born sentimentalists [*qingzhong*]. Blood is the stuff sentiment is made of. Thus shedding blood is in fact the working of sentiment. Sentiment's reach is infinite— downward into the private realm of romantic passion and upward into the fate of the state. . . . Those who shed plentiful blood are none other than men/women of sentiment [*duoqingren*]. . . . If one can shed blood for the sake of love, one can also shed blood for the love of country. By the same token, if one is unwilling to shed blood for love, how can we expect him or her to do so for the country? (Xu Zhenya 1994, 142)

As the somatic extension of sentiment, blood gives material expression to the essential oneness of romantic love and patriotic love. However, in employing the spatial metaphor to describe the flow of sentiment as "upward" and "downward," Xu implicitly privileges dying for the country (*xunguo*) over dying for love (*xunqing*). This is the reason why, despite the brevity of the battlefield passage, it looms so large in the teleological design of the story: One's sentimental experience is but a preparation for the ultimate sublime act of martyrdom. Naoki Sakai argues that national belonging is defined in terms of one's willingness both to kill and to be killed for the nation (as institutionalized in the practice of universal conscription). Insofar as "to belong" is always a matter of becoming, of acting, of killing and dying, the nation is a veritable "community of death." In the discourse of national martyrdom, a contingent, individual death is represented as a collective experience in which one becomes integrated with the body of the nation. In death at last, the schism between one's life as an individual and one's identity as a national subject becomes sutured (Sakai 1997, 181).[9]

In linking up "dying for love" and "dying for the country," the novel distances itself from older *xunqing* stories, the most celebrated of which is Jia

Baoyu's flight to religious transcendence (often treated as the spiritual equivalent of death) once his dream for a sentimental utopia is crushed by patriarchy. Xu believes that although Baoyu is laudable in "treating his own life as a stalk of feather" and "despising fame and fortune as a pair of thread-bare shoes," he is too myopic and fails to distinguish the "weighty" from the "petty" among love's many purposes (1994, 169). If Mengxia simply wallows in the luxury of grief or even follows Liniang to the grave, then he is only "adding one more ghost to the boundless sea of sentiment" (169). His death may still be meaningful within the traditional discourse of dying for love, but it cannot be made part of the collective representation of patriotism. But because he is "a man of supreme sentiment" (zhiqingren), Mengxia chooses instead to die for the revolutionary cause, turning an intensely private moment into a public statement proclaiming one's subjectivity and national belonging. The sentimental self, therefore, exchanges its life for a place in the discourse of nationalism; or to paraphrase Michel de Certeau, it submits its own body to be inscribed by the nationalist scriptural economy, as a "legible word" in its empowering language (1984, 140).

A short commentary published nearly a decade before the sensational success of Yu li hun envisions the new community of the nation as one suffused by sentiment. Descriptively entitled "Yixia xiaoshuo yu yanqing xiaoshuo ju shuguan shehui ganqing zhi su li" (Chivalric fiction and sentimental fiction have the power to instill social feeling, Zhongwai xiaoshuo lin 1, no. 7, 1907), the essay claims for the two genres named in the title a superior efficacy in cohering society and binding the average person to the nation: "To an ignoramus, words preaching duty, loyalty, and patriotism will go in one ear and come out the other. But the same person can be glued to tales about heroes and lovers. Why? Because of the power of sentiment" (Chen Pingyuan and Xia Xiaohong 1997, 228). Anticipating Yu li hun's message, the essayist asserts that there are only nameless heroes, but never feelingless ones. While chivalric fiction directly inspires people's love for the country and teaches the lower classes about morality and honor, romantic fiction uses love obliquely but effectively to articulate heroic ambitions. "The nation may be immense, the people may be heterogeneous, but nothing is beyond the reach of sentiment and nothing is unbridgeable by sentiment" (Chen Pingyuan and Xia Xiaohong 1997, 229). Although the author does not theorize the relationship between heroic and sentimental fiction, the two genres are nonetheless given equal status and are always mentioned in conjunction. Moreover, chivalric adventurism can translate directly into patriotism because it is, at least since Wen Kang, seldom conceived of without an affective substrate—"the loving heart"—which is imagined as infinite in its power to move and to inspire. Heroes must abound in feeling in order to move freely between the quotidian and the heroic, and between the spheres of the personal and the political. Sentiment, with its logic of universal equivalence and affinity, has become the locus in which much social and political hope is invested, not the least of which is the pursuit of modern nationhood.

In *Yu li hun* we see one of the earliest efforts to establish a continuum between love and patriotism, and its particular model of *ernü yingxiong* linking the personal and political in a gendered pattern reverberates across much of Butterfly literature. A core plot pattern emerges from these texts: on the one hand, the hero dies for the nation in full glory; the heroine, on the other hand, either follows him in death or remains in permanent mourning for him, making herself a living memorial of his sacrificial act. A story by Bao Tianxiao (1876–1973), "Ming hong" (Letters to the underworld, *Xiaoshuo daguan* nos. 2, 4, 1915), assumes the mournful voice of a widow addressing her husband who has been killed in the 1911 revolution. She has been writing to him, at his behest, every week and continues to do so even after his death, burning each letter in an incense burner. The letters give rueful accounts of their son's health and education (she is teaching him about *xiao* and *ti*, or filial and fraternal piety) and her longing for him (she goes over his diaries and poems again and again); she describes how she has sent him recent pictures of herself (that is, she has burned them); and so forth (Yu Runqi 1997b, 503–15). The gendered pattern of male sacrifice and female memory, however, departs from the usual Butterfly formula in which the woman dies for love and the man lives on to tell the story and to construct the meaning of their passionate existence (more on this in Chapter 3). A discomfort with this reversal of gender roles—that is, giving women the power of words while reducing men to mute corpses—in the Butterfly *ernü yingxiong* genre may be the reason behind an interesting dialogue between two Butterfly writers in the form of matching stories.

In 1915, Wang Dungen published a short story in *Libailiu* (no. 78) called "Xin xu" (A spiritual betrothal), which tells of the heroic death of a young man in the voice of his secret lover. A few weeks later, Zhou Shoujuan followed up with a sequel that puts the voice back into the mouth of the dead hero, now a wandering spirit. The female narrator in Wang's story tells her story as follows: Next to her family's new residence was a quiet family of mother and son. The son seemed to have a heavy heart (or, literally, he was a sentimentalist [*shangxinren*]), daily heaving pensive sighs over newspaper reports of the nation's internal and external troubles, and seldom entertaining guests. From a misdelivered piece of mail, she learned his English name, Paul Kong. She became very fond of him, convinced by her observation that he was a true patriot (*youguozhe*, literally, one who worries about the fate of his nation). When his mother died, her family helped him with the funeral. Then he suddenly departed, leaving only his maid behind. Later she moved to Guangzhou with her brother, and there she came upon a news report of the assassination of a warlord. The assassin turned out to be Paul, who was fatally injured and was dying in a hospital. By the time her brother and she arrived, he had already expired. She collapsed at his bedside, and blood came gushing out of her throat. Her brother explained to the puzzled physician: "My sister has long given her heart to Mr. Kong. It is a pity that he never knew about it." At this point the author steps in to vouch for the veracity of the story, claiming that it is the true story of a lady friend who is now thirty-one years of age and is quietly but determinedly living a widow's life (Yu Runqi 1997b, 744–47).

Perhaps disturbed by the implication that Paul died an unfeeling hero—that is, without having loved a woman—Zhou Shoujuan's story makes him speak up from beyond the grave: He has always known girl-next-door Tanying's feelings for him, and he would have certainly reciprocated it if it weren't for the graver task entrusted upon him by his martyred father to serve the fatherland. "When our nation is so beset by troubles, it is no time to pursue our private passion." Paul's ghost urges Tanying to transform her love for him into patriotic sentiment so that she would regard the nation as her "husband" just as he had regarded it as his "wife" (Yu Runqi 1997b, 816–20).

Men tend to be martyrs in patriotic stories because their individual identity is perceived to be continuous with the collective identity, something that is not usually the case with women. Women's primary role, then, is to introduce the element of discord and disruption, allowing the discontinuity between individual and collective identity to create dramatic conflict so that a stronger nationalist message can be sounded in the resolution. There is thus added piquancy when female characters are thrust onto the path to martyrdom. For example, a story entitled "Xing zai xiangjian" (Till we meet again, by Zhou Shoujuan, in *Libailiu*, no. 3, 1914) explicitly pits love against familial and national loyalty only to affirm the priority of the latter in the end. Guifang, an orphaned Chinese maiden, is passionately in love with a dashing

English diplomat named Freeman (*Fu-li-men*). However, she soon learns the painful truth that Freeman is the very person who fatally shot her father during the Boxers' siege of the foreign legations in Beijing. Her uncle, thrusting a bottle of poison before her, importunes her to place her "daughterly duty" above romantic passion (*ernü siqing*) and avenge her father. Guifang initially responds to the call of duty by vouching for the excellence of her English lover and the depth of their feelings, soliciting the following chastisement from the uncle: "Lass, you must remember that you're a Chinese. [And as a Chinese] you must obey your elders unconditionally. Tomorrow you shall dispose of him for good!" (Yu Runqi 1997a, 36). With a tumultuous heart, Guifang poisons the unsuspecting Freeman, and after giving her dead lover one last kiss, she passes out.

At first glance, the conflict of loyalties in this story seems to be that between *yi* (righteousness) and *zhong/xiao* (loyalty/filiality) frequently encountered in traditional chivalric fiction. However, by dwelling on Freeman's identity as an Englishman who has incurred a blood debt to the Chinese during a racially charged incident, the story calls into question the seamless continuum of *aiqing* and *aiguo* that underwrites *Yu li hun*'s male-centered sentimental heroism. Here, Guifang must renounce a full-fledged romance in order to authenticate her identity as a Chinese national. Moreover, in contrast to the May Fourth formulation, Chineseness is defined in particularistic terms—here in the terms of filial loyalty. What makes Guifang Chinese is not some abstract notion of citizenship, but her ability to abide by a nonnegotiable ethical command. This brings out an older, civilizational model of nationalism in which the Chinese nation is synonymous with civilized morality, whereas foreigners are barbarians who do not honor their parents, a model that is both at odds with and supplements the "family of nations" ideal. In the end, the anti–*Romeo and Juliet* denouement affirms the hierarchy that underlies the *ernü yingxiong* ideal: the demands of the nation (and those of the family) are such that the individual must be ready to sacrifice what is most precious to him or her—which in the Butterfly sentimental tradition is always love. The more majestic the power of love (so much so that it has conquered the barrier of race and nationality in this story), the more tragic its sacrifice and the more sublime the nation as a new form of human community.

For this reason, love across national boundaries is one of the few contexts in which we can catch a glimpse of the racial politics of Butterfly writers. These writers may be fascinated or even awestruck by the power of love to flourish between unlikely couples, but they are also apprehensive of the subversion of community founded on patriarchal rule and patrilineal descent. "Xin liao-zhai—Tang Sheng" (A new tale of the strange—Tang Sheng, by Pingdengge, *Xinxiaoshuo* no. 7, 1903) claims to be based on a true incident that took place in San Francisco. Tang Sheng, son of an overseas Chinese merchant, and Yi-niang, an American girl, have been lovers for ten years when the Boxer Upris-ing breaks out. As anti-Chinese racism escalates in the United States, Tang Sheng abruptly cuts off his relationship with Yiniang, ignoring her vows of love for China and her pleas to be treated as a Chinese. Despairing of moving him, Yiniang commits suicide. In her suicide note, she laments her fate as an American but utters not a word of resentment toward Tang Sheng. To honor her love for Tang and for China, her father donates her belongings to a Chi-nese school in San Francisco; Tang, for his part, never marries.

The author, whose pen name is Master of Equality Studio, commends Tang's action for "safeguarding the nation and preserving the race" (*baoguo cun-zhong*). To reinforce his interpretation, the author supplies a counterexample: In Honolulu, an aboriginal race has nearly died out because their women all seek to marry white men. In China, sycophancy has become a national voca-tion since the Boxer debacle, and there is little doubt that in less than a de-cade, the fate of racial extinction will also befall "our" people, who certainly deserve it for failing to maintain a firm racial boundary. The author then di-rects his attack to those overseas students who consort with the lowly women (*xiajian zhi shaonü*) of alien races. By subjecting themselves to sexual bondage with alien women, they have lost their freedom and turned against their fatherland (Yu Runqi 1997b, 1–4).

It is astonishing that the author can, in the space of one short story, give a rosy portrayal of Tang Sheng and Yiniang's interracial romance, and then con-demn across the board all Chinese-foreign liaisons as no better than client-prostitute relations. It is as if he felt impelled to quell his fascination for the fluid form of sociability exemplified by romantic love by returning to a con-ception of interpersonal relationships entirely defined by the dictates of na-tionality. When two nations turn hostile toward each other, a freely contracted relationship across the national divide is rendered politically suspect. And those who persist in such a relationship can do so only for base purposes. Para-doxically, for a relationship to qualify as a truly romantic one, it has to negate itself, even if this entails the death of one or both parties. Butterfly *ernü ying-xiong* stories are thus shot through with what David Denby has characterized as "the ideological complexity (or indeterminacy) of sentimental texts": "On the one hand, their representation of individual love appears to validate individual sentiment in the face of social pressures; on the other hand, they explicitly espouse, through plot and at a discursive level, an ideology of sacrifice and renunciation which appears to run counter to the primary sense of the text." Love remains the imaginative and emotional center of the text, but the perceived threat of lawless passion is neutralized through "the symbolism of closure, renunciation and death" (Denby 1994, 114).

In Hegel's view, however, this ideological indeterminacy is only a symptom of love's inherent weakness—its contingency as the caprice of personal fate:

> Those sufferings of love, those shattering hopes, that mere being in love, those endless griefs felt by a lover, that endless happiness and bliss which he foresees for himself, are in themselves of no universal interest but something affecting himself alone. Every man does have a heart for love and a right to become happy through it; but if here, precisely in this instance, under such and such circumstances, he does not achieve his end in relation to precisely this girl, then no wrong has occurred. For there is nothing inherently necessary in his taking a fancy for this girl alone, and we are therefore supposed to be interested in supreme contingency, in the man's caprice which has neither universality nor any scope beyond itself. This remains the aspect of coldness which freezes us despite all the heat of passion in its presentation. (1975, 567–68)

The Butterfly writers who espouse a more antagonistic view of the relationship between *aiqing* and *aiguo* would gladly second the thesis that there is no necessary reason why *this* woman must love *this* particular man and that its eclipse by the collective or universal interests of the family and nation incurs no wrong. When love is opposed to such interests, "its collisions always retain an aspect of contingency and lack of justification" (567). It only becomes heroic when it acknowledges the priority of patriotism and family duties and "engages in a fight with itself and the power of its own passion" (566).

It is also interesting that the author of "A New Tale of the Strange—Tang Sheng" imagines that an American woman would behave exactly as an idealized Confucian woman would when love has to be given up. Instead of affirming her own national loyalty and acting out her patriotic sentiment, Yiniang wishes only to adopt the political identity of her beloved, and when this is not possible, merely dies for love. As a rule, Butterfly patriotic stories foreground a male character's heroic act of rising above romantic love while being authenticated by it. By contrast, stories with a female protagonist usually dwell on her devotion to husband (alive or dead, married or prospective), parents, in-laws, or sons (rarely daughters). The relationship between "dying for the country" and "dying for love" on her part is discontinuous and problematic, or else it is a nonissue because she only dies for love. For example, in *Yu li hun*, though both Mengxia and Liniang receive much encomium from the author as *youqingren*, it is Mengxia who dies a hero's death on the battlefield, whereas Liniang dies a stereotypically romantic death.

It may be said that sentimental heroism, despite its universal pretensions, largely reproduces the patriarchal gender hierarchy by rendering women's claim to patriotism problematic. Although a man's primary identity may shift from the paterfamilias to romantic lover as the function of the family shifts from economic to emotional, his unquestioned status as master of the family (*jia*) and citizen of the state (*guo*) makes the transition from the private to the public a matter of course. Women's access to the nation, however, is invariably mediated through the family or the romantic nexus. Liniang is only able to demonstrate her "heroic" nature by prodding Mengxia on to leave her side in order to pursue loftier goals. Even if a woman is high-minded about national politics, she still has to act out her convictions through her father, husband, or son—either to make a hero of the latter, or to save the latter from the ignominy of becoming a *hanjian* (traitor).

• • •

The Butterfly discourse of love and heroism provides voluminous evidence that the rise of bourgeois commercial culture in the context of nationalism has entailed not a repudiation of the honor ethic but rather a commitment to reinventing the heroic tradition. Even though *The Sea of Regret* does not explicitly partake of the *ernü yingxiong* discourse, it nonetheless posits an ideal higher than romantic love, that is, the virtue of constancy. Likewise, Butterfly sentimental fiction grapples with the contradictory impulse to eulogize love and to subordinate it to something higher. The *ernü yingxiong* genre melds the impulse to transcend love with the encompassing narrative of nationalism, so that the imaginary community of nation becomes the unquestioned terminus of all passionate pursuits. As a result, the tendency of sentimental novels to embed social criticism within the personal and the everyday is overshadowed by the greater need to forge a homogeneous "society" coterminous with the nation. With the nation conceived as an extension of the family and patriotism an extension of filiality, gender and generational hierarchies quietly slip back into the imaginary community, perpetuating a gendered pattern of politics, morality, and transcendence.

For the same reason, Butterfly *ernü yingxiong* stories also represent an alternative nationalist imagination that incorporates rather than repudiating the narratives of the family. Unlike in most May Fourth stories, there is no fundamental chasm between love for one's nation and love for one's parents. Indeed, the two loves are often conceptualized as extensions, in different scales, of the same fundamental *qing*. The *ernü* in Butterfly stories achieves a degree of inclusiveness (romantic lovers, filial sons/daughters, and patriots) that is not only unprecedented, but also unmatched by later transformations. Filial piety is rarely left out of the moral economy of the *ernü yingxiong* paradigm: Guifang kills her English lover first and foremost to avenge her father; Paul Kong does not become an assassin until after his mother's death. In this, Butterfly writers are upholders of the Confucian structure of feeling, believing in the essential unity of all virtues and intent upon reconciling conflicts between equally cherished values. The idea of pursuing romantic love at the expense of filiality would have horrified them, and so would the notion that one's membership in the nation cancels out one's duty to obey one's parents.

Butterfly fiction's relatively fuzzy or elastic conception of community bears affinities with a current of nationalist thought that seeks to accommodate and appropriate existing forms of human solidarity. Sun Yat-sen, for example, is known for placing a high premium on the "family-ism and clan-ism" of the Chinese, which he believes can be enlarged and connected to modern nationalism. In this vision, a cohesive Chinese nation would emerge out of the gathering of hypertrophied clans, and become a modern gemeinschaft bound by "traditional feelings of solidarity" and governed by "a grand council of Chens, Wangs, and Zhangs" (Strand 1997). This narrative of community, however, is eventually repressed by both Sun himself and radical May Fourth nationalists who, discounting the ties that bind individuals to multiple communities, performatively characterize Chinese society as a "sheet of loose sand" in order to found a homogeneous nation on the assemblage of atomized individuals.

PART TWO

The Enlightenment Structure of Feeling

THREE

The Age of Romance

Part 2 explores how two new definitions of *qing*—the romantic and the psychoanalytic—replaced earlier ethico-cosmological definitions. While the romantic discourse of free love spearheaded the iconoclastic revolt against Confucian patriarchy, the psychoanalytic discourse gave *qing* a biological-materialist grounding as the expression of natural impulses that society unjustly repressed. Both, moreover, were bound up with the nationalist celebration of an intimate community in which *qing* was the universal currency. The nationalist definition will be taken up in Part 3. In Part 2, I propose the notion of "the enlightenment structure of feeling" to understand the radical experimentation with and contestation over new modes of subjectivity and sociality in May Fourth and post–May Fourth discourses on love.

In this chapter, I chart the evolution of the romantic genre and the construction of the romantic individual in the private sphere. I argue that the enlightenment structure of feeling radicalizes the individual as the basic and irreducible unit of moral choice and action. It breaks with the Confucian structure of feeling in staking uncompromising and nonnegotiable claims for individual freedom and autonomy. The freedom to choose one's marriage partner is seen as a fundamental right in the sense that individuals, inasmuch as they are autonomous moral agents, have the inalienable right to act without the deliberate obstruction from others, including parents. No claims that are based on ascriptive ties should be allowed to trump the voluntary expressions of the individual will. Romantic love is, therefore, a double-edged enterprise: on the one hand, it is about the thrills of courtship and heterosociability, on the other hand, it is about rebelling against parental authority and the courage to plunge into the exhilarating realms of "society" and "nation." In the latter sense, the numerous stories of "free love" produced in the 1920s are often less about freedom of love or marriage per se, and much less about libertarian sexual practice, than about the severance of ties with family, tradition, and locality and the forging of a national community whose claim on individual identity must override particularistic bonds.

Ideally, the romantic lover is an atomistic being shorn of all forms of dependency and obligation, a living signifier of freedom and autonomy, a self-sufficient and self-activating moral agent. Performatively, the enlightenment structure of feeling reduces the lover to a tabula rasa on which an altogether new vision of human solidarity may be imagined. It is in this sense that John Fitzgerald rightly regards the melancholy fiction of the May Fourth era as the birthplace of modern nationalism (1996, 92). But insofar as May Fourth fiction is also driven by the realist imperative, few romantic heroes and heroines are genuine atomistic beings ready to be claimed tout court by the nation. Love stories are soddened with melancholy because free love is a profoundly contradictory ideal. Existentially, free love is torn between the quest for autonomy on the one hand, and the need for recognition and the enjoyment of subjection on the other. Experientially, lovers are caught in between their embeddedness in a viscerally resilient web of social bonds on the one hand, and their romantic identity as autonomous individuals free to contract new, adventurous, and democratic forms of sociability. May Fourth romantics are first and foremost rebels who struggle to reject the Confucian family and its ethical and ritual codes. But the romantic rebels find themselves in search of a model on which to structure their brand new identity. On what basis should two strangers trust and bond with each other without the guarantee of objective institutions? What is the nature and goal of romantic happiness? How must the conflicting claims of freedom and solidarity be reconciled?

The texts that I choose to read closely in this chapter address these questions by wrestling with the twin goal of free love, attempting in their own ways to realize what Anthony Giddens calls the "democratization of intimacy" (1992). I trace the representation of love from a symbolic trope of freedom to a social field fraught with the complexity, perplexity, and power dynamics of modern life. Employing the categories of moral philosophy, I argue that love changed from a constitutive good or hypergood in the 1910s and 1920s to an ordinary lifegood in the 1930s and 1940s. The romantic genre, to be sure, did not flourish in a vacuum: social and political imperatives have continuously shaped it in different directions, creating controversies and often rendering it unrecognizable by conventional criteria. I will devote considerable attention to these forces in subsequent chapters. Here, I hope to show that the genre's popularity despite its growing disrepute bespeaks the urban middle class's insistence on the value and validity of ordinary life.

I begin with the notion of *le grand amour* in Alexandre Dumas *fils' La dame aux camélias* and Butterfly sentimental fiction. I then turn to Feng Yuanjun and Lu Xun's short stories about free love in conjunction with the romantic "bibles" of the May Fourth generation, *The Sorrows of Young Werther* and *A Doll's House*. Next I turn my attention to the critical treatment of love, marriage, and family in the writings of Ling Shuhua and Ding Ling. Finally, I examine, with reference to *Madame Bovary*, the permutation of love in metropolitan settings as "the affair" in the writings of Shi Zhecun, Zhang Henshui, and Zhang Ailing.

LE GRAND AMOUR

Charles Taylor uses "the constitutive good" or "moral source" to refer to that which constitutes the goodness of a certain action, motive, or lifestyle. A constitutive good, such as Plato's Idea and Christianity's God, compels our allegiance and empowers us to do good and to be good (1989, 93). Modernity, according to Taylor, is crucially marked by the gradual internalization of constitutive goods. This process begins in the rise of deism, an early modern school of thought that objectifies Providence and makes it immanent in the interlocking mechanisms of the universe that are intelligible to the rational human mind. In the post-Enlightenment age, it is taken for granted that constitutive goods reside not in an external entity, but in our rational faculty or in our expressive powers—our "inner nature." Taylor considers this a veritable revolution in moral consciousness, but he cautions us that an immanent ethic does not amount to a rejection of constitutive goods. The concepts of reason and nature do not function quite like God or Idea, but still perform analogous functions (94–95). It is in this framework that we can understand the tremendous appeal of translated novels like *La dame aux camélias* and *The Sorrows of Young Werther*. These novels, I argue, articulate a romantic moral theory in which our innate and inner capacity for feeling is a constitutive good.

The French novel *La dame aux camélias* was one of the first European novels translated into Chinese (by the intrepid Lin Shu). It instantly claimed a devoted and broad readership base, captivating readers with its poetics and ethics of modern love and inspiring local versions that sought to wed its romantic ethos to the indigenous *yanqing xiaoshuo* tradition. First published in 1848, the novel also deals with the paradigm shift in the domain of constitutive goods and the resulting conflict of values. Here, the romantic personality inhabits the character of Armand Duval, who wages a double-front battle in his tempestuous affair with the Parisian courtesan Marguerite Gautier: on the one hand, he faces his bourgeois father, who is wholly committed to rational order and respectability; on the other, he confronts the aristocracy whose licentious lifestyle keeps Marguerite a disposable object of pleasure. In falling in love with Marguerite and desiring to marry her, Armand challenges not only the aristocratic reduction of gender relations to temporal carnality and sportsmanship, but also the utilitarianism of the bourgeois marriage. The love affair between a tax collector's son and a courtesan also highlights the tension between a world of "surfaces" that operates on a nexus of money, ritual codes, practical rules, standards of distinction, intrigues, hierarchies, and calculation on the one hand, and a world of "depths" that defines itself against the former and celebrates constancy, disinterestedness, reciprocity, spiritual communion, and selfless sacrifice on the other.

Armand's love transforms Marguerite, a kept woman, into a romantic subject whose partnership, or whose ability to return his passionate gaze, is essential to his project of self-fashioning. He nearly succeeds in his battle with the aristocracy after literally removing Marguerite from Paris to the countryside, where they experiment with a new mode of gender relations in a state of nature. But unbeknownst to him, his effort is foiled by his father, who does not understand the transformative powers of the romantic enterprise and insists on pegging Marguerite to her discarded identity as a courtesan (and hence an unsuitable candidate for a bourgeois marriage). Marguerite asserts her romantic subjectivity by enacting "the heroism of renunciation" (Taylor 1989, 295): She gives up Armand and dies in abject loneliness, only to be immortalized by Dumas *fils'* contemplative narrative and in stage, operatic, film, and television adaptations, thereby attaining the exalted status of a true romantic subject.

The secret meeting between Marguerite and the elder Duval dramatizes a clash of values that has become all too familiar to us. Mr. Duval is eloquent in defending the hypergoods of the bourgeoisie: family bonds, career, prosperity, and respectability. Marguerite is not only made to recognize the legitimacy of these goods, but also to feel their irresistible magnetism to those who espouse them. Recognition of a rival hypergood often results in transvaluation, or a new perspective on previously held values. Although Marguerite is by no means ready to replace her own hypergoods—love, devotion, and companionship—with those of the bourgeoisie, she is forced to accept the relativity (and marginality) of the former and succumbs to the latter's demand for recognition and concession. As a fallen woman, Marguerite also responds intensely to Duval's performative "recognition" of the virtuous woman in her, aided by pleading teardrops and a paternal kiss on the forehead, and she rises to the occasion against her own interest. In sacrificing everything—including her own happiness—for love, she is the proverbial prostitute with a heart of gold. But it is more precise to locate her heroism in her ability to acknowledge and give priority to other people's hypergoods while remaining loyal, at least in spirit, if not in action, to her own.

The profound impact of *La dame* on modern Chinese literature has been noted and commented on by many scholars. Much of this commentary, however, limits itself to identifying precedence and influence, without delving into its role in the moral and epistemological transformation in early twentieth-century China. Some of the changes we can already identify in *Dream of the Red Chamber*, such as the confessional mode, the forging of new gender relations, and the heroism of renunciation. But this novel presented these techniques and problematics to Chinese readers in a new framework—romanticism. Together with other translated texts, it reshaped the terms and logic of the discourse of sentiment and helped to effect profound changes in conceptions of personhood, gender identity, and sociality. Above all, it codified a mode of fiction as well as a mode of living in which love is *le grand amour*, an all-consuming lifetime project. In this mode, life story is not only inseparable from romantic love, it is subsumed by the latter. Identity is constituted in memories of romantic love, in the dyadic relationship between a man and woman. Gender therefore emerges as the most significant marker of personhood. Love is also always singular: if one fails in the lifelong quest, or if love is terminated, one goes into an emotional remission either in death or solitude. True love, in other words, happens only once.

It is no accident that the romantic genre of the turn of the last century is overwhelming autobiographical and that autobiographical works are overwhelmingly devoted to the subject of love. Butterfly writers tirelessly reproduced the characters, plot elements, rhetoric, and underlying values of this genre so that a recognizable romantic convention was firmly in place by the late 1910s. Perry Link calls this convention a "composite myth," which unfolds on a six-phase Romantic Route through life: (1) extraordinary inborn gifts, (2) supersensitivity, (3) falling in love, (4) cruel fate, (5) worry and disease, and (6) destruction (1981, 65–77).

The man and woman of sentiment (*duoqingren* or *youqingren*) are the lonely wayfarers on the Romantic Route. Without exception, they are talented, handsome, and sensitive; they have sickly constitutions and frail physiques, and are susceptible to illness and melancholy. They weep a great deal; their tears drench their pillows and love letters. All in all, they live and die for *qing,* the one word that encapsulates their entire existence. To the extent to which their selfhood is defined by *qing*, they belong to an order of beings altogether different from the *wuqingren* (person without feeling). In the ultimate sentimental utopia, all the broken-hearted lovers (*qingchang shiyiren*) of the world would leave the hurly-burly of the mundane realm to join each other's company in a neverland appropriately called the Island of Sorrows (*hendao*). Such is the setting for Zhou Shoujuan's "The Gramophone Record":

> The island has a population of about a hundred thousand. Seventy thousand of them, male and female, are broken-hearted lovers from various countries; the rest are their family members and domestic servants, as well as coolie laborers. Even among the servants and laborers, there are plenty of those who have tasted the bitterness of *qing*. As for their nationalities, it is not easy to list them all in one breath. Beside those from the Chinese Republic, there are Americans, English, French, Germans, and other Europeans. Even the black race from Africa and the red race from South America make up a few hundred in number. These black and red people, though seemingly as ignorant as animals, actually know something about *qing* and have fled to the island with equally broken hearts. One knows from this that every human being, civilized or savage, is never exempt from the web of *qing*. After all, it is *qing* that accompanies all of us into the world at birth. (Zhou Shoujuan 1994, 167)

Here, the egalitarian aspiration of the sentimental utopia has an awkward moment as it tries to make claims for the class and racial Other. Nonetheless, the point is made: *qing* is a kingdom unto its own. In this kingdom, class and racial hierarchies are mitigated by the common quality of *qing* and the only real difference is between happiness and discontent: "the entire philosophy of life is bracketed within tears and laughter" (170).[1]

Other Butterfly stories may not take such imaginative flights of fancy, but the scenario they conjure up is no less mythopoetic in the sense that the hero and heroine always go through a similar series of tribulations and arrive at a predictably tragic end—usually death for the heroine and eternal solitude for the hero. The agent of fate usually assumes the form of an unsympathetic parent, a greedy relation, a jealous co-wife, indigence, ill health, superstition, evil customs (such as polygamy or child marriage), social turmoil, judicial injustice, miscommunication, and, sometimes, sheer accident. To prove her true passion, the heroine either dies of a sudden illness or commits suicide, often in a very public and demonstrative manner. The hero reciprocates through self-imposed solitude by either swearing lifetime celibacy or renouncing all worldly pursuits and disappearing into the mountains. For example, in a story called "Gebi meng" (Blood oath alliance, by Jingying nüshi, *Libailiu* no. 59, 1915), the wife of a scholar official is hounded to death by his mother, who objects to her courtesan past. The husband immediately withdraws from public service to become a farmer and vows never to marry again (Yu Runqi 1997b, 649–62). Similarly, in "The Gramophone Record," the protagonist, Qing Jiesheng, flees to the Island of Sorrows after the girl he loves is forced to marry someone else. He wastes away in melancholy and consumption, leaving behind a recorded testament of his undying love for the girl. Upon receiving the gramophone record and hearing his plaintive voice, the girl vomits blood and drops dead instantly. Such hyperbolic emplotment may not make good fiction, but it does make a very strong case for *qing* as a constitutive good.

The sacrificial woman and the solitary man populate the majority of Butterfly love stories, which are practically identical, save for the names of the characters and the type of trouble that crushes them. Although some of the more famous Butterfly novels are set against larger sociopolitical backgrounds, such as the Boxer Uprising and the 1911 Revolution, short stories seldom venture beyond the immediate circle of family, kinfolk, and neighbors, producing the illusion of a timeless and universal chronotope. When history is introduced, it functions as the agent of misfortune that changes characters' lives but not their persons. In other words, historical events do not bear upon the characters in such a way as to shed light on their personality or shape their identity as well as their relationships in any fundamental way. The narrator in "Jinqian xuelei" (Bloody tear stains on the shirt front, by Bi Hen, in *Minquansu* no. 9, 1915) visits his old schoolmate, Zhongshu, and is shocked by his disheveled appearance and solitary residence. Pointing to a woman's picture inscribed with elegiac poems, Zhongshu relates the tragic story of his life: During the 1911 Revolution, he became involved in some military action. After the uprising, he set out for home but was arrested and imprisoned in midjourney. Convinced that he could never get out alive, he wrote his wife a farewell letter. When she came to the city with the letter in her hand, rumor had it that he had been executed already. So she drowned herself in the Yangzi River. To this day Zhongshu is still in mourning for her (Yu Runqi 1997b, 690–95).

The gender divide in such stories is asymmetrical: the man becomes embroiled in a political situation while the woman suffers, often fatally, the consequences. For a woman, *qing* is always a matter of proper conduct, of acting out virtue with her body. She must be loyal, faithful, devoted, and self-sacrificing, so much so that only death—almost always self-induced—is adequate authentication of her identity as a woman of feeling. For a man, however, *qing* seems more of a matter of words. He somehow always manages to stay behind to tell the story, either directly to the reader, or to a framing narrator who invariably is also a man. A man of feeling does not just enact the heroism of renunciation; he also insists on immortalizing his love and sorrow in words. His life, in other words, is lived to be told as a story. We may trace this pattern of gender asymmetry to *La dame* as well as to *Dream,* in which Baoyu returns, after Daiyu's death, to his stone identity in the mythical realm to suffer eternal melancholy while hoping to transmit his story of unfulfilled love to the world of "red dust." Fu Lin, the author of *Stones in the Sea*, frames his novel with repeated declarations of his death-defying determination to commemorate love in writing (Wu Jianren and Fu Lin 1995, 23, 100).

Rey Chow takes issue with Butterfly writers for their fetishistic "staging of female trauma" as a means of wishfully reconstructing an idealized past, of recovering a tradition irrevocably lost (1991, 55–56). Indeed, in many ways, female characters are put on display as mute stick figures while a male voice-over is given the privilege of inscribing meaning and dispensing judgment.

Men, literally and figuratively, control the re-presentation of feeling. The inequality of subjectivity and agency is blatant. Chow also notes the unintended consequence of staging female suffering in "untried degrees of exuberance" and "in a popular, readable form": "What used to be unutterable, 'feminine' feelings were now put on a par with the heroic and patriotic, circulated, and made lucidly 'available' for the first time through the mass practices of reading and writing, activities that used to belong exclusively to the highbrow scholarly world" (55–56).

It is debatable as to what extent the feelings represented in Butterfly fiction are previously "unutterable," genuinely "feminine" feelings. To historicize feeling—precisely the goal of this project—one needs to resist the temptation to suppose that women have always had "feminine" feelings that are only now made public through representation. For all intents and purposes, the feelings are the invention of Butterfly writers for the purpose of articulating a new moral vision. The fact that women are predominantly represented as romantic lovers indeed signals a wide departure from their more conventional image as either filial paragons or sex objects. One critic in fact endorses the chaste image as a token of civilization because it shows respect, even reverence, toward women on the part of male authors. In contradistinction, "licentious tales" reduce women to playthings and assault female readers' self-esteem ("Xiaoshuo conghua," by Zhixin Zhuren, *Xin xiaoshuo* no. 20, 1905) (Chen Pingyuan and Xia Xiaohong 1997, 102–3).

On the whole, Butterfly writers strive to portray both men and women as sentimental beings, despite the persistent undercurrents of gender asymmetry. Perhaps this is why stories in which women are brutally victimized for the purpose of consolidating male bonding are by far in the smallest minority. As far as same-sex relationships are concerned, more common are benign tales of homosocial attachment among both men and women. In *Huangjin sui* (The money demon, 1913), for example, Chen Diexian relates his homosocial encounters with ease and candor. Upon meeting the charismatic Chishi, Chen feels instantly attracted to his free-spiritedness, and his feelings are warmly reciprocated. "This development brought out all the wildness of Chishi's nature. Clapping his hands and laughing, he announced, 'I always knew that true men of feeling wouldn't let themselves be restricted to love between the sexes. Provided they're kindred spirits, their sort of friendship also qualifies as love. From now on, when we drink we'll drink together, and when we go out somewhere, we'll go together'" (Chen Diexian 1999, 238). The absence of the pathologizing impulse that so troubled Foucault reminds one of Cao Xueqin's similar attitude toward Jia Baoyu's sentimental affairs with Qin Zhong and Liu Xianglian in *Dream*. Homosocial bonding is very much governed by the same rule as that governing the heterosexual relationship: Legitimacy is conferred on the grounds of sincerity and constancy, not sexual orientation. (Thus Xue Pan's promiscuous homosexual advances are met with both derision and brutal rebuff.) In portraying homosocial bonding as a legitimate manifestation of *qing*, Butterfly writers are in fact making literal the ecumenical claims of *qing*. For them, if *qing* is all-encompassing and omnipresent, there is no reason why it should not spring forth between two men or two women. However, in no sense is this an advocacy of plural sexualities or a critique of the institution of heterosexual marriage. The sanctity of marriage and family is affirmed in the sheer number of stories dedicated to the virtues of fidelity, chastity, and filial piety.

Having surveyed Butterfly romantic fiction, we can better understand the particular appeal of *La dame* among Butterfly writers and readers. First of all, love affairs set in the house of pleasure are familiar to late Qing–early Republican Chinese readers. Traditionally, courtesans have always played a special role in furnishing an emotional outlet for literati men who do not (and often cannot) expect an emotionally fulfilling life within the context of marriage and family. These women occupy a position vis-à-vis the man of feeling that is structurally similar to that occupied by his same-sex soul mates: They are the ones with whom he can forge freely chosen horizontal relationships, who make up his loyal and appreciative audience, to whom he dedicates longing verses, and whose lives he celebrates in laudatory biographies. Owing to their relatively unattached status, courtesans are imagined to possess a degree of emotional subjectivity and autonomy (in that they can ostensibly withhold attention/affection from a particular man) and to be capable of reciprocating men's emotional investment. This is precisely the premise of *La dame*.

La dame presents an at once strange and familiar world in which love and marriage are radically separate, and yet this separation is being questioned by the central character, Armand, who desires to actually marry the woman he loves. It is also a world in which identity is primarily predicated on a dyadic relationship between a man and woman and in which characters are first and foremost gendered beings whose lives are consumed by the singular goal of fulfilling heterosexual love. If Chen Diexian still tries to negotiate a compromise between a bisexual and multilateral definition of the self on the one hand

and a heterosexual and bilateral definition on the other, *La dame* cements the idea that a man of feeling needs to be appreciated and authenticated by a woman of feeling. And above all, *La dame* counteracts the prevailing tendency in the late Qing to represent the world of brothels and geisha houses as governed by crass gamesmanship, in which women are crafty, rapacious creatures who prey on unwary patrons, and in which men study brothel manuals in order to outwit and outmaneuver the women. The novel restores the house of pleasure as a sentimental arena in which purity of feeling lies beneath the facade of ruses and intrigues, and in which the noble ethics of care, devotion, and sacrifice readily burst forth when given the opportunity. The May Fourth generation would demand that this realm be relocated to the center of social and family life and that love precede and define marriage rather than running parallel with or antithetical to it. More crucially, May Fourth romanticism is part and parcel of the critique of tradition, and love, as a result, becomes a politicized symbol of the absolute hypergoods of the May Fourth modern: freedom, equality, rights.

I LOVE, THEREFORE I AM

Although the May Fourth generation most likely spent their youthful days devouring *La dame* and *Yu li hun*, the romantic hero with whom they most identified was not Armand or Mengxia, but Werther. Set against the background of the eighteenth-century cult of sensibility, *The Sorrows of Young Werther* showcases a new moral outlook in which the romantic feeling is the source of all that is good, truthful, and beautiful. Werther, the sentimental hero of the novel, attains greatness and achieves immortality not through the worldly pursuits that he so despises, but through "a certain nobility and purity of feeling" (Taylor 1989, 295). His extreme sensibility, melancholic temperament, and languid deportment were imitated the world over, not least in early twentieth-century China as the New Youth experienced the birth pangs of the modern subject, and as they sought to shift constitutive goods away from the traditional sources.

Translated into Chinese by Guo Moruo (1892–1978) in 1922, the novel has often been referred to as the bible of the romantic generation. Its impact goes beyond introducing the romantic ritual and idiom, supplying stirring maxims about modern love, and offering a negative role model (for the conservatives) for the impressionable young. Its significance, I submit, resides more crucially in the new moral framework that relocates constitutive goods in Nature, a pregnant trope encompassing both the natural and human world (as in "human nature"). The novel, therefore, gives us many memorable descriptions of the landscape that reflect the new orientation to Nature. Similarly, virginal women, children, and simple folk are also figured as the objective correlatives of the inner nature, or the heart—and hence the much-celebrated scene in which Werther falls in love with Charlotte while observing her handing out bread, with angelic beatitude, to her younger siblings. This "charming sight" clinches Charlotte's role as the Other in relation to whom Werther fine-tunes his sensibility and acts out the heroism of renunciation. Aligning himself with nature, women, children, and peasants, Werther defines his romantic self against the philistine, whose detestable characteristics are concentrated in Charlotte's intended, Albert. The rivalry between Werther and Albert, at an abstract level, is the rivalry between two competing constitutive goods: reason and nature, or human rationality and human emotion. Werther's suicide is the ultimate gesture of renunciation, and Wertherism becomes the modern mode of chivalry, admired and practiced by readers caught up in the global malady of the heart—the marking of sensibility as what makes life worthy and meaningful.

The Wertherian cult of the heart gives May Fourth youth a powerful weapon in their struggle to make the individual and heterosociability into the new organizing principle of Chinese society. In the May Fourth discourse, romantic love becomes a poignant symbol and a rallying point, standing for essential humanity and proclaiming the advent of a new life that is true to Nature. *Qing* is now always coupled with *ai* (love) or *yu* (desire) as in *aiqing* or *qingyu*, both of which have narrower connotations and are no longer cosmological categories that underwrite all human feelings. Another compound, *lian'ai*, referring (though not exclusively) to heterosexual romantic love, gains even wider usage. *Lian'ai* is also a highly charged term, and when preceded by *ziyou* (freedom), it becomes the battle cry of a generation of aspiring individualists seeking to break away from the Confucian family and patriarchal ideology.

The struggle to choose one's own mate, in open defiance of parental will, becomes the privileged site on which members of the May Fourth generation stage the morality play of the struggle between good and evil, nature and artifice, victim and persecutor, humanity and barbarity—that is, the free will and moral integrity of the individual on the one hand, and the hypocrisy and tyranny of family, society, and Confucian morality on the other. The center of conflict in May Fourth love stories is almost always situated between a pair of young lovers and their authoritarian parents. The lovers, by virtue of their passion alone, are inherently in the right; there is rarely any room for ambiguity. As one commentator puts it, the right and wrong in such stories are straightforward, because it is most "natural" that marriage should concern only the future spouses and nobody else (Zhong Mi 1919). Parents or parental figures are often supplied with an intention to persecute, something that is largely absent in Butterfly stories of tragic love. Parents, no longer the blind agent of some incomprehensible, impersonal, or anonymous force such as history, fate, or social convention, now act with a malicious will to power. Even when parental affection is acknowledged, it is so much a part of the patriarchal establishment that it usually comes not as a blessing but as a curse or burden for the young lovers.

In his inimitable style, Hegel offers a philosophical perspective on why romantic love becomes the code name for individual freedom and why it is able to bind a young man and woman together and pit them against the will of their elders and the family that has nurtured them. He begins with the peculiar dialectic of self-abnegation and self-affirmation in romantic love:

> What constitutes the infinity of love is this losing, in the other, one's consciousness of self, this splendour of disinterestedness and selflessness through which alone the person finds himself again and becomes a self, this self-forgetfulness in which the lover does not exist, live, and care for himself, but finds the roots of his being in another, and yet in this other does entirely enjoy precisely himself; and beauty is chiefly to be sought in the fact that this emotion does not remain mere impulse and emotion but that imagination builds its whole world up into this relation; everything else which by way of interests, circumstances, and aims belongs otherwise to actual being and life, it elevates into an adornment of this emotion; it tugs everything into this sphere and assigns a value to it only in its relation thereto. (1975, 563)

This intensely intersubjective dialectic gives rise to love's contingency that Hegel considers to be its fatal limitation.[2] Contingency here refers not so much to the notorious fickleness of the amorous heart as to the lack of universality—the kind of universality supposedly embedded in "the eternal interests and objective content of human existence, . . . family, political ends, country, duties arising from one's calling or class" (566–67). From the perspectives of such entities as the family and state, there is no absolute, objective reason why *this* man must love precisely *this* woman, or vice versa: "the endless stubbornness of necessarily finding his life, his supreme consciousness, precisely in this woman alone is seen to be an endless caprice of fate" (567). Thus in asserting one's subjectivity and freedom of choice through romantic love, one invariably runs up against the interests of objective institutions. Guided by the slogan "love is supreme" (lian'ai zhi shang), May Fourth romantics seek to tug everything into the sphere of love, not least to subordinate the claims of the family to the "vital right of subjective emotion" (566) or even outright repudiate them as the unjustified demands of egotistic parents. Love stories from this period are melodramatic not because of their improbable or sensational plots, but because of their unabashed moral Manicheanism. Evil not only has a human face, but is also as one-dimensional as the lovers themselves. Hence, despite their invariably unhappy endings, most May Fourth love stories read more like melodramas than tragedies.

The woman writer Feng Yuanjun's short story "Gejue" (Separation, in *Chuangzao jikan* 2:2, 1923) exemplifies the melodramatic temper of May Fourth love stories. The narrative is composed of a series of fragmentary and undated letters from the protagonist Junhua to her absent lover, Shizhen. Junhua and Shizhen have met in a modern school away from home and are passionately in love with each other. Their love affair has antagonized their parents, and until now, Junhua had not returned home for several years. Now she is locked in a room, fearfully expecting the imminent arrival of her fiancé—chosen for her by her mother. Alone in her "cell," Junhua longs for Shizhen, reminisces about their intimate but chaste romance, and contemplates the meaning of love. Characteristic of the May Fourth opposition of self and society, the narrative opens with a line that instantly pits the lovers against the rest of the world: "I never thought that despite all of our careful planning, we would still find ourselves defeated by society's backwardness."[3] The use of the plural first-person pronoun and the choice of words that conjure up a heroic struggle have the effect of rallying the reader immediately to the side of the valiant lovers-cum-fighters.

Furthermore, in deploying the epistolary form that addresses its intended recipient directly as "you," the narrative interpellates the reader in the position of the (absent) lover, who is also the confidant to her innermost feelings and accomplice to her rebellious thoughts. This form of address is markedly different from the structure of reception in Butterfly sentimental narratives where the narrator always steps between the characters and the reader to enact and channel sympathetic responses. At the diegetic level, the most immediate reason for Junhua's imprisonment is her mother's fury over a ten-day journey Junhua took with Shizhen, during which they "did nothing more than hug, kiss, and talk" (S, 111), an experience further recounted in a separate story entitled "Lüxing" (Journey). "She says that what we did was tantamount to illicit co-habitation, and that not only have I dishonored her, but even my ancestors in heaven are furious and ashamed of me. . . . How is it that our love—so sacred, noble, and innocent—has turned into something so condemned?" (S, 106).

The mother assumes that if the lovers have slept in the same hotel room, they must have had illicit sex, because "sacred, noble, and innocent" love has no conceptual footing in patriarchal ideology wherein sex—licit when it is for procreation and illicit when for pleasure—is the presumed object of all male-female associations. Love is intolerable because it stands for something greater and more threatening than immediate sexual gratification: individual liberty and autonomy.[4] Indeed, the very next sentence after the above-quoted question is a statement about the value of freedom: "Life can be sacrificed, but not one's will. If I can't have my freedom, I'd prefer to die" (S, 106). In the sequel, "Gejue zhihou" (In the wake of the separation), the same point is forcefully made again: "I love you [mother] and I love also my lover; but my greatest love is for my free will" (Feng Yuanjun 1997, 13).

European romanticist texts furnished an indispensable source of inspiration for the May Fourth discourse of love. One constantly comes across references to Goethe, Ibsen, Wordsworth, and Shelley (an exception is the Indian poet, Tagore, whose status as a Nobel laureate places him among the European giants). The disparate writings of these authors are effortlessly synthesized by their Chinese admirers as enunciating one single truth: the sanctity of individuality as supremely expressed in romantic love. Once so enshrined, love becomes an absolute value, an objective criterion that distinguishes truth from falsehood, good from evil, "us" from "them." The new valuation of love as a hypergood immediately renders other values suspect or incompatible with itself, even though Feng's story recognizes the validity of both motherly love and filial love. "I took the risk to come home in the hope that my love could be fulfilled on all sides. I did not realize that . . . [love's] various expressions can be mutually contradictory and intolerant" (S, 106).

This statement would have struck a Butterfly writer as erroneous because the central creed of the Confucian structure of feeling is precisely the unity of all virtuous sentiments, with an abstract *qing* as the constitutive good. We may recall how Dihua, the protagonist of *The Sea of Regret*, is matter-of-factly both a faithful lover *and* a filial daughter. The May Fourth inserts a wedge into the continuum of love and filiality and projects this new dichotomy as the combined product of Confucian intolerance and parental egoism.[5] Junhua thus resents her mother for taking her romantic love to be "a betrayal and an unfilial act," "a crime." Despairing of her mother's sympathy, Junhua contemplates escape to avoid the humiliation of being claimed, alive or dead, by her betrothed—her "worst enemy." But her thoughts quickly turn to death, foreshadowing her fate in the sequel, in which Junhua kills herself after an unsuccessful escape attempt. "We have trodden the bloody path of death in order to pursue our freedom to love. We should forge a way for other young people and wish them better success." She goes on to intone to Shizhen: "if I die . . . you must write out the history of our love, from the beginning to the end. You must organize and publish our six hundred love letters" (S, 113). The language here is unabashedly heroic, treating love as a lofty cause whose meaning and significance must be appropriately commemorated. The autobiographical impulse is rooted, as in *The Sorrows of Young Werther* and *Dream*, in the conviction that one's life is of interest to others simply because one has loved. Love ennobles, and love letters are the testaments to an authentic existence.

Apparently in a gesture to affirm the heroic nobility of love and defy the "debased outlook" of its detractors, Feng returns, after Junhua's suicide in the sequel, to the episode of the ten-day journey. This story supposedly shocked the reading public with its candid disclosure of physical intimacy—kisses, hugs, and chaste nestlings in bed—even though its avowed purpose is to prove love's innocence. Alone in their hotel room, the lovers prepare for bed by undressing each other. However, when Shizhen comes to the last layer of Junhua's clothes, he pauses and steps back gingerly and solemnly, murmuring that he cannot go on. The two of them stand motionless, as if overcome by some mysterious force. Junhua muses: "I do believe this to be the most exalted expression of the nobility of our souls and the purity of our love" (Feng Yuanjun 1997, 20). As they huddle together in bed, sex is both the closest and furthest thing on their minds, in the sense that their resolve to remain chaste is self-consciously made against the anticipated verdict to the contrary. Once again, they seek recourse to the Wertherian discourse that elevates love to the status of an absolute cause worthy not only of the sacrifice of desire, but of life itself: "In our embrace, we searched in our innermost souls for a place where absolute love can be realized. How tragic! How stirring! How sacred! I'm not afraid;

I'm not afraid at all! Life ought to be free; it ought to be like art. Is there a more glorious thing in the world than to die for love [*xun'ai de shiming*]?" (25).

The resolve to dedicate all to love becomes the high note of May Fourth romanticism. Everyday life, with its focus on reproduction, common routine, and the feminine sphere, holds little appeal. If the heroic life may be defined as one that "emphasizes the courage to struggle and achieve extraordinary goals, the quest for virtue, glory and fame, which contrasts with the lesser everyday pursuit of wealth, property and earthly love" (Featherstone 1995, 59–60), then it is ironic but logical that May Fourth romanticism, at least in its non-Freudian moments, should denigrate "earthly love" along with the pursuit of wealth (something parents are routinely accused of—Junhua's mother, for example, betroths her to the son of a rich merchant). In the story about the journey, Feng writes: "For the most part, human tragedies are generated by the unnatural relationship between people [*bu ziran de ren yu ren jian de guanxi*]. Our love has no use for that kind of unnatural relationship" (Feng Yuanjun 1997, 26). It is clear from the context that the "unnatural relationship" refers to what Mike Featherstone prefers to call "earthly love," or a sexual relationship. The distrust of sexuality seems to stem less from the age-old prohibition against lust than from romanticism's heroic aspirations, or the desire "to order and unify life, to form it from within in terms of some higher purpose which gives life a sense of destiny" (1995, 60).

As a rebel's cause, romantic love is caught in between the pursuit of a higher purpose and the affirmation of ordinary pleasures, including the pleasures of sociality and sexuality. Thanks to the increasing popularity of Freud, male writers such as Yu Dafu and Guo Moruo tended to take a more sanguine view of sexuality and its relationship to love, though this issue will kindle many rounds of debate in the 1920s and 1930s. Lu Xun, for his part, zoomed in on the inherent contradiction in the May Fourth ideal of free love that pinned so much hope—the hope of freedom, liberation, gender equality, and social transformation—on love. Can love shoulder such burdens? What or who may be sacrificed in the process?

TO BE OR NOT TO BE NORA

No other translated text electrified the May Fourth generation more than Henrik Ibsen's play *A Doll's House*. Translated into Chinese in 1918, it continued to "exercise a mesmeric effect in China well into the following decade" (Fitzgerald 1996, 99). Contemporary critics debated the symbolic meaning of Nora's captivity and escape—whether Nora symbolizes the oppression and emancipation of the individual as such, women in general, or the Chinese nation as a whole (Eide 1985, 195–204; Fitzgerald 1996, 99–100). For the same reason that most romantic stories ended with the denouement of escape, few May Fourth critics were inclined to speculate what happened to Nora after she left home. The exception was of course Lu Xun, whose stinging question in "Nala zouhou zenyang?" (What happens after Nora leaves home?, 1923) threw sobering cold water on the May Fourth appropriation of the play in the feverish campaign against the patriarchal family. If the family is the root of Nora's oppression, then her leaving the family should be the solution rather than the beginning of her problems. Prefiguring the socialist argument, Lu Xun plainly points out that the lack of economic independence fatally determines Nora's entrapment between the degradation of prostitution and the humiliation of resubmitting herself to the bondage of the bourgeois home:

> Since Nora has awakened it is hard for her to return to the dream world; hence all she can do is to leave. After leaving, though, she can hardly avoid going to the bad or returning. . . . To put it bluntly, what she needs is money. . . . The most important thing in society today seems to be economic rights. First, there must a fair sharing out between men and women in the family; secondly, men and women must have equal rights in society. (Lu Xun 1980, 87–88; 1998, 153–54)

Lu Xun suggests that Nora is oppressed not just as a woman, but as a member of the dispossessed class. This leads to a deeper question: What are the conditions of individual freedom? Is it predicated on the liberation of all oppressed social classes and groups? The May Fourth aspirants of free love apparently do not think so. Love for them *is* the ultimate affirmation of individual freedom and sovereignty. In identifying the family as their adversary, they believe that the battle is won once they succeed in breaking away from its claws and forming a free union. Young lovers dream of building a more rational and humane community of two—the companionate marriage—on the strength of the redemptive power of romantic love. But they are unprepared for the inherent risk of love or the cruel fact that subjective emotion, however rich, beautiful, and noble, does not constitute "the totality which an inherently concrete individual must be" (Hegel 1975, 567). To a large extent, the critique of romantic love turns on the whims of amatory fortune and where love stands vis-à-vis life's other goals, claims, and interests. In the Nora essay and in his 1925 short story, "Regret for the Past,"[6] Lu Xun questions love's pretension to realize individual autonomy and freedom as such— without a concomitant transformation of the socioeconomic system.

"Regret for the Past" is cast in the male protagonist Juansheng's retrospective voice. The story proper began about a year before, when Juansheng encouraged his lover, Zijun, to defy her family and join him in a free union. Their common-law marriage, however, quickly crumbled under the pressures of economic hardship and social isolation. Zijun returned home and soon died of ill health and humiliation. The narrative begins when Juansheng's thoughts, at the news of Zijun's death, are thrown back to their days together, from courtship to estrangement. At the end of the painful recollection, he reproaches himself for everything that has happened to Zijun. Lydia Liu argues that Juansheng's confessional gesture is really an attempt to assuage his guilty conscience of having abandoned Zijun to her death. He justifies his cruelty with repeated appeals to freedom, likening Zijun to a cage while implying that he is the entrapped bird seeking to break free (Liu 1995, 169). But there is more to the story than a critique of the male-centered discourse of love that "ironically reproduces the patriarchy it aims to overthrow" (167). In my view, it is also a profound reflection on the contradiction that inheres in the idea of free love.

At the start of his affair with Zijun, Juansheng is living alone in a grungy hostel room, away from home and unfettered by familial obligations. He is a free man, but also a lonely one. He speaks of how falling in love with Zijun has rescued him from the "dead quiet and emptiness" of his Spartan and solitary existence. For Zijun, free love is a matter of extricating herself from the authority of her uncle as well as a matter of experiencing the joy of a novel form of sociability sustained by the dialectic of self-denial and self-affirmation that Hegel speaks so eloquently of. Love makes them self-aware for the first time, and "they place their whole soul and world in this identity" (Hegel 1975, 563). At the peak of their passion, they seem to have indeed built a whole imaginative world on this dyadic relation alone, tugging the interests, circumstances, and aims of actual being and life into the sphere of love. Huddling together in their dingy nest, they seek support from each other to brace up against external pressures—her disapproving uncle, a snooty neighbor, and invidious glances on the street:

After we had gazed at each in silence for a moment, the shabby room would be filled with the sound of my voice as I held forth on the tyranny of the home, the need to break with tradition, the equality of men and women, Ibsen, Tagore and Shelley. . . . She would nod her head, smiling, her eyes filled with a childlike look of wonder.

"I'm my own mistress. None of them has any right to interfere with me." She came out with this statement clearly, firmly and gravely, after a thoughtful silence. (LX, 198)

In contrast to his ability to reproduce Zijun's words so precisely, the narrator confesses that he cannot remember how he declared his love for her. "Not only now—even just after it happened, my impression was very blurred" (LX, 199). He only vaguely recalls, much to his embarrassment then and now, his going down on one knee, mimicking the western courtship ritual he had seen in the movies. And yet he is able to recount in great detail Zijun's bodily and verbal reaction to his lectures on freedom. It seems that what Juansheng is seeking in free love is more freedom than love, or more self-affirmation than self-denial, especially in light of his unease with giving himself up to passion and his eagerness to put all that behind. He seeks to penetrate the consciousness of another with his "whole subjective personality" and to "constitute the other's real willing and knowing, striving and possessing" (Hegel 1975, 562), but he is reluctant to commit himself to the dialectical process of love, which entails, among other things, the renunciation of self-sufficiency.

Zijun, for her part, is far more willing and ready to find the roots of her being in Juansheng. She is said to remember every intimate detail of their romance: "She could recite all that I said non-stop, as if she had learned it by heart. She described all my actions in detail, to the life, like a film unfolding itself before my eyes, which included, naturally, that shallow scene from the movies which I was anxious to forget" (LX, 200). Thus, despite the male-centered perspective, the narrative gives a glimpse of how free love is experienced differently by Zijun. She is quoted twice declaring her autonomy and her defiance of her family, but it strikes the reader as a faint echo of the male narrator, who is bent upon vicariously liberating himself by liberating her. Her complete absorption in the courtship process, her nightly reenactment of the scene of proposal, and her insistence on the accurate rendition of history—"At night . . . I was often questioned and examined, or ordered to retell all that had been said on that occasion; but she often had to fill up gaps and correct my mistakes, as if I were a Grade D student" (LX)—all attest to a genuine enjoyment of love as well as confidence in the fulfillment it promises. For this reason, Zijun is able to derive tremendous pleasure from a moment which the narrator deems "ridiculous," even "contemptible," because it is a moment in which he acknowledges his emotional dependency and barters a piece of his autonomy for recognition and solidarity. Hegel shrewdly comments on the gender gap in the romantic enterprise:

> It is especially in female characters that love is supremely beautiful, since for them this surrender, this sacrifice, is the acme of their life, because they draw and expand the whole of their actual and spiritual life into this feeling, find a support for their existence in it alone, and, if they are touched by a misfortune in connection with it, dwindle away like a candle put out by the first unkind breeze. (1975, 563)

Needless to say, women's legendary, thorough surrender to love has less to do with their gendered nature than with the fact that life imposes fewer competing claims on them and that their "actual and spiritual life" has a much more restricted horizon. For a while, Zijun's total intoxication in the "acme" of her life renders her less vulnerable to the cutting glances in the street or their excommunication by family and friends. But once love is withdrawn from her, she does end up dwindling away tragically.

After considerable difficulty, the young couple settle down in a secluded lodging place. Zijun throws herself whole-heartedly into the daily routine of domestic life, with the apparent belief that because the love nest is of their own making, it promises only happiness. The troubles that emerge next, however, cannot be described simply as love worn thin. That Juansheng loses his job and is unable to shield their nest from the scourge of poverty is of course the turning point in their relationship, but more endemic problems have already reared their ugly heads before the calamity of unemployment strikes from outside. In a scene that recalls *La dame*, Zijun insists on selling her jewelry to help raise money for their lodging and furniture. Juansheng gives in to her wish, reasoning that "if she hadn't a share in our home, she would feel uncomfortable" (LX, 201). If one takes this to be an effort toward gender equalization, then it is puzzling that the couple unquestioningly adopt the sexual division of labor against which their idol, Nora, has rebelled. The home Nora walks out of is precisely the kind of home that Juansheng and Zijun embrace after their hard-won liberation from "tyranny" and "tradition."

After a short paragraph assuring the reader of the "tranquility and happiness" of their life together, Juansheng notes with regret that Zijun is being kept too busy by housekeeping to have any time to chat, read, or go out for walks. The renewal of love is being crowded out by the petty concerns of everyday life, which take their toll most immediately on Zijun's appearance. "Her ceaseless anxiety on this score [her mediocre cooking skills] made me anxious too, and in this way we shared the sweet and the bitter together. She kept at it so hard all day, perspiration made her short hair stick to her head, and her hands grew rough" (LX, 202). Once Juansheng is fired from his job, there is only bitterness left, which they find increasingly hard to share. Then, at the first sign of the disappearance of mutual accord, Juansheng begins to reminisce about the "peaceful life" back in the "quiet of my shabby room in the hostel" and fantasizes about "making a fresh start": "At any rate, I had got out of the cage [his old office], and must soar anew in the wide sky before it was too late, while I could still flap my wings" (LX, 204). As Lydia Liu (1995, 169) rightly argues, the renewed yearning for freedom in no time drives him to blame Zijun for his inability to take off and soar in the wide sky. More and more frequently, he finds himself fondly recalling his solitude of yore, something he has once dreaded and longed to escape. Everyday life, now inextricably associated with Zijun, suffocates him with the clutter of dishes and the smell of cooking smoke, disturbing his peace with a cacophony of animal and human noises. His displeasure with the annoyances, constraints, and boredom of the daily routine is never separate from his diminishing affection for Zijun, who has now stepped down from the pedestal as a "firm and fearless" New Woman to the mundane realm of biological and social reproduction:

> Then there was the never-ending business of eating every day. All Zijun's efforts seemed to be devoted to our meals. One ate to earn, and earned to eat; while Ahsui [her pet dog] and the hens had to be fed too. Apparently she had forgotten all she had ever learned, and did not realize that she was interrupting my train of thought when she called me to meals. And although as I sat down I sometimes showed a little displeasure, she paid no attention at all, but just went on munching away quite unconcerned. (LX, 205)

In Zijun's mindless immersion in daily drudgery, Juansheng finds the excuse for ceasing to love her. Convinced that he got along very well when he was on his own, Juansheng decides to fight his way out of the present impasse while he can still "flap his wings." The first step is to denounce love: "during the last half year for love—blind love—I had neglected all the important things in life. First and foremost, livelihood. A man must make a living before there can be any place for love" (LX, 207). In his materialist epiphany, love is no longer linked to freedom but to its antithesis—a besotted state of mind that blots out all matters of real import. In light of the essay on Nora, one cannot help sensing the author's endorsement of this reflection even as he mocks Juansheng's narcissism and hypocrisy. Finding himself caught in between the conflicting demands of freedom and love, he beats a reluctant retreat from love to recover what he truly values—his personal freedom.[7] Juansheng's choice may be morally unconscionable, but he remains true to May Fourth romanticism whereby one loves in order to be free. Love is jettisoned once it is realized that unfreedom can be more vicious than patriarchal oppression—especially for a man. But when he invokes the problem of livelihood, Juansheng is speaking only a half-truth. Losing his job also condemns Juansheng to a private existence, which is an intolerable condition for men who have always found their primary identity in the public realm. As Hannah Arendt states, "the life of a free man needed the presence of others. Freedom itself needed therefore a place where people could come together" (1963, 31). Hence Juansheng's fantasy about regaining a defining identity out in the real world—like "fishermen in the angry sea, soldiers in the trenches, dignitaries in their cars."

Zijun's degradation from an attractive New Woman to a vulgar housewife is more directly a product of the couple's unquestioning embracing of the bourgeois ideology of separate spheres—precisely what Nora rejects. "All the ideas and intelligent, fearless phrases she had learned were empty after all," for she has no more use for them as a private person. Condemned to the status of appendage, "all she could do was cling to someone else's clothing, making it difficult even for a fighter to struggle, and bringing ruin on both" (LX, 209). As Juansheng registers his resentment, it never crosses his mind that Zijun may have her own fantasies that have been censored by the domestic ideology they both take for granted. Free love as practiced by them is none so radical because the only "livelihood" it permits a woman is the conjugal family, whose daily grind paradoxically exposes the impossibility of love as a livelihood. Apparently not having lost all her courage, Zijun soon confronts Juansheng on his feeling toward her. He, with a solemn appeal to truth, confesses the cessation of his love and insinuates his desire for her departure. Once again he draws his weapon of suasion from Ibsen, casting the separation as a point from which to make a fresh start for both of them, although he cannot be said to be without a glimmer of knowledge of what awaits her outside their dingy nest. In the end, Juansheng repents and is pardoned by the author. Ah-sui, the exiled dog, miraculously returns to his side (perhaps signaling Zijun's pardon as well?), and he moves back to his hostel room, where he admits to finding only emptiness. Freedom now shamefully consorts with "oblivion" and "falsehood," and the road he has dreamed of embarking on "seems like a great, gray serpent, writhing and darting at [him]" (LX, 214–15).

The portentous ending seems to suggest that contrition and penance cannot redeem a botched romantic experiment. Lu Xun may forgive Juansheng who shares, though belatedly, his belief in the importance of economic freedom, but he is by no means ready to forgive the utopianism of free love and those who continue to trumpet its desirability while willfully ignoring its internal contradiction and its collisions with lived reality—either to delude themselves or to exploit the impressionable and gullible young. The husband in "A Happy Family" (1924) is one such person. He is a hack writer who spins the false yarn of "a happy family" in sheer bad faith, scornfully oblivious of the mundane details of daily life—the price of firewood, the storage of winter cabbage, the cry of a child. Above the drowning din of everyday living, he tries to keep afloat his dream vision of a conjugal family with all its bourgeois pomp, even though he can hardly find a realistic location in China for his story, nor can he keep the jarring but stubborn fragments of reality from irrupting into his savory fantasy. In the very first paragraph, Lu Xun makes it clear that the hack writer is bent on concocting a cheap story of conjugal bliss not because he believes in its reality, but because he knows how to cater to contemporary fads for a handsome remuneration.[8] If "Regret for the Past" reveals the tragedy of free love, then "A Happy Family" presents a burlesque. Lu Xun's own experiment with free love (see McDougall 2002) shows that it rarely reaches the height of tragedy, nor is it so absurd that one can dismiss it with a knowing chuckle. Writers after him continue to dramatize the existential quandary of free love and women writers, in particularly, begin to tell Zijun's story and expose the false promises of bourgeois marriage.

THE SEXUAL CONTRACT

In the late 1920s, it was commonly perceived that free love was in a state of crisis, and remedies came from all directions. Social conservatives wished to translate love into a communal ethic and purge all connotations of freedom and transgression from its semantic field. Radicals wanted to align love with collective political projects while reducing courtship and marriage to a bland routine. But despite the backlash against free love and the attempt to subsume it into the ethical and political, writers continued to engage the topic of love in its increasingly discredited sense—as romantic relationship between young men and women. Women writers, in particular, contributed to the staying power of the romantic genre by pondering love's role in women's struggle to achieve modern subjectivity. Their critique of love went beyond ethical and political considerations to expose the sexual contract underpinning the modern marriage and conjugal family.

In *The Money Demon*, the already married Chen Diexian tries to persuade Koto, a courtesan, to join his household as a concubine. Koto refuses, and Chen denounces her for being bedeviled by money (see Lee 2001). What Chen tries to achieve is the combining of the socioeconomic regime of marriage and the affective regime of romance—long considered separate and incompatible. Koto's preference for the status of a courtesan to that of a concubine is thus remarkably prescient of the problematic enterprise of the conjugal family. In marrying Chen, she would lose what little public existence she still enjoyed and the small measure of independence that being a courtesan afforded her. But Koto is decidedly in the minority in her rejection of the sexual contract. Many women do, willingly or unwillingly, forego what Koto holds so dear in exchange for the security and social status that a proper wife is able to enjoy and to which a concubine may have a partial claim. Women writers in the 1920s and 1930s, as I intend to show in this section, would dwell persistently on the promises and pitfalls of the sexual contract.

Rey Chow proposes the notion of "virtuous transaction" to read Ling Shuhua's "boudoir fiction" about middle- and upper-class women (1993). In Chow's view, women's relationship to patriarchy is one of contract or transaction whereby women behave virtuously and repress their true desires in exchange, in theory at least, for security, status, and domestic happiness. But more often than not, patriarchy simply fails to make good on its promises, and the specter of disappointment constitutes the oppressive backdrop of Ling's subdued portraitures of jittery, neurotic, and pathetically superstitious heroines. Although Chow does not invoke Carole Pateman's trenchant critique of the sexual contract, Ling's texts certainly support Pateman's argument that the bourgeois marriage is a faulty contract. For Pateman, a "contract is the specifically modern means of creating relationships of subordination," even though it is presented as the juridical expression of freedom (1988, 118). For example, the labor contract between the capitalist and the worker, or the contract between the prostitute and her client, is often touted as premised on individual free choice. Indeed, contractual relations gain their meaning in contradistinction to natural relations: they presuppose free relationships and political rights rather than ascriptive relationships and paternal rights. Pateman debunks the myth of the contact by pointing out that the "original contract" of western political theory is not just a social contract but also a sexual contract. The social contract effects the exchange of natural freedom for civil freedom protected by the state; the sexual contract establishes men's political rights over women and their orderly access to women's bodies (2).

The bourgeois marriage contract sanctions the sexual division of labor and the husband's ownership of the sexual property in his wife's person (Pateman 1988, 124). It is essentially a commercial transaction, for it is, until the last decades of the twentieth century, virtually the only way in which a woman could earn her livelihood in a socially accepted way. Thus women collectively are coerced into marriage even if a particular woman is free to remain single. The marriage contract is a kind of labor contract, but a wife's subordination to her husband is not the equivalent of that of a worker to a capitalist, because the employment contract presupposes the marriage contract. In other words, the construction of the "worker" presupposes that he is a man who has a woman (a housewife) to take care of his daily needs and to satisfy the reproductive imperative (131). Pateman makes the emphatic point that contract always generates political rights in the form of domination and subordination, and that it does not preclude inequality and coercion. Contract theory therefore ill serves feminism.

For our purpose, Pateman's critique alerts us to an aspect in women's writings that questions modern marriage as the natural destiny of the liberated woman. Scholars have tended to treat women's skeptical attitude toward marriage on an individualized basis, speaking of love lost or betrayed and resorting to such clichés as "marriage is the tomb of love." Taken collectively, women's writings expose the marriage contract as creating a relationship of civil subjection rather than solidifying the freedom that romantic love ushers in. In a bourgeois marriage, the wife is reduced to the status of property whose right of (sexual) access is reserved for the husband. She does not have jurisdiction over the property in her person, including her labor power. The wife is given a degree of moral authority within the household, but it is predicated on her renunciation of a role in the public domain and her willingness to endure "civil death." In other words, she gives up the right to contract out her labor power in exchange for a wage and secure a civil identity as a "worker." The marriage contract is about women's labor that is deliberately denied the name of "work" and that is dependent on the repressed connection between the private and civil spheres (135–36). The women writers whose works we examine below wrestle with the realization that bourgeois marriage is not the culmination of free love, but rather the negation of freedom and gender equality.

In Ling Shuhua's short story "Jiuhou" (Tipsy, 1928), Caitiao (wife) and Yongzhang (husband) are a loving couple whose conjugal relationship seems to be directly modeled on that between Helmer and Nora in *A Doll's House*. Indeed, Yongzhang so frequently heaps sentimental homilies on Caitiao that she feels vaguely uneasy, as if intertextual references to Ibsen's indictment of the hypocrisy of bourgeois marriage are poking at her consciousness. The culminating point of Yongzhang's devotion comes in the form of a New Year's "gift" as the couple relax together after hosting a successful dinner party: he tells Caitiao that she can have anything she wishes for the New Year. Caitiao is at the moment irresistibly drawn to a guest (by the name of Ziyi) who has passed out in a drunken stupor on their drawing room sofa:

> Ziyi's flushed cheeks looked as if they had been soaked through with rouge. His eyes, thoughtful and mysterious, were closed comfortably;. . . . Caitiao had never seen him like this before. Normally he looked so respectful and gentle, but now, after drinking, he looked sensuous and beautiful. After staring at him for a moment, Caitiao's face felt hot. She said:
> "I don't want anything [for the New Year]. I only want you to grant me one thing. It'll take just a second."
> "Tell me quickly please," replies Yongzhang gladly. "Whatever is mine, it's yours too. It's fine even if it should take a million years, let alone one second."
> "I want. . . . I'm too embarrassed to say it."
> "It's all right."
> "He . . . "
> "I'm sure he won't be awakened. Just say it."
> "I . . . I just want to kiss his face once. Would you let me?"
> "Really, Caitiao?"

"Yes. Really!" (Ling Shuhua 1984, 6–7; translation adapted from Chow 1993, 101)

The slumbering guest is here subjected to what might be called "Sophia's gaze"—made memorable in Ding Ling's "Miss Sophia's Diary" (see below)—whereby a man is reduced to his bodily features that are described in eroticized details. Caitiao gazes upon the reclining, feminized man in a boldly masculine manner and finds him "sensuous and beautiful." In doing so, she asserts her sexual agency: a married woman she may be, but she is still her own mistress and can still exercise control over her desires and inclinations as well as the use of her body. The myth of the marriage contract as a contract of freedom is temporarily upheld as her uxorious husband seems willing to accommodate her every wish, even one that most directly challenges his right of sexual property in his wife's person. After a moment's hesitation, Yongzhang grants her request. But Caitiao becomes hesitant and insists on Yongzhang's indirect participation—by walking her to the sofa. Yongzhang promises to lend her moral support by staying close by and watching her. The story abruptly ends with Caitiao declaring that she no longer wishes to kiss the man.

The anticlimax of the story has puzzled the critics. Rey Chow argues that Caitiao backs down because she realizes that her "improper wish" would amount to "a failure in wifely virtue" (1993, 101). The story thus demonstrates "the ideological limits that a Chinese woman internalizes in order to be a 'good' wife" (103). Again, Caitiao's "'adventure' is thwarted by the invisible contractual obligations she has made with society in terms of feminine virtue" (103). Chow finds the story "consciously conservative" because it shows a woman's "voluntary completion of a virtuous transaction" (103). To be sure, Caitiao's last-minute retreat can certainly be read as a cowering gesture, an inability to carry a transgressive act through, a capitulation to society. But I believe that there is more to the ending than this conservative reading allows. It is important to bear in mind that Caitiao's adventure is set in motion by Yongzhang's proffering of a New Year's gift. A gift is something that is bestowed upon us, something we do not acquire through an act of will. Marcel Mauss famously theorizes gift exchange as a kind of commerce that entails the obligation to give, to accept, and to reciprocate. And unlike the sale of a commodity, the giving of a gift establishes a social relationship between the donor and recipient. To this theorem Maurice Godelier adds the crucial reminder that there are different kinds of gifts, including gifts that manipulate an existing relationship, that humiliate the recipient or produce an oppressive sense of obligation, that establish and maintain hierarchies and inequality, and that confer authority and superiority on the donor (1999).[9]

The framing of Caitiao's abortive adventure as a gift from her husband renders problematic her claim to emotional autonomy. It serves as a reminder that the very possibility of her conceiving an improper wish is a gift of patriarchy that has already consigned her to the inferior position of a recipient. On the one hand, the husband, secure in his knowledge of proprietorship, further enhances his superior status by taking the moral high ground. On the other hand, Caitiao's ability to get away with a naughty whim only serves to prove her subjection to a relation of hierarchy and inequality. Her insistence that her husband play the role of spectator in her adventure is thus a tacit recognition of this basic condition—as if subconsciously, she understands perfectly well that what she is about to do is not an act of autonomous will, but rather a favor granted to her. Her recognition of the absurdity of the whole affair is most likely what causes her fluttering heart to calm down suddenly. Perhaps there is also a premonition of the terrible debt she would incur were she to accept the gift, of the oppressive sense of obligation she would have to live with and that would undermine any illusion of freedom and autonomy that she still needs to continue with the status quo. The story is conservative not in the sense that Caitiao so swiftly returns to the path of decorum, but in the sense that she chooses not to shatter that illusion. For all its apparent simplicity, the story is a poignant critique of the sexual contract. The notion of "virtuous transaction" is therefore highly ironic for women are never in a position—as juridical subjects—to negotiate contracts with patriarchy to begin with. The contract is an ex post facto fiction that demands that women live up to the terms of an agreement to which they have never given their consent.

A year before Ling Shuhua published "Tipsy," Ding Ling had dazzled critics and readers alike with "Miss Sophia's Diary" (1927). In recent years, "Diary" has become the locus classicus of women's literature in modern China, and its formal and thematic innovations have been amply commented on. I will not rehash the critical consensus on "Diary," most notably its daring and nuanced depictions of assertive and polymorphous feminine desires. Instead, I problematize the brusque way in which Sophia terminates her relationship with the dashing overseas Chinese man Ling Jishi—a relationship for which she has yearned throughout the story and has ardently pursued. In the last diary entry,

Sophia compels herself to face the truth that she does not love Ling Jishi and that she has been merely attracted to his handsome exterior. She cries out in agony, "How shall I analyze the psychology of a woman driven insane by the way a man looks? Of course I didn't love him, and the reason why is easy to explain: inside his beautiful appearance his soul is completely degraded!" (IMW 79). A few lines down, she resorts to even stronger language: "depths of . . . depravity"; a "wretched," "contemptible," "revolting," "pathetic man," "one of the vilest beasts." What kind of man is Ling that he deserves all these demeaning and vituperative epithets? What is the nature of his depravity? We find the clue in Sophia's many undelivered, accusatory questions for Ling: "Did you really think that all I desire is marriage and family? That all that amuses me is money? That all I'm proud of is my 'position'?" (IMW, 79).[10] We then trace this to a conversation between Ling and Sophia early in the text where Ling, quite innocently, tells Sophia what he holds dear in life and what he projects for their common future. Sophia recalls the gist of this conversation in a diary entry:

> All he wants is money. Money. A young wife to entertain his business associates in the living room, and several fat, fair-skinned, well-dressed little sons. What does love mean to him? Nothing more than spending money in a brothel, squandering it on a moment of carnal pleasure, or sitting on a soft sofa fondling scented flesh, a cigarette between his lips, his legs crossed casually, laughing and talking with his friends. When it's not fun anymore, never mind; he just runs home to his little wifey. He's passionate about the Debate Club, playing tennis matches, studying at Harvard, joining the foreign service, becoming an important statesman, or inheriting his father's business and becoming a rubber merchant. He wants to be a capitalist . . . that is the extent of his ambition! (IMW, 68)

This passage sketches out the kind of life that Armand's father would want him to have—the life of a bourgeois male (whatever his specific vocation) who shuttles between home, office, club, and (discreetly) brothel. Aside from the playboy aspect, it is also the kind of life that Albert proudly leads and from which Armand and Werther flee to prove themselves to be true romantics. However, while Armand and Werther may find the bourgeois male priggish and pathetically uninspiring, they do not necessarily deem him morally degenerate. As I have suggested, Marguerite in fact is quite willing to recognize the worth of bourgeois life (to other people). Werther, too, does not hold Albert in contempt, even though he despises everything Albert stands for and the latter's hold on Charlotte's heart injures him mortally.

The ferocity of Sophia's denunciation of Ling Jishi, then, cannot be casually explained away in terms of her disdain for a superficial man. Why and since when, we must ask, does the absence of romantic idealism become a moral liability? What makes Ling such a monster to Sophia that what he offers her is worse than a lonely death? Is Ling's monstrosity an alibi for her "twisted" will and "frustrated" sexuality (Barlow 2004, 137), or, perhaps more to the point, the castoff shell of herself as she tries to effect a painful sloughing off of her *nüxing* identity? But Sophia is a consumptive and is not likely to be reborn as a *funü*, or the socialist female subject. Never directly questioning the "conflation of 'liberation' and sexual desire" (153), Sophia is still very much a woman whose engendering is the effect of a voluntary embracing of "the phantom reality of erotic love" (144). To flee from Ling, the frail Sophia boards a southbound train and portentously declares that she will "squander" away the remaining days of her life somewhere where no one knows her (IMW, 81). One can hardly suppose that she would permit herself to enter into marriage-oriented romantic relationships again.

What Sophia has left behind, à la Nora, is the entire world of ordinary life as defined and sanctified by bourgeois ideology. Her violent disgust with Ling is thus an expression of her (and the author's) struggle with the radically shifting moral frameworks of her times. In the space of two or three years, Sophia would be reincarnated in Ding Ling's fiction as heroines who fight to win a public existence outside the domestic sphere; that public existence often takes the form of revolutionary activism (see Chapter 7). Critics have marveled at the 180-degree turn in Ding Ling's fiction within such a short time while contenting themselves with a purely biographical explanation (Ding Ling's first husband was executed by the KMT regime in 1927). But a careful reading of "Diary" reveals that Sophia is not so distant from the more fiery heroines of Ding Ling's later fiction. They all reject ordinary life as paltry and meaningless, and along with it, they denounce romantic love as futile, selfish, and retrograde. And in Ling Jishi we see early traces of the bourgeois male character (think of Zibin in Ding Ling's "Shanghai, Spring 1930" and Yu Yongze in Yang Mo's *The Song of Youth*) whose structurally determined ordinariness becomes almost an obscenity in official literary history.

THE AFFAIR

Ding Ling is probably registering a debt more to *La dame* than to *Dream* in casting Sophia as a consumptive. The turn-of-the-last-century European beliefs about tuberculosis conveniently link Sophia's immodest sexual appetite to her consumptive state. Barring a miraculous recovery, we can reasonably surmise that the still consumptive, and therefore still sexually voracious Sophia might manage to have an affair or two with men in the south, so long as they do not propose to her and hope to make her their little "wifey."

The affair is the guise that romantic love takes on once it has ceased to be *le grand amour* and made peace with the bourgeois social order. Instead of a lifetime project, the affair is brief, discrete, and repeatable. It is an adventure, set apart both spatially and temporally from the stream of concatenating events of everyday life. It is sought after for the temporary but intense stimulation, pleasure, and wonderment that it offers, not because it is a hypergood that supplies the meaning of life and claims uncontested supremacy and allegiance. It is, rather, a symptomatic product of love's quotidianization, of its irrevocable immersion in the phenomenology of everyday life. Romantic love now has to contend with such ordinary lifegoods as work, marriage, family life, stability, security, and solidarity. Idealized visions of romantic love still thrive in the semi-mythologized and highly commercialized world of urban leisure culture. What is "romantic" is still necessarily distinguished from what is everyday, but it is more and more associated with commodities and commodified leisure activities (Illouz 1997).

Shi Zhecun's short story "Meiyu zhi xi" (One evening in the rainy season, 1929) offers a pensive sketch of the novel experience of romance as a discrete and bounded adventure for the urban dweller.[11] The "I" narrator is a married man and office clerk who sports a complacent attitude toward his workaday routine. But when an opportunity for a possible romantic adventure presents itself, he is caught between conflicting impulses. One rainy evening, on his way home from work, he offers, after much hesitation, to share his umbrella with a young woman who has just stepped off a bus and who is unable to hail a rickshaw in the pouring rain. Throughout the duration of their shoulder-to-shoulder walk, he ruminates over the meaning of his action and indulges in shapeless, fragmentary fantasies. After they part, he heads home, a gratified, if slightly flustered and guilty, man. His brush with romance, if not quite an affair, qualifies as an adventure because it is clearly marked off from the everyday: the walk through deserted streets under the cover of the evening rain is a chronotope figuratively removed from the world of work and family life. It has a beginning and end, and what transpires in the walk has no material bearing on life: life goes on and is made more bearable by such unexpected, serendipitous adventures.[12]

The relativization of romantic love, or its demotion from a hypergood to an ordinary lifegood that must negotiate its claims with other, equally cherished lifegoods is a reflection of the condition of plural moral sources, or what Taylor calls "the fractured moral horizon," in the post-Enlightenment age. Taylor (1989, 410) speaks of the "tripartite 'map' of moral sources" that the nineteenth century bequeaths us: religious faith, scientific agnosticism, and culture/aesthetics. If religious faith appears to be a remnant from the pre-Enlightenment age, its hold on vast segments of the modern population has by no mean diminished. What has changed is that it is no longer the sole source of moral action and, fundamentalism excepted, has learned to live with other competing alternatives. The tension among the three sources accounts for much of our modern conflict.

The fractured moral horizon of modernity is most penetratingly illustrated in Gustave Flaubert's *Madame Bovary* (1857), which, not coincidentally, also documents with biting piquancy the transformation of romantic love from *le grand amour* to the affair.[13] If the novel is first and foremost an antiromantic critique, it also mourns the passing of *le grand amour* and the plight of those who are caught in its death throes. Emma Bovary stands for every hopeless romantic who finds herself stuck in a changed world where Enlightenment naturalism clamors to be the new religion of the age and religion aligns itself with the bourgeois valuation of ordinary life. It is significant that the novel begins and ends with Emma's husband, Charles Bovary, whose bovine complacency makes him a perfect icon of the petit bourgeois society against which Emma rebels. Charles's aspirations are quintessentially bourgeois: prosperous business, acquisition of property, affectionate family life, and well-nurtured children whose pursuit of the same aspirations makes happiness permanent.

As a woman, Emma cannot share her husband's thorough immersion in the joys of ordinary life. The narrative painstakingly delineates a personality whose education and disposition make her an inveterate dreamer who is unable to find contentment in provincial life. Critics often treat Emma as a generic figure of misguided idealism, but the novel is also emphatic in identifying the *gendered* cause of her discontentment: an educated farm daughter turned house-wife, her "theater and promenade" are but the window of her boudoir, a sym-bol of confinement and immobility. She rebels by being a negligent wife and mother and by seeking out romantic, adulterous adventures in imitation of all the romantic novels she has devoured.

If Emma's literature-inspired quest for romance makes her a case study of culture and aesthetics as a moral source, then Monsieur Homais, the town pharmacist and a self-important man of science, is a specimen of scientific agnosticism. He is fittingly cast as an Enlightenment doctrinaire who tire-lessly spouts pseudoscientific analyses of the world and who coerces the ser-vant boy Hippolyte to undergo a botched surgery that permanently cripples him. The agricultural show, on the other hand, is a collective celebration of the Enlightenment faith in bureaucratic rationality and technological progress. Flaubert artfully juxtaposes the proceedings of the agricultural show with Rodolphe's seduction of Emma, intermixing the presiding officials' stiff bombast about such earthy matters as animal husbandry with Rodolphe's honeyed fustian about the heart. The comic effect, however, barely conceals the sense of despair over the incompatibility of the two moral sources—the scientific/rational and the artistic/romantic—that is nevertheless the reality of modern life.

Emma's romantic quest is a gendered response to the alienation, fragmen-tation, and stifling homogeneity of bourgeois family life, while her relentless strivings make her unpardonably selfish and wreak irreparable havoc on her family. In this light, the novel is far from a one-dimensional indictment of ro-manticism. Rather, it is a profound reflection on the loss of moral certainty and its terrible and confusing consequences. It is not surprising, then, that re-ligion, alongside romance, is also a venue in which Emma seeks to escape the banality of everyday life. The novel's attitude toward religion is as skeptical as it is sardonic toward the Enlightenment, personifying them in the figures of Bournisien the priest and Homais, both being garrulous, quarrelsome, and petty-minded old men whose perpetual debate pauses only when their com-mon opponent, Emma, lies stiff and dead before them. Although it is easy to see how religion as an institution lets Emma down, it is hard to resist the temptation of attributing Emma's romantic debacle to the character flaws of individual men—her paramours Rodolphe and Léon. This may well be true, particularly in the case of Rodolphe, a rogue character who does not himself believe in the romantic notions with which he seduces Emma, which explains why he cruelly abandons her the moment he realizes that she is in it for real, not for the game of it.

But Léon, her second lover, seems to be a paler male version of herself, sharing her fondness for romantic literature and imagining her to be the romantic heroine of his dreams. However, when he is about to be promoted to chief clerk at his firm, Léon gives up his exalted sentiments and poetic imagination as well as Emma. He thus typifies that peculiarly Janus-faced modern man: the bourgeois as the bohemian, or an Armand finally reconciled to his father's world. It is not only nearly obligatory that a bourgeois man pass a period of his youth in "Bohemia," but even from within his banal commercial civilization, he wants to have a part in the "epiphanies of the creative imagination" (Taylor 1989, 424). Or as the narrator puts it mordantly: "every bourgeois in the flush of his youth, were it but for a day, a moment, has believed himself capable of immense passions, of lofty enterprises. The most mediocre libertine has dreamed of sultanas; every notary bears within him the debris of a poet" (Flaubert 1965, 211). Léon finds his inner poet by carrying on a clandestine affair with a woman who is also in search of grand passions. But as soon as the affair threatens to break out of the confines of the adventure, he beats a prudent, if cowardly, retreat. But if love has become something that the bourgeoisie cannot live with and cannot live without, it seems fated to become a game, and Léon is fated to degenerate into a duplicitous Rodolphe.

In the end, what ruins Emma is not adultery per se (Charles only discovers Emma's infidelity after her death), nor even her betrayal at the hands of her paramours, but her total lack of scruples in money matters and her compulsive, lavish expenditures. The novel seems to side with the bourgeois charge that the quest for hypergoods—here romantic love—necessarily entails the sacrifice of ordinary lifegoods—here a sound domestic economy. But it also points to the paradox that romance, the antithesis of instrumental reason, is increasingly bound up with the commercial civilization: Emma's adventures, in point of fact, are largely financed through loans from Lheureux, a shop owner and raptorial money lender. The bourgeois's bohemian fantasies would become the steadiest and inexhaustible source of capitalist profit. In the twentieth century, romance has indeed become not only impractical but also nearly unthinkable without the prompts and props supplied, ad nauseam, by commercial culture.

The affair as a commercially assisted experience of modernity is also taken up by Chinese writers. "Zai Bali daxiyuan" (At the Paris Theater, 1931), by

Shi Zhecun, is one of the many stories set in modern Shanghai that highlight love's new dependence on the consumption-oriented capitalist economy. Like Léon, the "I" narrator is a petit bourgeois who operates, in his everyday routine, by the principles of instrumental rationality, but who, in the space of this short stream-of-consciousness narrative, is out having a romantic adventure with a female acquaintance. Characteristically, their rendezvous takes place in a movie theater. Along with parks, cafés, dance halls, and department stores, movie theaters are a mainstay of commercialized leisure culture; in aggregate, these public/commercial spaces make up what historian Kathy Peiss calls a "heterosocial world" (quoted in Illouz 1997, 27), where men and women form ever-widening social circles outside the bounds of marriage and family. They can strike up relatively open romantic liaisons so long as they are discreet and do not turn rebellious. This is where one finds single, financially (semi-)independent women who wield as much, if not more, power and control over the terms and scope of romance as men have always done in such matters. Consequently, this is also where one finds the metropolitan personality, nearly always male and characterized by introspection, insecurity, paranoia, anxiety, hypersensitivity, timidity, tentativeness, and loneliness, all of which come to make up that uniquely modern psychological affliction—neurasthenia.

Throughout the extended monologue, which recounts the tryst between the "I" narrator and his female companion at the Paris Theater, the narrator obsessively tries to read the latter's mind as well as his own. First, he is taken by surprise when she beats him to the box office and purchases two tickets; he is then assailed by the thought that she considers him too poor or stingy, and by the suspicion that everyone around them has taken notice and is laughing up their sleeves at his embarrassment. In the same manner, every little gesture she makes and every staccato line she utters are chewed over in his mind with neurotic compulsion. The one central question for which he desperately seeks the answer is whether she loves him and vice versa. The sheer distance between this story and Butterfly and May Fourth love stories is only too apparent. In the latter, young people fall in love at first sight, and thereafter, the status of their love is never in doubt. What the lovers agonize over is how to overcome obstacles in order to bring their love to fruition. The lovers are transparent individuals who are no mystery to each other even if there can be misunderstanding or miscommunication between them.

Here, the man and woman out on a date are at full liberty to fall in love, and an entire leisure industry is in place to assist them in this enterprise. Yet they are plagued by uncertainties and paralyzed by their inability to communicate their feelings. The woman is a total enigma to the man, even though they are obviously no strangers to each other. Furthermore, he is not even sure of his own feelings for her, and he is at a total loss as to how and when to flirt, and whether he will be snubbed. Thus, instead of the abundance of words and profusion of emotions that characterize earlier love stories, the interaction between the protagonists of this story is characterized by taciturnity, awkwardness, and the folding up of the self that desperately yearns for connection and communication. They may be surrounded by thronging crowds, and yet they are essentially alone and very lonely. The man tries to counteract the sense of loneliness by turning inward and speaking loquaciously to himself and to his imaginary reader. And instead of reaching out to his companion in a genuinely communicative manner, he takes to indulging in what Leo Ou-fan Lee calls "kinky fetishism" (Lee 1999, 174): stealthily caressing and sucking her clammy handkerchief, exclaiming that her bodily fluids (sweat, spit, and snivel) taste marvelous, and imagining that he is embracing her naked body (Shi Zhecun 1991, 263).

If we are made privy to the neurotic psyche of the metropolitan man, the metropolitan woman remains at a narrative remove and tantalizingly opaque. Typically, she is economically and morally independent, cultured, willful, and haughty; she easily metamorphoses into a femme fatale—the modern incarnation of the fox spirit and ghostly maiden that haunt premodern erotic fiction. She is indeed such a figure in *Pinghu tongche* (Beijing-Shanghai express, 1935) by Zhang Henshui.[14] In this enormously popular novel, a young female con artist named Liu Jichun lays a sex trap for a wealthy banker named Hu Ziyun in a first-class compartment on the Beijing-Shanghai express train and makes off with his entire assets. Hu reappears several years later as a penniless bum in Shanghai and dies a pathetic death as he tries to make his way back north. The novel is a veritable parable of modernity. Rey Chow points out that the railway journey from Beijing to Shanghai spatially configures the two cities as the loci of tradition and modernity and that it is a one-way journey without return (1991, 76). She performs a highly sensitive reading of the ways in which Zhang Henshui paints modernity in its cacophonous and bewildering materiality: the noises, smells, bodily fluids, and objects that are thrown together haphazardly, without any regard for conventional boundaries (78–79). Although the division of the cars into three classes helps maintain a semblance of hierarchy and order, bodies and objects continue to jostle and commingle by accident or by design, leading ultimately to the undoing of Mr. Hu.

In addition to the myriad sensory stimuli with which it assails the passengers, the train is also a microcosm that displays how modernity both levels old distinctions and creates new ones. There is a good deal of commentary, either in direct authorial voice or in the conversations among the passengers who in one way or another have to cope with their enforced sociability, on how class and social status are made and remade on the train: Who rides in the first-class cars and who doesn't, who can finagle a free ticket and who can't or won't, who contributes positively to the train's ad hoc minisociety through generous and compassionate acts and who doesn't. The novel also highlights the allures and pitfalls of modern transportation and the capitalist economy. At the many stops en route, passengers would get off the train to sample local specialty snacks, having already amply discussed such things with fellow passengers and become familiar with the national lore of local color fostered by travel magazines. In an unprecedented manner, one comes into contact with a diversity of local cultures and customs in a matter of days. In this way also, localities are encased metonymically in a few snack carts in the stations, and people no longer have the time or motivation to experience a place by entering its concrete space and exploring its culture and history.

But above all, the capitalist economy renders wealth dangerously volatile and vulnerable. Unlike in traditional economies where wealth is reckoned in tangible estates and properties and intangible status (symbolic capital that can be converted to material capital when necessary), Hu's entire fortune comes in the form of stocks and bonds and cash, which he stores in a suitcase. He keeps a vigilant watch over it, and still Miss Liu manages to steal it from under his nose. Once he loses the suitcase, he loses everything and falls to the bottom rungs of the social ladder. This turn of fortune may seem overdramatized, for even the most thoroughgoing capitalist economy still has use for symbolic capital. Hu should be able to fall back on his social standing to absorb some of his loss. But the exaggeration makes a moral point: The money economy, the novel seems to intone, is what sustains modern life and what makes all that is solid melt into air.

Chow argues that the encounter between Hu and Liu stands for the conflict between tradition and modernity. According to her, between the two of them is "a struggle between the transparent complacency of a sign-reading 'subject' and the opaque fascination of 'objects' that are construed to be without consciousness"—here a solitary woman traveler (79). True, Hu's attitude toward gender relations is typical of "a traditional Chinese gentleman" (76): he welcomes an adventure to break up the monotony of the journey, so long as it is only an adventure. But he displays distinctively modern sensibilities in intuiting that an unattached and yet respectable woman (that is, the divorcée that Liu pretends to be) might not be adverse to the diversion of a one-night stand. (Liu displays her one-upmanship by leaving her pocketbook casually lying around so that he is induced to read her "private" correspondence, in which she expresses a yearning for sensual enjoyment without commitment or consequence.) He is also astutely aware of the troubled nature of modern marriages and understands that he can easily win over a divorced woman with sympathy (instead of the traditional attitude of animadversion). And last, he is conversant with the ritual of modern courtship, the stratagems of the "love game," and the protocols of the new heterosocial world. At times the novel reads like a manual on how to make a sexual conquest, with its patient disquisition on the requisite steps and proper pace of action (Zhang Henshui 1993, 28:54). One imagines that Hu is quite practiced in the art of seduction and has always been successful—until he meets his match in Liu.

If the heterosocial world allows for free and open association between the sexes, it is also a free-wheeling world where there is none of the traditional safeguards and where the amatory fortune is in full swing. One has only one's wits to rely on and strangers' words to go by, and the stakes are high: one gets a taste of the thrills of romance by losing oneself to another, thereby risking losing more than one is prepared to give up. Hu loses the game by being too cocksure, and his punishment seems out of proportion. But this is the risk that one takes when seeking out romantic adventures in this brave new world: Precisely because it is sealed off from the social world, every player is more or less an unknown entity and is not held accountable by anything but his or her own interests and desires. It is small wonder that crime fiction finds the romantic genre a genial partner and that the affair has become a privileged backdrop for intrigues and criminal conspiracies.

It may be argued that Hu is a traditional man because he has more than one wife at home. But it is clear in the novel that he never intends to take Liu into his household as another concubine, nor is he in the frame of mind to pursue freedom or transgress social boundaries by acting out a drama of *le grand amour* with her. He only wants to have an affair with her, anticipating the experience to be a game/adventure that is an end in itself. What he seeks is instant pleasure and escape, not lasting commitment or momentous self-sacrifice. Moreover, even with the limited resources available on the train only to first-class passengers, their romance is very much part and parcel of modern consumer culture. Name-brand cigarettes and liquor, for example, are indispensable props in their double-crossed seduction game. The novel is also peppered with references to leisure activities at movie theaters, dance halls, parks, and hotels—indeed, the couple plan to end their journey with a grand finale in a Shanghai hotel.

The modern woman, it seems, is opaque, intimidating, or downright predatory whenever the story is told from the male perspective. Women, however, do not always emerge from romantic adventures as victors. More often than not, because marriage is still largely the only vocation open to women, they enter into romantic/sexual liaisons with earnest expectations of marriage and as a result often end up bitterly disappointed and victimized. While men can lead a double life and make brief excursions into the world of adventurous affairs, for women, love is still a lifelong quest, the success or failure of which spells a lifetime of security (and perhaps happiness) or misery. This is the mismatched world in which the protagonists of Zhang Ailing's *Qingcheng zhi lian* (Love in a fallen city, 1943) find themselves.

Bai Liusu is a divorced woman who, at the beginning of the novel, is living with her uncharitable natal family. Her mother and her brothers and their wives consider her "spilled water" who no longer belongs at home and are scheming to marry her off again. To be sure, she can try to support herself by working as a governess or secretary, but she would instantly lose her "lady" status and destroy her prospect of marrying into a respectable family. Between a humble and unpredictable career as a working woman on the one hand, and a proper and secure career as a housewife on the other, Liusu makes a pragmatic, if not so courageous, choice. This, however, does not make her a "traditional" woman. First of all, it was she who initiated the divorce from her husband when she could no longer brook his philanderings and abuses. Second, she stoically wards off the pressure to return to her ex-husband's house to mourn his premature death as a widow in order to claim the property and privileges that are customarily accorded to the first wife. And last but not least, after she is thrust into the game of love with an overseas Chinese dandy named Fan Liuyuan, she proves quite his match in the diplomacy of love, in keeping up, in Fu Lei's words, "the pretty dialogue . . . games of make-believe and hide-and-seek . . . [the] luring and teasing, the trivial battles of attack and defense" (quoted in Lee 1999, 280). What she is faced with is a typical modern woman's predicament: how to secure one's life by securing the commitment of a man who excels in the modern mode of love—as an adventure, not a quest.

Liuyuan more than lives up to his reputation as a cad as he approaches his relationship with Liusu, much to the latter's distress, with a connoisseur's panache. They carry on their courtship while both are lodged in Hong Kong's Repulse Bay Hotel. The hotel is a typically modern locale of anonymity where one engages in self-fashioning and passing, experiments with alternative lifestyles, and strikes up casual and fleeting relationships. However good at the ritual of seduction and counterseduction, Liusu is keenly conscious of the prospect that their romance will only be the latest addition to Liuyuan's repertoire of repeatable affairs. To Liuyuan, Liusu is a mystery to be deciphered, a castle to be taken, a challenge to be overcome. Her "Oriental" charms, coming as she does from a traditional extended Shanghai family, add a good deal to her allure. He may even genuinely love her—the love game does not categorically foreclose sincere feelings—but he gives no indication of wishing to marry her, even after setting her up in an apartment. The turning point comes when Hong Kong comes under Japanese fire during World War II. Amid falling shells and whizzing bullets, romantic adventure loses its meaning. Staying alive and staying together become the only reality in times of war, for war has usurped all that once belonged outside the ordinary. With war raging as the most violent and destructive game that human beings play, or are forced to play, with one another, the lovers can no more afford to carry on their picayune games as they can survive on their own. They move back to the hotel, where there is a food supply, and when the fighting subsides, they return to their apartment, get married, and become engrossed with the nitty-gritty of eking out a livelihood in a troubled time.

The novel ends on an authorial note that has been the source of some controversy:

> Hong Kong's defeat had given her victory. But in this unreasonable world, who can say which was the cause and which the result? Who knows? Maybe it was in order to vindicate her that an entire city fell. Countless thousands of people dead, countless thousands of people suffering, and what followed was an earthshaking revolution. . . . Liusu did not feel that her place in history was anything remarkable. She just stood up smiling, and kicked the pan of mosquito incense under the table.
>
> The legendary beauties who felled cities and kingdoms were probably all like that. (Zhang Ailing 1989, 251; quoted in Lee 1999, 301)

It is easy to be rubbed the wrong way by the author's irreverent tone when speaking of the deaths and sufferings of thousands. Leo Ou-fan Lee, in defense of Zhang, believes that the reference to the legendary beauties is Zhang's way of delivering a critique of history by "applauding Liusu's victory: as if a city had fallen just to complete her romance and give her story a happy ending!" (1999, 302) Lee also praises Zhang for her "subversion of the grand narrative of modern Chinese history" (302). The ending therefore embeds two critiques. One is Zhang's turning on its head the ancient prejudice that women are the source of disorder. *Qingcheng qingguo* (beautiful women who topple cities and kingdoms) is a set phrase derived from legends warning of the dangers of women transgressing the boundaries between the inner and outer, private and public, and higher and lower. A ruler who allows his favorite consort's whims to impinge upon the affairs of the state is bound to abandon his kingdom to chaos (see Cass 1999, chapter 5).

Here, however, a disorder in the "kingdom" makes order/happiness possible for an ordinary woman. In my view, the perverse logic is more a critique of modernity than of "history" (Leo Lee seems to equate ideology or mythology with history). Modernity creates an impossible quandary for women in which marriage is their only respectable means of livelihood while men are permitted to have a double life, which means that *some* women, at least, have to forego the hope of marriage and respectability. History intervenes so that the paradoxical conditions of modernity are temporarily suspended. Suddenly the domestic bliss that has been casually and endlessly deferred threatens to be permanently out of reach. War creates a state of exception and puts an end to the love games that victimize women. Now the lovers must, as Liuyuan comments thoughtfully, cease to "talk about love" (*tan lian'ai*) and actually "make love" (*lian'ai*) (Zhang Ailing 1989, 250).

A second critique is directed against the nationalist credo that all Chinese share the same fate and that the defeat of China (and its ally, Great Britain, which ruled Hong Kong) means the end of happiness for all Chinese. Liusu finds happiness at the precise moment that her compatriots are dying and suffering in the thousands. It is thus a triumph of the personal, private, lower, and now over the public, political, higher, and world-historical. Zhang seems to say that personal happiness, especially as it pertains to women, does not necessarily hinge on collective (future) happiness and that individual freedom is not epiphenomenal to collective freedom, even though such is indeed the standard motif of the "grand narrative of Chinese history."

This challenge, one imagines, can be profoundly unsettling to the increasingly left-leaning critical circle.

• • •

The foregoing genealogy of romance draws a rough trajectory of love from *le grand amour* in Butterfly and May Fourth love stories to the affair in the writings of the so-called Shanghai School.[15] In the Confucian structure of feeling, *qing* is a cosmological category that functions as a constitutive good that theoretically informs all ethical feelings and actions. In the enlightenment structure of feeling, love is conjoined with individual freedom and is a hypergood that demands total faith and supreme sacrifices and subsumes all of life's purposes. It is enlisted in the critique of tradition as well as in the effort to legitimize new gender relations and the conjugal family. Its status as a hypergood, however, is always contested. The bourgeois affirmation of ordinary life has posed the greatest challenge to love's exclusionary claim to significance and has succeeded, in the age of commercial capitalism, in making love an ordinary lifegood that thrives in the niches of urban leisure culture. Romance is highly desirable, but it is no longer what singularly makes life worth living.

Romance, in the guise of the affair, extricates love from the moral-social matrix and delimits it as a discrete domain of experience centered on eroticism and gamesmanship. It owes a large credit to the popularity of Freud and the imported sexual sciences that enshrine sex as "a revelation of the self" (Sennett 1992, 7). Richard Sennett deplores the twentieth-century reification of sexuality as "an expressive state, rather than an expressive act": "sexuality *is*. We uncover it, we discover it, we come to terms with it, but we do not master it" (7). As a state of being rather than an activity, sexuality defines who we are. We are no longer enmeshed in a web of social ties and obligations but are wrapped in glorious isolation in our libido. Sennett asks us to consider how the modern usage of the affair has departed in connotation from the older term *seduction*. Seduction implies that the contracting of a sexual liaison has violated social codes and temporarily called all the other social relations of a person into question: one's spouse, children, and parents become implicated either symbolically through guilt or practically if the violation is discovered. The affair, however, "tamps down all these risks because it represses the idea that physical love is a social act; it is now a matter of an emotional affinity which *in esse* stands outside the web of other social relations in a person's life" (7–8).

This is also what most distinguishes the affair from *le grand amour*. In the latter, one's romantic identity is so bound up with one's social identities that a romantic involvement invariably has a life-changing ripple effect. Armand cannot continue his liaison with Marguerite for long without his father entering into the picture and attempting to rectify the father-son relation; Werther never entertains the possibility of becoming Charlotte's paramour and carrying on an affair parallel to her marriage to Albert; Mengxia and Liniang smother their budding love so that Liniang's identity as a chaste widow is not undermined; Junhua literally has to choose between lover and mother. Emma, however, carries on extramarital affairs with near impunity and Sophia freely chooses among eligible bachelors on whose bodies she stakes her claim to subjectivity and projects her erotic fantasies. In Liusu and Liuyuan's "city-toppling" affair, we see the two regimes of love coming to a head. Liusu wants it to be a seduction that, once legitimized by social and familial recognition, will be made permanent as *le grand amour*; Liuyuan, however, only intends to have a fling with an exotic Shanghai lady without the complications of reconfiguring all his other social relations and identities—including his identity as an unattached man. It takes something as extraordinary as a war to bridge the two regimes of love.

Romance tantalizes the bourgeoisie with promises of freedom and transgression without dislodging them from their complacency, comforts, and security. The tragicomedies of modern life are by and large structured around this ambiguity. Of the writers surveyed in this chapter, Zhang Ailing is perhaps the most artful chronicler of the transformations of intimacy and the dilemmas of the metropolitan personality who is incapable of the heroism of renunciation and yet yearns to be in touch with the heroic and transcendent. But in the 1940s, Zhang and a few other popular writers were a minority in their continued fascination with the quotidian dramas engendered by the plurality of moral sources on the fractured horizon of modernity. Many more writers, including Ding Ling, had chosen to throw in their lot with a new moral vision that gave unparalleled importance to collective political action and national liberation—the new hypergood of the revolutionary era. They also found a formula—"revolution + romance"—to articulate the transvaluative process in which the embracing of a new hypergood forces them to reevaluate life's meanings and to brand the May Fourth ideal of free love a delusion. This will be fully examined in Part 3.

Before the revolutionaries singularized the moral horizon, however, the discursive arena was abuzz with a heteroglossia of contentious voices debating love as a contested good and the inevitable clashes and compromises it introduced into modern moral life. It is to these debates that we turn in the next chapter.

FOUR

The Micropolitics of Love

In the late 1920s and 1930s, a conservative ethos permeated much of the social discourse on love, owing in part to the KMT regime's endorsement of Confucian revivalism tempered with a liberal dose of bourgeois family values. In its quest for a disciplinary society, the regime encouraged the conservative critique of free love as a conduit for unbridled egoism and the celebration of the family as the foundation of a new social ethic. The effort to place Confucianism on the altars of the state touched off a series of controversies in the public media among journalists, intellectuals, writers, and readers, who roughly fell into three camps: conservative, liberal or moderate, and radical. No one emerged as the unquestioned victor, although once the state began to clamp down on press freedom, the radical voices disappeared quickly. The conservatives continued to vie for dominance with the liberals in such cultural venues such as middlebrow fiction and leisure magazines that proliferated in the 1930s and persisted throughout the war years (1937–1949). The broad appeal of conservatism is partly attributable to its blending of a popularized version of May Fourth liberalism with older and still cherished Confucian values. As I will show in this chapter, even self-identified conservatives operated largely in a May Fourth or enlightenment framework, and what passed as a conservative position in the late 1920s could well have been alarmingly radical only a couple of decades ago.

The mantle of the May Fourth tradition, however, was claimed by a liberal intellectual contingent professing a firm faith in "free love," "love's supremacy" (*lian'ai zhishang zhuyi*), "the unity of body and soul" (*lingrou yizhi*), and the sanctity of heterosexual monogamy. They continued to denounce arranged marriages, parental authoritarianism, "feudal" customs, and Confucian kinship ethics (*lijiao*) and to lament young people's (especially women's) lack of freedom. They hurled criticism at the conservatives for being anachronistic, hypocritical, and insensitive to the plight of the victims of Confucian prejudices. They also castigated those who were insufficiently or insincerely committed to love, those who failed to live up to love's demand for sacrifice, and those who deviated from the path of normative happiness. At the same time, they came under full-throated attack from radical anarchists/socialists bent upon relegating love, along with all things "bourgeois," to the historical dustbin. In the late 1920s and early 1930s, the liberal camp that formed around *Xin nüxing* (The new woman) and its editor, Zhang Xichen (1889–1969), engaged in a two-pronged battle: with the conservatives on the relevance of Confucianism and the dialectic of sentiment and reason on the one hand, and with the radicals on the relative priority of love and sex, the status of chastity, and the class character of love on the other. The participants conducted their war of words not just through intellectually vigorous argumentation in the periodical press, but also through voluminous compilations (including translations) of histories, treatises, and instructional manuals on love, marriage, and sexuality.

There were also more topical debates that usually owed their origins to well publicized *affaires de coeur*. Although not without some share of sensationalism, the battle of discourse stirred up by these events explored issues closely related to the more philosophically oriented debates. Speaking in more empirical terms, the commentators on current affairs were equally concerned with questions such as: What is the nature of love? Can it become a source of moral action? How does one resolve love's conflict with life's other goals? What scientific and ethical principles should govern the realm of intimacy? Many positions and viewpoints were exchanged in the public media, though all seemed to agree that (sexual) love, rooted in human nature, is a legitimate good that should be regulated rather than ignored or suppressed. The debates, therefore, were keenly concerned with instating a set of rules that would ensure love's viability.

In this chapter, I first examine the ways in which a couple of real-life incidents set in motion sustained public reflections on the parameters of modern personhood and gender relations. Beginning with the "rules of love" debate ignited by the marriage of a Beijing University student, I draw attention to the give-and-take of public negotiations over the "rules of love" and the intellectual efforts to regulate everyday emotions and ethics through didactic self-help literature. I then turn to more theoretical debates among liberals, conservatives, and radicals over what should constitute the moral source of the modern subject.

THE RULES OF LOVE

The periodical press in early twentieth century was a vibrant public sphere for the construction of individual and collective identities (Lee 2001). Since late Qing writers invented the wildly popular genre of "scandal fiction" (*heimu xiaoshuo*), private lives were routinely thrown up to the scrutiny and judgment of "public opinion." A pattern emerged in the 1920s whereby segments of the reading public, scandalized by revelations of private entanglements, rose to question certain prevalent or emergent values. And given the centrality of women's issues in the May Fourth movement and beyond, these controversies were invariably tied to the profound impact of sociocultural change on women's lives. It is not an exaggeration to say that the May Fourth offensive on Confucianism was conducted over the dead bodies of what the editors of an anthology have called "new women martyrs" (Lan and Fong 1999, 76). While the circumstances of their deaths were vastly different, the meaning of their deaths as constructed by May Fourth activists lent urgency to the clarion call for radical change. The suicide of Zhao Shuzhen, for example, initiated the young Mao Zedong into the discursive battlefield of the New Culture Movement.

Reports of gruesome incidents of women's oppression continued to crop up in the liberal press throughout the 1920s. These incidents provided ammunition for the sustained critique of Confucianism and its present-day champions. In 1923, however, a scandal erupted into the public space that roused indignation and condemnation from both the liberal and conservative camps.

In this case, the female protagonist was not a mute and hapless victim of feudal customs; instead, she made a matrimonial choice that landed her in a comfortable social station at the expense of another man's rightful claims—or so thought the astonished public. The woman in question was Chen Shujun, a student at Beijing University. Chen Shujun came from a wealthy and influential family in south China and was one of first female students to enroll in Beijing University during the May Fourth Movement. Upon entering the university, she took up residence with a biology professor named Tan Xihong, who happened also to be her newly widowed brother-in-law.[1] Shortly afterward, she dissolved her engagement with a certain Shen Yuanpei and married the professor. Shen traveled to Beijing and took his grievance to the press, winning instant public sympathy for himself and inciting a chorus of public censure against Chen Shujun.

Just as the verdict against Chen seemed sealed in the court of public opinion, Zhang Jingsheng, who was teaching at Beijing University at the time and was on close terms with the Chen sisters, came to her defense in *Chenbao fukan*, a widely read and well-respected newspaper supplement. Zhang, who would himself a few years later become the bête noire of public discourse with the publication of *Xingshi* (Sex histories, 1926), went far beyond apologizing for the much-maligned couple, whom he calls "Miss B" and "A." Proposing four provocative "rules of love" (*aiqing dingze*) to justify Miss B's action, he used her case to illustrate a new pattern of gender relations. Zhang's bold attempt "prompted a massive response from the already agitated reading public"; the editor of *Chenbao fukan*, Sun Fuyuan, took a novel step and threw open his paper to all who wished to express an opinion on Miss B's case and on Zhang's "rules," allowing the debate to go on for months (Leary 1994, 141). A few initial responses further excoriated Miss B and A. Most of the letters, however, took issue with Zhang's four "rules of love," perhaps sensing their larger implications.[2]

Zhang Jingsheng claims that his four rules derive from sustained scientific studies of the biological, psychological, and social aspects of love. And yet the language he deploys to explain his rules is refreshingly plain: One, love is conditional (*you tiaojian de*). The conditions or criteria of love may include passion (*ganqing*), personality or character (*renge*), looks (*zhuangmao*), talents (*caineng*), reputation (*mingyu*), and wealth (*caichan*). The more one meets these criteria, the more successful one is likely be in the arena of love. Two, because love is conditional, it can also be compared. The person who best meets the criteria always wins out among competitors. Three, love is changeable. When we make comparisons, we are also making choices out of a natural desire for perfection. Thus love need not be steadfast and can indeed be transferred. Attractive persons will always be wooed by many, and they often change their mind when meeting a more eligible candidate. In the West, even marriages can be dissolved for this reason and it is considered quite normal. Four, conjugality is one kind of friendship, if only a more intense kind. Husband and wife can separate just like friends can part company. Those in love—whether they are married or not—must constantly strive to perfect themselves in order both to enjoy the pleasures of deepening love and to forestall competition from others. Euro-American couples respect each other and constantly encourage each other to improve themselves, because they know that love is changeable and husband and wife can part like friends. By contrast, if a marriage is not based on conditional love, then the husband and wife are reduced to the estate of the family and merely trade sex (ADT, 1–7).

Zhang Jingsheng goes on to argue that Miss B's action makes perfect sense when judged according to these rules. Unfortunately, Chinese society is composed of "inhumane" (*burendao*) families that are organized in ways contrary to the rules of love and that encourage men to become tyrants and women their servants. People reproach Miss B because they judge her by old moral standards (ADT, 8–9). Indeed, Miss B is not only pardonable, but also commendable. She is a new-style woman who loves freedom and understands the rules of love and who is capable of practicing her beliefs (*zhuyi*). Her change of heart was entirely determined by the comparative conditions of the two men: A is not only a congenial man, but his learning, talent, and status are high above those of Mr. Shen. It is only natural that she chose A for a husband (ADT, 10–11).

In proposing the rules of love, Zhang Jingsheng appears to be targeting two opponents: the older Confucian model of marriage and the ascendant romantic ideal of the love match. The fourth rule—that the conjugal relationship is akin to friendship—seems primarily addressed to the former. Under the Confucian model, marriage can only be legitimately contracted by parents and matchmakers because marriage is an alliance between two families. Affection matters naught because the union is never a matter of connecting two hearts. Zhang's formulation issues from the basic May Fourth conviction that romantic love should be the precondition and sole raison d'etre of marriage. As Eva Illouz points out, "if economic survival was the main vocation of pre-modern marriage, 'emotional survival' has become the main vocation of modern families who must maintain the dense emotional fabric of intimacy in everyday life" (1998, 169). Love can will a marriage into existence as imperiously as it can dissolve one. By equating marriage with friendship—the only social relationship in the Confucian paradigm that emphasizes personal worth and allows a degree of volition, contingency, and equality—Zhang is promoting the liberal model of marriage as a consensual union of two free, autonomous individuals drawn together by mutual affection and companionship. The ideal of companionate marriage has been so fervently embraced by the May Fourth generation that even the most vehement critics of Zhang are willing to concede the fourth rule to him—with some minor qualifications.

The other target at which Zhang seems to direct his polemics, however, is located within the May Fourth camp. Free love, as I have argued in Chapter 3, began its career in the May Fourth movement as a rallying point for individual freedom and family revolution. Its hallowed status as the symbol of a far-reaching social revolution went hand in hand with the May Fourth generation's need for an alternative principle on which to found a new moral order that was above and beyond the contingency of individual choices and yet amenable to individualist purposes. The most common refrain of the time is *lian'ai zhishang* (love is supreme), which asserts love's sanctity, inviolability, and immutability and enshrines love as the hypergood of the romantic generation. Unlike older hypergoods such as filial piety or loyalty, love's claim to moral supremacy is bolstered by a Wertherian cult of Nature: love springs from basic biological impulses, realizes the truth of human nature, and subtends moral knowledge that can be explored but neither altered nor obliterated. In order for young people to point to their heart and utter vows of eternality, love must be dissociated from worldly things that are by definition impermanent and corruptible. In other words, it must be a *hyper*good that stands *incomparably* higher than ordinary lifegoods.

The necessity to overcome what Hegel has defined as love's sine qua non—contingency—and to preserve love as an alternative foundation of ethics accounts for the assiduous effort on the part of May Fourth intellectuals to define love as "constancy" (*zhencao*). In elevating love as a sacrality, the May Fourth defenders of love's supremacy are remarkably reminiscent of the Confucian romantics we have encountered in Butterfly fiction. Despite their vastly different understandings of love and freedom as well as their different vocabularies and stylistic conventions, for many May Fourth writers, as for their Butterfly counterparts, constancy is the only acceptable rule of love. All prudential considerations that are tied to individual interests and inclinations are to be resolutely ejected from the moral lexicon of love.

In this spirit, Liang Guochang, the first reader to respond to Zhang Jingsheng, considers both A and Miss B blameworthy for violating the principle of constancy: A for remarrying immediately on the heel of his wife's death; and Miss B for unilaterally breaking her engagement with Shen. Liang admits that in the past constancy had been an unfair rule because it was required only of women ("chastity") and therefore became the instrument of their enslavement. But its unfortunate history does not mean that the principle itself is flawed. Once reformed and modernized, it is the highest human virtue and the surest guarantor of love's purity (ADT, 13–20). For him, constancy endows love with the crucial quality of permanence, thereby solidifying its claim to ethicality. His assumption, shared by most readers, is that hypergoods alone hold the moral meaning of life and guarantee happiness, and that all other considerations necessarily compromise virtue and happiness.

But moral philosophers have insisted that external goods such as wealth, reputation, health, even looks—things subject to "good fortune"—play an undeniable role in attaining worldly happiness and contentment (Berkowitz 1999, 10). And most people, by virtue of commonsense, have always acted on this knowledge in their choices. What Zhang Jingsheng is doing here is essentially lending a legitimizing voice to something that has shaped people's actions with or without explicit moral sanction. In so doing, he is trying to accomplish something rather postmodern: making love an ordinary lifegood, that is, adapting love for the domain of the everyday and making it perdure by acknowledging its relationship to the whims of "good fortune." In short, he is trying to affirm the moral worth of ordinary life while speaking the romantic language of love that has been increasingly pitted against the former and become increasingly hegemonic, oppressive, and inoperable. For Zhang, love must not only be the prerequisite for marriage, it must also thrive within marriage; but the purpose is to make married life emotionally fulfilling rather than consecrating it to an abstract principle and an impossible ideal. From here it is but a short path to the "lover system" that he would soon propose (see Lee 2006a).

In European history, once love became the legitimate motivation of marriage in the nineteenth century, it was, according to Eva Illouz, "incorporated in the domain of everyday life via the bourgeois sanctification of family and the everyday" (1998, 169). She writes, "in sharp contrast to chivalric or

Romantic or even Victorian love, which affirmed a heroic or 'authentic' self above and beyond the tribulations of everyday life, contemporary definitions of love are organized in the phenomenological and semantic categories of everyday life" (169). Similarly, whereas the May Fourth discourse affirms a heroic self beyond mundane concerns, Zhang's rules seek to incorporate love within the fluctuating boundaries of everyday life. He is bringing love down, as it were, from the pedestal of transcendental principle to a prudential plane, treating it not as a categorical imperative but as contingent on a variety of values, goods, and circumstances. He is suggesting that love should operate on a flexible set of strategies with which to make the best of what life chances to offer—to choose the most eligible marriage partner and to allow for margins of error and a chance to start anew—as much for the sake of perfecting love as for the sake of pursuing happiness.

Although apparently targeting different audiences, Zhang's four rules are internally consistent in the sense that they strive to define the marital relation as a more or less pure form of sociability, or what Anthony Giddens calls "pure relationship" (1992). In Zhang's view, passion is certainly of paramount import, but it cannot and should not become a first principle in the same way that birth or other ascriptive criteria tend to be. In other words, one cannot assume that passion, once it flowers, will be the permanent guarantor of a social bond. Instead, Zhang insists, a genuine social bond is a process in which the partners continually engage in what Erving Goffman calls "the presentation of self," which Richard Sennett emphatically distinguishes from the *representation* of the self. For Sennett, the latter grounds social relationships in supposedly open, unmediated expressions of personal feeling, or "personality," leading to the loss of "civility" (ability to interact with strangers qua strangers) and the inability to enact the art of public, impersonal expression, or playacting. More often than not, it short-circuits sociability by burdening it with expectations of trust, warmth, and security (1992, 33–42). By equating spouses with friends, Zhang is suggesting that the principle of sociability— the necessity to present oneself in the most creative and appealing ways instead of simply wearing one's heart on one's sleeve—applies to what moderns believe to be the most intimate relationship, precisely because intimacy obscures the contingent, and thus also creative, nature of sociability.

The adverse reaction to Miss B's matrimonial choice seems to have convinced Zhang Jingsheng that everyday life needs scientifically and philosophically sanctioned practical rules far more than it does romantic symbols that exact unnecessary sacrifices and that easily collapse under the weight of life's compounding exigencies. The romantic vision is fertile ground for both tragedy and farce. For the former, we may think of Lu Xun's "Regret for the Past," whose idealist hero ends up a nihilist; and for the latter, there is his "A Happy Family," in which the protagonist stubbornly turns his eyes away from the tribulations of everyday life (see Chapter 3). Though a visionary himself, Zhang is dissatisfied with the immanent ethics of love and its inability to withstand the abrasions of social reality. Pointing to one's heart to vouch for one's virtue convinces only the already converted, but to the skeptic, it can appear to be the wishful gesture of a deluded egoist, or worse still, the artful ploy of a dissembler. Zhang shrewdly realizes that the tenet of love's supremacy is self-defeating. Although a noble aspiration, its dogmatic denigration or repudiation of life's other goods and values and its desire to make love a guarantor of security and trust render love an inflexible and irrelevant ideal, good only for storybooks. In the practicality of everyday life, people are fully implicated in the socioeconomic and juridicoethical dimensions of gender relations. Indeed, not a few May Fourth intellectuals are known to have resigned themselves to their old-style marriages even as they indefatigably championed free love in their public personae.

Zhang's four rules acknowledge the mutability of life and attempt to effect a dialectic resolution of the sublime and the quotidian. They are built on romantic love's claim to ethicality (because it is always heartfelt, hence sincere) and rationalize the vagaries associated with its involuntary nature by introducing voluntary behavior such as comparison, competition, choice, and self-perfection. Moreover, in proposing rules for something that is supposed to be governed by impulse and spontaneity, Zhang gives due recognition to the theatrical or playful aspect of the romantic relationship as a form of sociability. Theorists of play have argued that it is the rules or conventions that allow players to distance their selves from the expressiveness of play and thereby experience the pleasures of risk-taking and social bonding (Sennett 1992, 316–23). Zhang seems to advise his readers that it is not enough simply to bring their raw selves to the arena of love, for genuine sociability requires self-distance. Rather, they need to take on a persona and present that persona to their object of desire in the most creative and appealing manner. The rules of love help them craft that essential mask of play. The rules, in short, are to be the technology of the self par excellence, an indispensable tool for navigating the brave new world of heterosociability.

In asking his readers to make rational deliberation on such matters as security, trust, self-improvement, and comfort, Zhang lays bare the bourgeois ideology that mystifies love in order to make marriage endure at all costs: on the one hand, love is "blind"; on the other hand, the knot thus "blindly" tied becomes ironclad in the name of "constancy." Zhang's critique of the increasingly sanctimonious discourse of love endears him to neither liberals nor conservatives. For rather than condemning love's fungibility or anti-institutional tendencies, he recognizes such qualities as the very reason why love cannot be turned into a new dogma delimiting the freedom of the individual. As a result, he ends up offending readers on both sides. The liberals are appalled by his irreverent subjection of love to the push and pull of everyday practicality; the conservatives are mortified by his endorsement of no-fault divorce—a practice that supposedly inevitably leads to the nightmarish scenario of a society of transitory marriages and broken families.

Zhang's radicalism thus has the effect of blurring the liberal-conservative fault line on the question of love. Indeed, the majority of the readers who sent in responses found themselves speaking a mixed language. Their criticisms can be consolidated into three basic points: One, Zhang Jingsheng's rules grant people carte blanche in an area on which society's stability and continuity depend. He encourages married women to go on "comparing" their spouses with other men and let such extraneous considerations as appearance, wealth, and reputation despoil their moral character as well as marriages (which apparently is far more disturbing than men comparing their wives with other women). If the only thing holding husband and wife together is a love that is not pledged to constancy, these readers pointedly ask Zhang, then is it acceptable to abandon one's spouse once her beauty has faded or once his wealth is depleted? Indeed, prostitutes and their clients are most adept at the art of measuring love by looks and money; aren't they the most adroit practitioners of love in Zhang's eyes? Is he not encouraging fickleness, vanity, avarice, and utilitarianism? Two, Zhang conflates the principle of constancy with the feudal ideology of "chastity" (*cong yi er zhong*, literally, one husband per lifetime). While chastity was an exclusively feminine obligation and contributed to women's oppression in the past, constancy in modern times applies to both men and women, enjoining them to pledge loyalty and preserve love against all odds. It does not absolutely rule out divorce and certainly does not condone vice—such as abuse, perfidy, crime, and alcoholism—in the name of permanence. Three, Zhang's rules issue forth from an elitist perspective (*guizu shi de lian'ai)*, because for him, the poor, the ugly, and the inept can never hope to know love, or even if they did, they would always face the danger of losing out to better-endowed competitors.

The first criticism is particularly widely shared by readers. They are greatly offended by Zhang Jingsheng's perceived attempt to steal a sacred ideal to whitewash Miss B's brazenly calculating choice. They are also upset with his suggestion that the rules apply to both courtship and marriage. For them, romantic play must stop at the gate of marriage. Once the vows are exchanged, love leaves the realm of impulse and fancy and enters that of the ethical, for one has presumably located the truth about oneself and come in touch with one's moral essence. To break the vow at this point would be to let contingencies and caprices compromise moral certitude. Dreading the specter of serial monogamy set in motion by the potentially endless chain of "comparisons," some readers propose a counterprinciple: love should be difficult to enter into and equally difficult to leave behind. The sole female participant in the debate, Xu Guangping (Lu Xun's common-law wife-to-be), writing under the pseudonym of Weixin Nüshi, used this principle to substantiate her doubt that there could be true love between A and Miss B given the brevity of their courtship (ADT, 67–75).

In his self-defense, Zhang Jingsheng declares that he is little interested in the metaphysics of love, thus avoiding the question that has preoccupied his contemporaries—how to tell true love from false love. Instead, he is merely trying to elucidate its rules in order to shed some light on Miss B's choice, while at the same time giving some guidance to today's lost generation. Zhang assures us that in knowing the rules, we can experience love more intimately, firmly, and gratifyingly, as is the case with music or landscape appreciation. Although anybody with ears can hear music, only those who understand music theory can really enjoy it. Likewise, anybody can see the landscape, but only those who understand the art of painting can appreciate it. By the same token, anyone can have sex, but only those who understand the rules of love can really experience its joy. On the contrary, people who hold love as mysterious can at best have some faint taste of love and at worst know only the stirrings of bestial impulses. Zhang ends his self-defense with a call to arms: "Young men and women, if you want to seek out true love, you have no choice but study the rules of love and use them as your guiding principles of action!" (ADT, 261–62).

It is interesting that Zhang Jingsheng does not fixate on the truth status of his theory. What he stresses is his conviction that all phenomena, or what he calls "totalities," whether of the natural or social world, can be rationally analyzed. In a matter of a few years, the will to knowledge would drive Zhang to produce the most sensational book on sex in modern Chinese history. Whether investigating love or sex, Zhang's goal is always the same: to produce a body of knowledge that would place the last terra incognita of human life under the conjoined spotlight of science and aesthetics. It will give people a tool to take control of their life—a tool that recognizes the flux of social relationships and is productive of life's possibilities. At the same time, it will also allow experts like Zhang himself to play tutor in governing the intimate conduct of the people. The rules of love are a prime example of biopolitics in that instead of mystifying or marginalizing love, they subject it to the normalizing regime of power/knowledge.

The rules of love would have been Zhang Jingsheng's answer to Lu Xun's searching question encrypted in the gloomy ending of "Regret for the Past." He would probably have gone so far as to say that the typical problems that tormented the youths of his time—lovesickness, loss of love (*shilian*), love triangle, love suicide, love murder, and so on—all grew out of their ignorance of love's rules. He would have been disturbed by the anguished cries against romantic love in literary journals, just as he would by the polarization of love and ethics in conservative circles. Although Zhang's pragmatic philosophy met with a great deal of resistance, the dialogue he opened up would go on.[3] And a steady trickle of sex scandals would continue to undermine any illusion of consensus on how the business of love should be conducted so that individuals may find happiness and society may find peace and order.

SCANDALOUS WOMEN

Like the Chen Shujun affair, the scandals that roiled the media in the 1920s and 1930s invariably involved women who played an aggressive role in love affairs. The public responses to these scandals offer us an oblique view of how society was adjusting to changing gender relations and patterns of intimacy. The generation of women who came of age in the May Fourth era seized upon free love as a powerful weapon in the struggle for individual rights and autonomy. Unlike political participation, economic independence, and education, freedom of love and marriage seemed a preeminently personal project accessible to all brave souls and least encumbered by the inertia of the social system.

For them, the personal was indeed the political, and the path to liberation began right at home, in the confrontation with their parents over the questions of whether, when, and whom to marry. By the late 1920s and early 1930s, however, the typical scenario had shifted from a daughter's rebellion against the family to a liberated woman's disastrous management of love life in the absence of familial supervision.[4] For conservatives, the sex scandals proved that women should never have been left to their own devices in the first place. Even liberal-minded critics were wont to interpret the scandals as evidence of women's immaturity, inexperience, and imbalance in navigating the minefield of love. But in terms of solution, public opinion was as divided as ever, and the issues raised in the "rules of love" debate continued to resurface.

The case of Tao Sijin and Liu Mengying took the problem of women's aggressive or transgressive behavior in love relations to a new height (or a new low, in the eyes of some observers). Tao and Liu were two female students sharing a rented quarter in the residence of Mr. Xu Qinwen, a writer and a common acquaintance of the two women. One day in 1932, a fierce quarrel erupted between the roommates, and Tao hacked Liu to death with a kitchen knife. The press positively jumped at the case, exploiting its sensational value for months on end. Xu Qinwen immediately came under suspicion in both the court of law and the court of public opinion for allegedly carrying on a love-triangle affair with the two women and allowing jealousy to fester and escalate into murder. Even after their diaries revealed that Tao and Liu had had an intense homosexual affair for over three years, Xu was still repeatedly subpoenaed and subsequently indicted on a total of ten charges in the criminal and civil courts. Xu ended up spending over ten months in jail. The "love triangle" paradigm was so powerful that it was enough for the district attorney of Hangxian to prosecute Xu for "being over thirty years of age but not married" and for "housing young women in his bachelor's abode" (Xu Qinwen 1937, 5).

In Xu Qinwen's account (who partly relied on the court's selective divulgence of the contents of the diaries), Tao and Liu were involved in a passionate affair and had gone to such lengths as taking an oath of devotion and procuring engagement rings. They were exceedingly proud of the strength, nobility, and intimacy of their lesbian love (*tongxing'ai*), and were exceedingly pained when signs of discord grew between them. Notwithstanding the revelation, the court as well as the public insisted on a heterosexual reading, even hinting that if it was not Xu (who had a sufficient alibi), then some other man must

have been the culprit. As an unwitting victim of judicial and popular prejudices, Xu was sympathetic toward the women and critical of the court's conservative presumptions as well as the media's feeding frenzy, even though he
himself also spilled considerable ink on the whole affair, including a series of
memoirs collected in *Wuqi zhi lei* (The guilt of bachelorhood, 1937) and a
novel called *Liangtiao qunzi* (Two skirts, 1934). In his memoirs, Xu gives anec-
dotal accounts of the litigation that dragged on for several years and offers a
pop-psychological analysis of "what went wrong" (Xu Qinwen 1937, 145–
50). Essentially, he echoes the common view that homosexuality is a mutation
of unfulfilled heterosexual desire and that it can be as "sharp" (*fengli*) in intensity and "absurd" (*huangmiu*) in expression as the latter (Zheng Ying 1930, 3).[5]

If Xu Qinwen's interest in the case was by default, then Pan Guangdan's
commentaries in his journal *Huanian* were more likely driven by professional
compulsion. Basing his diagnosis on court documents, newspaper reports,
and private correspondence with a friend in the know, Pan positively
identifies symptoms of paranoiac delusion, or "imperative hallucinations"
(English in the original), which he attributes to blistering jealousy fueled by
an inflaming passion (Pan Guangdan 1993, 8:437–38). As in his study of
Feng Xiaoqing (Chapter 5), Pan complements his diagnosis with prescriptions for social reform. He laments the near nonexistence of qualified psychi-
atrists who can be called upon by the court to ascertain the defendant's
mental state. Their expert opinion can mean the difference between life (reduced sentence or acquittal) and death (capital punishment) for the defendant (440–41). Even if the defendant is fortunate enough to be acquitted,
what measures are in place to prevent recidivism? "I would like to know how
society will accommodate her. Do we let her go home, go back to school, or
freely access other public facilities? Who can guarantee that she will not be
embroiled in homosexual love again and will not be driven by jealousy to
kill once more?" (441–42). Last, Pan points out that the school system is too
ill equipped to deal with the emotional disturbances of adolescence. The so-
called ethics directors (*xunyu zhuren*) know only how to conspire with laun-
dresses to keep track of the frequency of masturbation, but they have not a
clue as to how to help students manage their emotional life so that they will
have no need for masturbation.[6] By locating the roots of the problem in the
inadequacies of social institutions, Pan departs significantly from the prevailing moral responses that operate primarily in personal and polarizing
terms: romantic love corrupts moral character, and those who kill for love act

out of despicably selfish motives; whether homosexual or heterosexual, love cannot mitigate one's moral and judicial culpability.[7]

Tellingly, in another incident involving two women in the roles of aggressor and victim, the aggressor was hailed as a heroine thanks to her position *outside* a love triangle. Zhang Biyue and Zhang Bichi were sisters attending a middle school far away from home. Bichi, though already betrothed, became involved with their married teacher, Huang Changdian. After Biyue discovered the affair, Bichi fled to another city for fear of their parents' wrath. Biyue confronted Huang and shot him (though not fatally), and she was subsequently indicted and sentenced to jail. While serving her jail term, Biyue became a media sensation, and the public clamored for her release. Soon her school bailed her out. In a commentary in *Xin Nüxing*, a certain Fangxin Nüshi discerns three types of public reaction: The first type heaps adulation on Biyue, lauding her action as a frontal assault on free love. The author alerts us to the surprising fact that holding this view are not just Confucian moralists and old fogeys, but also self-styled "young fighters" (*qingnian zhishi men*). The second type of reaction blames Bichi for being a gull in allowing herself to be seduced by a married man. The third type, voiced mostly by the sisters' schoolmates, considers Huang the real villain who shamelessly tricked a schoolgirl into a phony engagement and thus deserved to be shot. Public sentiment, it seems, overwhelmingly favors Biyue, the attempted murderer. It is said that even Bing Xin (1900–1999) wrote to her in praise of her courage. The entertainment stage also put on a play celebrating her valiancy with the catchy title *Qingchang nüxia Zhang Biyue* (Zhang Biyue, woman warrior of the love scene) (Fangxin Nüshi 1929).

Rubbing against the grain of public enthusiasm, Fangxin Nüshi renders her own judgment as follows. In trying to frighten the so-called trend chasers with violence, Biyue has willfully intruded on her sister's right to love. Bichi is not blameless either: if she had the courage to love a married man and demand a divorce, she should also have the courage to confront her family upon discovery. Huang Changdian has been wrongly accused because he did not deceive Bichi about his marital status. Huang is to blame only because he tried to keep the affair secret. She ends her essay on an anxious note: "This incident shows how entrenched feudal forces still are in our society and how much our young people are still in its iron grip!" (Fangxin Nüshi 1929, 358).

This commentator was clearly disturbed by the fact that the lawbreaker was generously pardoned by public opinion while the victims, because they had violated the unwritten rules of love endorsed by conservatives and liberals alike, became the targets of public opprobrium. Biyue's apotheosis as a *xia* (warrior) shows that when a woman's agency is acknowledged and approved, it must be premised on her acting heroically *on behalf of* someone or something else. If Biyue and her sister had both been romantically involved with the teacher and the violence had been the fallout of triangle rivalry—as it would inevitably be interpreted—then the judgment would have been no more lenient than what was passed on Tao Sijin. Instead, Biyue fits neatly into the archetype of woman warrior who combines assertive agency with self-abnegation (recall Thirteenth Sister in *A Tale of Heroic Sons and Daughters*, discussed in Chapter 1). She is held up as the "best type of new woman for modern society" (*xian shehui xin nüzi zuihao de dianxing*). The new woman, it seems, finds her most noble calling in policing rather than traversing the "love scene" (*qingchang*). But the dissenting voice of Fangxin Nüshi indicates that not all women, in the post-Nora age, are willing to accept a role model whose claim to fame is an act of antiromantic bravado.

THE REGULATORY DISCOURSE

The high visibility of female players in sex scandals points to the fact that women's rise in the public arena is seldom unconnected to issues of love and sexuality (the exception being the filial heroine). The problem of love, conversely, is almost always discussed in conjunction with the woman question. Intellectuals and reformers who have taken an interest in the latter can hardly afford not to have an articulated position on the nature and rules of love. Wang Pingling (1898–1964) undertook just such a task in his somewhat misnamed book, *Zhongguo funü de lian'ai guan* (Chinese women's view of love).[8] The book's first few chapters, with headings like "The Greatness of Love," "The Origins of Love," "The Elements of Love," "An Analysis of Love's Power," and "The True Meaning of Love and Marriage," are a pastiche of liberal axioms culled from the writings of Ellen Key (1849–1926), Edward Carpenter (1844–1929), August Bebel (1840–1913), and their Chinese and Japanese interpreters. The middle chapters present a familiar narrative of women's oppression, written in the accusatory mode of May Fourth historiography. Toward the end, Wang proposes "the total solution" (*zong jiejue*) to the woman question, which turns out to be a step-by-step guide to courtship and marriage (Wang Pingling 1926, hereafter cited as ZFL).

To begin with, one needs to understand the crucial importance of "the budding phase of love" (*chulian*). Wang likens courtship (*tan lian'ai*) to detective work, casting lovers as both the detective and the mystery to be solved: The "budding phase" affords the best opportunity to conduct reconnaissance on each other's social background, learning, and moral character. One needs to listen to the words, watch the actions, and observe the habits of one's date. The key is to catch casual remarks and subconscious behavior, for these are most revealing of personal truth (*zhenxiang*) (ZFL, 59–60). At work here is the assumption that each person has a hidden truth not manifest in conscious speech and behavior. By advising young people to perform vigilant detective work on each other, Wang Pingling is essentially substituting the autonomous, interiorized self for the older notion of the person as an aggregate of status, social role, and material possession—circumstances and conditions that go-betweens or parents can easily ascertain. The minutiae of casual words and gestures have to be captured in close range and constant contact—a task that cannot possibly be delegated to a third party. But help is at hand in the form of guidebooks that vie to show the novice what qualities count as important, when to exchange vows, how to guard against impropriety, and how to decode the peculiarities, even the pathologies, of the "person in love."

Once in love, the challenge becomes how to sustain it. To avoid short-circuiting love, Wang suggests that lovers abide by the Way of the Mean (*zhongyong zhi dao*) by maintaining a semidetached relationship, even though this may well hinder the detective work he has recommended a few pages earlier. Underlying this contradiction is what Paula Fass (writing on American youth culture of the 1920s) calls "the haunting fear of sexual promiscuity" unleashed by the prospect of young people being left to judge for themselves, in their newly acquired isolated intimacy, "the degree and limits of permissible eroticism" (in Hoffman and Gjerde 2002, 196). Hence the voluminous effort to erect fences to keep in line the lovers out grazing the grassland of free sociability.

In a methodical fashion, Wang Pingling moves onto engagement and marriage. His central message here is ritual simplicity. He cautions against going beyond one's means to stage extravagant ceremonies merely to please one's fiancée or to elicit envy from the community (ZFL, 63). Wang's advocacy of ritual simplicity is consistent with his understanding of marriage as the fruition of spiritual love between two interiorized individuals, not as the alliance of rank and property between two families or clans. Indeed, if marriage is about love and love is about the invisible hummings of the heartstrings, ritual display is not only superfluous, but also invites suspicion that it is needed to cover up the desiccation of feeling. Wang's modern understanding of marriage leads to an enlightened position on divorce. Invoking Ellen Key's famous pronouncement that marriage without love is immoral, Wang affirms that the cessation of love fully justifies divorce (ZFL, 64–65). He is reticent on how love can be lost, but in his discussion of the love triangle, he discloses his subscription to Zhang Jingsheng's "rules": Love can be sustained only when such conditions as moral character, learning, beauty, and social background are well matched.

In his concluding chapter, Wang attempts to justify the enormous emphasis he has placed on love with a circular theory of women's emancipation, which goes like this: Chinese women have fallen to the status of victim of patriarchal oppression after being serially vanquished by men—first they lost their economic independence, which was their first line of defense (*di yi fangxian*), and then they lost educational, ethical, and political rights and were reduced to men's possessions. As patriarchal victims, they have no freedom of love and marriage. "Therefore," Wang forges on, "before their knowledge of love is formally rectified, that is, before true love and marriage become possible, Chinese women will not know enough to demand economic independence and educational rights. . . . Therefore, imparting to our women the true meaning and true essence of love is more urgent than discussing any other women's issues" (ZFL, 72). Not only would some of the women writers discussed in Chapter 3 be highly skeptical of such a claim, Wang's logically challenged argument also goes explicitly against the socialist contention that women's oppression is at bottom economic oppression, and that class revolution must take precedence over women's emancipation. Thus, on the one hand, his regulatory discourse of love and sexuality obscures the intersection of class and gender and depoliticizes the women's movement; on the other hand, it recognizes the specificity of women's issues and resists their subordination to questions of class and nation.

Another major effort at depoliticizing love and the woman question came from the journal that published Lu Xun's jaunty essay on Nora, *The Ladies' Journal* (Funü zazhi, 1915–1931). In the same year that Wang published *Chinese Women's View of Love*, the journal organized a special issue on love that attempted to secure love's position in ethical life by dissociating it altogether from eros. *Ladies' Journal* was the longest-running and most successful women's journal in Republican China. At a time when "the female press" was lively but volatile and when most publications sold only a few hundred or a few thousand copies, *Ladies' Journal* stood out with a sixteen-year consecutive publication history and circulation figures reaching as high as 10,000 (Nivard 1984, 37). Ironically, though not uncommonly, as Jacqueline Nivard notes, the journal not only had a nearly exclusively male editorial staff and pool of contributors, but 90 percent of its readership was probably also male. Her survey of the quick succession of editors reveals that these men came to the journal mostly through patronage networks, rather than on the strength of their feminist persuasion. In its initial phase, the journal was largely controlled by the members of the Southern Society (*Nanshe*) (a Butterfly establishment) with Wang Yunzhang (1884–1942) as the chief editor, who, in the words of Nivard, was "more a writer of love stories than a feminist" (44). Its advocacy of the "wise mother and able wife" paradigm was attacked during the May Fourth movement, and the editorship was transferred to a progressive coterie of intellectuals, including Zhang Xichen (1889–1969)[9] and Zhou Jianren (1888–1984). In their hands, the journal became more plugged into the international women's movement and began to cover such topics as love, marriage, divorce, education, work, sexuality, birth control, and prostitution.[10] The names of well-known international feminists frequently appeared in its pages. In 1925, the journal ran a special issue on "new sexual morality" (*xin xing daode*), provoking the anger of conservative readers with its attempt to liberalize traditional sexual codes (more in the next section). The Commercial Press obligingly replaced Zhang Xichen with Du Jiutian, an assistant in the press's natural sciences textbooks department. On Du's watch, discussions of free love, sexuality, and divorce largely disappeared, and the family and motherhood were reinstated as the privileged topics.

The special issue on love may be seen as Du's rejoinder to the earlier one on new sexual morality, but it eschews polemics and strives instead to affect a tone of scientific neutrality and moral ecumenicalism. A dozen expository essays expound on the history and nature of love; love's relationship to life, duty, and aesthetics; and the foundation and growth of love. Two dozen mostly personal narratives give sentimental accounts of loving relationships between family members and friends. The literary section is relatively small: a short story satirizing a peasant woman's ruinous, albeit improbable, desire for a diamond; a single-act play exposing the frivolity of free love; and a fable about how an honest coolie is blessed with love from a snail spirit. A contemporary commentator finds the entire issue a reactionary lightweight. He complains that although there is a "love" in every title and several "loves" in every line, there is little real substance. In particular, he objects to the essays penned by the chief editor, which he likens to lessons in a primary school textbook. The commentator also finds the various kinds of love celebrated in the issue alarmingly redolent of Confucian values (Wen Kai 1926).

The special issue is indeed a signpost of the post–May Fourth conservative realignment of the discourse of love. As radicals move increasingly to the frontier of sexuality, conservatives retool love as the moral sentiment par excellence, divesting it of any romantic/rebellious connotation and linking it up with bourgeois family values, often couched in Confucian rhetoric. Still, the essays borrow a good deal from the May Fourth critique of the patriarchal kinship system. An essay entitled "Fu'ai zhi jinxi guan" (Fatherly love, old and new), oddly placed in the personal narrative section, is a good case in point. Its author, Zhao Dongchen, not only cites Hu Shi's poem on modern fatherhood, but also echoes Lu Xun's essay on the same subject. In "Women xianzai zenyang zuo fuqin" (What is required of us fathers today, *Xin qingnian* 6:6, 1919), Lu Xun urges Chinese fathers to regard the parent-child relationship not as one of *en* (kindness, favor, bounty), but instead as one of *ai* (love) given without any expectation of return. This is because love is nature's design: "[The natural order] has no use for 'favors,' but provides living creatures with an instinct which we call 'love'. . . . When children are born, their parents instinctively love them and want them to live. . . . This love, free from any thought of barter or profit, is the tie that binds people together, the bond between all human beings" (Lu Xun 1980, 61, translation slightly modified). Lu goes on to cite Kong Rong (153–208), a Han dynasty descendant of Confucius, to the effect that a father does his son no special favor in begetting him in an act of lust. "Love alone is real," opines Lu Xun (130). The clichéd ring of the sentence notwithstanding, what Lu Xun is calling for is a kind of thorough reconceptualization of a basic human relationship that cultural historians have associated with the epistemic break of modernity—to wit, that ethical relationships should be a voluntary, creative enterprise rather than an inherited, preprogramed way of life.

Zhao Dongchen, too, quotes Kong Rong to debunk the ideology of *en*. He criticizes the notion of "raising sons to provide against old age" (*yang er fang lao*) as crass utilitarianism: "To hope to gain something from [the natural processes of] life is tantamount to buying and selling life itself. Fatherly love is pure, noble, and devoid of other purposes" (1926, 55–62). At work here is a distinctly modern idea of the family whose emergence in early modern Europe has been brilliantly documented by Philippe Ariès. Distancing itself from the traditional family as a genealogical and economic institution, the modern family endeavored to extricate itself from the "promiscuous sociability" in which family life had traditionally been embedded. It saw itself as primarily an emotional unit, private in its intimacy and sacrosanct in its values. The most important register of this change was the shift of emotional gravitas from the parent to the child: "the care expended on children inspired new feelings, a new emotional attitude . . . [which was] the modern concept of the family" (Ariès 1962, 412–13).[11] As a corollary, childhood was "discovered" as a distinct phase of personal growth, requiring its own clinical, pedagogical, and disciplinary regimes and authorizing new fields of knowledge, novel modes of literary and artistic production, and lucrative commercial niches.[12]

A roughly parallel shift is discernible in China since the late imperial times, marked most notably by the rise of the affective model of family—the centerpiece of the cult of *qing*. But the idea that the child is the unconditional recipient of parental love rather than the servitor of parental needs and beneficiary of parental benevolence only emerged in the early decades of the twentieth century. Tellingly, the shift of emphasis to fatherly love is accompanied by diminishing attention on the erstwhile all-important filial piety. It is indeed remarkable that of the twelve pieces dealing with parent-child relations, only two are about filial piety. The narratives of motherly and fatherly love, with the exception of Zhao's essay, are all told in the first person. The narrator either reminisces about the boundless love and care he or she has received from a parent, or describes some *tableau vivant* of parental affection witnessed in a public space. If the image of the loving mother is stereotypical, the affectionate father is surely a novelty—in Butterfly sentimental narratives, the father is mostly absent; in May Fourth romantic stories, he is usually a hardhearted tyrant. Here in the special issue, the father as fondly remembered by all three contributors is gentle, thoughtful, caring, forgiving, and open-minded. He sends his children to school, helps them with their lessons, nurses them in sickness, and even grants them freedom to choose their own marriage partner.

One author writes: "Father was the god of love: he loved not just us, but all our kinfolk and friends and all living creatures" (Yu Jing 1926, 68). It almost seems that Lu Xun's call for loving fathers is now being answered with personal testimonies and that his effort to tip the balance toward parental obligations (in the form of love) is reinforced in the disproportionate space devoted to fatherly love. Together, these essays transform a rigidly formal and hierarchical relationship into one of emotional reciprocity, but they also make it easy to defend the exercise of parental authority in the name of love. Indeed, it seems that all actions are potentially defensible in reference to emotional sincerity. One author, for example, lets his mother defend the practice of arranged marriage by appealing to love, thereby denying the possibility of parental wrongdoing altogether. He relates the episode in which his mother advises his lover to leave him and submit herself to an arranged marriage: "Nowadays there are those love-crazed young people who think arranged marriages are immoral and must be resisted. But really, how many parents have the heart deliberately to inflict mortal harm on their children? They are simply acting out of love; it's just that they have fallen behind the trends" (Wang Yunzhi 1926, 46). The need to validate parents is so strong that even the worst "crime" that can be perpetrated by them in May Fourth discourse is now rehabilitated as an old-fashioned act of love.

On the whole, the volume strikes a moderate pose from which to promote the middle-class ideal of the conjugal family, appropriating whatever elements from the Butterfly school and the May Fourth camp that are conducive to this ideal. The emphasis is not on the grand gestures of love as a lifelong project, or on the existential quandary of free love, but on the pious relationship between the generations and between the spouses—regardless of the manner in which the latter are brought together. Not surprisingly, two of the three entries on conjugal love show that arranged marriages—the anathema of the May Fourth generation—can very well be salvaged and transformed into model marriages. The picture of sweet and uplifting conjugality one finds here is a far cry from the anxiety, mistrust, and squalor that plague Juansheng and Zijun's free union in "Regret for the Past." One author tells us that his wife and he had seen each other only once before they were married through parental arrangement. But they fell in love at first sight and are as loving a couple as there ever was. His experience makes him doubt those proponents of "free love" who arbitrarily assert that "there can be no love to speak of in an arranged marriage" (Bao Sun 1926, 88). As such, love has gone from a rebel's byword to the most versatile apology for the status quo. For these authors at least, freedom *is* the law and love *is* duty.

The conjugal family as collectively imagined here does not reserve any space for the contractual model with its underlying principle of individual rights and freedom. There is no discussion of the management of marital property or the pros and cons of divorce. Unlike a 1918 household encyclopedia (see Lee 2001), the special issue pointedly shuns the economic dimension of the family and prefers to conceive of it entirely in affective terms. The essayists extol love as "the motive force of life," "the fountain spring of happiness," and "an indomitable and indestructible force." One author enumerates, point by point, how love is indispensable to life. First, Love is life's discipline. It keeps a person on the normal track of life: to be loved by parents when young, to love a man or woman when grown up, and to love one's children when old. Those deprived of love will sooner or later go astray. Second, love preserves life's harmony. Humankind is heading toward the Great Unity (*datong*) because people all share similar feelings and because love smoothes out our differences. Third, love is life's consolation by healing our psychological wounds. Fourth, love is life's delight. In families without love, men go out to gamble or visit brothels, causing calamities to befall their families. In an ideal family, if the wife is uneducated, the husband encourages her to study; if the husband studies too hard, the wife encourages him to engage in more outdoor activities. Life is thus made delightful. Finally, love is life's health for people in love will not become depressed. They are fit to pursue great enterprises and to sow healthy seeds in their progenies (Zhong Huanye 1926). In the conclusion, as is the usual practice, the author makes an impassioned plea: "Ambitious young men and women, make haste to revive your true nature [*benlai mianmu*]. The moment love is instated is the moment life is fulfilled. God of love, may you descend to save the four hundred million wretched souls!" (17). The hope invested in love is great indeed—it is not only to discipline the individual, enliven family life, and ensure happiness and continuity, but also to liberate an entire nation and lead its people to the Great Unity.

If the *Ladies' Journal* could still take for granted that a special issue on love would be welcomed by the readers, the editors of *All About Love Series* (Wei'ai congshu), a series devoted entirely to the topics of courtship and marriage, could not. In the series' foreword, the editors begin with a set of rhetorical questions that register a degree of uncertainty about love's relevance to the contemporary social world:

> What are our most urgent problems today?
> Political problems? Nay, let's leave them to zealous politicians. In the ebb and flow of political tides, these problems attract all the limelight. However,

in the future world of great unity, will not all political problems vanish like a puff of smoke?

Economic problems? Nay, it is not that we do not hear the cries for help from the slums or that we do not feel the friction of labor-capital disputes. But from our optimistic perspective, economic problems are at most an unfortunate, temporary phenomenon which the currents of world evolution will in time wash away.

What we believe to be the most important question today is still the question of love between the sexes. (Xinwenhua xuehui 1929)

The dismissal of political and economic problems is offhanded indeed, but, like Wang Pingling, the editors seem also to be saying that gender issues should not be driven off the edge of public discourse. In light of the growing hostility toward the topic of love in the late 1920s, the insistence on treating love as the most pressing question of the day is an important countervoice for all its hyperbole. In addition, the editors position their series against the sexological discourse of Zhang Jingsheng and company. Since the "rules of love" debate, Zhang has moved increasingly to the problem of sexuality. The confessional narratives he solicited and compiled in *Sex Histories* became the agent provocateur of a fierce media controversy as well as the wrath of the authorities. As the book's popularity continued to rise (so much so that it spawned many specious sequels), the clash between Zhang Jingsheng's aesthetic and populist project of sexuality and the new intellectual orthodoxy with Zhang Xichen, Zhou Jianren, and Zhou Zuoren at its core turned into a protracted battle of discourse in the late 1920s (see Leary 1994; Lee 2006a). Mainly on the defensive, Zhang Jingsheng became a foil for those wishing to stake out new niches in the wellsaturated market of self-help literature on love and sexuality. The editors of the *All About Love Series*, in this case, define their project as one that returns to the right track what has been derailed by Zhang Jingsheng:

Love has been a perennial concern of humanity. Is it not in response to the question of love that Plato advocated wife-sharing [*gongqi*] and that Confucius promoted ritualism [*lijiao*]?

In Europe and America, there have been some gains after many debates on this question. In China, the frenzied debate of the May Fourth era, which passed all too soon, has failed to establish a systematic theory. Worse still, the debate has now gone astray! The core of the question has been infiltrated by lascivious talk of "the third kind of fluid," "the fourth kind of fluid" and whatnot. Young people are no longer willing to pursue pure and healthy love and succumb instead to the reign of libido. This is heart sickening! It is our conviction that this pathological condition must be dealt with and that these absurd theories must be knocked down. (Xinwenhua xuehui 1929)

The editors know well that there is moral capital to be had in reacting indignantly to Zhang Jingsheng's open discussion of female sexuality—as in the reference to "the third kind of fluid"[13]—a discussion that challenges the prevailing construction of femininity as devotion and sacrifice. Wang Pingling's book, for example, makes no mention of female anatomy or sexuality. In the debate between Zhang Jingsheng and his critics, the pursuit of sexual pleasure is commonly denounced on two counts: One, it revives the feudal culture of sexual permissiveness, which was predicated on gender inequity and gross violations of eugenic principles; and two, it encourages egoism and the dereliction of duty. Nonetheless, the editors of the *All About Love Series* also know that the alternative is not silence or prohibition: "We cannot regard love as raging floods or fierce beasts and resort to absolute silence on the subject. We are well aware that the only way to knock down the unhealthy theories of love is to replace them with new, healthy ones. This is indeed our purpose in launching this series" (Xinwenhua xuehui 1929). Their new "theories," however, amount to a smattering of advice, instructions, platitudes, anecdotes, and love letters collected in some twenty slim volumes.

Most noteworthy is the fact that the entire series purports to be translations and/or compilations of foreign texts. Clearly, the editors are determined to exploit the cultural capital of the translated text. The unquestioned linkage between western science, objectivity, and truth is what Zhang Jingsheng gambled with when he sought to insert indigenous confessional narratives into an imported sexological framework in *Sex Histories*. None of his opponents paid much heed to his appeal to science, for what disconcerted them was his induction of the lay person's idiosyncratic voice into the chamber of knowledge heretofore exclusively inhabited by western thinkers and their Chinese interpreters. The *All About Love Series*, it seems, represented a renewed effort to stake out the field of sexual knowledge as essential to happiness but off-limits to amateurish improvisations.

Accordingly, the majority of the volumes fall into the category of how-to pamphlets dressed up as scientific treatises. With their contents overlapping a great deal, each of these pamphlets offers an assortment of bite-size knowledge of human anatomy, evolutionary psychology, sociobiology, eugenics, ethics, and codes of etiquette, with little concern for logic or coherence. The table of contents of the first volume, *Ai de chuxian* (The buddings of love), is a perfect specimen of topical anarchy and the haphazard manner in which these pamphlets are cobbled together: female pubescence, the first kiss, the anxieties of courtship, barbaric peoples' views of virginity and their marriage customs, the realization of love, the preparation for and growth of love, the basic problems of monogamy, women's difficulty in choosing husbands, the problem of virginity, the love of adult women. The contents of another volume, *Lian'ai shu* (The art of love, by Walter M. Gallichan), are no less chaotic. The chapter headings jump randomly from such general topics as love and life, rationalization of love's criteria, and the necessity of mutual understanding to issues of childhood sexuality and pubescence. On the whole, the "advice" these volumes have to offer seldom goes beyond the platitudes of the day— one could easily find dozens of such writings on any given day in popular magazines and newspaper supplements, particularly the ones targeting young readers.

The series' incoherence and repetitiveness are simply mind-numbing. Even when a title like *Lian'ai yu yule* (Love and amusement, by Bernhard A. Bauer) hints at a departure from the usual mishmash of pop psychology and hortatory bromides, the contents fail to deliver. And yet the fact that these volumes were pumped out one after another indicates that there was a receptive, if not avid, audience for such hodgepodge fare. Anything pertaining to love (with sex coyly tucked in), it seems, had some selling points, and readers just could not get enough of it. These texts are also self-perpetuating: the more rules and advice they offer, the more issues and topics they appropriate under the rubric of love, the more dependent the readers become, and the greater the need for such texts. When a pamphlet like *Jiewen de yishu* (The art of kissing) purports to initiate young acolytes into the "art" of kissing, it obliges them to accept that they do not already know how to kiss, or that even if they do, they have not been doing it properly or realizing its full artistic or erotic potential. Not only must they learn a neologism—*jiewen* instead of the folksy *qinzui*—they also need to learn all about its origins, techniques, positions, and etiquette as well as the "great question of why a kiss must be made into an art."

The power effect of such regulatory discourse is twofold: in the first place, it colonizes intimate experience and consolidates the authority of those with linguistic and institutional access to "western" knowledge; in the second place, it incites new practices and experiments that expand the pleasures of everyday living. Zhang Jingsheng's project of mining aesthetic potential in eroticism thus returns in the voice of the (foreign) authority and in a more bashful manner. Well aware of the power of the aesthetic, the editors regularly interlard scientific facts and moralistic harangues with tales of exotic customs and romantic adventures. The series also feature a selection of literary titles, ranging from a Shakespearean play to a collection of love epistles of notable westerners. In addition, the fact that *Lian'ai shu* boasts a special appendix containing "aphorisms of love" (*lian'ai geyan*) shows that the new orthodoxy of love is so well entrenched that its central creed can be condensed and packaged into a handful of aphorisms—something that necessarily presupposes a reservoir of widely shared assumptions. That love now has its own proverbs indicates how much one can take for granted certain (enlightenment) assumptions about love's place in the new social order. And yet, throughout the late 1920s, journalists, writers, and readers kept alive debates wherein they diverged widely on questions concerning the self, gender relations, and social roles. In the remaining sections of this chapter, I trace a couple of major threads of debate that raged principally in the pages of the journal *Xin nüxing*, with its chief editor Zhang Xichen as the primary combatant.

REDACTING CONFUCIANISM FOR THE AGE OF REASON

In 1927, Xia Mianzun (1886–1946), an accomplished educator and translator, contributed an essay to *Xin nüxing* defending the Japanese-inspired ideal of "wise mother and good wife" (*xianqi liangmu*). The essay is couched as a thought piece prompted by an overheard folk ditty, "Shi mang ge" (Ten busynesses). The ditty recounts the life of a typical Chinese woman who toils and moils all day, every day, to serve her in-laws, husband, children, and grandchildren, and then dies as empty-handed as she was born. Instead of reading it as a folk protest against women's status in patriarchal society in the manner of the May Fourth folklorists (Lee 2005), Xia prefers to see it as a glorification of women's "destiny"—marriage and motherhood. In his view, "self-sacrifice," the essence of "wise mother and good wife," is well captured in the title word "busyness" (*mang*). "Busyness" becomes a misery only for those self-awakened (*geren zijue*) women who are caught in the conflict between individualism and the species function. Thus the more awakened a woman is, the more she suffers. But because one cannot ask women to undo their self-awakening, Xia suggests that women turn their self-awareness inside out by regarding marriage and motherhood not as the shackles of unfreedom but as the very means of their self-realization (*ziji shixian*). From this, he leaps to the conclusion that the solution to the woman question lies entirely with women and that their biggest enemy is themselves—it is only due to their belittling of sacred duties as drudgery that they have fallen into their present lowly status (Xia Mianzun 1927).

At the end of the essay, Xia Mianzun addresses his female readers directly: "Ladies, you are 'busy' now and you will be 'busy' always. Why not try to realize yourselves in your 'busyness' and make society, the nation, and men recognize your value through your 'busyness'?" (1927, 481) Xia hopes that by investing self-worth in their social roles, or by internalizing the law as their own desire, women will be able to close the gap between the individual and the social order. Yet it is significant that even someone waving the conservative banner of "wise mother and good wife" feels compelled to speak the language of enlightenment—self-consciousness (*zijue*), self-realization (*ziji shixian*), and the like. In Xia Mianzun's effort to reconcile the conflict between individualism and the species function for women, we see the imprint of the enlightenment discourse of self-awakening that has irrevocably driven a wedge into the continuum of self and the social order. The greatest challenge for the conservatives is how to rearticulate the self-society continuum in the age of enlightenment.

In the late 1920s, this daunting task was taken up by Zhang Dongsun (1887–1973), the one-time editor of *Gaizao* (Reconstruction, a non-Marxist socialist magazine) and later cofounder (with Zhang Junmai) of the Guojia shehuidang (The national socialist party). In his essay, "You zili de wo dao zizhi de wo" (From the egotistic self to the rational self), Zhang equates the self-society opposition to antisocial egotism, a sure recipe for social anomie. "Chinese society of today is a cold and cruel place. There is no passion, sacrifice, friendship, gratitude, or cooperation; instead we have only self-serving, intrigue, propaganda, politicking, and treason. How has a kingdom of rites fallen into such a state?" (1926, 5). Zhang lays the blame squarely at the door of the modern individual who, by proclaiming him- or herself the victim of what used to stand for public good (family, community, morality), is heading down a doomed path of self-exile and destruction for all. Zhang searches for a way to salvage the "self" so that it does not automatically spell "selfishness," or a symptom of reason overturning the old moral order without supplying a new one in its stead, nor finding a new, greater self to overcome the deficiencies of the smaller self. Like Xia Mianzun, he concedes that the problem brought on by the rise of reason can only be resolved by the further growth of reason, not by turning back to the prereason state of nescience. Hence he proposes "rationalism" (*lizhi zhuyi*), which he defines as the expansion of knowledge through the discovery of a "greater self." Citing Socrates' maxim that virtue is knowledge, Zhang asserts that morality is only possible for the self-aware. Confucianism, so long as it is the conscious, rational choice of an individual, will regain its moral authority and become the healing force that China badly needs (Zhang Dongsun 1926).

With the dust of the May Fourth assault on Confucianism barely settled, Zhang Dongsun seems to want to avoid a head-on collision with a powerful historical verdict. He needs to somehow establish that the Confucianism so vilified by the May Fourth generation is not the Confucianism he is holding up as China's only hope. He suggests that long before the arrival of the West, Confucianism had already ceased to exert power and influence in Chinese society because it had fossilized—like "an empty shell"—into abstract principles and had become divorced from social praxis. He calls the process "the evaporation of Confucianism" (*lijiao de zhengteng*). By this logic, the malaise of Chinese society results not from "cannibalistic" Confucianism, as May Fourth intellectuals have alleged, but rather from its hollowed existence. Chinese society has long been overrun by rapacious egoism, and the coming of western material civilization is like striking sparks onto a pile of tinder.

Because western civilization only adds fuel to the fire, Confucianism remains the only alternative means to combat egotism. To do this, Confucianism needs to reach out to the ego that is mournfully wrapped up in its own feelings and desires. But Zhang Dongsun is keenly aware that he cannot afford to leave out of his moral scheme the most engrossing topic of the day: love. In a subsequent essay, he professes to take on the problem of love (*qinggan*); but with a rhetorical sleight of hand, he displaces it with a discourse on "bestiality" (*shouxing*). He explains that he is interested only in the kind of bestiality that cannot be punished by law, or what is called in English "instinct." To counter the May Fourth allegation of Confucianism as an artifice that smothers basic human instincts, Zhang employs the same quasi-scientific language to make the Kantian argument that instincts command no ethical authority. According to modern psychology, he notes, instincts are for the purposes of self-preservation and species continuity and are therefore neither good nor bad. Romanticism, therefore, has gotten it wrong by arguing that what is natural is good and that social problems stem from going against the grain of nature. On the contrary, Zhang maintains, by sublimating our basic instincts to nobler ends, we create culture and civilization. Confucianism has erred in stipulating the necessity of "minimizing desire" (*jieyu zhuyi*) because it discourages the spirit of progress and adventure. To remedy this, Zhang proposes "sublimationism" (*huayu zhuyi*), which allows reason to take control of passion and transform it for the good of society (Zhang Dongsun 1926).

Zhang Xichen responded to Zhang Dongsun's first essay by questioning his suggestion that ancient Chinese civilization was characterized by the non-discovery of the self (*meiwo*) and that, by implication, the ancients did not have selfish desires (*siyu*). For Zhang Xichen, the basic teachings of Confucianism are proof enough of the existence of desires. For example, the pillar of Confucianism, ancestor worship, can be shown to be entirely motivated by selfish purposes, such as the fear of unappeased ghosts harming the living or the fear of starvation in the afterlife if one's descendants fail to make offerings. In a characteristically May Fourth move, he charges Zhang Dongsun with hypocrisy: In truth, Zhang's brand of "rationalism" or "self-mastery" (*zizhi*) demands only others to master their desires so that they can be mastered by oneself. The only way, asserts Zhang Xichen, to achieve genuine, universal self-mastery is to overthrow the hypocritical doctrines of Confucianism (Zhang Xichen 1926a).[14]

It is interesting that Zhang Xichen does not question Zhang Dongsun's equation of "self" (*wo*) with "selfish desire." His spear of attack is instead thrust at the integrity of the speaker: the speaker's endorsement of an ethical system that imposes its most stringent codes on subaltern groups (women and youth). Zhang Dongsun's alleged exemption of himself from what he preaches proves his hypocrisy and thereby impairs his authority to legislate morality. The peculiar obsession with the question of motivation and the ubiquity of the charge of hypocrisy are uniquely modern phenomena—the inevitable product of modern epistemology that denies external or divine moral sources and that separates the inner and the outer, mind and body, word and action. It is clear that "selfishness" or "egotism" (*zisi*) is, by consensus of both sides of the debate, the most undesirable quality and thus the most damaging charge one can throw at one's opponent. Individualism must be condemned because it fosters selfishness in the name of freedom. Confucianism must be denounced because it masks selfishness beneath the rhetoric of self-sacrifice. On the surface, the debate circles around the question of whether Confucianism sublimates, masks, or, worst of all, thrives on selfish desires. But it is also a clash between two different visions of society—between, on the one hand, society seen as a basically fair totality in which a rational set of ethical principles guide and reward all who strive to be a moral person, and, on the other hand, society as a tension-charged field in which outmoded morality still holds sway because it benefits some at the expense of others. In the latter view, the call for self-mastery is inherently suspicious as a result of the conviction that no ethical law is universally binding in a hierarchical society. Men, for example, can demand women to "master" their desires while they indulge their own wildest fantasies. Sexual double standard, after all, has been the key note of the May Fourth project of "exposing" Confucian hypocrisy.

However, if Zhang Dongsun stakes the legitimacy of Confucianism on its ability to subjugate desire, then the most logical countermove would be to question his supposition that desire is the source of evil and that social order and progress require its subjugation. This is the move that the aesthetic theorist Zhu Guangqian (1897–1986) makes. In one of a series of letters addressed to an unidentified middle school student, Zhu invokes the antirationalist, antiteleological currents in western philosophy since the eighteenth century that see life as purposive without a purpose. Psychology has also demonstrated that the primary motive force of action is instinct or emotion, not reason. Freudian psychology, in particular, holds that action is driven by unconscious desires. Without art, religion, and emotion, the world of pure reason is a dull, cold, and cruel one. Reason urges us to do many things, but it is only when driven by emotion that we are able to do the tiniest fraction of them. For example, one knows very well one should help the poor, but unless one's sense of pity (*lianmin de qinggan*) is aroused by the sight of some miserable wretch, nine out of ten times, one will not give alms. Strictly speaking, the world of reason has only law not morality. What morality it does have is "the morality of reason" (*wen li de daode*), not "the morality of the heart" (*wen xin de daode*). The former gives mankind bondage, not happiness. For instance, when filial piety is regarded as a duty, it is the morality of reason. But if we see it as a kind of love that connects heart to heart and touches emotion with emotion, rather than as a quid pro quo transaction, then it is the morality of the heart. In a word, we must not only "know" the virtues, but also "feel" them (Zhu Guangqian 1928).

At a theoretical level, Zhu Guangqian's "morality of the heart" and Zhang Dongsun's "sublimationism" diverge on the fundamental question of whether morality is rooted in our affective nature or rational nature, a question that is derived, to begin with, from European philosophy. At the level of ethical praxis, the divergence is negligible. Both men characterize China as a "cold and cruel" place because of either too much desire or too much reason. Both attempt to effect a marriage of reason and desire, and neither is comfortable with one element unaided or unchecked by the other. Though couched in a more abstract language, their projects are essentially no different from the popular cultural concerns with the ethical propriety of emotion as well as the emotional authenticity of ethical relationships.

Still, the morality of the heart grants greater autonomy to the individual who alone can vouch for his or her "heart." Although both thinkers proceed from the enlightenment dichotomy of self and society, Zhu Guangqian is more troubled by the possibility of formalism and hypocrisy—of doing the bidding of moral codes without true feeling, of mechanically submitting the individual will to societal norms. But for the conservatives, aligning morality with feeling is akin to erecting the entire moral edifice on the shifting sand of individual whims. Extending Zhu's example of filial piety, Du Yaquan, the one-time editor of *Dongfang zazhi* (Eastern miscellany), argues that while it is certainly desirable to unite reason and sentiment in filial piety, duty must not be made contingent on personal feelings. Even when we do not "feel" the filial sentiment, we still must fulfill the duty of caring for our parents. Otherwise individual freedom would be divorced from societal constraints, and the consequence would be disastrous. Du grants that reason is born of the will to life (*shengming de yizhi*) and is thus a derivative force, but he contends that once reason has come into being, it should take charge of life, lest it be led astray by blind passions. In conclusion, Du sounds a conciliatory note: We should favor neither sentiment nor reason; rather, our goal is to reach a state in which we can "follow our heart's desires but never transgress the rules" (*cong xin suo yu bu yu ju*) (Du Yaquan 1928, 463).

Du Yaquan's evocation of a classical ideal echoes Xia Mianzun's formula of self-realization through self-sacrifice, or the internalization of ethical rules as one's own intimate desires. At this level, the conservatives are also pursuing a profoundly modern project, one that makes obligatory reference to the

emotional nature of the individual and that seeks to ground ethics in immanent experience. The conservatives and liberals may differ on whether Confucianism is capable of regeneration or whether some altogether new
paradigm is necessary, but they all seem to agree that an ethics that does not
speak to the "heart" or that is hostile toward "feeling" has no legitimacy.
This is perhaps why some of their arguments may appear pointless to later
observers. But the differences, even if only rhetorical, mattered a great deal
to these intellectual pugilists, for although they all agreed that love must be
made virtuous, they believed that what kind of love was validated and what
kind of rules were sanctioned would make a world of difference.

THE LIBERAL QUANDARY

In the wake of the collapse of the Confucian order, conservative and liberal
thinkers alike have agonized over the disappearance of a stable moral foundation on which to anchor the institutions of marriage and family. While the
conservatives have incorporated the enlightenment vocabulary of sentiment,
desire, and self-realization, liberals have also softened the barbed rhetoric of
May Fourth iconoclasm and have even resurrected the archvirtue of the Confucian structure of feeling: constancy or *zhencao*. *Zhencao* is constructed as a
distinctly modern virtue because it is voluntary and egalitarian. It becomes
the greatest moral capital for the exponents of "love's supremacy," for it allays,
or is hoped to allay, the anxiety engendered by love's Achilles' heel: its fungibility. Lest it sound too old-fashioned, the virtue of constancy is rearticulated
as the romantic imperative of uniting the body and the soul (*lingrou yizhi*).
The writings of Edward Carpenter, Ellen Key, Kuriyagawa Hakuson (1880–
1923), and others are frequently cited as the authoritative sources of the creed
that sublimated love is the foundation of modern morality because it facili-
tates the unity of reason and desire.

The Japanese literary critic Kuriyagawa Hakuson's historical treatise *Kindai no ren'ai kan* (Modern love) advances a three-stage evolutionary theory of
love. The first is the carnal stage that characterized antiquity. The eastern
moralists of today who fail to understand the meaning of the female/male relationship beyond sex and reproduction are still arrested in this stage. The
second stage is the Middle Ages, which boasted Christian puritanism, courtly
love, the worship of women, and the troubadour culture. In the final stage,

modern individualism gave rise to the ideal of the unity of body and soul.[15] Once love has evolved to this stage, it is a highly edifying force that purifies people's hearts and prompts them to do noble deeds. In marriage, love turns into mutual care between the spouses and then into parental love for children; it continues as filial love for parents and expands into love of one's kin, neighbors, compatriots, and all of humanity. Without love, marriage is legalized rape and long-term prostitution; without love, there is no morality (Kuriyagawa 1928, 16–20).

These last points echo the arguments of a generation of radical European social thinkers from Key to Ibsen, who have passionately critiqued bourgeois marriage for its suppression of individual freedom and women's rights. However, as a spokesman for the emerging bourgeoisie in East Asian societies, Kuriyagawa seeks to convert love from an iconoclastic emblem to a healing force that can bring Nora home again. He points out that for the awakened youths of the twentieth century, free love and marriage are no longer unattainable ideals. For this reason, Nora is already an outdated role model. Now the New Woman aspires to become the new wife and new mother (as opposed to the traditional "wise mother and good wife") who realizes herself through the gift of love as well as spiritual and carnal gratification. The same is also true for men—to sacrifice oneself for the woman one loves is the only way to realize one's manhood. Ibsen's Nora knows only the superficial self that is ultimately responsible for egocentrism. What she does not know is the dialectic of self-assertion in self-surrender, or finding oneself in one's lover and vice versa (21–25).

The repudiation of Nora should not surprise Chinese readers. Chinese detractors of the May Fourth icon have always been appalled by Nora's desertion of a family life made so sweet by her husband's dulcet vows of love and constant showers of affection. After all, many Chinese youths would have given anything for the life she rejects when she famously closes the door behind her. It did not take long for Nora to become an antiheroine, a symbol of individualism carried to excess. Once individualism was discredited, romantic love was in ever-greater need to form alliance with weighty concerns: morality ("constancy"), eugenics ("progress"), or nationalism ("national sympathy").

In an essay calling for the unity of body and soul, Chen Weibo considers the following forms of love unacceptable: love absolutism, love egoism, love suicide (*xunqing*), "sentimentalism" (English in the original), abstinence, promiscuity, and deviant sexualities (*jixing de xing shenghuo*). Invoking Ellen Key, he objects to "love for love's sake": Young people today tend to forget that love is a social act endowed with social values; too often, they seek private gratification in complete disregard for the higher goals of life (Chen Weibo 1927). It is in moments like this that the liberal/conservative distinction can hardly be maintained. Both share the desire to reconfigure love—which the May Fourth romantics have so successfully made into an anti-establishment force—as constitutive of society. This means treading an elusive center line that in fact amounts to a modern update of the Confucian structure of feeling. Once again, love is eulogized for its promise of virtue (self-sacrifice) rather than for its promise of freedom. Once again, love is the fount of moral sentiments and indispensable to domestic harmony and communal solidarity. It guarantees the unity of all virtues and turns the conjugal home into the site of the ultimate fulfillment of romantic dreams. If, in the May Fourth discourse, love means walking out of the patriarchal family, in the bourgeois update of the Confucian structure of feeling, love demands the embracing of the nuclear family. If filial piety was the reigning ethos of the the former, then conjugal love is to be the sovereign passion of the latter. But the crucial point is that conjugal love necessarily evolves to love across the generations and across social divides. It must not crowd out, undercut, or antagonize other familial and social feelings.

A great deal of discursive energy is spent on defining and balancing love's prosocial and antisocial tendencies, which paradoxically reinforces the distinction and engenders further discursive efforts aimed at its reconciliation. Increasingly, society is viewed as a collective of instinct-driven individuals, and the social order is precariously predicated on whether these individuals can rein in their inner beasts. Such a reductive view of society often leads to naive propositions as to how to solve China's social problems, or to the indiscriminate espousal of panaceas. The extreme popularity of eugenics is a good case in point. Both the conservative and liberal camps see eugenics as a scientifically sound way of making love morally and socially viable. For example, in a translated article featured in the *Ladies' Journal*'s special issue on love, Havelock Ellis (E-er-li-si) argues that eugenics is perfectly compatible with love because love necessarily involves making rational choices that take into consideration personal qualities, learning, and wealth. Moreover, eugenicists have been trying to transform eugenics into a new religion that promotes healthy matches (1926). Elsewhere, women's right to choose their own mates is also defended on eugenic grounds: the children of a freely formed union are far superior to those born of arranged marriages. Tani

Barlow thus coins the term "the eugenic subject" to characterize the new woman of the early twentieth century (2004, chapters 3 and 4).

The desire to legitimize love dulls even a rare and astute critique of eugenics by Zhang Xichen in reaction to Chen Jianshan's use of eugenics to attack free love. Chen Jianshan argues that from the eugenic point of view, free love is harmful to society and the nation because, contra Ellis, it is blind and irrational, concerned not with health but with passion alone. For this very reason, eugenics has not made significant inroads in the freest of all nations—the United States. The traditional marriage, in contrast, conforms much more closely to the principles of eugenics. This is because parents, especially enlightened parents of today, will always do their best to choose the most ideal (that is, eugenically sound) spouse for their children (Chen Jianshan 1924).[16]

Zhang Xichen dismisses Chen Jianshan's characterization of love as irrational. The thrust of his critique is largely humanist, defending the dignity of the individual and exposing the underlying antihumanist presumptions of eugenics. He presents the following points: All modern knowledge, including eugenics, is centered on "man." When Chen Jianshan asks that individual happiness be made subordinate to eugenic requirements, he is in fact treating human beings as dumb plants or livestock and placing the eugenicist in the role of horticulturist or animal farmer. But the eugenicist is human, not god; how can we know if what he considers eugenically sound is in the interest of everyone? Even if he is all-knowing, does he have the right to eliminate whomever does not meet his standards like the way one treats plants and animals? We moderns value intelligence over brute strength, so what criterion should we use in judging fitness? (Zhang Xichen 1925)

At this point, Zhang's polemic takes a 180-degree turn. Instead of continuing the line of critique he has forcefully advanced so far, he turns to Havelock Ellis (1859–1939), Zhou Jianren, and other psychologists, as if unable to dispense with the scientific mystique and unwilling, in the last analysis, to get on the wrong side of eugenics. His tone also becomes conciliatory: as long as people can transcend considerations of money and rank, real love is rarely antieugenic. Humans, like animals, have a natural preference for the beautiful and the strong. No one would deliberately choose someone with consumption or epilepsy for a spouse. Of course, there will always be those who make mistakes in marital choices. But mistakes are best addressed through education and other preventive measures, such as premarital physical examinations and forced sterilization of those with hereditary diseases. This is the way to accommodate both individual happiness and the happiness of the species (*zhongzu xingfu*) (Zhang Xichen 1925).

Despite his doubts about the moral integrity of eugenics, Zhang Xichen still finds it necessary to align love with basic eugenic principles. Earlier in the same year, Zhang Xichen, along with Zhou Jianren, had attempted to set down the parameters of a new liberal sexual ethics that turned as much on humanist principles as on eugenic ones ("Xin xing daode shi shenme?" [What is the new sexual morality?], *Funü zazhi* 11:1, 1925). Challenging the conventional assumption that morality consists of hard-and-fast rules of behavior laid down by ancient sages urging people to do good and shun evil, Zhang suggests that good and evil are relative terms. First, depending on one's perspective, sometimes the same deed can be both good and bad. For example, when a cat catches a mouse, it is a good deed for cat owners but a bad deed for the mouse. Second, the motive and outcome of an action are often at odds. Parents who arrange marriages for their beloved children out of benign motives often end up ruining their children's happiness for life (Zhang Xichen 1926b, 12–13).

Once he sets up the relativity of morality, Zhang Xichen is able to rework the conventional moral scheme. First he takes on the dichotomy of egotism and altruism by asserting that the two are mutually complementary. On the one hand, egotism is not immoral so long as it harms no one else; on the other hand, if one ignores one's own welfare, one is in no position to do good for others (13–14). The defense of egotism responds to the conservative formula of "individualism = egotism = selfishness." By blurring the boundary between egoism and altruism, Zhang Xichen makes it possible to ground morality in love without obliterating love's private, personal dimensions. In other words, he does not have to cleanse love of all traces of self-interest in order to defend its ethicality (a move that Zhang Jingsheng made a few years back to the consternation of the reading public). Applying this new criterion of morality to sexuality, Zhang Xichen defends the possibility of morally responsible sexual freedom. He explains that what does not harm society and other individuals cannot be immoral. Consensual sex between an adult male and female is a private matter that should be left to the parties themselves. If an unfaithful spouse grants his or her partner the right to divorce, or if the three parties of a triangle work out some arrangement to the satisfaction of all and without harming society and other individuals, they cannot be considered immoral either (19–20).

What Zhang Xichen is advancing here is a utilitarian brand of moral philosophy. He states it clearly: The goal of morality is to increase the overall happiness and reduce the overall pain in society. In pursuing this goal, we place the welfare of humanity above all other considerations and the welfare of the majority above that of the minority. This means that sometimes it is necessary to sacrifice the happiness of an "unhealthy" (that is, eugenically unfit) minority for the sake of the majority's happiness (13). Yet our received sexual morality does just the opposite. To give one example, it demands that all men, even those with hereditary diseases, marry and produce offspring. As a result, deformity plagues the race. To give another example, society condemns children born out of wedlock as "illegitimate" and their parents (especially the mother) as immoral, but it condones the so-called legal couple for recklessly breeding litters of children and then abandoning them to disease, deformity, mendicancy, banditry, and prostitution. For the sake of our future, such topsy-turvy morality must be reformed! (15–16).

The Confucian imperative to continue the patriline is both incomprehensible and reprehensible within Zhang's enlightenment framework, which places the individual in a universal collectivity (society, nation, human race). Between the individual and the collectivity, there are only other individuals in relation to whom one must exercise moral restraints. There is little concern with reconciling love with other familial affections, particularly filial piety. Even the newly recuperated virtue of constancy is not a moral principle sui generis. Because virtue is but a means to achieve the greatest happiness of the greatest number, the breach of fidelity is not immoral so long as the sum total of happiness is not diminished as a result. Small wonder that Zhang, to his indignation, is accused of endorsing polygamy by Chen Bainian (1925).[17] For conservative thinkers, the move to relativize and privatize morality is a dangerous step. Without of a set of binding principles emanating from a source higher than individual human agents (such as Heaven, the Way, the Sages, Reason), morality will, they fear, degenerate into a convenient tool used arbitrarily to justify all kinds of unspeakable deeds—including sexual profligacy under the shield of individual happiness. But the proponents of new sexual morality deny that immanent morality is necessarily arbitrary by stressing that it grows out of the scientific study of the human body and mind and hence is firmly grounded in the objective truths about human nature.

Such is Zhou Jianren's line of argument in his "Xing daode zhi kexue de biaozhun" (The scientific criteria of sexual morality, *Funü zazhi* 11:1, 1925). As a eugenicist, Zhou is not entirely comfortable with leaving sexual matters wholly to private individuals. Advocating socialized child care, he argues that while sexuality is a private matter, the consequences of sexuality concern the future of the race; therefore, national interests must be taken into consideration in matters of childbirth and child rearing. But Zhou also opposes enforcing chastity, regardless of the net gain or loss of happiness (in Zhang Xichen 1926b, 28–29). That Zhang Xichen and Zhou Jianren approve of practices that are easily construed as promiscuous and then righteously dismiss the charge of defending immorality has everything to do with their sense of empowerment from the intersecting discourses of humanism, science, and nationalism.

SEX RADICALISM

Just as the liberals seemed to be gaining the upper hand in the battle of discourse, they found themselves embroiled in bitter disputes over the gender and class ramifications of new sexual morality, particularly the much-vaunted unity of body and soul. This time their opponents came from the radical anarchist camp who, in calling for the abolition of all conventional social institutions, rejected the dualism of reason and sentiment as a phony problem, a subterfuge of bourgeois ideology. Emboldened by the latest convergence of psychoanalytic and Marxist theory on the theme of repression, a group of romantic anarchists unfurled a banner of sexual revolution that shocked and scandalized their contemporaries. The central planks of their platform denounced love as a bourgeois conceit and sought to disentangle sex from the imbricated discourse of love, morality, and social order. They made extensive use of evolutionary psychology to establish the independent legitimacy of sexuality, which in turn became the centerpiece of anarchism's libertarian, or what Foucault has called "Freudo-Marxist," philosophy of life.

The anarchist assault on liberal orthodoxy began in the mid-1920s with a subtle semantic shift: love (*lian'ai*) in the anarchist parlance was increasingly equated with "reason" or "morality"—as a social artifice erected to repress the primal sexual instinct (*yu*). In the preface to the Chinese translation of Tayama Katai's (1871–1930) novel *Futon*, Guangtao substitutes the opposition of love (*ai*) and sexuality (*yu*) for the more familiar one of reason and sentiment. In a gleeful tone, he reminds us that however sacred love is said to be, it cannot escape an ugly battle with desire. In an apparent reference to the tormented state of mind of the novel's protagonist, he suggests that if we could just break free of all moral constraints and abandon ourselves to our desires, we would retain more humanity than those who cleave to the hypocritical life of love. And our lives would also be more fulfilled (Guangtao 1926). What is relatively new here is the assertion that sexual desire is what defines humanity, not because it is necessarily good or beautiful, but because it is simply "there," because it is the truth. As human beings, we have no choice but to resign to our essential humanity (what Zhang Dongsun prefers to call "bestiality"). In embracing our sexuality, we embrace our humanity.

Also new in the anarchist discourse of sexuality is the assumption that the human body is but "a structure of finely attuned cogs and wheels, an intricate machinery which could be adjusted and regulated" (Dikötter 1995, 21), and that to deem one particular organ or mechanism "immoral" is simply beside the point. Another author puts it more starkly: "Love is a mechanical function. When the sexual organs are mature, a man and a woman will be drawn to each other instinctually. The so-called 'spiritual love' is a fraud" (Peng Zhao-liang 1926, 29). Mao Yibo concurs that love is a function of reflexes (*fanshe zuoyong*), the result of tactile contact and sensorial stimulation. Sexual love is simply a kind of reflex found between the sexes. There is nothing mysterious about it (Mao Yibo 1926).

This line of argument signals an important shift from the regime of morality that has dominated the liberal/conservative debate to the "regime of truth," though liberals such as Zhang Xichen and Zhou Jianren have on occasions also deployed the regime of truth to defend their "new sexual morality." In terms of the history of sexuality, this parallels the two-century-long process in Europe of medicalizing large areas of human experience previously dominated by moral-theological discourses (Davidson 2001). That the radicals openly profess the desire to shed all moral constraints and to give a free rein to sexual instincts shows that the issue of morality has become irrelevant so long as they feel truth is on their side. Immorality is no longer a meaningful charge. Ren Chang, for example, matter-of-factly advocates multiple sexual partnerships, or what some might call promiscuity: As a result of social evolution, there is a new division of labor with regard to the fulfillment of our needs. We should not expect one partner to meet all of our demands, for it would be tantamount to asking one's tailor to cook one's meals too. I can be A's carnal partner and B's spiritual partner simultaneously and remain faithful to both of them, just as I can belong to several organizations at the same time. We must do away with the notion of ego and cease to regard our lover as our property. Instead we should share him or her with others, just like we do a piece of artwork. Instead of the usual prayer, "may all lovers under heaven happily unite in matrimony," let us wish that "all lovers under heaven happily meet and enjoy one another" (Ren Chang 1926, 7).

The functionalist parceling out of emotional needs leaves no room for the Hegelian dialectic of love. What is obviated in the mechanical conception of the person as an aggregate of discrete needs are all the perplexing questions of individual identity, self-worth, and voluntary sociality. The radicals' in-your-face approach startled their contemporaries, but their exultation over the emancipatory potential of sex was part and parcel of a flourishing discourse of sexuality. According to Frank Dikötter, it was a discourse that encompassed talk of sex as a sign of liberation, commercial exploitation of sex-related topics, the nationalist agenda to regulate sexual conduct, and a faith in science to dismantle tradition. The producers of this discourse were a diverse group—journalists, social reformers, professional writers, educators, and ideologues who articulated a multiplicity of viewpoints and spoke from a variety of cultural locations (1995, 1–5). The anarchists represented the most radical end of the spectrum, their radicalism being a function of their fundamental opposition to the principle of private property and the capitalist social system. Marriage was heavily targeted because it institutionalized the private ownership of one human being by another or by an institution (the patriarchal family). For a woman who had no other means of livelihood, marriage amounted to lifetime prostitution. Both the May Fourth rebels and their liberal, pro-feminist inheritors (including women writers) had argued similar positions before, but their proposed remedies had rarely entertained the option of eliminating the institution of marriage altogether. The anarchists saw nothing in marriage, not even the most idealized form of companionate marriage, that did not violate their vision of a humane society of freedom, dignity, and spontaneity. Likewise, all doctrines and practices that ran counter to the overarching goals of universal freedom were resolutely rejected. These include, in Lu Jianbo's reckoning, marriage, puritanism, chastity, proprietorship of love, singleness, birth control, and all forms of sexual deviancy (Lu Jianbo 1926).[18]

On the whole, the anarchist critique takes the form of a militant attack on all things bourgeois. What counts as bourgeois is rather ill defined, but insofar as gender relations are concerned, constancy, spiritual love, the unity of body and soul, and related precepts are the usual suspects. In the exchange between Zhang Xichen and Chen Bainian mentioned above, Zhang's attempt to liberalize "sexual morality" was construed by the latter as a new defense of polygamy—or worse, as advocating sexual anarchism. Qiandi,[19] however, sees no anarchist message in Zhang's suggestion that constancy is a question of taste (*quwei*), faith, or idiosyncrasy (*jiepi*), that is, a matter of free will and free choice. He insists that this admittedly permissive view of constancy is still hitched to bourgeois pseudomorality and can still be deployed as a sexist trap for women (1927). As if to forestall all such "fresh" fences erected in defense of love, Qiandi advances a tendentious theory of antilove (*fei lian'ai lun*) that initiates a new round of debates (*fei lian'ai lunzhan*) in *Xin nüxing* among himself, Zhang Xichen, and others.

Qiandi breaks his theory of antilove into three components, the first of which is antilove and anticonstancy. In accordance with the mechanical understanding of the human body, he affirms that sex is a purely physical act that has nothing to do with love. Constancy, on the other hand, is only relevant to gods, ghosts, kings, and heroes, not to biological facts. Whether old-fashioned or newfangled, unilateral, or bilateral, constancy is but a dignified name used to cover up exploitation and oppression. Second, romantic love is not the sole foundation of civilization. Not only can civilizational values be born of same-sex relationships, but there are also plenty of bachelor philosophers, writers, and scientists who have made great contributions to human civilization. Finally, romantic love and human love (*renlei ai*) are incompatible. "Love" is the code word for the sex life of the leisure classes. The wage laborer has no way of knowing the love that is supposed to be rich in spiritual and cultural significance. Love thus thrives on and consolidates the capitalist relation of production. Once capitalism is overthrown, there will be only "sexual friendship" (English in the original) or "human love" between the sexes (Qiandi 1928).

Key to Qiandi's case against romantic love is the charge that it is antithetical to "human love," a point he derives from the Japanese sociologist Yoneda Shōtarō's (1873–1945) treatise *Ren'ai no kachi* (The value of love). Yoneda grounds his theory in a strenuously maintained distinction between "romantic love" (*lian'ai*) and "human love" (*renlei ai*): The former is the possessive relationship between a man and woman and the latter is a person's love for all humanity, regardless of sex. The two kinds of love are mutually exclusive and one does not grow out of the other. He even posits a separate origin for "human love": "sociality" (*shehui qinhe*). Sustained by "life force" not used for sexual purposes, sociality is the foundation of truth, beauty, and goodness

(Yoneda 1927). Yoneda's dualist thesis rends asunder the liberal camp's painstakingly established affinity between love and sociality. Deprived of the claim to larger relevance and wider application and forcibly pushed back into the murky pit of "selfishness" or "egotism," romantic love is scarcely defensible. Qiandi goes a step further than Yoneda to deny the very possibility of romantic attachment by rejecting the concept of the heart, for so long as the heart holds a place in the discourse of love, there is always the potential for sociality. Qiandi wants to reduce all contact between the sexes to the accidental, impulsive, and purely biological act of sexual intercourse. Once he denudes love of social significance, he is able to denounce it as a castle in the air, an ideological fiction of the bourgeoisie.

Zhang Xichen summarizes Qiandi's arguments in six points and poses questions to each. In the next issue of *Xin nüxing*, Qiandi replies and Zhang follows up, all in the special column created for the debate: "Fei lian'ai lunzhan" (A debate on the theory of antilove). Lu Jianbo (1904–?), another vocal anarchist and active participant in the debate, comes to Qiandi's reinforcement. He too grounds the critique of capitalism in a naturalist philosophy: Sexual desire is the basic nature (*benxing*) of all creatures, human beings included. The present economic system not only restricts sexual freedom, but also protects the private ownership of sex. To bring down this citadel, we must not only destroy existing gender ideology, but more importantly, we must demolish the economic foundation of the current social order. In addition, we need to demystify sex, treating it as ordinary as eating and regarding kissing, hugging, or what Zhang Jingsheng calls "erotic play" (*qingwan*) as natural expressions of human affection and intimacy. In the free society of the future, there will be no more spouses, only companions and lovers. This will be the ultimate human fulfillment and the ultimate harmony of the sexes (Lu Jianbo 1928).

The anarchist insistence on conjoining sexual and class inequities in their analysis can be read as a response to Lu Xun's question of what happens after Nora leaves home. While conservatives and liberals have proposed to bring Nora back to reformed or liberalized domesticity, the anarchists view it as a new form of bondage. Instead, they propose to overhaul the entire social system so that Nora will find not only economic independence (so that she will not "go to the bad"), but also genuine personal and sexual freedom (so that she need not "return home"). Before the anarchists, few readers in China seem to have appreciated Ibsen's indictment of bourgeois domestic ideology. The May

Fourth generation appropriated the play for their agenda of rebelling against the Confucian family. The irony is that they fought for precisely what Nora left behind: the bourgeois family that concealed the relations of inequality and exploitation beneath the naturalizing rhetoric of love and gender roles. Once the anarchists rejected the legitimacy of the conjugal family, love is repudiated as part of its ideological camouflage, a heap of lies covering up the unnatural and unjustified private ownership of sex.

The anarchist no-nonsense take on sex proved highly offensive to the liberal sensibility. In what he hoped to be the final word in the debate, Zhang Xichen mounted a wistful defense of private property. In his view, those advocating promiscuity (*zajiao*, communal sex) mistakenly believe that society restricts sexual freedom (*xingyu de ziyou*). As a matter of fact, human beings have long been liberated in the realm of pure carnality in that there are many ways of achieving gratification, but not in terms of freedom of love (*lian'ai de ziyou*). True, love is a product of the capitalist system of private property; but are all things under capitalism worthless? Capitalism's art of love is as useful to us as its science and technology. Ignoring Lu Jianbo's reference to "erotic play," Zhang asks, if sex is just sex, how come food is never just food but is elaborately prepared in a variety of culinary traditions and consumed in diverse social contexts? At the end of the essay, Zhang confesses somewhat dourly that if the future proletarian society will have food and sex only for the sake of assuaging hunger and lust, then he would rather settle for the present bourgeois society (Zhang Xichen 1928). The prospect of communal sex holds as little attraction for a liberal as for a conservative. But surprisingly, the radicals and conservatives share a common critique: that romantic love is antisocial and detrimental to the public good. Their respective conceptions of public good are of course very different, but their verdict of love's social deficiencies forces the liberal camp to be increasingly conciliatory. Zhang Xichen's defense ends with a less-than-principled assertion of personal preference. Another liberal who jumps in at the tail end of the debate concedes that love may be antisocial, but reassures the reader that it is only a temporary condition. Moreover, love may require leisure, but it need not be the monopoly of the leisure classes. Movies and parks are the ingredients of only one kind of love life; the working class also has its own, simpler (*pusude*) kind of love (Hong Jun 1928).

But what is the working class's simpler kind of love like? Insofar as the romantic genre is concerned, the literary landscape is inhabited by urbanites who may not all qualify as members of the "leisure class" but who are none-theless eager practitioners of bourgeois love. The new genre of proletarian literature (*puluo wenxue*) has by and large shied away from the sentimental and the erotic in an effort to distance itself from modernist and middlebrow urban fiction. The thorny question of love and class is not to be resolved until the ascendancy of socialist realism.

• • •

This chapter begins with a discussion of real-life incidents that sparked pub-lic debates on the rules of love and sex. These and other similar incidents are what James Lull and Stephen Hinerman call "media scandals"—private acts that offend the dominant morality of a community and that, once publicized in narrative form by the media, "produc[e] a range of effects from ideological and cultural retrenchment to disruption and change" (1997, 3). The media scandal usually dramatizes a basic moral dilemma and taps into "fundamen-tal and powerful cognitive-emotional structures" (20). In shocking the pub-lic, it brings changing mores into sharp focus, thus compelling people to reexamine and renegotiate the basic terms and parameters of morality. At a time when love was eulogized as transcendent, sacrosanct, and immutable, Chen Shujun's decision to leave her fiancé to marry a professor was deeply unsettling to the public, as we have seen in the ensuing debate. Most readers resisted Zhang Jingsheng's effort to reform sexual morality and clang to the romantic ideal of constancy. But each subsequent scandal chipped away at the romantic redoubt, and some of Zhang's proposals made a stealthy come-back in the self-help literature and subsequent debates.

Armed with the conviction that love has rules and that happiness depends on their mastery, guidebooks set out to rid love of its rebellious and utopian edges and "incorporate [it] in the discourse and phenomenological properties of daily life" (Illouz 1998, 170). They break down the topic of love into ever more categories, identify ever more pitfalls on its path, propose ever more dos and don'ts, and spice up their instruction with ever more juicy anecdotes. The unprecedented attention devoted to the daily business of love contributed to the quotidianization of love and the affirmation of the everyday. When intel-lectual and political elites in the 1930s and 1940s promoted the grand narra-tive of revolution, they came up against a proliferating and resilient discourse of the everyday, a discourse that saw meaning and fulfillment in ordinary life whose central ingredients were romance, marriage, family life, work, and lei-sure. To discourage this consuming interest in the quotidian, revolutionaries on both the left and right denounced love as a frivolous bourgeois pursuit, a distraction from nobler purposes in life. In their effort to define a higher and more meaningful life, they sought to strip love of its protean meanings and reduce it to a mechanical routine. In this they were indebted to the anarchists who, even more than the conservatives, discredited love's claim to ethicality and nobility.

By the mid-1930s, the anarchists had mostly dropped out of public dis-course. Although they may have foundered on their unabashed utopianism, they certainly tapped into the hopes and frustrations of many young urbanites who were trying to chart a new course in the unfamiliar territory of gender re-lations outside the Confucian kinship structure. They were able to fuse the "minor chronicle of sex" (Foucault's phrase) with the anarcho-socialist cri-tique of capitalism. Although they were unable to prevail against the conser-vative-liberal block thanks to the ideological backing of a conservative regime and the swelling middle-class rank,[20] the anarchists were able to re-kindle radical idealism among educated youth, producing a discursive legacy with which the revolutionary ideologies of the 1930s had to reckon.

FIVE

The Historical Epistemology of Sex

The anarchists' advocacy of free sex proceeded directly from the repressive hypothesis, or the idea that there is a timeless, primordial sexuality that has been silenced by civilization. For Foucault, the repressive hypothesis is built on a juridical model of power. Sexuality in this model is external to power—power understood as rules and prohibitions enforcing order and control in society. The corollary thesis is that sexual liberation will necessarily follow upon the rejection of law and the dismantling of the repressive machinery—capitalism, morality, and family—so that "man can be reconciled with himself, once again find his nature or renew contact with his roots and restore a full and positive relationship with himself" (Foucault 1990a, 2).

Anarchist or not, intellectuals in the 1920s and 1930s pursued a foundational understanding of sex inspired by psychoanalysis and sought to discover a deep history of (repressed) sex in the annals of the Chinese past. Their narratives, however, betray a conceptual muddling of sex and sexuality and a kind of epistemological anachronism to which much contemporary scholarship on the subject is still not immune. Arnold I. Davidson points out that as a nineteenth-century invention, the concept of sexuality presupposes "a psychiatric style of reasoning" that locates sexuality in impulses, tastes, attitudes, and psychic traits. It is therefore unavailable to earlier times when sex identity was exclusively linked to the anatomical features of the body. Any discussion of pre-nineteenth-century sexuality, particularly in the language of modern sexology, psychiatry, or psychoanalysis, is therefore highly problematic, leading, at worst, to a "disfiguring, disabling anachronism" (1987, 18).[1] Davidson (2001) calls for a method he terms "historical epistemology" that probes the conditions of possibility of knowledge, or how a mode or area of human experience becomes problematized as a candidate for the judgment of truth or falsehood.[2] The modern sexual sciences turn "sex" into such a candidate, dislodging it from the older discursive arena of theology and morality and erecting on it the entire edifice of modern subjectivity. Psychoanalysis, for one, is not just a new science that grants us greater access to our sexual truths, but is also a new "style of reasoning" that ushers in a whole new apparatus of orientation, identity, authenticity, and normality.

Davidson builds his historical epistemology on Foucault's work on the history of the discourse of sexuality. Foucault characterizes the medical sciences that emerged in nineteenth-century Europe as a "game of truth," in contradistinction to what he calls *ars erotica*, an ethicoaesthetic regime that supposedly governed sex and desire in ancient Greece and Rome as well as "Oriental" societies such as China, Japan, and India. In the erotic art, pleasure is the supreme principle, defined not in relation to law or utility, but in relation to itself—"its intensity, its specific quality, its duration, its reverberations in the body and soul"—and truth is subordinated to the pleasure principle and the pedagogic imperative (Foucault 1990a, 57). This mildly Orientalist moment in Foucault serves to accentuate the historicity of the sexual sciences, or the *scientia sexualis*, with their peculiar procedure of truth production—confession —that bears little resemblance to the art of initiation and the transmission of erotic knowledge from body to body.

It is important to keep in mind that *ars erotica* did not exhaust classical and nonwestern approaches to sex and desire. Before the emergence of sexuality in eighteenth- and nineteenth-century Europe and its global dissemination in the twentieth century, the experiences of sex and desire have been, for the most part, organized by moral, theological, and medicinal theories of virtue and vice, salvation and sin, order and chaos, mastery and dissolution, health and decay. That is why when Foucault turned to ancient Greece and Rome in search of a history of the "desiring man," he found himself no longer writing about sexuality but about ethics. Here, *ars erotica* was only a subset, along with cuisine, exercise, reading and writing, of an encompassing concern with the art of living, or how to turn one's life into a work of art. In the introduction to the second volume of the history of sexuality as well as in several interviews, Foucault endeavors to justify the shift. He explains that he is not interested in sexuality as such—"sex is boring" (1997, 253)—as much as he is in how sexual matters come to be constituted as an "ethical substance"—that part of oneself that becomes the locus of ethical work. The shift to the ethical is necessitated by the fact that sexual behavior in Greek and Roman antiquities was part of a moral and aesthetic regime of life rather than a separate medical or psychological problem. A man's sexual preference did not have a truth value or a foundational status: a male-male sexual liaison did not brand a man as a "homosexual," nor did idiosyncratic sexual practices render a man a "pervert." Before the nineteenth century, sexual behavior was largely a matter of (compulsory) ethical choices that indexed a person's relationship to him- or herself, to a moral community, and/or to God or the gods. For this reason, as Davidson points out, such notions as chastity and virginity that for us necessarily pertain to the sexual were in fact moral categories that addressed the relationship of the will to the flesh (1987, 37).

The modern invention of sexuality was by and large a process in which the medical discourse took over large areas that had previously been the domains of morality and religion. In the conceptual space created by modern psychology, the discourse of sexuality took on "a positivity, a being true-or-false" (Davidson 1987, 23) while repudiating the older moral framework of good and evil. Richard von Krafft-Ebing, for example, glossed "chastity" as "anesthesia of the sexual instinct" in his monumental *Psychopathia Sexualis* (38), implying that the ethical imperative of being chaste amounted to a denial of what was natural and essential to humans, a denial that inevitably engendered forms of psychopathology. Likewise, when Freud defined "love" as "lust plus the ordeal of civility" (quoted in Solomon 1991, 506), he was calling attention to civilization's onerous constraints on the sexual life of the moderns. However, just because the medical discourse rejected older sexual morality does not mean that it did not operate in a moral framework of its own. As Foucault has shown so well, the language of truth spoken by modern sexual science was motivated by a simultaneously emancipatory and normative ethic—the free and healthy expression of our (hetero)sexual "nature." This

was the case in the interwar years when cultural critics held Christian morality responsible for the decline of western civilization and western manhood,
and called for sexual liberation as the path to universal human emancipation
(and also, as Wilhelm Reich hoped, doing away with homosexuality and por-
nography). This was also the case when liberal intellectuals in China attacked
Confucian morality or when anarchists repudiated bourgeois ideology for re-
pressing spontaneous sexuality. Whether employing an explicitly psychological or psychoanalytical language, they were mobilizing the regime of truth
given birth to by *scientia sexualis*.

The introduction of the sexual sciences, particularly Freudian psychoanalysis, in China in the first decades of the twentieth century played a crucial role
in displacing the indigenous ethical/cultivational discourse on sex and the
body. The imported discourse of sexuality also became bound up with a
whole range of issues and agendas, from anti-Confucian iconoclasm,
women's liberation, family reform, universal education, and eugenics, to nationalism and state-building. In particular, the Freudian theory inspired a
flood of psychoanalytic reinterpretations or rewritings of premodern literary
and historical texts. Whereas Freud used the Oedipal myth to articulate a
modern "truth" about the developmental dynamics of sexuality on the
assumption that ontogeny recapitulated phylogeny, the mostly western-
educated May Fourth intellectuals set out to "make sense" of early texts—
texts that seemed tantalizingly reticent about those aspects they had come to
equate with personal truth: emotion, love, and sexual desire. They diagnosed
these texts as symptomatic and read between the lines in order to fill in the
psychological gaps and disclose the repressed (sexual) truths. In their hands,
psychoanalysis was divorced from its clinical setting and retooled as a critical
hermeneutic strategy. It served the enlightenment agenda of displacing both
the Confucian moral discourse of sex/lust and the cultivational discourse of
health/generativity[3] with a scientific discourse of sexuality.

In the light of Foucault's critique,[4] how do we read psychoanalytic criticism
that uses precisely the repressive hypothesis to achieve emancipatory goals? How
are the psychoanalytic terms and theories of sexuality brought to bear on premodern texts, myths, or legends, and with what consequences? To explore these
questions, I examine the psychoanalytic project that seeks to advance an emancipatory politics of the body by unearthing muffled desires and diagnosing defor-
mities in the lives of mythohistorical figures. Specifically, I propose to examine
three instances in which western-educated intellectuals use Freudian theory to

reinterpret or rewrite early Chinese legends or tales. These cases highlight the problematic use of psychoanalysis across times and cultures and foreground the linkage between power and knowledge. I hope to show in this chapter that psychoanalysis was deployed in the May Fourth movement and beyond to popularize a new sexual subject whose personal truth resided in its heterosexuality. The validity or ineluctability of the sexual subject was established by psychoanalyzing the premodern person, revealing him or her to be au fond a sexual being whose realization had to await the age of enlightenment, science, and progress.

THE POETESS DIAGNOSED

The localization of Freud in China has of late received considerable scholarly attention in the field of Chinese studies (see Dikötter 1995; Lee 1999; Shih 2001; Sun Naixiu 1995; Zhang 1992).[5] Yet it seems that too much has been made of how accurately the Chinese understood Freud or how much they could stomach the so-called pan-sexualism (*fanxing zhuyi*) of psychoanalysis. The imported discourse of sexuality in early twentieth-century China was part of a profound paradigm shift in the conceptions of self, gender, and community. As a result, Freudian theory was useful not for its practical effectiveness as a therapeutic tool, but for its epistemological transitivity. Alongside and sometimes in place of love, sexuality became another archsymbol of all that was repressed in a puritanical social order. Various forms of the repressive hypothesis began to take shape around this newfound rebel's cause. As a kind of compulsive iteration of the founding gesture immortalized by Lu Xun's "madman" who scrutinizes Confucian classics only to find "cannibalism" (*chiren*) in between lines preaching "benevolence and morality," intellectuals surveyed historical records and descried repressed sexuality throughout the "dark" ages.

In denouncing Confucian morality, the May Fourth generation found in Freudian theory a powerful and prepossessing language—the language of science—to make their case. It allowed the iconoclasts to discredit the moral framework in which sex and gender were embedded by asserting that Confucianism ran counter to basic human (sexual) nature. The mantle of scientific neutrality, however, masked a different moral framework in which they made their case for sexual liberation—a framework first articulated in the Romanticist valuation of Nature (including our "inner nature") as a constitutive good. Their consuming desire to dismantle the Confucian moral order blinded them to their own strong commitment to an alternative set of ethical ideals—their own "regime of truth"—encoded in the bourgeois apparatus of sexuality. With determination, they pursued the ideal of the nuclear family in which the husband-wife and parent-child relations were to be organized entirely by "love" rather than by socioeconomic principles or the ethical prescriptions of chastity and filial piety. The conjugal/oedipal family as the emancipation of nature/sexuality became a potent icon against which the "traditional extended family" was ever harshly judged and critiqued.

In this context, the repressive hypothesis was an effective weapon in challenging the prohibition of sexual expressiveness within the terms of Confucian orthodoxy. But its essentialist notion of sexuality and juridical model of power also had the effect of flattening the historical terrain and precluding a critique of its own normative thrust. Not only were May Fourth intellectuals reticent about the *ars erotica* tradition,[6] they were also highly ambivalent toward the cult of *qing*. As I have argued in Chapter 1, men or women of feeling may be regarded as the first modern subjects insofar as they locate their moral source intrinsically rather than extrinsically. Nonetheless, this subject was not a sexual subject to the extent to which there was no separate category of sexuality and to which sex was subordinate to the ethical discourse of love as moral sentiment. The cult of *qing* inaugurated a new regime of truth, but it did not turn on a hermeneutics of the body and its desires. Familiar Confucian virtues such as chastity remained central to the cult of *qing* but acquired a different reality: instead of being a moral code whose binding power was vested in an external source—the heavenly principle—chastity was now a voluntary ethical choice, the outcome of the moral will's ability to check desire's propinquity to excess.

This aptly illustrates Foucault's conviction that although ethical codes have remained relatively stable and simple, their underlying realities are always multilayered and fungible (1990b, 28). Still, the yoking of love to virtue ill served the May Fourth anti-Confucian agenda and ill suited the goal of replacing the moral theory of sex and desire with a scientific one. For the intellectuals, "chastity" was a moralistic conceit, an ethical injunction that twisted the true shape of desire out of recognition, and an artifice that impeded the natural, spontaneous expressions of sexuality for the sake of maintaining an orderly and stable civilization. They were therefore unable to accommodate the emotional realities that the cult of *qing* had injected into Confucian moral theory. The premodern man and woman of feeling were enigmatic anomalies for them, requiring the penetrating scrutiny of the psychoanalytic gaze.

A case in point is Pan Guangdan's (1899–1967)psychobiographical study of Feng Xiaoqing (1595–1612),[7] a legendary poetess of the late Ming dynasty (1368–1644). At the age of fifteen, Xiaoqing was bought by a certain Feng Yuanjiang as a concubine. Feng's principal wife forced her to live alone in a villa on the West Lake in Hangzhou and forbade her husband to see her. Having learned to read and write from her mother, who had been a lady tutor, Xiaoqing preoccupied herself with reading, writing, and painting, and found some solace in the company of a lady friend, Madame Yang. After Madame Yang followed her husband (an official) to another post, Xiaoqing wasted away in loneliness and died of consumption at the age of seventeen. Her poems—the few that supposedly survived the fire set by the jealous wife—became widely circulated, and she soon acquired a cult status, inspiring many commemorative poems, several biographies, and more than a dozen plays.[8]

As a beautiful and talented woman who died young in tragic circumstances, Xiaoqing was a prime candidate for romantic mythopoeia by self-styled men of feeling. The myth, or what Dorothy Ko calls the "Xiaoqing lore," that immediately sprang to life after her death and grew unstoppably (despite her marital family's effort to squelch it) became a prominent component of the cult of *qing*. Her biographers and other myth makers overwhelmingly anchored the meaning of her life in *qing*, laying a great deal of stress on her fascination with *The Peony Pavilion*. As we have seen in Chapter 1, the play creates one of the most memorable heroines on Chinese stage—Du Liniang—whose arduous search for romantic happiness drives her to traverse the boundaries of dream and reality, life and death. Before she dies of lovesickness, Du Liniang paints her own portrait, thereby leaving behind a visual testament to her passionate existence and a clue to guide her lover onto the path to sexual congress in the netherworld.

In most accounts, Xiaoqing is said to be a devotee of *The Peony Pavilion*. Aware of her imminent death, Xiaoqing commissioned a painter to draw her portrait and made him repeat his work three times before she was satisfied. Like Liniang, she consecrated the portrait with incense and pear juice, then lay down to die. Her self-fashioning after a literary heroine became fertile ground on which to elaborate a poetics of sentiment. Xiaoqing's literati admirers suggested that because her learning was nearly exclusively derived from *The Peony Pavilion*—deemed by orthodox Confucians as indecent reading matter for well-born ladies—her death was no less than a heroic choice to die for love. In this way, her refusal to remarry despite her status as a virtual widow and despite her friend Madame Yang's urgings attested to her true devotion to the supreme principle of *qing*.

Pan Guangdan, however, takes exception to the Xiaoqing myth. Instead, he proceeds from the repressive hypothesis and what might be called "anachronistic psychological realism," which attributes sexual motivations to myths, legends, and historical events to make psychological "sense" of the latter; and he arrives at the conclusion that Xiaoqing died from neither lovesickness nor the persecution of the termagant wife, but from pathological narcissism. He begins his study with an expository chapter on the psychoanalytic theory of sexual development, invoking authorities like Freud and Hirschfeld. He then presents his diagnostic reading by first quoting a passage from a biographical source that describes the solitary Xiaoqing thus: "She often enjoyed talking to her reflection in the lake. Surrounded by flowers in the light of the setting sun, or as clouds floated on the surface of the clear water, she would gaze upon her reflection and carry on an absorbing dialogue with herself. But when the maid peeked at her, she would stop at once, though traces of tears and dark frowns would still linger."[9] Clearly, Pan explains, Xiaoqing's narcissism is not of the same order as the normal adolescent self-absorption. First of all, she is said to enjoy *talking* to her reflection *often*—which tells us that she attributes a separate personality to her reflection and that this is a repetitive, compulsive behavior, not an occasional indulgence. Second, she *promptly stops* her solipsistic conversation when the maid peeks at her, minding the latter's intrusion just as a pair of lovers would in their secret tryst. Last, Xiaoqing appears to be exceedingly pained by her reflection—perhaps because she knows too well that her object of love is but a specular image.

To quell any further doubt about his diagnosis, Pan quotes from Xiaoqing's tiny oeuvre:

With fresh make-up I vie with the beauties in the pictures,
Knowing not how I would fare.
To the spring lakeside I drag my emaciated body
To take pity in you as you in me take pity. (FXQ, 23)

Pan's clinching evidence is the thrice-drawn portrait. Already, Xiaoqing is known to have made herself up beautifully every day and dressed in her best even during the worst stages of her illness. With no one around her to appreciate her beauty, the only explanation, in Pan's view, is her narcissistic desire to please her one and only object of love—herself (FXQ, 25). Though practically an invalid, she sat for her portrait and insisted on its conveying a likeness of both appearance (*xing*) and spirit (*shen*). To achieve this end, she rallied herself to enact daily life rituals for the painter: fanning the tea kettle, organizing her books, smoothing out the folds of her petticoat, or mixing the painter's colors for him (FXQ, 25). For Pan, this only makes sense if we see the painting not simply as a self-portrait, but as the portrait of Xiaoqing's lover—hence her self-forgetful fastidiousness and demand for perfection.

Scrutinizing her poems, her farewell letter to Madame Yang, and her biographies for traces of her psyche, Pan is convinced that Xiaoqing was keenly aware of the burning intensity of her desire even if she might not have been able to pinpoint the precise nature of her condition, to wit, her narcissistic desire, which took her own self as its object (FXQ, 32). He asks, given her status as an abandoned concubine, what prevented her from seeking the usual recourse of remarriage, or taking shelter in religion, especially since she was already conversant in Buddhist scriptures and enjoyed the occasional company of a nun friend in her lonely residence? She must have had some inkling of her "sexual pathology" (*xing xinli biantai*), a condition for which neither remarriage nor religion could offer any therapeutic redress (FXQ, 27–29). Her precocity and astute self-intuition enabled her to arrive at the following self-diagnosis in her letter to Madame Yang: "Amorous thoughts and tender words rush into my mind at the least provocation; I'm afraid this is because my nature refuses to be silenced" (FXQ, 33). For Pan, frank and revealing passages like this mark the pinnacle of women's literature in China.

When it comes to the etiology of narcissism, Pan Guangdan employs a developmental scheme that he calls "the stream of libido." Xiaoqing, he begins, married at the tender age of fifteen. With her frail constitution, she could hardly have withstood the "sudden onslaught of sexual experience" (*xing jingyan zhi rouning*), which was made doubly crushing by her husband's libertine lifestyle. As a result, her stream of libido was forced to flow backward, and in an environment of idleness and boredom, most of it ended up in the stage of narcissism (FXQ, 33–34). Pan also detects faint traces of mother complex and homosexuality, and he has a ready explanation for this too: while most of Xiaoqing's stream of libido reconcentrated in the stage of narcissism, some of it regressed to the stage of mother fixation and some to that of homosexuality (FXQ, 35). Homosexuality, moreover, could also have been a result of "transference," that is, of Xiaoqing acting out her mother-complex vis-à-vis the maternal figure of Madame Yang.

Thus flourishing psychoanalytic and sexological concepts, Pan reads Xiaoqing's writings and biographical sources as symptomatic evidence of her pathologies. For him, there can be only one conclusion: Xiaoqing's symptoms are the symptoms of frustrated sexual desires, of a blocked "stream of libido" that could not run a normal course under the repressive machinery of the Confucian family system. He writes in the afterword:

> My readers should be familiar with our society's long-standing attitude toward women. In a word, it is incomprehension (*bu liangjie*). Among the educated classes, the moralists regard women as inauspicious creatures and the bohemian literati treat them as playthings. . . . One need only take a hasty survey of Qing women's poetry anthologies to realize the sheer number of women who were frail and depressed, especially among the educated classes. It had everything to do with the unnatural inhibition of sexual development. . . . For several thousand years, countless Chinese women have perished senselessly; Xiaoqing was but a drop in the vast ocean [of victims]. (FXQ, 39)[10]

Here Pan gives a modern explication to the popular myth of *hongyan boming* (beautiful women die young): Beautiful and talented women like Xiaoqing were unable to fulfill themselves sexually or intellectually and were therefore doomed to suffer unremitting melancholy and depression, which often cost them their fragile lives. The only way to rescue women from Xiaoqing's fate is to reform society's view on sex and sexual development (FXQ, 40). Now donning the hat of a socially engaged critic, Pan Guangdan advocates sex education, coed schooling, and open social intercourse between men and women as ways to pave the developmental path to normal, healthy heterosexuality (FXQ, 40–41).[11]

It becomes clear from this final message why it is necessary for Pan to psychoanalyze Xiaoqing and diagnose her as a neurotic (read a sufferer, a victim). Pan decidedly does not see himself as the latest admirer, following a long lineage of men of feeling, to add more grist to the mill of the Xiaoqing lore. He considers those gushy literati paying poetic tribute to Xiaoqing as merely motivated by rudimentary sympathy for her sufferings, not by genuine understanding of her psychological condition. Perusing the abundant homilies dedicated to her memory, he finds only idle speculations and total misapprehensions (FXQ, 39–40). Pan's antipathy toward what might be considered as

六八五 · 小青

女才子

小青

Figure 5.1. Xiaoqing at lakeside. Illustration from the *Book of Talented Women* (reprinted in *Zhongguo gudian wenxue banhua xuanji*, vol. 1, ed. Fu Xihua; Shanghai: Shanghai renmin meishu chubanshe, 1981).

Figure 5.2. Xiaoqing in front of the mirror. Illustration by Wen Yiduo for the first edition of Pan Guangdan's *An Analysis of Xiaoqing* (Shanghai: Xinyue shudian, 1927).

a countercultural construction of Xiaoqing as a woman of feeling is somewhat puzzling. The explanation, in my view, needs to be sought in the momentous epistemic shift that I have spoken of earlier. It must have appeared to Pan that the sentimental homilies have a way of clinging to a moral/spiritual language and never getting at the roots of the problem, which for a psychoanalytically inclined mind invariably lie in sexuality. Pan's dissatisfaction with the fatuous literati thus has less to do with his impatience with sentimentalism than with his intolerance for a human ontology that does not locate the truth of the individual in sexuality. The contrast between the older iconography associated with the Xiaoqing lore and the drawing that appears in the 1927 edition of Pan's book sheds light on this disjunction in historical epistemology (Figures 5.1 and 5.2).

In traditional Chinese painting, the human figure is merged into the landscape in such a way that it constitutes no separate locus of meaning apart from the ontic universe. This holds true for portraits as well as for landscape paintings. For example, in Figure 5.1, the portrait of Xiaoqing seeks to express the harmony between human and nature by blending the flowing folds of the robe into the texture of the adjacent rock. The art historian John Hay (1994) has argued that the body in traditional Chinese narrative and pictorial arts is a body dispersed in metaphors of nature, in folds of drapery, and in the texture of topographical surroundings. Note that Xiaoqing is fully clothed, and her bodily contours are also blended into those of her garments. Loneliness and melancholy are conveyed in the forlorn figure she cuts among a tree, a rock, some reeds, and a vast lake—pictorial metaphors that echo the resonances between humans and the cosmos. Yet there is nothing in the picture that might induce the viewer to speculate about her inner turbulence—note that the picture does not even show us her reflection in the water which might then form a circuit of gaze and thereby call attention to her emotional and psychological state.

In contrast, the drawing by Wen Yiduo (1899–1946)[12] aims to achieve precisely this effect (Figure 5.2). Here, contrary to the biographical assertions about her fastidiousness, Xiaoqing appears disheveled and despondent, sitting in front of a mirror with her robe hanging loosely and one shoulder exposed. She is gazing intently at her reflection with two fingers suggestively touching her lower lip. This emphasis of the face—refracted and redoubled by the mirror—calls to mind Arnold Davidson's argument that the modern iconographical representation of sexuality tends to concentrate on the face and/or the upper body as the expressive locus of psychologically defined personality (Davidson 1987, 27). Whereas the dispersed body in the older iconography of Xiaoqing is a body expressed *through* clothing and the ambiance, the "objective body" in Wen Yiduo's illustration is a body revealed *from* clothing, a body that seeks to assert its sexual truth from underneath the concealing artifice of society, a body that invites us to play the part of voyeur by turning its back to us only to allow us a tantalizing glimpse. The facial and bodily details can serve no other purpose than to call attention to her sexuality, her obstructed stream of libido, and her pathological narcissism. Moreover, the contrast of darkness and light not only creates the illusion of spatial and psychological depths, but also conjures the tragic struggle between individual desire and an oppressive social order.

If the first reason behind Pan's dissatisfaction with the myth of Xiaoqing is an epistemological one, then the second reason must be sought in the political nature of Pan's psychoanalytic project: to discredit the traditional social order by exposing its oppression of women. The cult of *qing* appropriates Xiaoqing in its effort to enshrine love as a hypergood. But in doing so, it also glorifies female sacrifice and elevates the beautiful but ill-fated woman of feeling to an exalted subject position without fundamentally questioning the Confucian gender system. The woman of feeling becomes a new kind of female deity that supplements rather than undermines the male-dominated pantheon of power. As a May Fourth intellectual whose rebellion against tradition usually begins with an attack on its treatment of women, Pan cannot allow that there be any viable subject position for women within the Confucian order. Hence his project to demystify Xiaoqing the goddess of love, to restore her human vulnerability, and to unveil her deep psychic sufferings beneath the glittering halo thrust upon her by a hypocritical society. Pan wishes to show that with regard to women, there is no possibility of unfettered humanity in traditional China.

THE SHREW REHABILITATED

Pan Guangdan's study seeks to deflate an exalted icon of "traditional" culture. The embedded question in his project is this: if extraordinary women patronized by literati and hallowed as romantic heroines turn out to be victims of psychopathological disorders, how much worse must ordinary women have had it? Bleak images of the latter abound in May Fourth literature: Lu Xun's

"The New Year's Sacrifice" and Rou Shi's "A Slave-Mother" come immediately to mind. Though there is little doubt that Confucian patriarchy is the institutional source of women's oppression, in stories like "The New Year's Sacrifice," there is also the disturbing presence of elderly women who ally themselves with patriarchy and in fact act as the chief enforcers of its regulative code and executors of its punitive laws. The figure of the mother or mother-in-law in May Fourth texts are often starkly negative and unredeemable. A Six Dynasties narrative ballad that tells of a willful mother-in-law who forces her son to divorce his wife is thus duly appreciated by May Fourth radicals as a folk indictment of parental authoritarianism in the old family system and repeatedly put on stage by the practitioners of the modern spoken drama.

The ballad in question is *Kongque dongnan fei* (Southeast flies the peacock, third century CE).[13] The longest narrative poem in traditional China, it relates the foreshortened marriage between Jiao Zhongqing, the magistrate of Lujiang prefecture, and Liu Lanzhi, daughter of a gentry family. Zhongqing and Lanzhi are properly married and a loving, companionate couple. Zhongqing's widowed mother, Mother Jiao (*Jiaomu*), however, conceives a dislike for Lanzhi and is bent on sending her packing. The ballad opens in the voice of Lanzhi protesting to Zhongqing of her innocence and her dutifulness in serving the Jiao family. Zhongqing pleads on her behalf to his mother, adding that he would never marry another woman, which only infuriates the old lady. After returning to her natal family, Lanzhi is pressured by her brother to remarry, and in desperation, she drowns herself. Learning of Lanzhi's death, the grief-stricken Zhongqing hangs himself, fulfilling the pact they have made in secret.

The ballad is remarkable for its representation of conjugal attachment in the face of the kinship system's cruel indifference to personal feelings. The subtlety with which it captures the emotional upheavals that rile the star-crossed couple is unsurpassed in medieval narratives. For example, knowing that he cannot contest Mother Jiao's authority, Zhongqing asks Lanzhi to return to her natal family temporarily and promises to go fetch her in no time. Lanzhi replies by enumerating her belongings and lamenting that they make a meager present to his next bride—her sense of mistrust and anguish is all the more palpable for not being named. In their secret tête-à-tête after Lanzhi has consented, to appease her family, to marry a country squire, Zhongqing congratulates her on her good fortune in a sarcastic tone that so needles Lanzhi that she promptly proposes a double suicide to honor their love. For these reasons, the appeal of the ballad to the May Fourth sensibility is quite apparent. Not only does the fetching portrayal of the couple speak to the May Fourth valorization of conjugal love, but the hardly justified action of the mother-in-law and its tragic consequence bring to the fore what the May Fourth generation loathe the most about the traditional family: the older generation's wanton exercise of power and authority and the depredation of the young (and female) as servile and expendable appendages. Small wonder that most stage adaptations of this ballad emphasize Mother Jiao's villainous role in destroying the young couple's conjugal happiness. In place of the ballad's rueful but more or less neutral tone, the modern plays exult in the struggle between good and evil, flattening out such ambiguous characters as Lanzhi's mother, who on two occasions turns importuning matchmakers away, to Lanzhi's relief. Thanks indeed to such renditions, *Jiaomu* is still a moniker for wicked mothers-in-law to this day.

Yuan Changying,[14] however, went against the grain when she published her three-act play "Kongque dongnan fei" in 1929. Both Jingyuan Zhang and Elisabeth Eide have noted that Yuan reinterprets the ballad by justifying Mother Jiao's action through Freudian theory (Eide 1989; Zhang 1992, 79–81). In the preface to the play, Yuan explains how she came upon the Freudian interpretation:

> Of course, from ancient time on, mothers-in-law in China have had absolute authority over their daughters-in-law. Mother Jiao's dismissing of Lanzhi could be nothing more than an assertion of such authority. But such answers could not satisfy me. I knew that there were psychological factors in human relations. Mother Jiao's dislike of Lanzhi was natural from the psychological perspective. My own experience and my observation of others told me that the reason why female in-laws could not get along well with each other is jealousy. (Yuan Changying 1985; quoted in Zhang 1992, 80)

This insight came to Yuan suddenly upon waking from sleep, after she has been pondering the ballad for some time, unsure of how to commence her adaptation. As we make our way through this preface, we quite reasonably expect some momentous epiphany at the end. But instead we are given "jealousy" (*chicu*), an apparently bland and clichéd explanation for intrafamilial conflicts. But it would have been quite novel in the 1920s to filter familial relationships—a realm usually governed by ethical discourse—through the cold lens of psychology, with its personality types and (admittedly reductive) categories of interpersonal dynamics. The disarmingly simple notion of "jealousy" in fact indexes the transition of the family from a regime of alliance to a regime of affect and sexuality. Foucault tells us that the bourgeois family is the anchor of the modern apparatus of sexuality, functioning at once as the "obligatory locus of affects, feelings, love" and the "incestuous" site of sexuality (1990a, 108). In placing incest at the heart of sexuality, "as the principle of its formation and the key to its intelligibility," psychoanalysis guarantees that "one would find the parents-children relationship at the root of everyone's sexuality" (113). The oedipal idea that the relationship between a mother and son could be sexual rather than ethical (or chastely sentimental) could well have been a Copernican revolution in the domestic realm.

Yuan's play concentrates its psychological insights on the mother-son relationship while treating the conjugal relationship in the standard idiom of May Fourth romanticism. As the play opens, we are immediately plunged into the queasy intimacy between Mother Jiao and Zhongqing, who is sick in bed; we have every reason to believe that his illness is in large part brought about by Mother Jiao's obsessive attention. Mother Jiao simultaneously infantilizes Zhongqing (as when she lovingly chides him for being "naughty") and sexualizes him (by stroking his luxuriant mane), transferring all her unfulfilled desires and longings onto him. Feeling suffocated by her love, Zhongqing intimates his desire to leave her side, only to invite an outburst of impassioned protests. In the end, she grudgingly consents to taking in a bride for him because it is recommended as the only way to contravene his lingering illness (*chongxi*). The youthful attraction and growing bond between Zhongqing and Lanzhi eat deeply into Mother Jiao, and she strikes back by ordering Lanzhi's divorce.

In the original ballad, Mother Jiao invokes Lanzhi's sloth and lack of decorum as reasons for her dismissal while in the same breath promising to seek the hand of a neighbor's daughter for Zhongqing. She comes off as imperious and unsympathetic, but there is no suggestion that she feels threatened by her daughter-in-law as a rival for Zhongqing's affection. In Chapter 1, we discussed the discursive silence on the conjugal relation in Confucian sentimentality. Mother Jiao's inclemency in the ballad can very well be read as a punitive response to an emotional reality that is illegitimate and without a proper name. The couple's devotion to each other has transgressed a boundary that is not explicitly drawn, and therefore their punishment can only be meted out with an alibi, as it were.

In Yuan's play, Mother Jiao torments Lanzhi with a monomaniacal fixation that can only be explained by Lanzhi's presence in the family as an alternative center of emotional gravity, not by any (imaginary) acts of ritual impropriety or disobedience. The last straw comes in the middle of act 2. Zhongqing, upon returning home from official duty, heads straight to his wife's apartment and is seen hugging, kissing, and comforting an aggrieved Lanzhi by servants. The intimate details create a sexual undercurrent insinuating that Mother Jiao's sense of injury goes far deeper than the recognition of a breach of decorum— Zhongqing should have paid her a visit first. It is a feeling of sexual defeat and loss that devastates her very core of being. Granny, the elderly neighbor woman who, according to Eide, plays the role of a Greek chorus, explains Mother Jiao's psychology to Zhongqing's teenage sister: "It's too embarrassing to spell it all out. . . . We widows pour all our affections on our children and they become our spiritual lovers [jingshen shang de qingren]. . . . Then our lonely hearts are pushed out of our sons' affections by their wives and there is no place for us to turn. Young widows have it the worst" (Yuan Changying 1985, 30). The sister observes that Granny's words are unpleasant but to the point: "Mother loves brother indeed a bit too excessively" (30). This exchange is of course intended for the readers, lest they fail to grasp the psychological argument of the play: Under the sway of universal psychological law, Mother Jiao cannot be held responsible for what she cannot help but do; her action is compelled by an inner force that instinctively defends its own interests. In going along with this inner compulsion, Mother Jiao, truculent as she may be, is merely being true to her nature. Refusing to swallow her defeat and humiliation and refusing to go on with the hypocritical life of virtuous widowhood, she strikes back:

> Gods of Heaven and Earth! You allot us mothers every hardship. We suffer and we endure, yet what is our reward? The reward is that our sons get snatched from our bosoms and delivered into somebody else's! Is this fair? If there is even a little justice on Earth, why aren't we allowed to keep this one speck of happiness that we eke out of all our pain? And if your laws and commands really are so unfair, why shouldn't the mothers of this world revolt? I . . . I dare to be a rebel against Heaven! (Yuan Changying 1985, 22; translation adapted from Dooling and Torgeson 1998, 232)

In portraying Mother Jiao as a victim *and* a rebel, Yuan Changying introduces a feminist reading of the ballad that is largely absent in contemporaneous adaptations that focus on the intergenerational conflict. For Yuan, repressive mothers and mothers-in-law may be a product of their ascension to positions of power and authority, but this does not lift them out of their victim status or alleviate their misery. In particular, the proscription against widow remarriage results in tortured psyche and deformed sexuality, which women are expected to endure alone and in utter silence. In acting out her incestuous desire, Mother Jiao rebels against the code of silence. She thus joins the company of disreputable women from Chinese mytho-history who are granted agency, subjecthood, and dignity in their twentieth-century reincarnations by way of a voice that was denied them in the past. Yomi Braester makes this point with regard to Ouyang Yuqian's (1889–1962) theatrical adaptation of the story of Pan Jinlian—an infamous adulteress who poisons her husband and is then brutally killed by her brother-in-law Wu Song. In *The Water Margin*, Pan's confession is omitted through indirect speech. In Ouyang's version, she is given her own voice and allowed to turn her confession of crime (of loving Wu Song as well as murdering her husband) into both a climax of erotic gratification and a *j'accuse* against patriarchy (Braester 2003, 60–61).

In a way, Ouyang's task is easier than that of Yuan. His Freudian rendition of Pan Jinlian gives us a love-crazed woman who merges Eros and Thanatos and who defiantly acts out her desire under a falling blade. As she meets her violent death, the fact that she has victimized someone else would have receded quietly to the background because *her* victim is a man whom she does not love, but to whom she is forced to provide wifely services for a lifetime. Pan has become a stereotypical heroine who dies for liberty and love. Mother Jiao, however, forces us to grapple much harder with the human cost of her rebellion: in pursuing an unrequited love, she ruthlessly snuffs out the budding conjugal happiness of a young couple (who, in the May Fourth ethical universe, have certain legitimacy and rights that Pan Jinlian's husband does not). For Yuan, patriarchy's crime against women is therefore twofold: it not only wrecks countless women's lives by depriving them of emotional and erotic fulfillment, but it also turns them into self-destructive persecutors of those weaker and more vulnerable than themselves.

In this light, Freudian theory seems to serve well Yuan's feminist critique. Eide considers the play one of the first self-consciously feminist appropriations of Freudian themes in Chinese: "To show that the Confucian society was repressive was nothing new in the May Fourth period, but . . . to interpret female frustration as a perversion of natural desires was less common" (1989, 69). She regards Yuan's effort less than successful on stylistic grounds. The gestures are overly dramatic, and the descent "into Freudian subconsciousness quickly deteriorates to rhetorical declamations superimposed on the theme [of women's plight in traditional China]" (70). But perhaps there is more to the apparent mismatch than artistic ineptitude. Yuan is said to be fastidious in keeping the play faithful to the ballad, especially in the areas of setting, costume, and speech pattern. Thus as far as she is concerned, the Freudian element is not "superimposed" onto the play as something alien that may or may not mesh with the original text; rather, it represents universal reason that helps unearth the unspoken and unspeakable truth in a tale of desire and repression.[15] With the aid of Freudian theory, she rehabilitates Mother Jiao by revealing who she really is: a widow who transfers her libidinal energies onto her son because society allows her no other outlets.

But the moment of truth also discloses the limits of the Freudian interpretation: It reduces the mother-son bond to a matter of physiological instincts. The anthropologist Margery Wolf proposes the notion of the "uterine family" to understand the close bond between mothers and sons in traditional Chinese families (1972). As an essential outsider in the virilocal, exogamous marriage system, a daughter-in-law's best hope for integration into her marital family is in bearing sons whose role in continuing the patriline helps secure a stable subject position for the mother. Mothers therefore have more than a psychosexual need to cultivate close ties with their sons, but not with their daughters. Destined to be married out, daughters are at a structural, rather than erotic, disadvantage in winning their mothers' affections. Psychoanalysis, however, would have us accept the uterine family simply because the mother-son relationship can be conveniently mapped onto an oedipal heterosexual typography. It therefore precludes social analysis and blinds us to the structural determinations of women's oppression. Instead, we are led to suppose that had Mother Jiao been able to remarry after the untimely death of her husband, she would not have had to resort to the perversity of taking her son for a substitute lover. Marriage, it seems, is the magical cure for women's psychosexual disorders. But Nora would certainly beg to differ.

THE BUTCHER DISSECTED

The two cases already discussed represent the typical early use of psychoanalytic theory in China, which, as Jingyuan Zhang has pointed out, was mostly limited to psychobiographical investigations of authors and characters. But

despite the reductive crudeness of these investigations, psychoanalysis stimulated a new understanding of the human subject as a "process of reconstruction" rather than a static, unitary presence (1992, 147, 152). The modern
(sexual) subject it helped to invent was immediately subject to modernist
experiment. Indeed, The use of psychoanalysis in biographical or critical
studies was a minor phenomenon compared with the extensive invocation of
psychoanalytic concepts and principles in modernist fiction. The leading
modernist writer Shi Zhecun, for example, is known for the explicitly and
self-consciously psychoanalytic quality of his fiction, which has been much
commented on (and admired) by his fellow writers (see, for example, Su
Xuelin 1983) and which has also invited much conscientiously psychoanalytic criticism from contemporary scholars (Jones 1994; Lee 1999; Shih
2001; Zhang 1992).

In 1932, Shi Zhecun published a short story entitled "Shi Xiu" in *Xiaoshuo
yuebao* (Short story monthly). It turns an infamous episode of sex and violence
from the fourteenth-century picaresque novel *The Water Margin* into a modern psychological story. As such it lends itself extremely well to the critical
exercise of identifying key Freudian themes and fleshing out the characters'
psychological makeup and textual/sexual symbolisms. But if Pan Guangdan
and Yuan Changying have a feminist agenda to pursue in their diagnostic rewritings, what is Shi's purpose in stitching together a Freudian narrative out
of a disturbing old tale? At the most immediate level, it is a diagnostic/thera-
peutic effort that attempts to account for the seemingly gratuitous violence in
the original tale through a narrative talking through. In the process, the
moral framework that underpins the original tale is replaced with a new
framework that speaks to modernism's fascination with the sexual subject. To
show how psychoanalysis enables this process of displacement, we begin with
a closer look at the original story with an eye to its twentieth-century Freudian metamorphosis—a task slighted by critics who are more drawn to the
"modernity" of Shi Zhecun's fiction.

In *The Water Margin*, over a hundred men from all walks of life who are on
the run from the law gather on Mount Liang to form a robber band. They organize themselves by the code of sworn brotherhood and lead a riotous life
replete with convivial bacchanalias, raids on the rich, and skirmishes with
imperial troops until finally making peace with the state. The brotherhood
is mythologized as what Victor Turner calls "communitas," in which the
norms that govern institutionalized social relationships are abrogated and in

which the boisterous outlaws fashion "an alternative and more 'liberated' way of being socially human" (1982, 51). They usually begin as decent, upright fellows (if a bit headstrong) who are fond of liquor and the martial arts. Their run-ins with the law are usually the result of their trying, perhaps too rashly, to right a wrong or defend themselves against evildoers. A common pattern features the righteous slaying of an adulterous woman, which leaves the hero only one recourse: fleeing to Mount Liang to escape prosecution.

In deploying misogyny as a plot device, the novel reproduces the patriarchal exclusion and denigration of women. Under patriarchy, men negotiate their relationship to one another through the negated currency of women's reproductive capacity (the "traffic in women"), and in some circumstances, they forge fraternal bonds over the dead bodies of ritually sacrificed women. Sworn brotherhood is a particularly virulent form of fraternal organization in that fictive kinship is particularly dependent on the sacrificial logic. Anthropologists have argued that ritual sacrifice allows men to overcome the fatal flaw of their having being born of women, to relate to one another as members of an indivisible and enduring body social, and to orchestrate their own symbolic rebirth as producers of a sacred social order that transcends the finality and contingency of biological reproduction (Block and Parry 1982; Jay 1992).

The sacrificial victim need not necessarily be a woman, but more often than not, it is. Song Geng provides abundant examples from *The Romance of the Three Kingdoms* and *The Water Margin* in which men extravagantly demonstrate the priority of the male bond above familial ties. Liu Bei, for example, comforts his lieutenant and blood brother Zhang Fei after the loss of a city together with Liu's wives and children with the following line: "Brothers are like arms and legs; wives and children are merely garments. You may mend your torn dress, but who can re-attach a lost limb?" (quoted in Song 2004, 160) On the basis of examples such as this, Song argues that "the male-male bond does not need to use woman as the medium" because the homosocial discourse is fundamentally hostile toward women and heterosexuality (174). But women do not have to be a positive presence to be a medium of homosociality; rather, they serve to fortify the male bond precisely by their absence, or by their summary relegation to the private, the immanent, and the finite. In other words, men achieve transcendence by denying women access to the transcendental.

The story of Shi Xiu from *The Water Margin* well illustrates the centrality of sacrifice in the phantasm of a fraternal utopia. Shi Xiu enters the picture as a vagabond from a humble origin (he is the son of a butcher). Selling firewood on the street for a living, he perchance ingratiates himself to a town executioner named Yang Xiong by extricating the latter from a terrible scrape. The grateful Yang pledges brotherhood with Shi, brings him home, and sets him to work in his family butcher shop. In Yang's frequent absences on official duty, his wife Pan Qiaoyun contracts a liaison with a wayward monk, and their goings-on are carefully observed by Shi Xiu. Shi reports the affair to Yang, but Qiaoyun turns the tables on him by accusing him of impropriety. Shi is obliged to move out, but he is resolved to clear his name and to vindicate his "brother" Yang Xiong's shame of cuckoldry. He lays a trap for and murders the monk and his accomplice, shows their bloody garments to Yang as evidence, and councils the enraged Yang on how best to dispose of Qiaoyun and her conniving maid. The episode ends with the two men on a hill in a suburb, hacking the two hapless women to pieces and then taking off for Mount Liang.

Although the story devotes extensive narration to the secretive scheming and slow unfolding of the adulterous affair, its authorial sympathy is decidedly invested in the two "brothers." The language of brotherly loyalty suggests a strong homosocial bonding between the two heroes, particularly when a potential conflict is afoot, or when one swallows a wrongful accusation to avoid washing the other's dirty linen in public, or when one is looking out for the other's interest against his immediate feelings. For example, before Yang Xiong, goaded on by Shi Xiu, disembowels Qiaoyun, he solemnly pronounces her crime and punishment: "Harlot, you had me confused. I nearly fell for your lies. *You've sullied my brother's name* and you're sure to kill me if you get the chance. My best bet is to strike first. What kind of heart has a bitch like you? I want to see for myself!" (Shi Nai'an 1993, 747, emphasis added; hereafter cited as WM). It seems that Qiaoyun's worst crime is not so much adultery as her attempt to alienate the homosocial bond. For this "crime," she pays with her life in a gruesome execution: "[Yang Xiong] sliced her open from breast to belly, hauled out her organs, hung them on the tree, and cut her into seven parts" (WM, 747).

In the process of discovering the adulterous plot, Shi Xiu's affection for Yang Xiong grows in portion to his rising anger and repulsion over Qiaoyun's reckless indulgence in lust. The illicit affair is portrayed in a harshly condemnatory language. The lovers are said to be driven into brazen abandon by sheer concupiscence. The monk is referred to as a "scoundrel," a "rogue," or a "shaven-pate," and his murder by a righteous hero amounts to a verdict of monasticism as counterfeit manhood/brotherhood.[16] The tale of Shi Xiu and Yang Xiong constructs the fiction of brotherhood by narrating its genesis in acts of mutual care and assistance and its fortification in the ritual killings of saboteurs and counterfeiters. Through their shared participation in a forbidden act of violence, Shi and Yang affirm their parity (against their disparate social origins) and precipitate their rebirth as gallant heroes destined for the utopian space of Mount Liang. The novel's sacrificial logic—manifested in misogyny and anticlericalism—needs to be understood in relation to its endorsement of male homosociality and the honor ethic.

In traditional Chinese society, homosociality tended to encompass the erotic, social, economic, and political realms as a principle of forging solidarities beyond kinship. It is not necessarily the polar opposite of homosexuality, as it tends to be in contemporary western societies. Eve Kosofsky Sedgwick points out that even though "male bonding" is structurally predicated on intense homophobia in our society, in ancient Greek and tribal societies, there is usually a fluid continuum between "men-promoting-the-interests-of-men" and "men-loving-men" (1985, 5).[17] Although sodomy was intermittently prohibited in imperial penal codes, homoerotic practices were discreetly tolerated in both sexes within and without heterosexual institutions—so long as they did not upset the normative patterns of domination (Sommer 2000, 114–18). In its more militant expression as fictive brotherhood, homosociality takes on a defensive posture with regard to heterosexuality and spares no effort in building male honor and intimacy on a sacrificial logic. Although this defensive posture often results in brutal violence, it rarely assumes the form of sexual aggression—in marked contrast to the logic of male bonding structured along the heterosexual/homosexual dichotomy as operative in, for example, instances of fraternity gang rape on American university campuses.[18]

The homosocial continuum, however, becomes highly problematic with the essentialization and medicalization of sex in the early twentieth century.[19] Homosexuality and heterosexuality are now mutually exclusive identity categories, and homophobia becomes the underside of the discourse of normality. Male bonding still requires the present absence of a woman, but she is now the object of desire for the men and the spoil of male rivalry. Violence against women in this new framework must necessarily take on a sexual overtone, if it is not outright rape. With the woman posited as the (ostensible) telos of their contest, intimacy and mutual assistance between men are relieved of the homosexual suspicion. Once taken out of the framework of homosociality,

Qiaoyun's violent death in the hands of the two men appears utterly senseless —until it is placed within the interpretive framework of heterosexual rivalry. The rewriting of historical texts thus both creates such conundrums and renders them intelligible in the modern epistemological framework. Hence in Shi Zhecun's Freudian version, Shi Xiu becomes a robustly heterosexual man whose inhibitions turn him into a vindictive sadist-cum-voyeur.

The transmutation begins with the objectification of the female body from the perspective of a desiring male gaze. Recall that the body in traditional Chinese aesthetics is a body dispersed in natural metaphors, garment folds, and topographical texture. It is rarely an objective or revealed body in the mimetic tradition of western art. When a female character is introduced—and only if her appearance is of narrative significance as, say, in an erotic novel— an elaborate inventory of her physiological features, ornaments, and clothes may be given not in order to form a coherent image of the body-object, but as "items in the woman's native dowry" (Hay 1994, 56). It is therefore significant that in the novel Qiaoyun's appearance is never described, though one obtains the impression very quickly from her words and actions that she is a vivacious and resourceful woman who gets what she wants—for better or for worse.[20] Her features do not matter precisely because the episode does not turn on a heterosexual axis—the adultery implicates the heroes only in a negative way. Rather, the novel's homosocial orientation underscores the fact that Shi Xiu's features are more often commented on. For example, when Yang Xiong first presents Shi Xiu to his father-in-law, the latter is at once taken in by Shi's good looks and his being "a big, heroic type" (WM, 715). When Shi Xiu kowtows to Qiaoyun (who is his senior by rank) in the introduction scene, the narrative uses a familiar simile—"like pushing a gold mountain, like felling a jade pillar"—to accentuate his manly physique and fine features.

In Shi Zhecun's version, there is no mention of Shi Xiu's appearance and his corporeality is dematerialized into a voracious gaze under which Qiaoyun's body materializes into a shapely, avoirdupois object. The modern regime of seeing frames the reader's first encounter with her, as Shi Xiu lies wide awake in bed recalling her image to mind. The description begins in the classical style of dispersing the body in the accoutrements, but it quickly takes us behind her slightly slouched, diaphanous blouse to feel her milky white skin. Under the modern gaze, clothes reveal more than they conceal, and the reader is invited, with Shi Xiu, to see straight through them to the alluring somatic reality. Again as Shi Xiu lies in bed trying to sort out the flux of sensations and urges that have assailed him during his first day at the Yang residence, he fantasizes seeing Qiaoyun, in her breezy evening gown, cross a threshold with a lamp in her hand and, having dropped one of her embroidered slippers, try to hook it back on with her bare foot. "O yes, he saw this smooth, round, and exquisitely shapely foot reaching backward, her body leaning forward, her left hand holding the lamp, and her right hand extending out for balance—this delicate posture that irresistibly aroused his tender pity" (Shi Zhecun 1991, 174, hereafter SX). Here, Qiaoyun's body not only has a distinct shape but also obeys the laws of physics. It is an isolated body, unconnected to the natural ambiance or social context—note that the scene is set in the liminal space of fantastic darkness. Its exposed part—the bare foot—is exposed not for the purpose of advancing the plot, but is served up for fetishistic contemplation.[21]

Shi Xiu's intensely heterosexual desire and its perversion suffuse the Freudian story, to the exclusion of much that is central to the source text—the meeting and bonding of the two heroes, the running of the butcher shop, the unfolding of the adulterous affair, the misunderstanding and reconciliation between the two men, and their eventual escape to Mount Liang. Instead, the narrative begins with Shi Xiu's reflection on his past and present circumstances, stays with his psychological anguish and struggle, and ends with his pleasurable sensations at the sight of Qiaoyun's mangled body. As William Schaefer aptly puts it, Shi Zhecun's narrative follows "Shi Xiu's point of view so closely that the reader is almost suffocated in his thoughts and actions" (1998, 38). Andrew F. Jones also notes how Shi's narrator "usurps the voice and athletic prose" of the novel and overwhelms "islands of accurately rendered premodern vernacular dialogues" with lengthy and contemplative delineations of Shi Xiu's heterosexual desire (1994, 577).

Indeed, the fast-paced and action-packed narration of the novel is deliberately slowed down and streamlined in order to allow for the full psychological complexity of Shi Xiu's character to emerge. The Freudian narrative is fully absorbed with capturing the overt and covert workings of desire: its incandescent flames, its dark undercurrents, and its grotesque eruptions. The narrative repeatedly identifies Shi Xiu as a "passionate," "fiery," and "hardy" warrior, his breast aflame with passion and his mind teetering on the verge of insanity from the raging war of desire and morality. We witness him go from a timid young man hopelessly smitten by his sworn brother's voluptuous wife, to a bumbling, self-defeating seducer caught in "the magic net of angst and the scorching heat of desire" (SX, 187), to someone with a demonic obsession with desire itself that soon manifests itself in his fetishistic fascination with blood, and finally to a sadistic monster who orchestrates a grisly murder in order to taste voyeuristic ecstasy.

In order to seal Shi Xiu's heterosexual nature—against his image in the novel as a chaste and circumspect young man impervious to the charms of the fair sex—the author also invents a whole episode of Shi Xiu spending a night with a prostitute at a brothel. In this episode, the prostitute inadvertently cuts her finger while peeling an apple, and the oozing blood triggers Shi Xiu's sadistic fantasy. Then at the murder scene on the hill, as he contemplates Qiaoyun's "pinkish" dismembered limbs, Shi Xiu feels an intense sensation of joy; and seeing a flock of ravens descend upon the entrails hanging on a tree, he murmurs to himself: "it must be delicious" (SX, 209). With this disarmingly simple sentence, the story ends. The story has no more need to go on because the author has furnished, by way of psychoanalysis, an explanation for Shi Xiu's seemingly inexplicable urge to have Qiaoyun so violently eliminated: to wit, Shi Xiu is a sexual pervert and blood-fetishist who can only find gratification in a bloodbath, and whose perverse pleasure grows in direct proportion to the ghastliness of the killing.

In the novel, the double murder is explicitly recognized as a crime with legal consequences that the heroes must try to elude. In Shi Zhecun's version, the focus is shifted from the crime to criminality, particularly the psychological underpinnings of criminality. In casting violence as a way of fulfilling perverted heterosexual desire, Shi Zhecun diagnoses misogyny as a discrete psychological disorder—sadism, or sadistic neurotic obsession. Insofar as Shi Xiu does not himself perform the butchering but rather takes pleasure in the role of instigator-cum-witness, his sadism is overlaid with another psychopathological condition: voyeurism. Both sadism and voyeurism are well-identified forms of sexual "perversion" in psychoanalytic literature. The interest in perversion, in fact, was fundamental to the rise of sexuality insofar as (hetero)sexuality only became a normative truth regime when opposed to perversion as a threatening deviation. It follows that perversion as a medical construct could not be anterior to the invention of sexuality. Arnold I. Davidson shows how the notion of perversion before the nineteenth century bore no intrinsic connection to sexual desire, but was rather a moral/theological concept connoting any act of the human will that was contrary to God. Thus the noun *pervert* was the antonym to *convert*, referring to someone who was turned from good to evil (1987, 45–46).

Foucault tells us that it was the nineteenth-century discourse of sexuality that brought the pervert into being as a distinct kind of individual whose sexual pathologies told his essential truth and no part of whose being could be unaffected by this truth (1990a, 43). The pathologizing of criminality, therefore, boils down to the revelation of the dark sexual mysteries of the criminal as pervert. But in exposing Shi Xiu as a pervert, Shi Zhecun imposes the entire apparatus of modern sexuality onto a terrain where inner depths, layered consciousness, the divorce of sexual aim and sexual object, the disarticulation of sexuality from genitality, and so on are all alien ideas. Perversion as such is not left "blank," "hidden," or "submerged" in the novel, as some critics have argued, but simply does not belong in the novel's conceptual space. Perversion is transplanted there not as the missing piece of a puzzle, but as the building block of a new overarching framework to refigure that conceptual space. Andrew Jones makes a similar point in his reading of "Shi Xiu": "in forcing tradition to yield up its dirty psychic secrets, they [Shi Zhecun's rewritings of traditional tales] also stage the advent of a modern humanist epistemological regime in China" (1994, 594). My contention is that the rewritings inscribe onto tradition the "collective cultural unconscious" (594) that they purport to discover. The conflicts between the self and an array of sociocultural institutions such as religion, race, or the code of brotherhood, which supposedly structure the " cultural unconscious," are not anterior to the psychoanalytic intervention, but rather its effect, or symptom. In other words, tradition may well have its share of "dirty secrets," but what it "yields" under psychoanalytic interrogation is only the countertransferential symptoms of the analyst that encode the entire apparatus of modern sexual subjectivity. In this light, Shi Zhecun is pursuing a characteristically May Fourth critique of the Confucian tradition. A May Fourth critic would have no trouble reading this story as an indictment of a repressive social order that turns a bashful young man into a horrific criminal.[22]

But for a number of contemporary scholars, Shi Zhecun is also engaged in the modernist project of deconstructing the enlightenment model of the coherent and unified subject that has been arduously pursued by the modernizing intellectuals of the May Fourth generation and promoted by the nationalist ideology of the state. They often cite his nonfiction writings where he professes a keen interest in such psychological phenomena as "split personalities" (*erchong renge*) and "neurasthenia" (*shenjing shuairuo*). Shi Zhecun's fiction, likewise, portrays the "neurotic agitation" of the metropolitan personality with a sensitivity and finesse unrivaled by his contemporaries. As Schaefer (1998) has shown, Shi Zhecun employs a number of interwar modernist techniques and thematics to critique the ideology of sacrifice—be it racial nationalism or secret brotherhood—for its ritual exclusion of the alien, the impure, and the heterogeneous. The subject in Shi's fiction is not just ec-centric and under siege by uncanny intra- and extrapsychic forces, but also the battered product of the violent repression of the Other. Although at the narrative level Shi's texts largely rely on the technique of psychological realism, thematically and ideologically, they often rub against the grain of the dominant narratives of enlightenment and nationalism.[23] In particular, his choice to retell a disturbing episode from *The Water Margin* allows him to cast a jaundiced eye at the modernizing intellectuals' enthusiasm to recuperate the novel as an indigenous narrative of popular sovereignty and China's answer to *The Social Contract*.

But Shi Zhecun's modernist sensibilities seem to short-circuit when it comes to making psychological or emotional sense of male homosociality, a form of patrilineal solidarity that requires the sacrifice of sexualized women but does not define itself in the all-consuming terms of modern sexuality. In the novel, sex (or, rather, lust) is an element of impurity—standing for biological contingency and finality—that has to be purged from the fraternal order in order to guarantee the latter's integrity and permanence. Indeed, the monk's pursuit of lust renders the monastic fraternity inauthentic and himself a filthy scoundrel who deserves to be violently ejected from the company of men. The two heroes, by contrast, are stoically invulnerable to Qiaoyun's charms and end up eliminating her in order to cleanse the pollution that her desires and wiles have cast over their manly covenant. Once Shi Zhecun brings (hetero)sexuality to bear on the episode as both the theme and its interpretation, the homosocial imperative is merely redolent of latent homosexuality and can no longer be linked in any meaningful way to the killing of the adulterous woman.

It is most probably for this reason that Shi Zhecun excises some of the lines in which the two heroes express admiration, concern, or loyalty to each other, though he keeps their affectionate term of address—"brother"—intact. He deletes, for example, the line uttered by Yang Xiong immediately before he executes Qiaoyun, "You've sullied my brother's name." At the same time, he makes Shi Xiu express contempt for the inept and short-fused Yang Xiong. More than once, Shi Xiu laments the fact that so fetchingly beautiful a woman as Qiaoyun should have to make do with a flabby, sallow-skinned fellow with sparse eyebrows and tattoos on the arms (SX, 172–73).[24] When he tries to remind himself of his indebtedness to Yang Xiong and to recognize the latter as a magnanimous gallant, Qiaoyun's image immediately rushes in, crowding out any generous thoughts of Yang he might be entertaining. For most of the story, Shi Xiu is simply too consumed with his desire and obsession to think much about his benefactor, let alone have tender feelings for him. When he finally convinces Yang Xiong of the affair and helps him plot the murder, he is shown to be consciously manipulating the simple-minded Yang Xiong while calling him, sotto voce, "a good-for-nothing," "a stupid boor" (SX, 203). The omission of the two men's journey to Mount Liang at the end also precludes the possibility of a homosocial happily-ever-after.

Thus, while Shi Zhecun's story indicts the novel's violence against women by "adulterating" its voice and by "revealing" what is hidden beneath the code of brotherly righteousness (Schaefer 1998, 61), the rewriting also exerts a kind of violence in rendering the patrilineal mode of sociality an epistemological impossibility and thereby undermining its own critique of the sacrificial logic. The reduction of masculinity to normative heterosexuality also reinforces a gender essentialism that defines gender exclusively in terms of binary and teleological sexuality. In retelling a tale of desire and violence in which women are the sexual objects-cum-victims of perverted men, Shi Zhecun also reductively attributes women's oppression to a puritanism that supposedly vitiates men's psychosexual well-being. As a corollary, he seems to agree with Yuan Changying that normal heterosexual relationships with saner and gentler men, wrought by the insights of psychoanalysis, are women's best hope for liberation.

● ● ●

My object in this chapter has primarily been to explore the May Fourth mobilization of the repressive hypothesis and the mechanisms and implications of psychoanalyzing premodern texts. I do so in the light of Foucault's critique of psychoanalysis and the repressive hypothesis. The primary target of Foucault's critique, as is well known, is the effects of power produced by psychoanalysis, especially in consolidating the bourgeois nuclear family as a regime of sexuality. He reserves his harshest criticism for what he calls "Freudo-Marxists" who celebrate libido as the unproblematic force of liberation and who operate on the repressive hypothesis that presupposes the mutual exclusion of power and pleasure. Much of his criticism is equally valid with regard to the May Fourth discourse of truth and emancipation. But if Foucault has taught us anything, it is that resistance need not be exclusively sought in the psyche, the unconscious, the drive, or in "forms of sexual pleasure which are pushed to the sidelines of the norm" (Jacqueline Rose, quoted in Butler 1997, 97).

In all three case studies presented in this chapter, psychoanalysis plays a double role. As a modern liberatory discourse that pits pleasure against power, it is fervently embraced by modernizing and modernist intellectuals alike for its emancipatory promises. In psychoanalyzing early texts, they mobilize the repressive hypothesis to critique the Confucian moral order and promote enlightenment humanist ethics and epistemology. From the narcissistic poetess to the incestuous mother and to the sadistic butcher and his prey, all are victims of a cannibalistic tradition. But in identifying repressed heterosexual desire as "a single locus of Revolt" (Foucault's phrase), psychoanalysis reductively inscribes the modern subject in the power regime of the family—the locus of affect as well as heteronormativity and reproductive rationality. Moreover, psychoanalytically framed resistance cannot evade the fatal flaw of collapsing psyche and culture as a homogenous process governed by the principles of transference and displacement (Meltzer 1987, 215). The May Fourth emancipatory project thus comes to rest on the facile procedure of exposing one thing as being really something else: Xiaoqing's melancholy poetry is symptomatic of her narcissistic neurosis; Mother Jiao's intolerance of her daughter-in-law stems from her sexual jealousy; and Shi Xiu's misogyny is really a displacement of his obsessional neurosis. Instead of freeing the (sexual) truth from textual obfuscation, psychoanalytic criticism inflicts a violence of interpretation that obscures the political and social determinations of oppression and victimization.[25]

The psychoanalytic critics and authors in our case studies proceed unswervingly along the subject-desire-truth axis. They condemn traditional society as ignorant (no knowledge of the unconscious) and repressed (in the juridical sense of the word), pity women for having to bear the brunt of ignorance and repression, and use psychoanalysis to "clear the way for sex by telling what was hidden" (Baudrillard 1987, 28).[26] They denounce the traditional extended family and fictive brotherhood as not only misogynist but fundamentally antisexuality and antiscience. But the desire they seek to liberate/proliferate is eminently yoked to a normative heterosexual paradigm. The modern sexual subject they conjure up is one that locates its personal truth in its heterosexuality and that pursues liberatory politics in the oedipal family by submitting to the laws of sexual hygiene, reproductive sciences, and bourgeois gender ideology. In condemning older, moral modes of organizing sex and pleasure simply as repressive, they preclude recognition of their own situatedness in the apparatus of power and obviate a critique of gender oppression not grounded in sexuality.

PART THREE

The Revolutionary Structure of Feeling

The Problem of National Sympathy

As the enlightenment structure of feeling brought the romantic and psycho-analytic definitions of love into the discourse of the everyday, it also presupposed a third, nationalist definition that both underwrote and undermined the ideals of free love and liberated sexuality. It is fitting, then, to return to the May Fourth period as we seek to understand how the discourse of love could have accommodated two apparently contradictory ideologies: nationalism and individualism. It has been commonly recognized that nationalism and individualism were inseparable in May Fourth thought. Indeed, nationalism was the strongest ally of May Fourth rebels in their struggle against the patriarchal family and in their quest for free love. The new discourse of national character that it authorized did much to delegitimize Confucian ideology by disclosing traditional society for "what it was": a realm devoid of human feelings and solidarities. In Part 3, I turn my attention first to the critique of tradition within the problematic of a nationalist regime of feeling, or national sympathy, and then to the negotiations of the personal and political, and the recrudescence of heroism in revolutionary discourses.

In this chapter, I take up the intersection of nationalism and love from the vantage point of the discourse of national character centering on the question of sympathy. In the first section, I set up the discursive context by reading two instances of the global discourse of national character—one missionary and one colonial—that establish sympathy as a crucial signifier of nationhood. But my focus here is the founding father of modern Chinese literature, Lu Xun, whose profound reflections on the subject of love and sympathy have not been rigorously explored, the immense scholarship already dedicated to him notwithstanding. Through a rereading of the "Preface to *Call to Arms*," "Medicine," and "The True Story of Ah Q," I argue that modern Chinese literature was born as a discourse of lack that portrayed grassroots society as unfeeling and that envisioned the mission of literature as a sentimental project—to make Chinese feel for and identify with one another as conationals by replacing kinship and locality-based identities with universal, sentiment-based identities. In the second part of this chapter, I examine specific May Fourth criticisms contending that the Chinese were incapable of genuine love because the Chinese family fostered hypocrisy. Treating *hypocrisy* as a keyword of the May Fourth discourse of love, I aim to understand the ways in which the obsession with unmasking the "pseudo-moralist" contributed to the sentimental reconstruction of self and nation. In the final section, I demonstrate the hegemonic effect of the discourse of national sympathy through a symptomatic reading of Yu Dafu's short story "Sinking" as a narrative of failed sociability.

SYMPATHY AND NATIONAL CHARACTER

Let us recall Liu Tieyun's remarks on weeping cited in the Introduction. Liu makes the startling assertion that a person's moral worth should be measured by his or her capacity to weep rather than by the degree to which he or she fulfills socially prescribed duties and obligations. As I have suggested, what Liu is proposing is a new way of imagining the individual self and his or her relationship to a larger community. Tears are the sign of a spiritual nature, an interiority, a subjectivity. Liu wants to have us believe that if we can weep for ourselves and our kin, we can extend this ability to feel others' pain and misery and shed tears across the barriers of class, race, and religion. The ability to transcend social boundaries is indeed the most recognizable requirement of Enlightenment humanism. Still, Liu is operating within the framework of the Confucian structure of feeling, given his desire to construct a continuous chain of affinities from the individual person to the universe without excluding the intermediate realms and without positing the inevitability of conflict. The epistemic break of the May Fourth, however, introduces the dialectic of individualism and universalism. The individual is defined as an autonomous being with reference not to a skein of overlapping social groups, but to a universal realm—humanity—whereby the only legitimate boundaries belong to the nation-state. Feeling is now an experiential index to a person's membership in common humanity, rather than in any particularistic group smaller than a nation. The individual's sentimental experience is always already, in the words of David Denby, "informed by and contributing to universal categories" (1994, 241). Conversely, universalism requires that the individual shed all concrete forms of identification and become a wholly unattached, atomized being. The truly universal is also the most visceral and most immediate, that which can be shared, without mediation, by an infinitude of individuals. Arguing that the sentimental dialectic of the individual and the universal is the structuring grammar of the narratives of the French Revolution, David Denby writes:

> Individual and universal are the twin poles of meaning in the sentimental text: in *this* weeping child, *this* grieving mother, *this* father repenting his cruelty to his daughter, we are encouraged to read the sufferings of *humanity* as a whole, just as the individual act of generosity towards the victim figures the universal virtues of *bienfaisance* and *sensibilité*. Moreover, the reaction of an observer to the sufferings of the individual victim functions as a sign, an indication, a proof of the existence of that universal category, for it is humanity, sensibility which are perceived as the bridge between the two individuals; they are the condition of a humane social order. [Sensibility] is that which makes them universally generalizable, the essential and irreducible humanity of each individual, whatever his or her social position, being the guarantee of this infinite mirroring and extension. (1994, 140)

The universalist ideal of Enlightenment humanism is frequently debunked and revealed to be a fragile illusion barely masking the fault lines of gender, class, and race. Richard Rorty, for example, strongly objects to the notion of "human race" as the ultimate and most exalted basis for forging human solidarity. Still, he concedes that universalistic abstractions such as the Christian notion of "child of God," the Enlightenment notion of "humanity," and the Kantian notion of "rational being" have played a crucial role in history by keeping the way "open for political and cultural change by providing a fuzzy but inspiring *locus imaginarius* (e.g., *absolute* truth, *pure* art, humanity *as such*)" (1989, 195). One arena in which fuzzy but inspiring abstractions like "humanity" have been indispensable is the imagining of the national community, which, despite its boundedness, enlists the service of Enlightenment humanism to aid the battle against its rivals: families, clans, native places, and so on. Because of its predilection to operate in universalistic terms (what others have called its transnational impulses), nationalism arrogates to itself a superior status over older forms of community and effectively masks new forms of conflict and oppression engendered by its not-so-universalist policies and practices. It replaces existing blood- and territory-based principles of identity with the infinitely individualizable and universalizable principle of sentiment. Indeed, the notion of common humanity is precisely what informs the early twentieth-century discourse of national character, wherein the alleged inability to identify or sympathize with "man" as such is taken to be a fatal flaw in the national character and an indication of failed nationhood.

Arthur Smith, an American missionary and author of *Chinese Characteristics* (1894), devotes a lengthy chapter to the problem of the "absence of sympathy" as one among the manifold moral and cultural defects of "the Chinese people." He enumerates the many instances of the Chinese indifference to the suffering of fellow creatures and their cruel treatment of the weak and the helpless, be they strangers, cripples, paupers, sick people, women, children, or prisoners. Defining sympathy as "fellow-feeling," he argues that although the Chinese do practice a certain amount of benevolence (defined as "well-wishing"), they are "conspicuous for a deficiency of sympathy" (1894, 194, hereafter cited as CC). He attributes this to the dire poverty in which the masses of the Chinese people are mired and which has the effect of inuring them to the "most pitiable exhibitions of suffering of every conceivable variety" (CC, 195). The upshot is that there is a constant "social war" waged between the strong and the weak, the rich and the poor, the privileged and the deprived. Given this deplorable state of affairs, Smith prognosticates that the blighted empire needs a large dose of "human sympathy" more than it does weaponry, industry, or technology:

> China has many needs, among which her leading statesmen place armies, navies, arsenals. To her foreign wellwishers it is plain that she needs a currency, railways, and scientific instruction. But does not a deeper diagnosis of the conditions of the Empire indicate that one of her profoundest needs is more

human sympathy? She needs to feel with childhood that sympathy which for eighteen centuries has been one of the choicest possessions of races and peoples which once knew it not. She needs to feel sympathy for wives and for mothers, a sympathy which eighteen centuries have done so much to develop and to deepen. She needs to feel sympathy for man as man, to learn that quality of mercy which . . . Christianity has cultivated until it has become the fairest plant that ever bloomed upon the earth. (CC, 215–16)

The idea of sympathy as the fundamental criterion of humanity can be traced to Rousseau, whose concept of pity inaugurated the most basic tenet of Enlightenment humanism—the universal identity and parity of "men." The sympathy one person feels for another in spite of the differences that separate them is taken to be the most telling proof of common humanity; or, as Denby (1994) puts it, it is what makes human beings universally generalizable. That sympathy transcends the primordial bonds of blood and proximity becomes a privileged trope in articulating the difference between civilization and barbarity, between humanity and subhumanity, and between universalism and particularism. Rousseau maintains that a man is in his most primitive state if he is without the ability to perceive resemblances, to understand what he shares in common with another who is not his kin, and to pity others by the transport of imagination and identification:

> Apply these ideas [of common humanity] to the first men, and you will see the reason for their barbarousness. Never having seen anything but what was around them, they did not know even that; they did not know themselves. They had the idea of a father, of a son, of a brother, but not of a man. Their cabin held all their fellows; a stranger, a beast, a monster, were the same thing for them: outside of themselves and their family, the entire universe was nothing to them. (1998, 306)

Smith's exhortation of the Chinese to "feel sympathy for man as man" comes out of this humanist aspiration to universalize human subjectivity and sociality. This is precisely why his theory of national character, condemnatory as it is, proves useful for Chinese nationalists, who substitute the "nation" for the "human race" while retaining the rhetorical power of universal humanism. By promoting sympathetic identification among citizens across class, ethnicity, region, gender, and kinship divides, nationalism attempts to remove or de-privilege all prior claims on individual identity. Chinese people must not only have the idea of a father, a son, a brother, a neighbor, and a fellow villager, but also that of a fellow countryman, a Chinese as such. Their fellow beings must not be limited to those in their house, or even those in their village or town, but must include, as John Stuart Mill puts it, all "those who live under the same government, and are contained within the same natural or historical boundaries" (quoted in Sakai 1997, 146). Fellow Chinese, even if they do not and cannot all know one another, must not treat one another as monsters and beasts. They must demonstrate a veritable national feeling, as befits a modern nation.

Nationalist ideology represents the modern nation as a transparent community united in its affections and its commitment to abstract, universal values. Its members identify with one another primordially, regardless of each person's particular location in the social, economic, and political structures. Jean-Luc Nancy suggests that the idea of a primordial community is the invention of modern society trying to cope with the "harsh reality" of the modern experience: "Community, far from being what society has crushed or lost, is *what happens to us . . . in the wake of society*" (1991, 11). Modern society, in its effort to disavow historicity and unevenness, projects the image of an organic community "made up principally of the sharing, diffusion, or impregnation of an identity by a plurality wherein each member identifies himself only through the supplementary mediation of his identification with the living body of the community. In the motto of the Republic, *fraternity* designates community: the model of the family and of love" (9). The nation sees itself precisely as rooted in such an organic community, where individual identity is mediated through the body politic and where the collectivity constitutes each individual's ultimate truth and commands his or her unconditional loyalty. From the "sharing, diffusion, or impregnation" of national identity modeled on family and love, one derives the "national feeling" or "national sympathy" that binds the national community together in space as well as in time. John Stuart Mill gives one of the earliest definitions of the nation in terms of a particular "feeling": "We mean, that one part of the community do not consider themselves as foreigners with regard to another part; that they set a value on their connection; feel that they are one people, that their lot is cast together" (quoted in Sakai 1997, 146–47).

The nation as a community of feeling is what Richard Sennett calls "the modern gemeinschaft community" in which people share the fantasy that they have "the same impulse life, the same motivational structure," in which "open social relations are possible as opposed to groups in which partial, mechanical, or emotionally indifferent ones prevail" (1992, 310–11). Nationalist discourse also constructs the nation as a totality that subsumes all forms of sociality to the state and stigmatizes "any social relation that [is] not confined by the dictates of nationality" (Sakai 1997, 138). Individual, contingent encounters are abstracted as synecdoches of national encounters that must follow a fixed script, whereas personal exchanges of sympathetic feeling across national boundaries are discouraged, if not outlawed. As Naoki Sakai points out, the principle of national sympathy demands that the circuit of feeling be coterminous with the boundaries of the nation as defined by the state, that one extends sympathy to one's fellow countrymen and antipathy to those designated as enemies of the nation, and that one maintains a practical, interactive, and empathetic relation with one's fellow countrymen, and an epistemic, objectifying, and antipathetic relation with outsiders (1997, 142). The construction of national community thus involves a two-pronged strategy: demonstrating a strong and enduring presence of sympathy within the nation, and delineating the limits of sympathy without. Watsuji Tetsurō's (1889–1960) theory of climate and national character deploys precisely this strategy—the celebration of the richness of Japanese feeling is juxtaposed with a discussion of "the abandonment of emotion" (Harootunian 2000, 281) among the Chinese. The discourse of cultural difference in effect serves to mark the limits of national sympathy, of the impossibility of a practical encounter across the national borders.

Watsuji's *Fūdo* (Climate and culture), first published as a series of articles and then as a book in 1935, is an attempt to rearticulate Japan's relationship to the West and its Orient—the Asian continent—in geocultural terms.[1] Watsuji opens his disquisition on the "emotional vitality and sensitivity" of the Japanese with the assertion that man is a social animal and that his distinctive way of life is best manifested in the male-female relationship. The "national spirit of Japan" is thus located in the ways in which men and women love each other. Owing to the doubling of tropical and arctic climates on the Japanese archipelago, the Japanese people have loved both calmly and violently since the days of the *Kojiki* and *Nihon shoki*. This unique combination of tranquillity and savagery is most characteristic of the Japanese type of love and is found in neither India nor China (1971, 138–39). For Watsuji, "Japanese love" is a naturalized and naturalizing metaphor that signifies the transhistorical essence of Japanese nationhood. In this way, nationalist ideology turns love into a cultural strategy, investing it with the quintessentially nationalist burden of embodying the continuity of national culture.

If the vitality of emotion attests to Japan's status as a nation par excellence, then the lack of emotion that Watsuji believes characterizes Chinese culture necessarily hinders China's bid for modern nationhood. Proceeding from the climatic determinism that drives the principal arguments of his book, Watsuji reaches the conclusion of emotional deficiency from observing the "monotonous" landscape of the lower Yangzi Valley: "the vastness of the Chinese continent is only revealed in the form of a vague and little-changing monotony":

> While it is true that the Chinese are unemotional this does not mean that they have no emotional life; their emotional life may be called unemotional. Those who express themselves in terms of a dull monotony see no cause for change of the kind that would react on and agitate their emotions. Here Chinese and Japanese are poles apart, for the latter is possessed of a rich temperamental diversity which thrives on change. The picture of the Chinese, bird-cage in hand, gazing up blankly at the sky all day long is strange in Japanese eyes, for, to the latter such a leisurely rhythm of life seems to lack all sensitivity. (127)

In keeping with his conviction that climate does not exist apart from history and that the climatic constraints on human existence are manifested historically, Watsuji reviews Chinese political history from the feudal ages through the imperial reigns to the modern semicolonial era. He asserts that the anarchic tendency of the Chinese as well as their capacity to maintain economic integration through kinship and regional ties alone have led ultimately to the paralysis of the nation. The imperial state itself was perennially without law, and its relationship to society was essentially predatory. After the collapse of the empire, the new state, consisting of financial and military cliques perpetually at war with each other, colluded with western colonial powers at the expense of the Chinese people. With the exception of a few percipient leaders such as Sun Yat-sen, "the Chinese people felt no strong concern about this [imperialist] economic pressure." Their time-honored ability to survive under a predatory state has habituated them to such pressure. And without a rich endowment of emotion, the Chinese are not capable of feeling that their lot is somehow cast together. While crediting Sun Yat-sen for correctly diagnosing China's colonial status, Watsuji blames his nationalist movement for entangling China more deeply with western capital, clearly with a view of Japan's imminent role as China's "liberator": "as long as the power that drove this [nationalist] movement was directed to intensifying the colonial nature of China, this nationalist awakening could not develop into a true movement for the liberation of China from her colonial status. The Chinaman's lack of emotion finally drove him to extreme distress" (132). The Chinese nationalists seek out colonial powers for support because there is an absence of emotional bonding between the leaders and the people of the nation. Watsuji suggests that China's hope lies in Japan, which has kept alive the "genius of the China that existed between the [Qin] and Song dynasties": "By acknowledging this, the Chinese could restore the power and grandeur of their noble culture of the past, lost from the China of today" (133).

Although Watsuji's most immediate evidence for the paucity of Chinese emotion is the putative monotony of the lower Yangzi Valley landscape, it is evident that he did not formulate his theory of emotion and culture entirely on the basis of his firsthand knowledge of China. Lydia Liu informs us that Smith's *Chinese Characteristics* was translated into Japanese only six years after its original publication (1890) and became the "the master text" (Lu Xun's words) on which many "China hands" based their sweeping pronouncements on the Chinese (Liu 1995, 52). Watsuji's book is therefore very much part of the global discourse of national character partaken of by colonialists (or colonial aspirants), missionaries, and (semi)colonial intellectuals alike. It is interesting that although both Smith and Watsuji locate the failure of the Chinese nation in its lack of emotion/sympathy, neither finds it logical to point to "national sympathy" as the way to overcome China's world-historical failure. While Watsuji holds up "Japan" as the answer, Smith prescribes "Christianity." Signs of an emerging national feeling, on the other hand, are dismissed as inauthentic and xenophobic. In the context of discussing the absence of public spirit among the Chinese, Arthur Smith wonders if the Chinese can be said to be patriotic: "There is undoubtedly a strong national feeling, especially among the literary classes, and to this feeling much of the hostility exhibited to foreigners and their inventions is to be traced" (CC, 111–12). This "strong national feeling" is to Smith somehow less than "national feeling" proper. Instead, he prefers to see it partly as "misapprehension" and partly as "race hatred." The rhetorical dithering is characteristic of the colonial ambivalence towards the possibility of nationhood among the colonized (or semicolonized). Partha Chatterjee points to the colonial perception of India as a congeries of fragmentary, particularistic communities "so insular in their differences with one another as to be incapable of being merged into larger, more modern political identities" (1993, 224). This is because colonial thought could not seriously entertain the idea that the colonized might, in a mimetic fashion, create a true political community, that is, the nation, thereby removing the ideological justification of the colonial presence (224).

The double bind of colonial thought is hardly disguised in Smith's studied reservation: "But that any considerable body of Chinese are actuated by a desire to serve their country, because it is their country, aside from the prospect of emolument, is a proposition which will require much more proof than has yet been offered to secure its acceptance by any one who knows the Chinese" (CC, 112). He gives an example to demonstrate how ordinary Chinese decidedly do not see themselves as "one people" bound by common interests and emotional affinity. According to him, during the second Opium War, coolie work was done for the allied troops by Chinese subjects hired in Hong Kong. But when these same coolies were captured by the Chinese army, they were sent back to the British ranks with their queues cut off (CC, 113–14). Smith's message is thus: It was bad enough for Chinese coolies to assist foreigners in attacking their own country, but for the Chinese government to throw these wretches back into the arms of the enemy is no less than the gravest violation of the principle of national sympathy. By cutting off their queues, the Qing government was effectively disowning these coolies as Chinese (since wearing a queue was mandatory for all male subjects of the Qing empire). Thus ruthlessly cast off, can they ever be expected to identify with "China" and show concern for the fate of their "fellow Chinese"?[2]

The missionary discourse on Chinese national character was obviously targeted at the readership back home or foreign missionaries, travelers, and sojourners in China. It had as much to do with the self-fashioning of the "West" (or "the Anglo-Saxon race" in Smith's language) as with the desire to "understand" China. By the same token, Japanese cultural theorists, directly or indirectly endorsing Japan's colonial policy in China, adopted this discourse to configure a series of relations of hierarchy that consigned China always to the second term: subject/object, civilized/barbarous, colonizer/colonized, disciplined/anarchic, sympathetic/apathetic. But the discourse of national character did not remain the sole preserve of the missionaries and Japanese. Modern Chinese intellectuals also seized upon this discourse to lay claim to national identity and to articulate their historical agency vis-á-vis the "Chinese people." The idea of the lack of sympathy was echoed as a commonplace truism that was nonetheless painfully corroborated by personal experience.

In the first decade of the twentieth century, the young Lu Xun, a medical student in Japan, made the momentous decision to become a writer after a traumatic encounter with the Chinese lack of sympathy. It was likely during this period (1902–1909) that he read the Japanese translation of Smith's book. Its impact on him can be gauged by the fact that till his dying day, he had wished that other Chinese would read it too: "I still have hopes that someone will eventually start translating Smith's *Chinese Characteristics* [into Chinese], because this book offers insights that would lead us to analyze, question, improve, and transform ourselves. Rather than clamoring for recognition and praise from others, we must struggle with ourselves and find out what it means to be Chinese" (quoted in Liu 1995, 53).[3] Fully aware that the book contained "miscellaneous errors," Lu Xun nonetheless deemed it necessary for the Chinese to interrogate themselves in the terms framed by the discourse of national character, that is, as *Chinese*, a race or ethnos defined by their supposedly common characteristics.

What Lu Xun is calling for is collective self-awareness, or the ability to return or even to adopt the Other's gaze. The technology of the self that he sees best suited for this purpose is none other than the endlessly proliferating discourse on national character, which has made "China" an eminent reality. He believes that, by subjecting themselves to the effect of this discourse, the Chinese will finally performatively lay claim to that "reality" and "find out what it means to be Chinese." In other words, they can empower themselves, paradoxically enough, by Orientalizing themselves. Lu's own literary career pioneered this self-Orientalizing project that would continue to define the self-perception of Chinese intellectuals for generations to come. However, as the many studies of Lu Xun have shown, his efforts to "dissect" the Chinese mind, to delve into the root of the Chinese malady, and to capture that all pervasive and yet always elusive national character often end up a deconstructive reinvention of the Orientalist discourse, exposing the ambivalent self-positioning of the modern intellectuals in their pursuit of national sympathy.

Nearly all studies of Lu Xun (or of modern Chinese literature, for that matter) begin with the obligatory slide show episode in the preface to his first short story collection, *Nahan* (Call to arms, 1922). As an explanation for his decision to abandon medical study and take up literature, Lu relates how he was mortified to observe the indifference with which a crowd of Chinese spectators looked on an execution of an alleged Chinese spy by a squadron of Japanese soldiers during the Russo-Japanese war (1904–1905).[4] In many ways, the passage relating this episode has become not only the founding text of modern Chinese literature, but also the mission statement of modern

Chinese intellectuals. It is therefore necessary to scrutinize once again that paradigmatic moment of awakening:

> This was during the Russo-Japanese War, so there were many war slides [after the lecture], and I had to join in the clapping and cheering in the lecture hall along with the other students. One day I unexpectedly saw on slide many Chinese whom I had not seen for a long time. One of them was bound, while many others stood around him. They were all strong fellows but appeared completely apathetic. According to the commentary, the one with his hands bound was a spy working for the Russians, who was to have his head cut off by the Japanese military as a warning to others, while the Chinese beside him had come to enjoy the spectacle.
>
> Before the term was over I had left [Sendai] for Tokyo, because after this film I felt that medical science was not so important after all. The people of a weak and backward country, however strong and healthy they may be, can only serve to be made examples of, or to witness such futile spectacles; and it doesn't really matter how many of them die of illness. The most important thing, therefore, was to change their spirit, and since at that time I felt that literature was the best means to this end, I determined to promote a literary movement. (LX, 2, translation slightly modified)

A photograph bearing a striking resemblance to the scene in question was discovered by a Japanese scholar in the 1980s. It shows a blindfolded and bound man kneeling on the ground about to receive a blow from a sword-wielding Japanese officer. Looking on in the background are seven or eight Japanese soldiers and immediately behind them some Chinese identifiable by their hairstyle and clothes. The caption reads, "Execution of a Russian spy. Among the audience were also soldiers laughing (shot outside the town of Kaiyuan, Manchuria, on March 20, 1905)" (Liu 1995, 62). Although it is difficult to discern the precise expressions of the Chinese spectators, it is clear that some of them are stretching their necks to get a better view of the execution. The caption of the photograph does not identify the unlucky "spy" as Chinese, though it might well have been a matter of common sense at the time. Still, it is noteworthy that the first thing Lu Xun saw (or recalled to have seen) was simply "many Chinese" (*xuduo Zhongguo ren*). Although another might see an executioner, a victim, and spectators, for Lu Xun, there were only two kinds of people on the screen: the Chinese and the Japanese.

In another recounting of the same episode, Lu Xun writes: "In these lantern slides there were also scenes of some Chinese who had acted as spies for the Russians and were captured by the Japanese and shot, while other Chinese looked on. And there was I, too, in the classroom. 'Banzai!' the students clapped their hands and cheered" (Lu Xun 1980, 409). This time Lu Xun could not join the clapping and cheering along with his fellow students; instead, he found the cheering "particularly jarring." The appearance of Chinese faces on the screen, or what Rey Chow calls the medium of "technologized visuality" (1995, 5), had irrevocably reconfigured his relationship to his classmates: in the lecture hall were no longer simply fellow students, but a Chinese student and Japanese students belonging to different, mutually exclusive regimes of national sympathy. It is perhaps not too far-fetched to say that Lu Xun *became* a Chinese precisely at this traumatic moment of recognition and sympathy. He expected that the other Chinese in the scene would feel the same, only to be appalled by the perception that the latter not only showed no sign of sympathy, but had apparently "come to enjoy the spectacle" (*shangjian zhe shizhong de shengju*).

Both Rey Chow and Yomi Braester fault Lu Xun scholars for having overlooked the relationship between visuality and spectatorship in this well-parsed passage. Chow calls our attention to the significance of the medium at the founding moment of modern Chinese literature: "Lu Xun discovers what it means to 'be Chinese' in the modern world by watching film" (1995, 9). Again, "'being Chinese' would henceforth carry in it the imagistic memory— the memorable image—of this violence. National self-consciousness is thus not only a matter of watching 'China' being represented on the screen; it is, more precisely, watching oneself—as a film, as a spectacle, as something always already watched" (9). Braester discloses the "critical blindness to the author's manipulative description of the photograph" by showing how Lu Xun shifts our attention away from the execution itself—which contains "riveting details"—to the spectators on and off the screen, particularly to the grating contrast between a crowd of passive spectators and a lone but active witness of history in the midst of another crowd (2003, 38–39; see also Yue 1999, 82–83). Concurring with Susan Sontag, who famously wrote that "without a politics, photographs of the slaughter-bench of history will most likely be experienced as, simply, unreal or as a demoralizing emotional blow" (1977, 19) and that "all photographs wait to be explained or falsified by their captions" (2003, 10), Braester argues that Lu Xun politicizes the slide image by writing a national message over the marginalized visual content (2003, 40). To push this point further, we can say that Lu Xun, to cope with the "emotional blow"

dealt by the violent image, is simultaneously adopting and resisting the "jingo-
ist gaze" of the camera (Yue 1999, 81) by averting his eyes from the "slaughter-bench of history" toward the peripheries. The reconstruction of the scene
nearly twenty years later also amounts to an act of writing back, from his new
nationalist subject position, at the caption/commentary that had inscribed
the image with a blustering imperialist message.

While Chow and others criticize scholars for accepting prima facie Lu
Xun's famous gloss of the Chinese spectators as being marked by profound apathy and for ignoring the fact that it is a "retroactive attempt to verbalize and
narrativize a mute visual event" (7), they tend not to question his representation of his own reaction as a moment of *nationalist* awakening. In my view, it is
Lu Xun who tells us that "China" is being represented on the screen—by a few
poker-faced men looking on an act of violence. It is precisely because of their
failure to recognize the victim as one of their own that they are irrevocably
constituted as Chinese—but not without the mediating gaze of Lu Xun the
spectator and the would-be writer. Thus it is quite beside the point to read the
episode or image apart from Lu Xun's poignant reconstruction of its
significance in the preface. Chow questions Lu's reading of apathy into the on-
lookers' inscrutable miens: "how does Lu Xun, looking at the screen, know
that the Chinese observers *are* apathetic? How do we know that the looks on
their faces mean that they are apathetic?" (7). Gang Yue too asks how Lu Xun
could detect "enjoyment" in those blank countenances (Yue 1999, 80). Perhaps Lu Xun's uncanny physiognomic ability owes something to the discourse
of national character. Precisely because the Chinese have already been pro-
nounced apathetic by the likes of Smith, what Lu Xun sees on the screen can be
none other than apathy—here made permanent and irrefutable by the immobility of the medium. Indeed, the shock of recognition, the sense of déjà vu,
must have been so strong that Lu Xun's recollection verges on the paranoid:
rather than being pained, repulsed, and galvanized into action, the Chinese
bystanders apparently have come positively to enjoy the spectacle.

The absence of a circuit of sympathy between the spectators and victim
launches Lu Xun's lifelong search for the meaning of national identity. For
him, as for Smith and Watsuji, the failure of sympathy signifies nothing less
than the failure of the nation. Yet unlike the latter, he is determined to instill
national sympathy in his fellow countrymen, or in his own words, to "change
their spirit." To crudely paraphrase Lu Xun, a Chinese who cannot identify
with another Chinese is not worth saving ("it doesn't really matter how many

of them die of illness"). To put it even more crudely and within view of Lu Xun's early attraction to social Darwinism: People who do not possess a genuine national feeling do not deserve to live—they are not properly human. China's most urgent need is therefore not material progress or institutional reforms, but a spiritual revolution that will jolt the slumbering souls of the Chinese to the recognition that their lot is cast together. Once they are restored to their national being, they will refuse to be "made examples of" and "to witness . . . futile spectacles" without proper patriotic reactions. In a word, they will cease to be *a-pathetic* and become *sym-pathetic*.

Despite the vast difference in circumstances, the slide show episode has something in common with the story about the "Chinese coolies" alluded to by Arthur Smith. Both stories are used to illustrate the absence of national sympathy among the Chinese. As a missionary, Smith can only bring himself to prescribing Christianity-inflected "human sympathy"; he takes the trouble to acknowledge manifestations of a "national feeling" only to deny their authenticity. Ironically, Lu Xun's literary experimentation also brings him to question the possibility of national sympathy. "[While] Smith can walk away from his critique . . . content in the knowledge that salvation is at hand," writes Theodore Huters, "for Lu Xun, such salvation seems inconceivable, and this painful consciousness surely lies at the heart of the agonizing deferral of resolution and suspension of closure that constitutes the aesthetic fulcrum of his most enduring work" (1998, 579). In stories such as "Medicine" and "The True Story of Ah Q," the idea of national sympathy dims before the chasms that crisscross the social terrain and the complex patterns of oppression and victimization. In its place, the crowd figures prominently as a counter-community, a tumorous growth in the body politic that inhibits the formation of a national community of sympathy and that renders fictional resolution and closure impossible. In his dogged refusal to romanticize the victim as innocence incarnate or the crowd as the embodiment of collective will and common sentiment, Lu Xun seems to acknowledge that the dream of national sympathy is powerless to overcome the intersecting levels of contradictions in Chinese society.

Under Lu Xun's pen, the victim is often faceless or out of focus (as in his recounting of the slide show), and the crowd is depicted with clinical precision. By foregrounding the dynamic of ritual victimization in a usually anonymous and typified locality, Lu Xun shifts the line of conflict from between society and state to within the social realm between the sadistic crowd and its victim.

The highly allegorical story entitled "Yao" (Medicine, 1919), for instance, is deliberately written from an angle that eschews the distinction between the Manchu and Han, or the conflict between the ruling regime and the republican revolutionaries, by placing the Manchu state in the shadowy background. Instead, the narrative focuses on the gulf separating the revolutionaries and the masses, even though both are at the mercy of the repressive state. In this story, the masses are figured as the spectators in the crowd who not only do not sympathize with the revolutionary martyr named Xia, but also enjoy the spectacle of his execution and cannibalize his decapitated body. Epitomizing the apathetic, uncomprehending, and cannibalisitc crowd is the Hua family, whose surname, combined with Xia, has traditionally stood for the Han Chinese ethnos. However, while Xia sacrifices his life for the cause of anti-Manchu nationalism, the Hua family is engrossed in its desire to perpetuate the family line by attempting to salvage the life of its consumptive heir, Little Chuan—clearly the personification of a moribund China.

The story opens with Old Chuan, the father, heading off to the execution ground to procure medicine for his son. The medicine turns out to be a steamed bun dipped in the blood of the freshly executed prisoner, Xia—a supposedly effective remedy for consumption. The crowd scene is depicted solely through the eyes of Old Chuan, who timidly stays at a distance from the semicircle of spectators. When one of the men turns around to look at Old Chuan, his eyes are said to shine with a "lustful light, like a famished person's at the sight of food" (LX, 26). Thus the crowd's cannibalism is not only directed toward the prisoner, but also toward its own members. In the slide show that changed Lu Xun's life, the act of violence is visually in the foreground, though Lu Xun seemed less disturbed by the horror of violence than by the reaction (or lack thereof) of the Chinese spectators in the background. Here Lu Xun conceals the execution from the reader's mind's eye altogether, as Old Chuan can only see the back of people's heads. What is described, briefly but memorably, are the engrossed onlookers: "Craning their necks as far as they would go, they looked like so many ducks held and lifted by some invisible hand. For a moment all was still; then a sound was heard, and a stir swept through the on-lookers. There was a rumble as they pushed back, sweeping past Old Chuan and nearly knocking him down" (LX, 26).

The crowd is thus depicted as the true victimizer, and its ubiquitous presence and complicity seem far more frightful than the state's reign of terror. It is for this reason that we speak of the crowd and its victim, rather than the crowd, the victim, and the victimizer (the executioner and, by extension, the Manchu state). It matters little who precisely is the executioner—he commits the act of killing swiftly, sells the bloody bun to Old Chuan, and is out of the picture. It is the crowd that prolongs the moment of victimization by reveling in the spectacle of violence long after the event itself. The next day, the crowd reassembles in Old Chuan's teahouse to carry on the violence—the violence of language. As the customers speak uncomprehendingly of Xia's revolutionary activities, jealously of his uncle who has pocketed the cash reward for turning him in to the authorities, and approvingly of the jailer's abuse of him, the effect of apathy or antipathy seems far more devastating than the execution itself.

The chasm that hopelessly separates the revolutionaries and the ordinary folks is rendered literal on the burial ground, where Xia and Little Chuan's remains lie on different sides of a path: "Left of the path were buried executed criminals or those who had died of neglect in prison. Right of the path were paupers' graves. The serried ranks of grave mounds on both sides looked like the rolls laid out for a rich man's birthday" (LX, 31). Needless to say, Xia's grave is on the left side and Little Chuan's on the right. However, their posthumous division based on the distinction between criminals and law-abiding subjects is rendered totally superfluous by the fact that both are the victims of the ruling elite and that the vastly different circumstances of their deaths mean absolutely nothing in the latter's eyes. Both are mere sacrificial offerings for "a rich man's birthday." However, instead of recognizing the "rich man"—the Manchu rulers or foreign imperialists—as their common enemy, the Chinese, bent on perpetuating spurious distinctions and cannibalizing one another, continue to offer up sacrificial victims for the maintenance of a violent social order.

The final segment of the story is a lengthy meditation on whether the chasm between the Huas and Xias can be bridged. Significantly, when the two bereaved mothers come to offer sacrifice to their respective sons, the path is momentarily crossed over. Startled by the sight of a wreath laid anonymously on her son's grave, Mother Xia nearly faints. Little Chuan's mother steps across the path to console her. Yet as soon as she becomes aware of the fact that no wreath has been laid on her own son's grave, this fleeting moment of sympathy quickly dissipates and gives way to a vague sense of jealousy: "Suddenly she had a sense of futility and stopped feeling curious about the wreath" (LX, 32). When Mother Xia appeals to her son's spirit to communicate with her through a crow and fails to meet with any response, Little Chuan's mother feels "somehow as if a load had been lifted from her mind" (33). Also lifted is the hope that the two mothers might come together and form an affective alliance—as the basis for political action—out of their common suffering and oppression.

The unaccounted appearance of the wreath has been interpreted by both Lu Xun and his commentators as the clue to a hope never entirely given up on the part of the author: even if the Hua family, their associates, and the nameless crowd do not harbor any sympathy for Xia, at least *someone* out there does. The wreath reassures the reader that the revolutionary martyr is, after all, properly mourned for—by someone who understands and identifies with his nationalist aspirations and will likely carry on his unfinished task. The crow that refuses to answer to Mother Xia's (superstitious) supplication has been taken as a harbinger of the onslaught of revolution—it takes off towards the "far horizon" only after the two mothers have left the graveyard, leaving them to their bewilderment, mutual suspicion, and repressed memories of cannibalism.

The revolutionary's hope that his blood will serve as spiritual medicine for the afflicted souls of the masses is ironically and cruelly realized when the masses, represented by the Hua family, take his medicine in the literal sense. However, if the Huas are only the unwitting victimizer of one of their own kind, and therefore may still be brought to the realization of their "true" bond with the Xias, then the villagers in "A Q zhengzhuan" (The true story of Ah Q, 1921) completely negate the possibility of an ignorant/innocent victimizer. Here victimization is always an act of malice. The story paints a bleak portrait of the village of Weizhuang (a no-name village, or an all-Chinese village) where people have only envy and contempt for one another. It also offers a veiled but no less devastating critique of the 1911 Revolution as one that grossly simplified and misdiagnosed the ills of Chinese society as rooted in racial antagonism instead of in the Chinese character. With his caricature panorama of Weizhuang, Lu Xun wishes to turn the Chinese gaze back from the "tartars" or "foreign devils" and upon the Ah Qs and the "Imitation Foreign Devils" in every village and town. Ah Q, the most celebrated John Chinaman in modern Chinese literature, has long been associated with the birth of the "native" discourse of national character. But as Lydia Liu points out, Ah Q has rather a hybrid origin; he is more precisely the product of a translingual discourse of national character that circulated among Euro-Americans, Japanese, and Chinese (Liu 1995, chapter 2).

Whether or not Lu Xun had read Arthur Smith before he wrote this story, Ah Q seems to walk straight out of the pages of *Chinese Characteristics*. In fact, most of the "characteristics" identified by Smith and other Orientalists can be, with little or slight modification, used to describe Ah Q and the denizens of Weizhuang, most notably Ah Q's complete lack of emotion and sympathy. As Marston Anderson observes, Ah Q is victimized by the whole village society as "an all-purpose scapegoat" because of his status as a transient scavenger; but he in turn seeks to victimize those who are even more powerless than himself or those who are distrusted by the village society (for example, the novice nun): "He is no mere victim of the social order but very much a participant in it" (1990, 81). The narrative thus refuses to invite pity from readers who are predisposed to assume innocence on the part of victim and to root for the underdog. Even in the final moment of his life, Ah Q is unable to solicit sympathetic identification. The "gaping spectators" who have gathered to "enjoy" the spectacle of his execution are depicted as senseless and cannibalistic as ever: "Now [Ah Q] saw eyes more terrible even than the wolf's: dull yet penetrating eyes that, having devoured his words, still seemed eager to devour something beyond his flesh and blood. And these eyes kept following him at a set distance. These eyes seemed to have merged into one, biting into his soul" (LX, 111–12).

The crowd is portrayed as the most insidious victimizer. Yet, among its ranks is one of Ah Q's former victims: Amah Wu, the maidservant to whom he once unsuccessfully made love. When the crisscrossing lines of oppression and victimization are so woven into the social fabric, with whom should one sympathize? How indeed does one draw the line of sympathy and antipathy? Why does the ritualized elimination of a scapegoat bring together the villagers not as an affective community but as a cannibalistic crowd with an insatiable appetite—much as the overthrowing of the Manchu rule has not brought about a cohesive Chinese nation but instead left the new Republic mired in unending internecine strife? By embedding these questions in his narrative, Lu Xun seems to be commenting on his own nationalist project to change the "spiritual nature" of the Chinese people. He seems to question the tendency (himself not exempted) to attribute historically and socially generated problems to the absence of sympathy or lack of emotion, and suggest that, without radically transforming the basic structures of society, sympathy will always be out of place, so to speak, and remain a sentimental solution.

THE INVENTION OF HYPOCRISY

Lu Xun's incomparable stature in modern Chinese literary history undoubtedly has a great deal to do with his remarkable capacity for self-interrogation and his inveterate skepticism toward utopianism (see Anderson 1990; Huters 2005). But his professed interest in the discourse of national character and his powerful representations of Chinese society as a realm of apathy and antipathy set the basic tenor of much May Fourth social discourse. Setting out to find a community, he finds only the crowd. Like Ah Q, the crowd is also a translingual creation—the product of turn-of-the-last-century discourse of social psychology (see Sun 2002). For the self-styled observer of the urban psyche, the crowd is the antithesis of the community, of civilized sociability. It is, in the words of Richard Sennett, "the mode in which the most venal passions of man are most spontaneously expressed" (1992, 299).

But in the eyes of May Fourth critics, the Chinese are not just ruthless as mobs on the street; they are equally so as private individuals. In other words, if the Chinese can be "expressive" only in a predatory way in public, their ritualistic mode of interaction in the private sphere is no less destructive. What, then, of all the Confucian talk of benevolence and piety and sacrifice? The answer is familiar to all students of the May Fourth movement: it was nothing but hypocrisy. In the radical periodical press, iconoclastic intellectuals concentrated their attack on the Confucian family as an institution of suffocating formality, accusing Confucian ethics of encouraging hypocrisy and devaluing spontaneous, sincere feelings.

Writing for *Xinchao* (Renaissance), Gu Chengwu denounces the Confucian family as a "feelingless plaything" (*wuqing de wanwu*) plagued by statusism (*mingfen zhuyi*), conventionalism (*xisu zhuyi*), and fatalism (*yunming zhuyi*). One evil consequence is the absence of love (*aiqing*). Originally Confucianism had advocated the "gradation of love by blood ties" (*qin qin zhi ai*), which means that the closest kin are bound by the most sincere love, which diminishes by degree as blood ties thin out. But the Confucianists use "the hierarchy of generations" (*beifen*) to replace the gradation of love: No matter how one's elders ill-use one, one must treat them with "the most sincere love"; even if one does not feel it, one must make a show of it (*aiqing de xingshi*). Otherwise one would commit a punishable offense. This is like a novice in a theatrical troupe who is taught to act out grand gestures of loyalty, filial piety, chastity, and righteousness (*zhong, xiao, jie, yi*). One would be laughed at if one pointed out that he was acting without true emotion. Likewise, all our family requires of us is just this—perfection in the formality of love (*youfen wuqing*) (Gu Chengwu 1919).

The critique of formalism presupposes a fundamental division between private sentiment and its public expression. Indeed, it is only within the framework of the enlightenment structure of feeling that posits the binarisms of morality and sentiment, of *li* and *qing* that notions like *xuwei* (hypocrisy) and *wei daoxue* or *jia daoxue* (pseudo-moralist) make sense. Feeling or love is accorded a kind of ontological authenticity and appealed to as the touchstone of personal truth. Hence its "repression" by *li* is cast as not only unjust and cruel, but also unnatural and inhuman, and herein lies the ethical basis of May Fourth iconoclasm. The analogy of the Confucian family to theater is a good indication of how much public expression or performance of feeling is subordinated to an inner reality and deprived of authenticity.

In his ambitious chronicle of the decline of the "public" in the West, Richard Sennett highlights the ways in which the classic ideal of the *theatrum mundi* became discredited in the nineteenth century. The traumas of capitalism stimulated a reversal in the relative moral value of the public (epitomized by the city street) and the private (the family): while the family was increasingly idealized as a refuge or a locus of emotional and psychological authenticity, public life became synonymous with coldness, cruelty, and cutthroat competition. When the private became "a moral yardstick with which to measure the public realm," the very legitimacy of the public order, or the res publica, was thrown into question (1992, 20). Sennett links the eclipse of the public to the belief that social meanings were generated not in the rule-bound, civility-governed, and conventionalized interactions among people in their public personae, but in the unmediated expressions of individual, private feelings. Beginning with Rousseau and increasingly in the nineteenth century, the greatest vice of public life was thought to be its impersonality or theatricality—precisely what had used to be its source of strength and vitality. Playing one's social role in public was now necessarily an impersonal, inauthentic, and hence morally inferior way of being. The important point for us is the hypothesis that "theatricality has a special, hostile relation to intimacy" (37). In prescribing a theatrical —that is, role oriented—mode of interaction, the Confucian family suffers a similar fate of being discredited as a territory hostile to intimacy and authenticity. Insofar as it anchors the continuum of the family-state, the Confucian family has always been a public institution. But in the May Fourth framework, it also becomes the locus of an inauthentic public. One need only think of Ba Jin's (b.1904) *Family* (Jia, 1933) to appreciate its new signification as a sepulchral realm where spontaneous, authentic feelings are mercilessly squelched by ritualism and hypocrisy.

As might be expected, the accusation of hypocrisy also has its counterpart in the colonial discourse of national character. Arthur Smith, for example, has plenty to complain about the "absence of sincerity" among the Chinese. In an indignant and yet resigned manner, Smith speaks of the impossibility of ever getting simple and straight facts from any Chinese person. Anticipating Lu Xun's Madman who scrutinizes the Confucian classics to find only "eat-people" (*chiren*), Smith declares that anyone who peruses the classics with a discerning eye "will be able to read between the lines much indirection, prevarication, and falsehood" (CC, 267). While it is exasperating enough that the Chinese would indulge in the license for lying and would not flinch when being called liars, what is worse is that "the ordinary speech of the Chinese is so full of insincerity, which yet does not rise to the dignity of falsehood, that it is very difficult to learn the truth in almost any case" (CC, 271).

As an illustration of the bewildering misalignment between language and feeling, Smith cites an allegedly Chinese tale that mocks the stilted politesse of the elite. In the story, a gentleman caller is shown into the reception hall of his host. His arrival alarms a rat on the beam, which in turn upsets a jar of oil, which then precisely falls on the guest and soils his fine robes. Smith goes on:

> Just as the face of the guest was purple with rage at this disaster, the host entered, when the proper salutations were performed, after which the guest proceeded to explain the situation. "As I entered your honourable apartment and seated myself under your honourable beam, I inadvertently terrified your honourable rat, which fled and upset your honourable oil-jar upon my mean and insignificant clothing, which is the reason of my contemptible appearance in your honourable presence." (CC, 275)

To Smith, this tale perfectly illustrates the befuddling nature of the Chinese language and the sheer distance between expression and inner feeling. And he apparently delights in drawing ammunition from the Chinese themselves to show up their many shortcomings. That all the maddening instances of insincerity and hypocrisy do not seem to bother the Chinese very much is then taken as manifestation of their duplicity and moral depravity. One could argue that for a Chinese audience, the guest's speech, other than its excessive use of honorifics, may well be the most emotionally appropriate response to the situation. In Smith's eye, however, when anger is felt but not forthrightly expressed, language has failed affect, and the person has become an emotional and psychological fraud.

In condemning Chinese insincerity, Smith is operating in what Arjun Appadurai calls the modern West's "embodied doxa," which opposes inner feelings to their public expressions (1990, 92). For Appadurai, this is often misrepresented as a general theory about the relationship between affect and expression. In particular, he notes that the concept of hypocrisy accentuates a number of cross-cultural issues involving the topography of the self, the problems of staging and representation, and the authenticity of public expression. Seen in this light, both the colonial discourse of insincerity and the May Fourth discourse of hypocrisy amount to an attempt to impose the Enlightenment "topography of the self" onto the terrain of Confucian sentimentality where "real feeling" is at most a misnomer and carries none of the ontological weight attributed to it in the modern episteme.

Through the prism of the enlightenment structure of feeling, the Confucian family as a theatrical community of sentiment becomes absurdly mechanical, hypocritical, as well as oppressive. The institution of arranged marriage, in particular, comes to be seen as the epitome of Confucianism's contemptuous disregard for personal feelings. One critic writes that marriage in China is like a puppet show, totally mechanical, passive, and commodified (Qu Shiying 1920). Another critic catalogues four types of marriage and condemns them all as inhumane (*fei renge de*): these are superstitious marriages, marriages of status, marriages of property, and marriages of carnal desire. A humane marriage, he avers (citing Edward Carpenter), is the bodily and spiritual union of one independent person (*renge*) with another (Yi Jiayue 1919). Tian Han (1898–1968) echoes this opinion in his call to legitimize consensual marriage. For him, love among the myriad creatures of the universe is never secretive, so must love between a man and woman be made open. Secretive love is repressed love and the breeding ground for miseries and sins. Citing Percy Shelley and Ellen Key, Tian proclaims: "We don't want '*marriage by capture*,' '*marriage by purchase*,' or '*marriage by service*.' We want '*marriage by consent*'!" (1919, italicized phrases are in English in the original).

In their critique of hypocrisy, these and other May Fourth–era writers portray Confucian marriage as nothing but property exchange, social climbing, superstition, or male desire; missing is the element of love, the one thing that all marriages, in the eyes of the romantics, should be about. Their critique partakes of what Alasdair MacIntyre calls "the modern moral scheme" consisting of three key concepts: rights, protest, and unmasking. In this scheme, "natural rights" or "human rights" are universally and equally attached to all individuals and define the parameters of individual moral stances. An individual will "protest" against all perceived incursions of rights by other individuals or by social institutions, and he or she often does so by revealing that such incursions are in fact utilitarian profit-seeking or the base pursuit of desire. We have seen these strategies in operation in the debates among the liberals, conservatives, and radicals in Chapter 4. Confucian ritualism, for example, is habitually accused of serving the interests of the patriarchal family and gratifying male desire at the expense of women's basic human rights. Within the discursive limits of modernity, one's moral rectitude is no longer guaranteed by a transcendental authority, but relies solely on one's claim of sincerity. Hence the accusation of insincerity, of saying one thing while meaning another, of harboring ulterior motives behind showy words, is highly damaging. Any pursuit of a higher purpose or hypergood, any effort to (re)invent a grand narrative will have to weather such damaging accusations from detractors. The major contending protagonists of modernity are all prepared to claim that their opponents merely offer a rhetorical mask of morality that conceals what are in fact the preferences of arbitrary will and desire (MacIntyre 1984, 68–70).

MacIntyre's mistrust of modernity aside, unmasking is indeed a privileged polemical strategy of the May Fourth radicals, for whom the most effective way to defeat their conservative opponents—no less "protagonists of modernity" than themselves—is to disclose the putative material or libidinal motives behind their moralistic defense of old values. Lu Xun's story "Soap" (Feizao), for example, is just such an exercise in unmasking the main character Siming's sexual longings for the beggar girl whom he and his cohort at the Moral Reform Literary Society wish to apotheosize as a filial exemplar (LX, 164–75). Prasenjit Duara reads the story as aspersions cast on such "modern gentry patriarchs" like Kang Youwei, whom Lu Xun saw as deploying the language of morality to exploit and oppress women (2003, 137). Indeed, in "My Views on Chastity" (1918), Lu Xun takes the moralists to task for demanding women to be chaste while they themselves practice polygamy: "Men cannot make rules for women that they do not keep themselves"

(Lan and Fong 1999, 12). He ends the essay with a characteristically May Fourth enjoinment: "We must tear off every mask" (17).[5] Likewise, conservative backlashes against free love in the post–May Fourth era effected a reversal with essentially the same rhetorical weapon of unmasking. The end result is that "hypocrisy" becomes one of the most used and abused epithets in the moral lexicon of modernity.

In her comparative study of the French and American Revolutions, Hannah Arendt points out that the Reign of Terror in the former case stemmed directly from Robespierre's war on hypocrisy. In identifying the heart as the sole source of political virtue, the French revolutionaries turned the Revolution into a frightful, boundless, and self-defeating hunt for hypocrites (1963, 97). Arendt writes: "War on hypocrisy was war declared upon society as the eighteenth century knew it. . . . Their [the men of the Revolution] favoured simile was that the Revolution offered the opportunity of tearing the mask of hypocrisy off the face of French society, of exposing its rottenness, and, finally, of tearing the façade of corruption down and of exposing behind it the unspoiled, honest face of the *peuple*" (105–6). Arendt reminds us that hypocrisy is not identical to the deceit of the liar or the duplicity of the cheat. Rather, when the hypocrite pretends to virtue, he is said to be playacting (*hypocrite* in Greek means "playactor"): "The hypocrite's crime is that he bears false witness against himself. What makes it so plausible to assume that hypocrisy is the vice of vices is that integrity can indeed exist under the cover of all other vices except this one. . . . only the hypocrite is really rotten to the core" (103).

Ultimately, Arendt admits, the reason why hypocrisy, the vice that pays compliment to virtue and that covers up vices, could become the vice of all vices and the phantom target of revolutionary frenzy has to be sought in the metaphysical problem of the relationship between being and appearance (101), or as Appadurai contends, in the Enlightenment "topography of the self" (1990, 93). The May Fourth hunt for Confucian hypocrisy may not match the feverish abandon with which the French Revolutionaries ferreted out the hypocritical patriot, but the movement certainly sees itself as an epic struggle to eliminate a vice that threatens the possibility of national regeneration. Intellectuals also resort to the language of the theater to expose the illusions, dark motives, and chameleon disguises of the Confucian order. In so doing, they introduce to their readers a revolutionary episteme predicated on the radical dichotomy of being and appearance. If in traditional societies, lying and make-believe were "not considered crimes . . . unless they involved wilful deception and bearing false witness" and hypocrisy was a scarcely conceivable phenomenon (102–3), in the new frame of reference, being untrue to others and to oneself while pretending to be otherwise undermines the entire moral and conceptual edifice of the modern project.

The most despised hypocrite in May Fourth discourse is the smug Confucian who spouts moral catechisms to oppress others, but who allows himself wide latitude in his sex life, even if only in fantasy. It is perhaps not so curious that Lu Xun's satire of the Chinese everyman should feature a chapter on love, in which Ah Q's erotic yearnings provide the occasion for staging and denouncing Confucian hypocrisy. The chapter is ironically entitled "The Tragedy of Love," which narrates Ah Q's foiled attempt at erotic fulfillment. Normally, Ah Q is too preoccupied with securing the next meal, dodging abuses at the hands of fellow villagers, and indulging in real or imaginary victories over his "enemies." Occasionally, however, some mysterious stirrings from down within would direct his thoughts to women. At practically the rock bottom of the village pecking order, Ah Q nonetheless feels infinitely superior to all women, to whom he adopts the supercilious attitude commonly attributed to Confucian moralists in the May Fourth period: "His view was, 'All nuns must carry on in secret with monks. If a woman walks alone on the street, she must want to seduce bad men. When a man and a woman talk together, it must be to arrange to meet'" (LX, 80). As if to mock the solemn heading "The Tragedy of Love," Ah Q is simply incapable of conceiving of the male-female relationship beyond crude sexual gratification. Hence his plea for "love" can only take the form of asking the maidservant Amah Wu to sleep with him, sending her off screaming and inviting a good thrashing from her master.

The crude equation of love with sex is a familiar critique of Confucianism.[6] In this episode, Ah Q is the caricature personification of the Confucian moral economy in which romantic love is not a lifegood and in which nonkin men and women are forbidden to interact openly and freely as social equals. Predictably, Ah Q's quest for "love" turns into a farce, testifying to the sheer improbability of romantic love within the moral universe of Weizhuang, and by implication, of traditional China. For all their elaborate talk of morality and emotion, the Chinese are shown to have never known love before. And if they have never truly loved another person who is not their kin, how can they be expected to love their country made up of strangers?

That the Chinese have never known love before is a familiar refrain of the time; and we hear it in Shi Heng's essay entitled "Lian'ai geming lun" (The revolution of love, in *Juewu*). According to Shi, there is no love among the Chinese because the Chinese do not understand the meaning of love. The truth is that love is a hypocritical formality for the Chinese who have no opportunity to express genuine love. Confucianism regards women as lesser beings; and so long as there is no equality between women and men, there is no love to speak of. At most, men are allowed to pursue their passion outside of loveless marriages. But this is not an option for women. "Love is free, but where is freedom in a Chinese person's love? Love is voluntary, but where is the free will in a Chinese person's love?" (Meisheng, 1923, 4:75). Shi Heng concludes that the revolution of love will do away with all false morality, evil customs, and the unnatural and inhuman marriage system and will establish new, equal, and free unions founded on true love. To do this, he reminds us, one must begin with women's emancipation, which means open social intercourse, equal opportunities for employment and education, and freedom of marriage and divorce (Meisheng, 1923, 4:78–79).

The emancipation of women is arguably the most visible, most compelling, and most championed causes of the May Fourth movement. Although not all writers go to the length of prescribing concrete measures such as education, work, and child care, women's oppression is for many of them the crux of China's problems. However, the woman question is rarely separate from that other great preoccupation of the May Fourth generation: the subordination of the young to the old in the patriarchal family system. Small wonder then that women are mostly cast in the role of persecuted daughters fighting their parents (often mothers) for freedom of love. Parents, as a result, often become the embodiment of Confucian hypocrisy. Hu Shi's one-act play, "Zhongsheng dashi" (The greatest event in life, 1919), provides a textbook example of parents whose duplicitous conduct is a product of the hypocritical moral order.

As a work of literature, the play does not have much to recommend it. But its significance in the history of modern Chinese literature is sealed by its forceful articulation of the conflict of the generations as synecdochical of the conflict between authenticity and hypocrisy. As the play opens, Tian Yamei is debating her mother over her desire to marry her lover, a Mr. Chen. Mrs. Tian has just consulted a fortune-teller and learned that Yamei's horoscope is incompatible with that of Mr. Chen. Yamei is incensed at her mother's "superstitious" activities and upbraids her: "Have you forgotten that father doesn't allow them [fortune-tellers] in the house?" When the father comes home, he too scolds his wife, who attempts to show him the divinatory verse she has obtained from the

Temple of Guanyin: "It's precisely because it is the greatest event in our daughter's life that we as parents must be particularly thoughtful and sober. This business of plaster Bodhisattvas and fortune-telling is all just a swindle. . . . From now on, I'm not going to allow any more of this superstitious talk. We're finished with plaster Bodhisattvas and blind fortune-tellers once and for all. And we're going to discuss this marriage properly" (Gunn 1983, 5–6). The father's enlightened stance, however, is revealed to be a sham when he too opposes Yamei's marriage, citing the "fact" that the Tians and Chens belonged to the same clan two thousand years ago and reminding her that "Chinese custom forbids persons of the same family to marry" (7). Failing to shake her father from his resolve to observe the "laws laid down by our own clan ancestors," Yamei elopes with her lover. Although the father's motive remains obscure, his hypocrisy of denouncing one set of superstitious beliefs while upholding another is the central target of the play's critique—far more so than the mother's naive faith in "plaster Bodhisattvas and blind fortune-tellers." The play thus mobilizes the tripartite modern moral scheme—rights, protest, and unmasking—to show that behind high-sounding moral rhetoric lie the preferences of arbitrary will and irrational tradition, or the rotten core of Confucian hypocrisy.

The play, like so many May Fourth texts, also enacts the triumph of the national community over parochial forms of sociality. Etienne Balibar sees in the ascendancy of the national form, supplemented by the modern idea of race, the demise of "private genealogies":

> The idea of a racial community makes its appearance when the frontiers of kinship dissolve at the level of the clan, the neighbourhood community and, theoretically at least, the social class, to be imaginarily transferred to the threshold of nationality: that is to say, when nothing prevents marriage with any of one's "fellow citizens" whenever, and when, on the contrary, such a marriage seems the only one that is "normal" or "natural." (Balibar and Wallerstein, 1991, 100)

The idea of "rights" in May Fourth discourse is driven home first and foremost as the rights to marry any of one's fellow citizens, regardless of genealogy or social station. In this play, private genealogies, either the overtly superstitious kind or the ostensibly rational (but nonetheless bogus) kind, are shown to be totally irrelevant. It is in this sense that marriage between two individuals becomes a national affair and that lovers' melancholy ruminations can be the incubator of patriotism. In this way, May Fourth love stories come to structure a new nationalist consciousness.

In May Fourth discourse, parents' inability to love their sons and daughter and to facilitate free love is not so much a personal failure as a failure of the Confucian family system. The goal of rebellion, then, is to flee the family as the site of unfeeling cruelty and inhumanity, or the site of unfreedom. As we have shown in Chapter 3, the new heterosocial world became the arena where hopes of freedom and romantic fulfillment were invested and also where the risks and frustrations of free sociability were encountered. Idealistic youth driven by an ardent faith in the nobility and utopian promise of love found themselves unprepared for the inherently adventurous and gamelike qualities of romantic love. Having fled the theatrical impersonality of their traditional families, they yearned for a community of intimacy—a *gemeinschaft*—in the heterosocial world, only to experience what Sennett calls "the tyranny of intimacy." Just as community (gemeinschaft) became a weapon of critique against society (gesellschaft) for nineteenth-century bourgeoisie, the nation was to be their critique of the family in the name of love. For this they were willing to forego a freer but also riskier form of sociability. In the final section of this chapter, we look at how the problem of free love becomes implicated in the debilitating discourse of national sympathy.

LOVE AND GEMEINSCHAFT

When Lu Xun excoriated the Chinese for failing to display the requisite qualities of a modern nation, he was partaking of the fantasy that the modern nation is a gemeinschaft whose members have "the same impulse life [and] the same motivational structure" (Sennett 1992, 311). The "gemeinschaft," which requires the full disclosure of feeling to others, is thus the antithesis of the Confucian social order against which the May Fourth generation rebelled. The nation as gemeinschaft is crucial for understanding why May Fourth romantic fiction is so conducive to the imaginings of modern nationalism: the key is that both are premised on a code of intimacy as the only authentic and morally legitimate mode of constructing social relationships. A lover's search for a soul mate to whom he or she can disclose in full his or her feeling carries a logical affinity with a patriot's search for conationals with whom he or she may share the ecstasy of communal intimacy. Failure in either pursuit can also easily turn into resentment against an unresponsive lover or an incohesive motherland. Unrequited love as the code word for failed sociability, then, is the key to unlock the conundrum of love and nationalism, or *why* the discourse of nationalism is mobilized to articulate a preeminently personal crisis, in Yu Dafu's short story "Chenlun" (Sinking, 1921).

In the opening passages of the story, we find a lugubrious youth—a Chinese student in Japan—taking a solitary stroll in what may well be the ultimate hostile world: a foreign country that has colonial designs on China and is not coy about holding the Chinese in a racist regard. But our protagonist tells us that he is also alienated from the social circle of fellow Chinese students. The posture he strikes is that of Rousseau—the reveler in the woods and the critic of urban gregariousness. His yearning for intimacy and authenticity estranges him from an impersonal world which demands playacting and distance from the self. "Lately he has been feeling pitifully lonesome. His emotional precocity had placed him at constant odds with his fellow men. . . . Amidst the half-ripened rice fields . . . he was seen strolling with a pocket edition of Wordsworth" (Lau et al. 1981, 125, hereafter cited as SK). While seeking emotional refuge in European romanticism and the idyllic serenity of country homes, the protagonist cries out for a soul mate to whom he can unbosom himself: "I want neither knowledge nor fame. All I want is a 'heart' that can understand and comfort me, a warm and passionate heart and the sympathy that it generates and the love born of that sympathy!. . . . O ye Heavens above. . . . I shall be wholly content if you can grant me an Eve from the Garden of Eden, allowing me to possess her body and soul" (SK, 128).

The yearning to possess a woman "body and soul" signals an important distinction between Yu Dafu's protagonist and older types of man of feeling. The former is a new breed of romantic beings versed in the psychoanalytic theory of sexuality. Abandoning the once sacred dichotomy of love and desire, Yu Dafu's story gives "candid descriptions of masturbation, voyeurism, impotence, and morbid sensibilities" (Liu 1995, 143). What Feng Yuanjun has referred to obliquely as "unnatural" (see Chapter 3) is for him the very essence of human nature for whose rectification he is willing to rock the entire moral edifice. It is crucial to note that sexuality in this story is almost exclusively "pathological," and self-consciously so. The discourse of abnormal sexuality, unlike that of forbidden love, does not at first seem to have a clearly identified critical object. Instead, the narrator seems to take perverse pleasure in self-diagnosis and heedless self-revelation, with the aid of a psychoanalytic lingo studded with English words like *hypochondria* and *megalomania*. But Chinese critics then and now are quick to read irreverent and subversive implications into Yu's exhibitionism. Guo Moruo, a fellow romanticist and leftist critic, remarks: "For those hypocritical literati, those pseudo-moralists and pseudo-scholars who have been cowering in their antediluvian carapaces, Yu Dafu's courageous self-exposure struck like a flash of lightening, setting them ablaze with indignation" (quoted in Sun Zhongtian 1996, 4). A 1990s commentator echoes this view: "In the manner of the Renaissance humanists, Yu Dafu uses his natural, spontaneous self to defy the shackles of feudal ethics and moral-ity" (quoted in Sun Zhongtian 1996, 4).

The frankness of Yu's text is thus taken as a courageous challenge against the hypocrisy of the "pseudo-moralists." The assumption is that the latter are equally motivated by, if not consumed with, sexual desires but are too conceited to own up to this essential human truth. Instead, like Siming in "Soap," they mouth banalities about purity and chastity and contribute to the withering of the human spirit among the Chinese. The teenage protago-nist's anguished struggles with his pubescent body become, for these critics, the first volleys of the monumental struggle to tear off the masks of morality and to emancipate humanity. But instead of running up against parental au-thoritarianism or Confucian hypocrisy, the protagonist's sexual awakening is hemmed in by the project of national sympathy.

The most salient point of this story, which no critic has ever failed to com-ment on, is that it is set in Japan and the object of the adolescent protagonist's desire is Japanese women. What has not been emphasized is the fact that the specter of national sympathy looms so large that his search for recognition, sympathy, and love on the personal level is cast as an impossible dream—so near and yet so unreachable. Every fleeting presence of Japanese girls would cause his breathing to quicken. Yet their "ogling" could never, as he bitterly berates himself, be intended for him. "They are Japanese, and of course they don't have any sympathy for you" (SK, 127). Paradoxically, the limits of na-tional sympathy become a source of consolation for the want of personal sym-pathy. With the nation as the hegemonic referent, the sense of frustration is readily turned outward so that his failure to win love and sympathy from Japanese girls is a consequence of his national identity as a despised China-man, rather than, possibly, that of his personal traits (a timid introvert?). Hence the outburst: "China, O my China! Why don't you grow rich and strong? I cannot bear your shame in silence any longer!" (SK, 128). This line is repeated like a refrain in the text; again and again, "China" fills in to bear the brunt of failed sociability. In invoking China, the protagonist is able to lose himself in the fraternal community of national sympathy—even if it can only be presently experienced as a lack. It is a trauma—the trauma of Chineseness—that he willingly inflicts upon himself because it can be shared and because, through sharing, it connects him to a collective project that renders his personal failures insignificant. The invocation of China is thus a cop-out, a scapegoating gesture that absolves the self of the burden of free sociality.

Unable to endure the pains of stirring desire, guilt, and frustration, the protagonist abandons school and wanders to a seaside resort. At a wine shop, he becomes intensely drawn to a waitress. Still, the specter of national sympathy so clouds his vision that he sees not just a waitress, but a *Japanese* waitress from whose body emanates "a uniquely Japanese scent of flesh." He is thus caught in the quandary of desiring her as a woman and fearing/resenting her as a Japanese: "She squatted by him and served him most attentively. He wanted to look closely at her and confide in her all his troubles. But in reality he didn't even dare look her in the eye, much less talk to her. And so, like a mute, all he did was look furtively at the delicate, white hands resting upon her knees and that portion of a pink petticoat not covered by her kimono" (SK, 138–39). The eroticization of the feminine Other clashes painfully with the perceived inferiority of the desiring male subject. His aching ability to appreciate "the special charm of Japanese women" (SK, 139) only sharpens the pulsating agony over his inability to assert his masculine proprietorship to possess that charm. Soon even the possibility of passing for a Japanese man is denied him:

> It was specifically the corner of the waitress's petticoat that was perturbing him now. The more he wanted to talk to her, the more tongue-tied he became. His embarrassment was apparently making the waitress a little impatient, for she asked, "Where are you from?"
> At this, his pallid face reddened again; he stammered and stammered but couldn't give a forthright answer. He was once again standing on the guillotine. For the Japanese look down upon Chinese just as we look down upon pigs and dogs. They call us Shinajin, "Chinamen," a term more derogatory than "knave" in Chinese. And now he had to confess before this pretty young girl that he was a Shinajin.
> "O China, my China, why don't you grow strong!"
> His body was trembling convulsively and tears were again about to roll down. (SK, 139)

The intersection of the patriarchal gender hierarchy with the discourse of national character and colonial ideology creates the impossible subject position of being a man and a *Shinajin*, a paradox that renders the narrator literally speechless as well as impotent. Or as Shu-mei Shih puts it, "[China's] national weakness conditions a symbolic castration of the Chinese male" (2001, 116).[7] After the above exchange, the waitress's withholding of hospitality and sexual favors is easily construed by the protagonist as a gesture of racial discrimination, though this is not apparent from the narrated sequence itself. The point is that neither he nor the waitress is able to overcome the limits of national sympathy and freely enact an instance of sociality based not on the dictates of nationality but on the practical, everyday (including erotic) interaction between a man and woman.

What critics have rarely dwelt upon is the sense of compulsion on the part of the protagonist to own up to his nationality. What makes confession his sole modus operandi of associating with strangers? What has happened to the art of passing, of make-believe? I argue that the regime of national sympathy—here precipitated by colonial racism—has thoroughly deprived him of the art of play-acting, of mask-wearing, and of self-distancing that Sennett considers essential to pure sociability. In other words, he is incapable of contracting social relations without reference to his essential being—his Chineseness. An apparently innocuous question like "where are you from" elicits from him not some clever riposte or innocent bluffing, but a relentless self-inquest and an embarrassing loss of expressiveness. Instead of seeking recourse to the art of tarrying, he surrenders himself to the guillotine of authenticity. When he places the whole weight of his selfhood on what is by nature a transient form of sociability—the encounter between a bar girl and her patron—sociability is crushed, and so is his self.

In the end, utterly broke and shame-stricken, he drowns himself in the sea after uttering these famous last words: "O China, my China, you are the cause of my death!. . . . I wish you could become rich and strong soon!. . . . Many, many of your children are still suffering" (SK, 141). The protagonist's suicide has been commonly read as a protest against China's impotence in the international Darwinian struggle for survival. On a different level, it can also be read as a denunciation of the nation as a destructive gemeinschaft. By calling out to China in his dying moment, he uses his own death to attest to the hegemony of national identity that has so subjugated him that his hope to achieve personal happiness is entirely contingent upon China's global standing. In this sense, the story is also an antidote to the romantic notion of love as an angel of freedom. Here, love can barely raise its fair head in front of the beast of national belonging.

• • •

In conflating the crises of personhood, manhood, and nationhood, Yu Dafu gives us a poignant testimonial of the crippling effect of national sympathy on the autobiographical self. The epiphanic ending of "Sinking" refers us back to the slide show episode in which the young Lu Xun awakens to his Chineseness. Lu Xun responded to the trauma of awakening by embracing the problem of national character and by waging a war on the "hypocrisy" of Chinese society. In doing so, he and his fellow writers bequeathed to us a vision of Chinese society as hopelessly plagued by hypocrisy, fractured by familial narcissism and parochialism, and devoid of affective identification across social divisions. The nationalist definition of love was thus inaugurated as a discourse of lack, of deplorable absence, of fatal inadequacy. And it was precisely on this discourse of lack that modern Chinese literature was founded and its mission defined by its founding fathers and mothers: to fill the arid Chinese hearts with love and sympathy, to make them identify with each other and feel for each other's pain, and to galvanize the "sheet of loose sand" into a community of sympathy.

The quest for national sympathy hegemonized the May Fourth project of emancipatory subjectivity and sociality and laid the groundwork for the revolutionary structure of feeling. The awakenings chronicled in romantic fiction were ones in which individuals awakened not only to their individual rights and autonomy, but also to their direct interpellation by the nation, and to their unmediated relationship to humanity as such. In their own ways, writers like Lu Xun and Yu Dafu grappled with the double-edged implications of national sympathy. Their fiction, therefore, is caught between the yearning for an intimate community and the apprehension that the "modern gemeinschaft is a state of feeling 'bigger' than action" (Sennett 1992: 311) and that it threatens to metamorphose into a monster that devours its own children.

SEVEN

Revolution of the Heart

"Revolution" (*geming*), like free love, was a highly charged and versatile term in the May Fourth lexicon. Owing its modern usage to the French Revolution on the world stage and to the anti-Manchu uprisings of 1911 in China, revolution in the May Fourth era came to be dissociated from direct political action but retained its crucial connotation of a brand-new beginning (Arendt 1963, 28–29).[1] It was frequently coupled with love, marriage, and family to signal the advent of broad social change. In the mid-1920s, however, as the Nationalist Party (KMT) consolidated its power in the south, launched the Northern Expedition, and proceeded to purge leftists among its ranks in the bloodbath of 1927, the idea of revolution began to move back into the political realm. Japan's annexation of Manchuria and bombing attacks on Shanghai also brought war and destruction closer than ever to home. In this atmosphere of danger, risk, and anxiety, it appeared that the art of kissing, the pangs of lost love, and the intrigue of love triangle that had captivated the public for a decade were sorely out of place, luxuries that brought shame or suspicion rather than distinction upon the pursuants. But is not love the defining quality of modern personhood? Is it not the hallmark of individual freedom? How and why has it become a dispensable luxury item, something that must be relinquished in a time of crisis? Are not the goals of revolution universal emancipation and freedom? If love must be subordinated to revolution or deferred to a postrevolutionary utopia, what has become of the May Fourth understanding of love, and what has come to take its place?

A new fiction genre or formula, "revolution + romance," rose to the fore to engage these questions and to offer practical as well as fantastic solutions. The genre became a smashing success, reflecting in part the radicalization of the intelligentsia in the late 1920s and the reassessment of the relative significance of the private sphere of sentiments versus the public realm of political ideas and activities. Writers on both ends of the ideological spectrum contributed to the genre's success, and its stubborn popularity bespoke as much revolutionary fervor as a reluctance to relinquish the discourse of love. When party ideologues sought to shore up the ideological base for mobilization purposes, they found themselves compelled to speak the language of love in order to secure a discursive footing in the all-pervasive social discourse of love. They wrote prescriptive texts in an effort to convince their comrades that revolution was not only a legitimate player in the field of love, but also the ultimate solution to the romantic crisis. Taking their cue from the anarchist critique that radically separated love and sex, political ideologues called for the postponement of love and the subordination of sexual relationships to the revolutionary agenda. In this chapter, I read a selection of prescriptive texts in conjunction with literary examples of "revolution + romance." I ask how revolution and love are theorized as a hierarchical binary and how revolutionary literature struggles to construct a new heroic subject—the modern *ernü yingxiong*.

THE BIRTH OF A LITERARY FORMULA

As early as the mid-1920s, KMT reformers and educators began to form a distinct voice in the debate on the nature and rules of love. In an essay about love among Chinese youth, Yang Xianjiang, editor of *Xuesheng zazhi* (Student magazine), takes the typical May Fourth position in faulting ritual and lucre for obstructing romantic happiness. His proposed remedies are commonplace enough: open social intercourse, education for women, freedom of choice, and economic independence. He also shares the assumption with his contemporaries that love is a natural instinct that must be properly managed rather than suppressed. His views, however, become more distinctive when he moves to the subject of the "revolutionary youth" (*geming qingnian*). For a revolutionary youth, he argues, love, marriage and sex are three different things. Love poses a grave threat to the revolution because it diminishes the revolutionary zeal and induces treason, discord, suicide, and murder. In other words, it restricts one's attention to personal loss and gain, thereby causing one to lose sight of the larger enterprise. The only way to prevent love from taking over one's life is to subordinate marriage to the interest of the revolution. This entails several precautionary measures: (1) One should marry only one's comrade or at least a sympathizer; (2) wedding ceremonies are not necessary; (3) both parties must be willing; and (4) if the marriage comes into conflict with the collective interest, it must be dissolved (Yang Xianjiang 1925). The scenario of the organizational marriage alarmed a liberal critic who saw in the revolutionary repudiation of love traces of Confucian puritanism—the proscription of individual freedom and the equation of marriage with the species function (Gao Shan 1926).

To be sure, in the May Fourth parlance, Confucianism is mostly a code word for everything that the liberals and radicals find objectionable, or, as they prefer, "feudal" (*fengjian*). In previous chapters, we have seen how frequently it is mobilized as a denunciatory epithet in the battle of discourse. Yang Xianjiang, unexceptionally, positions himself against Confucianism at the outset with a routine denunciation of its evils to signal his progressive stance. But his critic apparently still feels it is damaging enough to label him a Confucian puritan. And it does seem to work. Subsequent efforts to advance the revolutionary position frequently have to contend with the accusation of puritanism. And the challenge is not so much to prove that revolution is pro-love as to construct a paradigm that is sufficiently different from and superior to the bourgeois pursuit of the conjugal family and the anarchist pursuit of sexual freedom.

Hong Ruizhao, a KMT propagandist, rose to the challenge with a tract called *Geming yu lian'ai* (Revolution and love, 1928).[2] It is a remarkable effort to effect what Laclau and Mouffe call "a unified chain of equivalence" in a heterogeneous field by imposing a hegemonic dichotomy—revolution versus love—and by translating it into the moral dichotomy of the public good versus private interest. In the preface, Hong notes with some alarm that ever since "the tidal waves" of free love came crashing ashore in China and awakened millions of slumbering men and women, the names of Key, Ibsen, and Bebel have been lingering on everyone's lips, and romantic literature advocating "love's supremacy" has been all the rage. Among the youth who are as extravagantly romantic as they are fervently revolutionary, the relationship between revolution and love has become a most urgent problem that demands an immediate solution (Hong Ruizhao 1928, 1–2, hereafter cited as GL).

Hong Ruizhao makes it clear that he is out to refute the "pathological exaggeration of love's powers" (*lian'ai kuada kuang*) among modern individualists and to debunk the grandiloquent tune sung by some of his comrades to the effect that love and revolution are complementary and that love abets rather than obstructs revolution (GL, 2–3). What he is taking on is not only the May Fourth cult of free love, but also the growing trend of revolutionary romanticism spearheaded by the members of the Creation Society, particularly Yu Dafu and Jiang Guangci. Revolutionary romanticism has been in the making since the Butterfly revival of the *ernü yingxiong* ideal, but the May Fourth romanticists decisively shifted the meaning of *ernü* from filial piety to romantic passion and made love the inner essence of the revolutionary spirit. Yu Dafu, for example, believed that romantic passion is the touchstone of a true revolutionary:

> A truly revolutionary poem is not one which rattles with pistols and grenades or contains the word "revolution" repeated hundreds of times. But speak out your genuine sentiments under no disguise, emit your passion as if it were a lava from volcano—this is the paramount duty of a poet. The emergence of a revolutionary career is possible only for that little passion, the cultivation of which is inseparable from the tender and pure love of a woman. That passion, if extended, is ardent enough to burn down the palaces of a despot and powerful enough to destroy the Bastille. (quoted in Lee 1973, 274)

Jiang Guangci puts it even more succinctly: "All revolutionaries are romantic. Without being romantic, who would come to start a revolution? . . . Idealism, passion, discontent with the status quo and a desire to create something better—here you have the spirit of romanticism" (quoted in Lee 1973, 273).

Much like Butterfly sentimental heroism, Yu Dafu and Jiang Guangci's brand of romanticism assumes an unproblematic affinity between romantic love and revolutionary fervor, idealizing revolution as an abstract, sublime moment of transcendence, a moment that lends legitimacy and meaning to the sentimental existence. In their writings, the narrative attention lingers on the winding path of love that leads up to the heroic finale. And heroism almost always culminates in isolated instances of martyrdom. There is virtually no description of collective action, or of the ways in which revolution becomes "work" entwined with everyday life including romantic life, or of the ideological complexity of revolutionary politics. The prospect of burning down palaces and storming the Bastille is always far on the horizon, more a figure of speech than a goal of action.

The leftist critic Qian Xingcun credits Jiang Guangci's novella "Ye ji" (Seaside commemoration, 1927) for setting the irreversible trend of "revolution + romance" (see Yang Yi 1998, 1:72). Let us take a close look at how the first "revolution + romance" story changes the terms of the discourse and why this change might have discomfited the likes of Hong Ruizhao. The story is presented as a document *trouvé* and self-consciously distinguished from the run-of-the-mill triangle love stories that saturate the market. Narrated in retrospect, the story begins with a secretive and intensely emotional remembrance ritual on the dark seashore of Shanghai. The object of the commemoration is a female revolutionary named Zhang Shujun, a victim of the bloody massacre of 1927. The narrator, Chen Jixia, who identifies himself as a revolutionary writer without any party affiliation, has known Shujun for some years as the daughter of his landlord family in whose residence he takes his room and board. Shujun is a spirited, sympathetic, but plain-featured schoolteacher. She quickly discovers Jixia's identity as the author of revolutionary literature and falls passionately in love with him. Jixia, however, finds her unattractive and remains emotionally unresponsive to her overtures, even though he is not above experiencing (involuntary) arousal when in close proximity to her sexually ripened body. Spurned but not discouraged, Shujun devotes herself to political activities that eventually cost her her life. Meanwhile, Jixia begins to court another schoolteacher whose virginal charms catch his fancy. Zheng Yuxian, on whom he eagerly projects the fantasy of conjugal bliss, turns out to be a feeble-minded woman who readily deserts him when his revolutionary ideals prove a liability.

Curtly jilted by Yuxian, Jixia begins to question not only his judgment but also the extent to which he understands his own heart. He realizes that while he was bent upon wooing Yuxian and deluding himself that Yuxian loved the revolutionary in him, his heart had already been taken captive by

Shujun—the true revolutionary. What drives him to the seaside is more than the regret of having failed to requite a woman's sincere love. It is also the remorse of self-betrayal: in choosing to love Yuxian, Jixia affirms the wrong side of himself, the side that is rooted in his bourgeois identity—his status, income, and reputation—and in his bourgeois mentality that impels him to seek in a woman a partner with whom to build a private love nest. Having lost Shujun, he resolves to make his heart a permanent tomb for her wandering soul (her corpse is never recovered) and thus redeem himself by reaffirming the revolutionary in him. The seaside ritual is thus the modern equivalent of following a loved one in death. In keeping an eternal vigil for a revolutionary martyr, Jixia also gives over his soul to the revolution, achieving a kind of spiritual transcendence of which he is incapable when confronted with a female revolutionary in the flesh.

The story changes the terms of the romantic discourse by stripping love of its potential for transcendence. Not only is love shamefully brittle and shallow, it also blinds the lover as to where the true source of life's meaning lies. Instead of inspiring noble acts of devotion and sacrifice and ushering young people onto the path of progress, love leads them to the dead end of history. Only revolution, Jiang Guangci suggests, can fulfill the role of secular salvation. But nowhere in Jiang's writing, or in most "revolution + romance" stories for that matter, does it appear that revolution is poised to replace love or that young men and women no longer relate to one another as sexual beings and are instead fully prepared to realize themselves exclusively in revolutionary work (for such characters, we have to await the arrival of socialist realism). If anything, much of the fictional space is dedicated to love's agonies in the face of revolution's rival claim to meaning and transcendence and the latter's imperious drive to curtail individual freedom. In his personal life, in fact, Jiang chose to honor love, freedom, and creativity over revolution: finding himself unable to handle the onerous tasks of organized politics and lamenting the diminishing space left for romance and writing, he quit the Communist Party—a move that incurred the furor of the party, which immediately expelled him as a traitor (Lee 1973, 218–21; D. Wang 2004, 93).

Indeed, as revolution ceases to be an abstract ideal and enters the everyday as "work"—attending meetings, mobilizing, handing out leaflets, and so on—it also runs up against love as a formidable rival. For more than two decades, thanks to the indefatigable efforts of romance writers and guidebook authors, love has come to structure the urban middle classes' ethical, social, and fantasy life. Moreover, its articulated visions of the ideal social order—the community of love—rejects violence and subversion as a way of life (see Lee 2006b). For the revolutionaries, therefore, love poses the greatest obstacle to their project of politicizing both aesthetics and everyday life. Their tactic is to exploit the basic tension between the affirmation of ordinary life—the dignity and worth of ordinary family life and work—and the aspiration for a higher life, a tension that has always informed the discourse of love. By equating the revolutionary project with the higher life, they peremptorily reduce love to a one-dimensional experience pertaining only to the lower and narrower sphere of the private individual, an unregenerate preoccupation that prevents one from rising above the pettiness of ordinary life and merging with the grand and heroic. Thus as revolution attempts to colonize daily life, daily life as the urban middle classes know it is denied of any intrinsic meaning or value.

The delegitimation of the everyday is cast as a historical necessity by both political parties. Hong Ruizhao alludes to "a war of pens" (*bizhan*) on the problem of love among his comrades at the Whampoa Military Academy, noting with disappointment that nothing conclusive was reached in the debate. Now he is compelled to cite a "reactionary agitprop booklet" of the Communist Party. Notwithstanding its overall "mendaciousness," the booklet makes one reasonable point: that love must make way for revolution in the present political climate of anti-imperialism and antiwarlordism.[3] Hong underscores this point with a logic that informs much of modern political messianism, or what Charles Taylor prefers to call "millenarism":

> The millenarist scenario describes a moment of crisis, one in which acute conflict is about to break out, one in which the world is polarized as never before between good and evil. It is a moment in which the suffering and tribulation of the good dramatically increases. But at the same time, it promises an unprecedented victory over evil, and hence a new age of sanctity and happiness unparalleled in history. (1989, 387)

Thus Hong justifies his demand for renouncing love—something he admits is basic to humanity—as warranted by the "transitory" period of crisis. But the key here is that the postulation of crisis is deemed sufficient to sanction all draconian measures as noble sacrifices, as necessary tribulations before the coming "age of sanctity and happiness." Therefore, the present suffering must not be viewed as a necessary evil to be endured for a better future, but rather as the showdown between virtue and vice. The revolution does not compromise its nobility for eclipsing love because love, as Hong intends to show by drawing on contemporary polemics, has degenerated into egotism, an ignoble passion fundamentally at odds with the welfare of humanity. In opposing romantic love, the revolution is calling forth "the goodness of uncorrupted nature" (Taylor 1989, 387) latent in all virtuous people—their "human love."

The notion of human love comes from the Japanese sociologist Yoneda Shōtarō. We have seen in Chapter 4 that the anarchists borrowed Yoneda's dualist theory of affect in their critique of romantic love. For Yoneda, romantic love is a selfish passion fundamentally opposed to "human love," the abstract love for all human beings qua human beings. Departing from Freud's monist view of human sexuality, Yoneda maintains that human love is rooted in a separate psychosomatic reality—"social affinity"—that is not libidinally derived (1927). From this, Hong concludes that there is no room for love in a society wherein sociality (*qunxing*) is fully developed (GL, 12). It now appears that the renunciation of love is far from a temporary expediency, but mandated by the laws of evolution.

Hong assures the reader that he does not wish to eliminate romantic love; all he asks for is the recognition that love is only one small part of life, not its entirety, nor its *summum bonum* (GL, 40). Hence it is absurd to believe that love should reign supreme and that all else must be subjected to its vagaries. Hong disapprovingly mentions the example of a certain Mr. Fang, the political liaison officer of the Hangzhou Public Security Bureau, who killed himself because he was unable to endure the torment of a love triangle. Hong finds it deplorable that a promising young revolutionary like Mr. Fang should die for two scrappy women when he could have given his life to the battle against reactionaries. This is all because the meaning of love has been blown out of proportion (GL, 35–36). The only way to keep love in its proper, subdued place is to enforce monogamous marriage with little or no freedom of divorce. Once subjugated by marriage, love will actually work to stabilize society because research has shown that singles are much more prone to criminality than married people (GL, 38–39).

In a chapter called "Psychological Remedies" (*Xinli de jiuji*), Hong Ruizhao rejects revolutionary puritanism as a viable solution because it is based on the false opposition of reason and passion. There is no need to proscribe passion because passion can be easily made an ally of reason. Here he introduces another hypostatized concept, "ethical passion" (*yiwu ganqing*), purportedly borrowed from a certain American philosopher: "Ethical passion

. . . is the awakened portion of our experience. Under its sway, we feel compelled to do the right thing" (GL, 44). Hong explains that the deeply felt impulse to do the right thing—redressing a wrong or taking part in national salvation—is what defines the true nature of a revolutionary (*gemingxing*). Revolution, therefore, is never simply a matter of responding to external command, but one of passionate striving (GL, 45), much in the same manner that *qing* is conceptualized as a moral sentiment in the Confucian structure of feeling. Like Yu Dafu and Jiang Guangci, Hong too calls for uniting revolution and (ethical) passion, but he is not inclined to link "the tender and pure love of a woman" directly to political action. At best, love can fortify a marriage against the socially destructive practice of divorce; at worst, it corrupts the comrades and makes them susceptible to Communist sex traps (GL, 37). Thus, although love adds little to the revolution, it is too potent a force to be left to its own devices.

The concluding chapter accordingly switches to the chatty mode of self-help literature. Hong Ruizhao's advice is nothing out of the ordinary: in choosing marriage partners, we must prudently stay away from the vain and arrogant types, from those unsympathetic to the revolution and from those melancholy and sickly "scholars and beauties" (who are bad news for the future of the race). In short, revolutionaries should always marry sensible and robust fellow revolutionaries. But are there enough sensible and robust female comrades for revolutionary men to choose from? As if in anticipation of this question, Hong supplies in the appendix a separate treatise on "the question of love among revolutionary women" (a reprint of an essay he published in *Zhongyang banyuekan*, no. 20). Here, he wrestles with the contradictory subject positions opened up to women in the revolution. On the one hand, Hong applauds women's effort to break out of the patriarchal family in order to join the revolution and to serve society and the nation. On the other hand, fearful of the coalescence of an independent, liberal feminist movement, he locates women's "new mission" (*xin shimin*) squarely within the conjugal family.

The reason why women need to be redomesticated is sought in science. Although dismissive of Freud's theory of love, Hong Ruizhao finds it convenient to endorse the psychoanalytic "insight" that women are enslaved to their emotions. It is therefore to be expected that female revolutionaries will frequently stumble over the question of desire. Compounding the problem is that fact that once they have embraced the idea of liberation, they are easily misled into believing that liberty extends to the realm of sexuality. What they fail to realize is that when they encounter problems in love, it is not just they who are in trouble—they have also placed their offspring, and by extension the entire race, in danger. For the sake of the nation, Hong intones, we ought to impose the code of chastity among unmarried and married women alike. We ought also to urge revolutionary women to fulfill their "heaven-endowed duties": marriage, child rearing, and domestic management (GL, 85–87).

Under the rubric of revolution, Hong Ruizhao assembles an argument for organizational rationality and discipline by synthesizing ideas from conservatives, liberals, anarchists, and even the communists, as well as by freely mixing Wnlightenment humanism, sexual psychology, psychoanalysis, sociology, and eugenics. Ultimately, I submit, the revolutionary discourse is able to triumph over the contending discourses because it offers both a radical project of political renewal and a conservative social program (particularly in the form of matrimonial discipline). As such, it promises a total solution to the romantic crisis—the insecurity, mistrust, duplicity, and betrayal that have come to be so ineluctably associated with the romantic experience. Although the bourgeois ideal of the conjugal family has broad appeal, it is unable to eliminate the role of amatory fortune or the contingency of personal inclinations and interests. It is for this reason that Zhang Jingsheng's rules of love prove so galling to liberals and conservatives alike.

As romantic love seems to flounder as the spiritual pillar of modern life, party ideologues mobilize a new heroic discourse to supply a grand moral purpose to life—the liberation of the Chinese nation from the "corrupt servants of tyranny" (Taylor 1989, 387). Whether it is the KMT speaking of eliminating the warlords and communist bandits or the CCP speaking of overthrowing the three titanic forces oppressing the Chinese masses (imperialism, feudalism, and capitalism), the language is always Rousseauian, prophesying the battle "between virtue, patriotism, and freedom, on one side, and vice, treason, and tyranny, on the other" (387). Both parties promise a new republic of virtue in which every individual will be able to "reconcile reason and passion and merge the smaller self with the greater self" (GL, 6).

The appeal of the revolutionary promise is discernible in the shifting patterns of romantic fiction. More and more "revolution + romance" stories gravitate toward a political denouement. The typical plot line begins with a thwarted romance or a love triangle and ends with the jilted, disappointed, or disillusioned party taking leave of the scene of love and joining the revolution— either the Northern Expedition, the communist underground labor movement, or the war of resistance against the Japanese invasion. Still, revolution remains an "ending" that brings the plot to a halt; it is not a player in the story proper. There is no representation of the "greater self" in action. The heroic subjectivity remains unapologetically individualistic and intensely private—as epitomized in the ending of Jiang Guangci's "Seaside Commemoration," where revolutionary epiphany is a thoroughly introspective experience. The narrator takes up neither arms (to become a fighter) nor the bullhorn (to become a labor agitator); instead, he brings rose wine and flowers to the shore to commune with the fallen heroine's soul and to bemoan the romance that never was. Revolution, it seems, is no more than a mode of feeling. It supplements rather than constituting romantic subjectivity. For all its high-flying rhetoric, Jiang's story celebrates the heart more than anything else.[4] Most writers of "revolution + romance" stories who came after him stayed more or less within the parameters he established, although a few began to explore the question of when revolution ceased to be romanticism by another name and when its exigencies rendered love experientially superfluous and historically counterrevolutionary.

THE LOGIC OF THE SUPPLEMENT

After nearly a decade of backlash against the May Fourth ideal of free love, the intellectual ethos of the 1930s seems to have turned decidedly against all love-related issues. Yang Sao, the translator of a Russian article on marriage, has to attach a self-conscious note defending the necessity of his endeavor (1930). It is hard to imagine earlier authors writing on the same topic needing to make a similarly rueful plea for attention. In an elegiac tone, Leo Ou-fan Lee singles out the year 1931 as the end of the "journey of sentiment" in modern China: "With the death of [Xu Zhimo] in 1931 . . . , an extraordinary decade of emotional commotion came to an end" (1973, 271). Ding Ling, whose celebrated entry into the literary scene had been marked by her daring explorations of feminine desire, produced some unflattering portrayals of love in the late 1920s. Her 1928 short story "Shujia zhong" (Summer vacation), for example, is just such a scathing critique of love—here same-sex love among female schoolteachers—as a frivolous game played by characters thoroughly bored by life. Tze-lan Sang finds the story "chilling" in its contempt for female homoeroticism, but she also recognizes that Ding Ling is taking an increasingly dim view of all forms of romantic attachment (2003, 151–53). Tani Barlow believes that Ding Ling both laments the injurious effects of sexual repression and is alarmed by the ugly guises that desire tends to assume. She writes:

> "Summer Break" illustrates the severe penalties Ding Ling's stories imposed on nüxing [the sexualized female subject]. Zhiqing [a character in the story] and the rest, the blind and the sighted, those in darkness and those who saw the light, exist inside a repetitious cycle that they compulsively initiate: neurasthenic collapse, rally, fantastic erotic pleasure, dreams of self-directed change, disappointment, self-loathing, relapse. . . . In the late 1920s Ding Ling's stories hinted that individual sexuality is at issue in many ugly behaviors, ranging from female Don Juanism, to homoeroticism, to masturbatory sexual phantasmagoria. (2004, 43)

Like Sang, Barlow does not consider this story a targeted attack on homosexuality. In her view, Ding Ling finds same-sex attraction "understandable but compensatory," and her narratives chide "such erotic affairs in the same tone as they criticiz[e] women's failure to will action in other life experiences" (406, n63). Indeed, homosexuality here is only a demeaning trope to ridicule the paltriness and frivolity of love. Ding Ling apparently wants us to see the grotesque consequences of chronically lacking higher ambitions or higher purposes in life—and love is decidedly not among them. Hence, when temporarily deprived of male associates and released from the routine of work, these women simply turn to each other for emotional and sexual relief. And instead of finding happiness, they become embroiled in endless cycles of jealousy, betrayal, and resentment. Barlow succinctly sums up Ding Ling's contribution to the "revolution + romance" theme: "In Ding Ling's hands, 'love' was becoming a catchall for all personal indulgences balanced not against revolution, actually, but against a large, diffuse matter of praxis on behalf of all progressive communities larger than the self" (167).

In a different story, Ding Ling ponders the baleful impact of melancholic romantic fiction, including her own, upon the younger generation:

> We wrote some things and people read them, but after all that time, nothing at all has changed. Besides the money we got for it, can you see any other meaning to it? It's true that some readers were moved by a particular anecdote or passage, but look at the kind of readers they were! Nothing but petty bourgeois students in high school and beyond who have just reached adolescence

and are prone to melancholy. . . . I now realize that we've actually done harm by dragging younger people into our old rut of sentimentalism, individualism, discontent, and pent-up anxiety! . . . What's their way out? They can only sink deeper and deeper into their own rage. They can't see the connection between their suffering and society. (Ding Ling 1989, 115–16; hereafter IMW)

Whereas once writers proudly proclaim themselves sentimentalists or individualists and poured out their "sorrows" to showcase their boundless interiority, now their lovesick groans have become "the lingering vestige of a gilded and irresponsible world of the past" (Lee 1973, 272). Lydia Liu points out that the general intellectual climate of the late 1920s has become less and less hospitable to the idea of "individualism" (1995, 95–98). From Hu Shi's hierarchy of the "greater self" (*dawo*) and "smaller self" (*xiaowo*) and Chen Duxiu's denunciation of laissez-faire individualism to Deng Feihuang's critique of individualism as a bourgeois ideology, the individual has become the Other of an emerging heroic collectivity, be it the "Chinese nation" or the "laboring classes." Revolutionaries on both the left and right claim to embody the "greater self," grounding their legitimacy in some version of social collectivism while lashing out against those with liberal tendencies as bourgeois romantics. The word *romantic,* as Zhu Ziqing puts it, is now "reduced to slander and a curse" (quoted in Lee 1973, 273). To be a romantic is to ally oneself with the regressive classes, the reactionary political cause, or the unjust social system that progressives are seeking to overthrow. It is tantamount to declaring oneself the enemy of history.

The urgent need to take leave of the sentimental preoccupations of the "individual" is expressed in a poem called "Lian'ai yu geming" (Love and revolution). The poet Wu Menghui cries out fervidly: "Love?/The world has not been made just! . . . /Class struggle has begun/Our brethren are shedding tears and blood;/My love, let us take leave of our passion/For what we need is "love" no more! . . . /My love, pray turn away your cherry lips/For it is the enemy's blood-smeared throat that I desire to kiss!" (1927). It would be hard to find a more striking juxtaposition than that of a lover's cherry lips and a bloody gash on an enemy's throat. The contrast highlights the courage and sacrifice in the poet's eroticized preference for the latter. One is to go straight from the lover's embrace to the battlefield, and those who are too fainthearted to make such a heroic leap become the butt of satire.

One month later, the same journal that published the poem carried a satirical piece entitled "Lian'ai shang wei chenggong, tongzhi bu xu nuli" (Love has yet to succeed; my fellow comrades, you needn't exert yourselves). The title is a facetious play on Sun Yat-sen's testament urging the Nationalist Party to carry on the revolutionary enterprise—"The revolution has yet to succeed; my comrades, you must strive to carry it on" (*Geming shang wei chenggong, tongzhi reng xu nuli*). The essayist targets his satire at those who, despite the unfinished nature of the revolution, indulge in romantic play. He ventriloquizes: "Comrade, if you have not succeeded in love, never mind about the revolution. . . . For when the revolution does come about, others will traipse off to cuddle with their loved ones while you yourself still have to endure loneliness and ennui. What good is revolution to you anyway?" (Xiugu 1928, 194). Love is accused of being a cover for egotism, myopia, and pusillanimity— the chief characteristics of an "individualist." In contrast to Yu Dafu and Jiang Guangci's vision of the romantic lover as (potentially) the most ardent revolutionary, the individual in love is portrayed in this satire as apathetic to anything beyond his or her private emotional gratification. The author goes on to mimic the voice of the "love-supremacist": "The revolutionary enterprise of our time should begin with the 'completion of love.' We can put to rest such slogans as 'Down with the warlords! Down with the imperialists!'" Singling out those who are supposedly most susceptible to the lures of individualism, the author ends the essay with mock advice: "Allow me to offer a word of advice to students, merchants, and the petit bourgeoisie: Make haste to make love while you still have a few bucks; once you have all secured a lover, then come and join the revolution hand in hand" (Xiugu 1928, 195).

The characterization of love as a leisure activity of the moneyed and propertied classes echoes an important question in contemporary debates: is love a universal experience or a class-specific privilege? Leftist and anarchist polemicists generally adhere to the conviction that only the bourgeoisie can afford the luxury of romantic love, and that the high premium it places on chastity and fidelity is but an ideological ruse to protect the institution of marriage. The anarchists carry the logic furthest to conclude that the proletariat can dispense with the hypocrisy of sexual morality and truly emancipate themselves by practicing free sex (see Chapter 4). Although both liberals and conservatives are appalled by the anarchist assault on marriage and family, the association of romantic love with the bourgeois class has acquired a kind of truth effect. The romantic lover is increasingly stereotyped as a selfish, possessive, and potentially treacherous egotist bent on pleasure seeking, oblivious to mounting social and political crises, and devoid of idealism and a sense of moral responsibility. As such, he or she is exiled from the realm of the sublime, where a true revolutionary is necessarily one who has been tempered by and transcended the flames of love.

Ding Ling's "Yijiusanling nian chun Shanghai" (Shanghai, spring 1930, 1930), from which the above quotation on the futility of writing is taken, presents two mirroring stories which Tani Barlow believes belong together "by force of a certain intellectual logic" (in IMW, 112).[5] This intellectual logic is precisely the bankruptcy of romantic love, and by extension, of the bourgeois class in the broad historical scheme of things. The first segment chronicles the gradual awakening of a bourgeois woman, Meilin, from "her enthrallment to bourgeois 'love'" (in IMW, 113). Like "Regret for the Past," the story begins with the aftermath of free love, though the flashbacks to the days of courtship are more perfunctory. Meilin cohabits with Zibin, who is set up in the story as the archetypal bourgeois intellectual: talented, proud, materialistic, cynical, and totally self-absorbed. Unlike Juansheng and Zijun, Meilin and Zibin are comfortably well off, thanks to Zibin's successful literary career and thanks to the relaxed social attitude toward free love (at least within their own circle of friends). Thus the deterioration of their relationship, in the total absence of external pressure, is emphatically laid at the foot of romantic love—a false idol that turns out to be incapable of sustaining a social bond or endowing life with lasting meaning.

Throughout the story, Ding Ling carefully notes the small comforts and luxuries that the romantic pair enjoys: dainty dresses, chilled fruit cocktails, gourmet candies, movies, and leisurely strolls. Nonetheless, their health slowly declines, their minds grow more and more restive, and visits from friends become less and less frequent. Zibin alienates Ruoquan, the friend whose speech we have quoted, by ridiculing "proletarian literature"; he further isolates himself by launching loose-cannon attacks on the leftist literary scene as a whole. His progressive friends admire his literary talent, but regrettably regard him as "belong[ing] to a different age" (IMW, 121). Shut up in his study, Zibin finds himself unaccountably plagued by a vague sense of unhappiness: "All he knew was that nothing felt right, that words could not describe his unhappy feeling" (IMW, 124). His creativity wanes and his mind turns "blank" as soon as he grabs his pen. He cannot find any relief from his "self-inflicted" misery in his relationship with Meilin—"the woman had never understood him" (IMW, 118). Keeping his mental troubles to himself, "he pampered her, petted and amused her, and satisfied all her

material wants. But he only wanted her to love his ideas and what he loved."
It is an exact replica of the relationship between Helmer and Nora in *A Doll's House*—the stereotypical bourgeois couple brought together by superficial attraction rather than by intellectual compatibility and affinity.

Meilin's awakening, first set in motion by Ruoquan's remarks, inversely parallels Zibin's self-withdrawal. Although nothing cataclysmic has taken place, she reaches an epiphanic moment when all of a sudden her "muddle-headed" thinking about love and happiness falls apart:

> In the past, having read a lot of classical and romantic fiction, her ideal had been to throw over everything for love. Once she fell in love with him, she really had left everything behind and plunged into his embrace. She had gone along quite happily the whole time thinking muddle-headedly that she was fortunate. But now things were different. She needed something else! She wanted her own place in society. She wanted to have contact with many, many people. Even though they loved each other, she could no longer be locked up in the house as one man's after-work amusement. (IMW, 125)

Once Meilin decides that "a life of leisure was no longer acceptable" and that "the role of wife, the role of lover, did not satisfy her" (IMW, 133), she seeks out Ruoquan, who eagerly inducts her into the activist circle. This option is clearly not available to Zijun in "Regret for the Past." Zijun's only discursive resource—one that she mobilizes successfully against the traditional family—is the Nora model constructed by the May Fourth discourse of emancipation. For her, free love is the solution to life's problems and not a problem itself. As such, love exhausts life's meaning and purpose for her. Thus, when Juansheng withdraws his love, life has come to an end, and the only thing left to do is to die. Because she sees no life outside of love, she never appears to yearn for a place of her own in society, or to "have contact with many, many people." This is precisely what Meilin strives for and has the means of attaining, thanks to the rise of the revolutionary discourse.

While Zibin frets in his study trying to commence a new novel featuring "a Chinese Don Quixote" (IMW, 136), Meilin is attending a meeting of a Communist Party study group. In contrast to the strained relationship between her and Zibin, here she feels instantly absorbed into the camaraderie: "Aside from Ruoquan, she did not know anyone there, but she did not feel awkward. On the contrary, she felt quite comfortable because she and they were all 'comrades'" (IMW, 136). She listens with rapt attention to a speech given by a young printer on the "the world's political and economic situation" (IMW, 136). Immediately afterward, she requests to work in a factory to become "proletarianized." The story ends on a May Day with a petrified Zibin reading a note left by Meilin informing him that she is at the moment "on the [avenue] as assigned by the organization to carry out [a communist] movement" (IMW, 138).

The element of fantasy is obvious in the character of Meilin (not to mention the printer who can perorate on world politics and economy). But Zibin is no less tendentiously portrayed. Like Ding Ling's morose adolescent reader of romantic fiction, he is too myopic to see the connection between individual unhappiness and the injustices of the social system. Happiness eludes him notwithstanding all his possessions—love, fame, and material comforts. Simply by virtue of the fact that he has turned his back on history, he is doomed to unremitting misery. That vague sense of discontent which he cannot name may well be unconscious guilt under the censorious gaze of history. Interestingly enough, the figure of the abject bourgeois is equally vilified as the Other of progressivism/nationalism in both KMT and CCP discourses, as evidenced by Hong Ruizhao's approving invocation of his enemy's propaganda material. It does not have to be gendered male, either. In the second segment of the story, the bourgeois lover is a woman named Mary who refuses "to relinquish what the romantic age has made available to her . . . [the] world of feminine pleasure and sensuousness" (Tang 2000, 119). Barlow observes how well Mary and Zibin would suit each other: it is as if Mary, "the hyper-feminine, tortured, essentially sexual creature of imported European literature," is authored by Zibin, "the treaty port literary star" (1989, 29). But the mismatch is intentional—it is to facilitate Ding Ling's exploration of the dialectic of love and revolution.

Whereas the story of Meilin stops abruptly at the point of awakening and does not show how revolutionary work is to be incorporated into daily life and how she is to negotiate the inevitable clashes, the second segment takes up these questions by beginning with an already awakened protagonist. It seems that Ding Ling is more comfortable dealing with new questions in the framework of a more conventional distribution of gender roles whereby the man represents the enlightened, progressive, and universal force and the woman stands for its antithesis. The story of Wang Wei and Mary shows in no uncertain terms how love, with its insatiable demand for time, attention, and money, obstructs the daily work of revolution—meetings, study sessions, the drafting of "planning outlines, organizational outlines, manifestoes, and correspondence," and "practical struggles" (IMW, 140, 141). Keeping the lovers together is but a tenuous passion that is more a remnant of a romantic past (periodically renewed by their youthful sexuality) than a deeply spiritual bond. Mary is said to love no one but herself and enjoys ease, comfort, and the excitement of erotic pleasures (IMW, 147, 157). Wang Wei, for his part, is keenly interested in "the world economy, politics, and how to liberate the laboring masses." He wishes he could discuss these issues with Mary, but he could do no more than "suffer in patience the torture of her love" (IMW, 149).

With the authorial sympathy clearly invested in Wang Wei, Mary's feminist protest of sorts is presented as a temper tantrum, a caricature version of Meilin's soliloquy of awakening[6]:

> I make you suffer? Nonsense! It's you who has made me suffer! What pain do you have? During the day, you go out to 'work.' You have a lot of comrades! You have hope! You have goals! At night you come home and rest. You have a woman whom you can kiss anytime you want! As for me, I have nothing. All day I roam around. I have boredom, loneliness, and the deep regret that comes from losing my love! (IMW, 162–63)

The protest is not only framed as the ravings of an "angry," "irrational," and "hysterical" woman, but also intended to be a self-indictment. Mary's problem is exactly as she describes: she has no hopes and no goals, only self-induced boredom and loneliness. Ding Ling offers a proto-Marxist explanation to her problem: she is a bourgeois woman who is incapable of seeing beyond herself and achieving, as a female bus conductor in the story does, "simple, clear understanding of politics that result[s] from having class consciousness" (IMW, 142). But the difference between the bus conductor and Mary is more than "class consciousness": The former has a salaried job that affords her not only a measure of economic independence, but also a public persona and access to the political sphere. Unlike Mary the housewife, the bus conductor has transcended the debilitating privacy of a natural person without a public existence. In other words, she has realized Meilin's dream of having "her own place in society" and having "contact with many, many people." Ding Ling, however, does not advance such a liberal-feminist argument; rather, she abides by the class analysis and reiterates it in Wang Wei's recognition of the class-determined incompatibility between himself and Mary: "If Mary were a peasant girl, a factory worker, or a high school student, then they would get along very well because there would be only one idea, one outlook. He would lead her and she would obey" (IMW, 156). As a last resort, Wang Wei suggests that Mary go to one of his meetings. Mary goes along only because she would not miss any opportunity to parade her beauty and possibly make a conquest. Little does she know that the revolution has completely reinvented the terms of gender relations. The rules of the game have so changed that she simply makes a fool of herself. She is painfully aware that her beauty is met with utter indifference from everybody attending the meeting, and that while they look "dynamic, vigorous, and full of vitality," she alone does not have this quality (IMW, 157).

Xiaobing Tang reads the second segment as a dramatization of the disciplining of the male revolutionary body in the face of the temptations of feminine desire and city life. He argues that "the fact that [Wang Wei] is constantly exhausted and unavailable, emotionally as well as physically, to a desiring Mary becomes one effective way for him to safeguard his commitment through disciplining his body" (2000, 118). Precisely because Wang Wei has shifted the locus of a higher life from romance to revolution and is determined to spare no effort in pursuit of this higher life, he can make no allowances for competing goals and claims. Daily life is only meaningful to him to the extent that it is colonized by revolutionary work. Failing to make the same transfer and unable to take leave of the picayune pleasures of city life, Mary deserts Wang Wei in the end and is last seen shopping in Shanghai's affluent quarters with another man in tow. Meanwhile, Wang Wei devotes himself wholeheartedly to his revolutionary work, and the story ends with his arrest while taking part in anti-imperialist protests on the street. Their divergent paths seem to affirm that romance has no place in revolution, but a barely developed subplot featuring a comrade of Wang's and the afore-mentioned bus conductor offers a glimmer of possibility. Their romance is successful because the woman, unlike Mary, is "a true revolutionary" (IMW, 169) and because they have, from the same baseline of class consciousness, managed to merge love with work. Yet the fact that their romance is only invoked rather than dramatized indicates that perhaps Ding Ling is not too sure how a revolutionary romance would operate in a day-to-day context. Or perhaps she cannot trust herself to the task of representation out of a vague awareness that "revolutionary romance" is an ideological fiction that would stretch the realist mode beyond the limits of verisimilitude and good faith. After all, the prospect of a romance with only "one idea [and] one outlook" and in which the man leads and the woman obeys may not be too amenable to the mimetic mode or even palatable to a sophisticated urban readership accustomed to romance's excitingly equalizing effects and its mystique of risk and unpredictability.

Given the evident discomfort with yoking together revolution and romance, why then the persistence of the formula? If love has become such a suspect topic, why is it not cast off altogether? Why does not love, in the first segment of "Shanghai, Spring 1930," end at the moment of awakening? For all her resemblance to Nora, Meilin does not walk out of her love nest in a gesture of protest. Perhaps the author does not wish to lead the reader unnecessarily to surmise how Meilin will survive on her own, how she will guard her body/chastity, or whether she will embark on an alarming path of sexual liberation/dissolution. Such anxieties are not unreasonable on the part of a readership steeped in romantic fiction of love entanglements centering on female characters. Indeed, if this story were given a coda by the notorious romancer Zhang Ziping (1883–1959), Meilin would most certainly become romantically involved either with Ruoquan, who is already awakened and thus no longer bourgeois, or with the remarkably knowledgeable (and hence her intellectual match) printer. But Ding Ling at this stage in her career is decidedly not interested in such complications. Her central concern is not whether a woman can find the "right man," which still treats love as the ultimate goal, but whether romance as a lifestyle and ethical ideal can be reconciled with revolution.

Thus, the ending is more about transferring the primary locus of Meilin's identity from the home (love) to the street (revolution) than about leaving one man behind in order to join another man. Xiaobing Tang focuses on the "corporeal reorientation" of the male body (particularly that of Wang Wei), but it is apparent that Ding Ling is equally concerned with the subversive potential of the newly mobilized female body and the need to keep it tractable. Mary, however, whose "repetition of Nora's action becomes a sign of resistance against the historical tide—the revolutionary ideology" (Liu 2003, 133), is allowed to go off with another man because she has chosen to go against the "historical tide" that renders her decadence irrelevant.

By contrast, instead of abandoning her common-law husband to his bourgeois miasma, Meilin stays with him (thus allaying the reader's anxieties about her sexuality) but relocates her identity in her underground political activism. In place of Nora's forceful slamming of the door are constant protestations of "deep love" for Zibin, even after her awakening: "Yes, she still loved

Zibin and, no, she would never leave him, of that she was certain" (IMW, 125). And in her note to Zibin, she writes: "when I come back we can have a rational discussion. We should both criticize each other very sincerely and thoroughly. I have a lot of things to tell you, some about myself and some about you" (IMW, 138). Thus we are assured that after the May Day demonstration, Meilin will return to her abject bourgeois lover to help him see the light through "rational discussion," and that her sexuality will be well contained in the bourgeois home and will not hinder the blossoming of her political identity.

Once again, we find the sexual politics of the left fall into line with that of the right. Hong Ruizhao, the KMT propagandist, also wants women to take part in revolutionary activities while being true to their feminine destiny. Love must be made subordinate to revolution, but it is useful in shoring up the institutions of marriage and family against the anti-institutional pursuit of sexual liberation. But there is an even deeper reason why love and revolution are so persistently juxtaposed and why their dialectical relationship proves so irresistible to the narrative imagination. This has to do with love's fundamental place in the constitution of the modern subject. The revolutionary self, insofar as it is a modern subject, compulsively harks back to romantic love because it cannot define itself without reference to an interiority long conceptualized as an emotional terrain, vast, deep, and mysterious. People might disagree on whether the inner terrain is ruled by the libido, the élan vital, or "human love," but few would dispute its centrality in making a person into a "self," a subject endowed with freedom, rights, and agency. The revolutionary subject may define his or her "self" primarily in collective terms (as in the "greater self" or "proletarian self"), but it is still unable to dispense with a sentiment-based inner realm. Love, after all, has been the modus vivendi of the modern self. The revolutionary subject needs first of all to establish itself as an affective subject, one that feels, loves, and, as it is increasingly necessary, hates; one that is capable of loyalty, devotion and self-sacrifice; *and* one that can transcend its (class) limitations and empathize with the suffering masses. In going straight from the lover's embrace to the crucible of the battlefield (real or symbolic), the bourgeois intellectual constructs him or herself as the revolutionary subject par excellence. This subject, in short, is the new *ernü yingxiong*.

In Chapter 2, we discussed how the modern hero is no longer a misogynist murderer, as in older chivalric stories, but rather a tender-hearted man of sentiment. *Yu li hun*, for example, insists that Mengxia's eventual martyrdom is fundamentally connected to his identity as an passionate lover. Love and pa-triotism are placed on a fluid, mutually authenticating continuum, for in the Confucian structure of feeling, all virtues are ideally unified. The May Fourth generation rejected this holistic paradigm, particularly the pivotal place of filial piety, and introduced their own problematic of the dialectic of love and national sympathy. The social discourse of love in the 1920s further disrupted the love-patriotism continuum with a differentiated and ever ramifying cate-gory of "love." As love was made part of everyday life, it was simultaneously regarded as the antithesis of a new heroic ethic—the revolution—as well as its internal supplement. The "revolution + romance" formula emerged to fashion the new *ernü yingxiong*, and more often than not it was caught in the paradox of dramatizing the antagonism of love and revolution while at the same time averring their essential oneness.

Hu Chunbing's play, *Ai de geming* (The revolution of love, 1931), is a good example of the formula from the right. Zhong Sanmin is the rebellious son of a well-to-do compradore merchant. His name, Zhong (invoking *Zhongguo*, China) Sanmin (invoking Sun Yat-sen's *sanmin zhuyi*, the Three People's Prin-ciples), marks him more as a character type—a Nationalist patriot—than a rounded or layered personality. He despises his father and the latter's impetu-ous foreign boss, ignores the overtures of a flirtatious socialite, and steadfastly courts a free-spirited New Woman appositely named Hua Ziyou (free China). In a botched insurrection, Sanmin is arrested, and after being rescued by com-rades, he is forced to go into hiding. At last the revolution[7] succeeds, and San-min returns home victoriously to drive out the foreign boss, save his family from ruinous incrimination, and finally secure Ziyou's love. In a climactic scene, Sanmin rips up the foreign boss's business contract with his father and proclaims: "This is the time we Chinese tear our slave indentures into shreds!" (Hu Chunbing 1931, 90).

Like earlier romantic stories, the play takes pains to establish Sanmin's foremost identity as a lover. In his student days in Japan he had been involved with a Japanese woman, whom he gave up when he returned to China to join the revolution. His return, therefore, was accompanied by the ritualized ges-ture of renouncing one's right to contract intimate ties with a foreign na-tional, as well as by the determination to contain the universalist aspiration of love within the limits dictated by the nation-state. Quite predictably, in a cri-sis scene, the Japanese woman, like the return of the repressed, turns up unan-nounced to haunt him, putting his new regime of national sympathy to test.

By now Sanmin is courting Ziyou, whose symbolic status allows Sanmin to reconcile private passion with public commitment. The ease with which he does this is evident in his declaration: "I love Ziyou! I want revolution!" (24). In loving Ziyou, whose name literalizes the goal of the Nationalist revolution, Sanmin transforms himself into a modern *ernü yingxiong*.

The happy ending of the play affirms the possibility of uniting private passion and political commitment. And yet the highly symbolic nature of the characters belies the facile optimism, making it imperative that personal happiness is not only contingent upon revolutionary success, but also dependent on the revolution for its very definition. Ideally, there should be nothing really private about "private passion." To colonize the shifting field of individual identity, to give it a fixed principle, a permanent structure, and a coherent meaning, revolutionary nationalism revives the discourse of *ernü yingxiong* because it establishes love as equivalential with *and* subordinate to patriotism, that is, as a supplement. Here, the notion of "supplement" grants us greater analytic purchase than that of "sublimation." Ban Wang uses sublimation to understand the exuberance of emotion in such revolutionary literature as Yang Mo's (1914–1995) *Qingchun zhi ge* (Song of youth, 1958). For him, the romantic impulse is never simply repressed out of existence, but is co-opted by politics through sublimation—that is, the rechanneling of libidinal energy into politically acceptable outlets (2003, 473). Hence an important plot element in "revolution + romance" stories is the heroine's transferring of love from an undeserving bourgeois to a magnetic revolutionary, thereby unifying private passions with political ideals.

Although I agree that a process of sublimation is certainly at work, the term does not capture the persistently ambivalent standing of love in revolutionary literature. The supplementary logic enables us to discern the doublespeak of "revolution + romance": on the one hand, love must be recognizable in the conventions of romantic love stories—to wit, the revolutionary lovers must still be erotic beings rather than robotic sloganeers, and their relationship must still be dyadic and suffused with the usual gamut of romantic sensations: adoration, elation, self-denial, ecstasy, jealousy. On the other hand, love must be denied of its centrality or claim to transcendence; the lovers must not die for love. In short, as the internal supplement to revolution, love is simultaneously affirmed and disavowed; it is co-opted as an indispensable ally and repudiated as an intransigent rival.

The supplementary logic becomes fully operational in the inherently polysemic and heteroglossic world of representation where there is always room for play. Love can still be the all-consuming topic even if it is to be supplanted by revolution in the end. Mao Dun (1896–1981) clearly recognizes the dangerous latitude afforded by the formula and makes a rectification attempt in his self-appointed role as the cultural czar of the left. In an essay entitled "'Geming' yu 'lian'ai' de gongshi" (On the formula of revolution and romance, 1935), Mao Dun points out that there are three variations of the "revolution + romance" theme. In the first, most popular, type, the protagonist engages in both revolution and love, experiences the conflict between the two pursuits, and finally relinquishes love for the sake of revolution. In a less common variant, the emphasis is no longer on the conflict but on the complementarity of love and revolution. Usually there would be one woman being wooed by several men, and she would pick out the most revolutionary one among them. Of late a third type has emerged, showing how love grows among men and women who are engaged in the same revolutionary work. Mao Dun unambiguously endorses the last type. In the first type, he argues, love is in the foreground whereas revolution is but a cloak (*waitao*) or a backdrop (*peicheng*). The second type gives revolution and love equal emphasis, thus creating the impression that love is as important as revolution and that it constitutes a significant dimension of life. In the third type, by contrast, revolution is the only meaningful pursuit in life; love is but a routine affair, like eating and sleeping. The poet afflicted with the "pathology of love" (*lian'ai bing*) may think this attitude blasphemous, but under the bright light of revolution, love is indeed nothing more than an everyday business, and certainly not worth going crazy for (Mao Dun 1935). Hong Ruizhao would have been pleased by the equation of love with eating and sleeping—something one cannot do without but must not be accorded undue significance lest it challenge revolution's monopoly on the meaning of life, or the "higher life."

Eager to sing the valediction to "revolution + romance," Mao Dun directs his ire against Chen Quan's[8] novel *Geming de qian yimu* (On the eve of the revolution, 1934, hereafter cited as GQY) for stubbornly clinging to the lonely path of the most incorrect type in which revolution serves as the deus ex machina to resolve a romantic impasse. Set in the years immediately before the Nationalist revolution, the novel chronicles a love triangle among a female student (Zhang Mengpin), a Beijing University professor (Xu Hengshan), and a graduate of Qinghua University (Chen Linghua). The story begins with Linghua and Mengpin's romance in the typically May Fourth fashion: chaste meetings, youthful frolicking, exchange of ideas, secret longings, intimations of love, and painful parting. One quality, however, distinguishes it from a typical May Fourth love story: there are no authoritarian parents meddling in young people's matrimonial affairs. The picture of domestic harmony presented in the novel reflects both the author's distance from May Fourth iconoclasm and the KMT's profamily ideological orientation.

No sooner than their romance begins in an Edenlike setting do Linghua and Mengpin have to part company—Linghua is due to leave for America for a lengthy study-abroad program. Uncertain as to whether he should propose to Mengpin before leaving the country, Linghua consults his best friend, Hengshan, a self-proclaimed bachelor for life, and receives the following advice:

> Just think of the situation in China today. Domestically we are tyrannized by warlords and politicians; internationally we are oppressed by imperialists. Our compatriots live and die like beasts of burden in wars, floods, coldness, hunger, and sickness. Still more, our glorious ancestral land is everywhere in the grip of the white man. How can we have the peace of mind to indulge in romance? Linghua, you are very talented and you ought to dedicate yourself to national salvation, instead of becoming infatuated with a woman (GQY, 585).

While Linghua is abroad, Hengshan becomes acquainted with Mengpin and is hopelessly smitten by her, not knowing that she is Linghua's girlfriend. During a demonstration against the warlord regime, Hengshan injures himself to save Mengpin and wins the latter's gratitude and daily visits to his sickbed. At this juncture, Linghua unexpectedly returns to China. Having ascertained that Mengpin's heart still belongs to Linghua, Hengshan decides to withdraw and begins to entertain suicidal thoughts. But rather than die for love, he resolves to die for the country: "The revolutionary banners have been unfurled in the South and the revolutionary fighters have readied themselves for bloody battles. Why not change my name and join the army? I will then honor my friendship with Linghua, do my best by Mengpin, and repay my homeland with my own body! Go, go, go join the revolution!" (GQY, 650).

At the beginning of the story, Hengshan is a determined antiromanticist; halfway through the novel, he is made to recant his vows, plunge headlong into "the sea of love," and then solemnly renounce it to extricate himself from a moral dilemma. The entire triangle plot seems to be set up to highlight Hengshan's identity as an *ernü yingxiong*, which accounts for its contrived feel. Immediately before he declares his love for Mengpin, Hengshan explains that *ernü* and *yingxiong* are inseparable: "The more intrepid a man is, the more easily he is ensnared in the web of love, for puissance is meaningless if not appreciated by a beautiful woman" (GQY, 645). The echoes of Yu Dafu and Jiang Guangci can be easily registered. And as for Yu and Jiang, the subtext in such pronouncements is the idea that the revolutionary identity is grounded in love. And here is the crux of Mao Dun's objection to the novel. He derides it as "a hysterical romance" and complains that, notwithstanding the title, "there is no sign of revolution until the very last page . . . when [Hengshan] decides to withdraw from the 'arena of love' and humors himself with the thought of joining the revolution—as if only romantic losers become revolutionaries!" (Mao Dun 1992).

This scenario directly contradicts the only "revolution + romance" formula that Mao Dun approves of: the situation in which love grows spontaneously out of revolutionary comradeship. So long as revolution is the top priority, love can be tolerated as a necessary fact of life. But the romantic loser-turned-revolutionary seems to operate by a different logic: that heroic action serves only to supplement romantic subjectivity. In other words, the hero renounces love only because it proves unattainable. Its unattainability in turn reinforces its exalted status among life's many goods and goals, as something whose value can only be affirmed through the supreme sacrifice of life itself. Mao Dun has a point here: revolution is never integrated into the plot at the diegetic level; the narrative is unabashedly preoccupied with the business of love and courtship. A political protest is briefly invoked, but it is only to facilitate the encounter between the professor and the female student. His unrequited love blossoms in a hospital ward—a clichéd romantic setting—rather than in "revolutionary work," as Mao Dun prefers.

Ironically, Mao Dun's own fictional output up to this point has more or less adhered to the love → disappointment → revolutionary activism pattern that he so resolutely repudiates in the essay.[9] *Rainbow* (1930), for example, gestures toward a revolutionary romance between the New Woman Mei and her political leader Liang Gangfu, but it halts abruptly at the point of Mei's first real political action in the May Thirtieth demonstration (Mao Dun 1992). Marston Anderson believes that Mao Dun's inability to bring most of his novels to a structural completion is a sign of his failure to reconcile the "conflict between the ideal and the real, that is, between the clarity of structural pattern on the one hand and the refractoriness of an empirically observed social environment on the other" (1990, 129). David Wang makes a similar point about Mao Dun's vacillation between "History [*sic*] as something in which he believes" and "history as something he sees and feels" (1992, 40). Like Ding Ling, Mao Dun seems daunted by the challenge of representing love that is not just supplementary to but fully reconciled to revolution—something Hu Chunbing is able to do only by reducing his characters to symbolic ciphers and by avoiding the phenomenology of everyday life altogether. Also like Ding Ling, Mao Dun cannot seem to trust his ability to keep love at the mundane level of eating and sleeping so that it does not contest the supremacy of revolution, nor does he find the realist mode adequate to the daunting task of reconciling emotional subjectivity and revolutionary anonymity.

THE REVOLUTIONARY PAS DE DEUX

In his essay on "revolution + romance," Mao Dun chastises Chen Quan for treading a lonely path, implying that progressive writers have gladly abandoned the formula—or, rather, they have given up writing about themselves altogether, since the formula is first and foremost preoccupied with the intellectual "self." He holds up Nie Gannu's (1903–1986) "Liang tiao lu" (Two paths, 1933) as a promising attempt at bringing a new perspective to bear on gender relations (Mao Dun 1935). Nie's story, set in the countryside, cannot be farther afield from the vast majority of "revolution + romance" stories about educated urbanites. The protagonists of "Two Paths" are a rural couple brought together through family arrangement at a young age. The husband tries to assume the role of the authoritarian patriarch and lord it over the wife. When the communists come, the wife becomes an activist, only to be betrayed by her husband and killed by KMT soldiers, who subsequently drive the communists away (Nie Gannu 1980, 36–63). Needless to say, the idea of love has absolutely no relevance in their life, and the word never appears in this stark tale of gender oppression and political violence. The conjugal relation is entirely shorn of its emotional qualities and is used to figure life-and-death class antagonism. Increasingly, even such "case studies" of peasant or worker characters give way to representation of politicized masses and their anonymous heroism. In Ding Ling's "Shui" (Water, 1931), for example, "characters find their identity only in the context of the crowd and its collective intentions" (Anderson 1990, 185). No one here dreams romantic dreams. Love is firmly rejected as a bourgeois delusion, and heterosociability is erased to make room for collective political action.

Although feasible for a short story, depersonalized, anonymous, and collective portrayals are difficult to sustain in an extended narrative space—so long as realism's raison d'être is to represent human dramas. Leftist writers are apparently aware of this difficulty, and few have attempted to produce a full-length equivalent of "Water." The solution, as shown in Hu Chunbing's play, is to feature characters who are "types," that is, individuals who are embodiments of ideological categories, individuals without the refractoriness of individuality. But should such typified individuals have love life? If so, should their love life be made to weather the same storms of uncertainty, mistrust, and betrayal that have tormented countless fictional lovers? To what extent should gender and eros be allowed to emerge as technologies of self? Why should a typical female worker love precisely *this* typical male worker, and no one else? To love a typical character is necessarily to love the ideological collectivity that she or he represents, not his or her personal qualities or idiosyncrasies. Hence, love in socialist realism is by definition class love, even if it manifests itself phenomenologically as romantic or sexual love. This is indeed how socialist realism rewrites the *ernü yingxiong* model, of which the successful first example is perhaps *Xin ernü yingxiong zhuan* (A new tale of heroic sons and daughters, 1949), coauthored by the husband-and-wife team of Kong Jue and Yuan Jing.[10]

The novel's resemblance to the predecessor that it deliberately invokes—Wen Kang's *A Tale of Heroic Sons and Daughters*—hardly extends beyond the stylistic, though this may well be chiefly responsible for its popularity. Robert Hegel perceptively sorts out familiar character types, settings, plot devices, as well as narrative techniques that the novel draws from traditional vernacular fiction and southern *chuanqi* drama, noting especially the action-packed narration with its quick tempo and the use of songs, poems, or slogans as epigraphs to set the tone for the chapters (1984, 210–12). The *New Tale* is set in the marshland surrounding the Baiyang Lake in Hebei during the war of resistance against Japan. Meek and befuddled, the villagers find themselves the target of competing mobilization efforts from the KMT and CCP. Local thugs and operators quickly form militias and attach themselves to KMT organizations, using resistance as a front to bully the villagers and extort grains from them. As the Japanese intensify their "combing" campaigns (*saodang*), these ragtag troops are easily co-opted by the invaders. The CCP-led resistance, on the other hand, relying on the honest and newly awakened villagers, score victory after victory in their clashes with the Japanese and their Chinese allies and is eventually able to wipe out the Japanese presence in the region.

As might be expected, the novel features a bevy of positive peasant and cadre characters, a few middle-of-the-road characters, and several evildoers. It begins with a budding romance between two peasant youths, Niu Dashui and Yang Xiaomei. A few glimpses and a few good words casually heard favorably incline them to each other. But Xiaomei is forced by her family to marry the ne'er-do-well Zhang Jinlong, and Dashui is soon engaged to marry a girl in a neighboring village. On his way to fetch his bride, Dashui learns that she has been raped by a contingent of Japanese soldiers and has drowned herself in shame. The enraged Dashui then joins the CCP-led resistance movement. Xiaomei, too, joins the movement, having been practically abandoned by her husband, who is now a sharpshooter in the local KMT-backed militia. In their revolutionary work together, Dashui and Xiaomei look out for each other and mature politically. A warm feeling grows between them, though neither has the time or energy to cultivate or even acknowledge it. After Zhang Jinlong formally defects to the puppet regiment, Xiaomei divorces him even though she is carrying his child.

The novel then devotes about 10 pages, out of a total of 270 pages, to Dashui and Xiaomei's marriage. It is brought about, however, not by their own initiative. Observing how well they suit each other and how effectively they work together, the avuncular guerrilla leader inquires about their feelings and suggests that they get to know each other better and tie the knot when the circumstances permit. No words of tenderness are exchanged between the prospective spouses; instead, they sheepishly and matter-of-factly blurt out their thoughts:

> "I have a very good impression of Comrade Xiaomei. She works hard and aggressively; she's considerate of all the cadres. She didn't let Jinlong's family prevent her from joining the resistance. . . . " Dashui faltered. "Anyhow, she's wonderful! I don't know how to put it. . . . "
>
> . . . .
>
> "I completely approve of Comrade Dashui. I think he's splendid. He's solid as a rock. When the Japanese tortured him so cruelly, he didn't give an inch! He does fine work and learns better than I. I have no objections either!" (DS, 227)

Thereafter, Dashui and Xiaomei exchange a letter or two while working on separate projects. The letters are formalistic, containing courteous greetings, inquiries of health and work, and discussions of official business. Tenderness pokes through only fleetingly when Dashui importunes Xiaomei to come to him to discuss a matter face to face: "Come quickly! Definitely come! I still have much more to talk to you about!" (DS, 245). At their wedding ceremony, Dashui and Xiaomei are teasingly called upon to report their "courtship history" (*lian'ai jingguo*). Dashui insists that they have worked together for years "like brother and sister" and never kissed each other or even held hands. But pressed, he admits that he has been in love with Xiaomei for quite a long time. Left alone, the couple affirm their feelings for each other and mutually commiserate their past sufferings. Still, their pillow talk maintains a fine balance between lines like "you're so strong, so good" and "only the revolution was able to bring us together" (DS, 257–58). As if to mirror this balance, the chapter is entitled "Love and Hate," and it devotes precisely half of the chapter to the guerrilla's foiling of Zhang Jinlong's revenge attack. But of course the novel as a whole can hardly be said to be equally divided between romance and revolution.

Guo Moruo wrote a preface for the novel when it was first published in 1949, praising its skillful implementation of Mao's Yan'an directives for literature and art and urging its readers to take Dashui and Xiaomei as their role models. The characters in the novel are, in his words, "all ordinary sons and daughters and at the same time heroes committed to the collective" (DS, 1). The merging of the ordinary and the extraordinary seems to take us full circle back to Wen Kang. Indeed, in both novels, the protagonists are less lovers than heroes. But in Wen Kang, heroism requires a reaffirmation of the traditional family order and renunciation of the *jianghu*. The identity of the heroes is firmly rooted in the familial context and their heroic accomplishments in the public world are an extension of their domestic virtues. In the *New Tale*, Dashui and Xiaomei are first and foremost revolutionaries whose identity is forged in the crucible of the resistance movement. Their marriage renders them human and brings heroism to the realm of the ordinary. Unlike ascetic religions, revolution does not necessarily require its practitioners to "exit" the mundane realm; rather, it aims to revolutionize society itself so that there will no longer be an outside, an exterior to revolution. The couple do not have a separate existence outside their revolutionary career, nor do they derive meaning or value from any other source—least of all their sexual union. To be true to its name, revolution must be total.

As such, the novel fits Mao Dun's prescription close to a T. First of all, it decidedly tips the scale of representation from romance to revolution—here the resistance movement—so that revolution is the central drama rather than an afterthought. Second, neither Dashui nor Xiaomei can be called romantic losers because they were never in love with their first spouse/fiancé to begin with. The apparent love triangle among Dashui, Xiaomei, and Zhang Jinlong is more accurately an allegory of class struggle: Zhang's attempt to regain Xiaomei is motivated not by love but by hatred and possessiveness. Xiaomei repels him not simply because she loves Dashui more (she does—but that is beside the point) but because she is repulsed by what Zhang stands for: the self-serving land-owning class and their running dogs that oppress the peasantry and betray the Chinese nation by collaborating with the invaders.[11] Joining the resistance movement is therefore not a convenient resolution of romantic crises, but is rather motivated by patriotic sentiments and class consciousness (hence Dashui's refusal to be inducted into the reactionary militia that promises good pay and easy access to loose women). To this extent, the characters are degendered: they interrelate primarily as political rather than sexual beings. This is also borne out by Xiaomei's treatment at the hands of He Shixiong, the ringleader of the puppet troops, after they captured her and her baby. He repeatedly subjects Xiaomei to interrogation and physical torture while trying to break her will by appealing to her maternal instincts. But never once does he betray any intention to subject her to sexual assaults, attesting to the displacement of the war between the sexes by class warfare.

Third, although love grows imperceptibly between Dashui and Xiaomei, it never clamors for attention nor presses forth any demands that might weaken their commitment to the political enterprise. It is indeed treated as a routine affair like eating and sleeping, something that can and should be taken care of efficiently so that one can get on with more pressing and more important tasks. The individual characters still retain their smaller selves and are capable of affixing their affections on a particular person, which involves an appreciation of not just revolutionary credentials, but also individuality. But the feeling between the couple is only an intensified version of the general goodwill that permeates the revolutionary camaraderie. This is why when Dashui expresses gratitude to Xiaomei for all the "love and care" she lavished on him after he was tortured by the Japanese, Xiaomei replies: "Revolutionaries are one big family—everyone is a dear relative!" (DS, 257–58). In the same way that the smaller self provides local habitation for the greater self, love is a local manifestation of class solidarity and patriotism. It is only meaningful when fused with the revolutionary passion that propels the struggle for liberation. It seems that leftist intellectuals have finally found a way to write about their peasant others without depriving them of that all-important modern signifier: feeling. At last, the peasant characters in *A New Tale of Heroic Sons and Daughters* seem to have mastered the revolutionary pas de deux of love and heroism.

THE SOCIALIST GRAMMAR OF EMOTION

Our genealogy has arrived at the moment when the revolutionary discourse seems to have perfected a poetics of love that is eminently serviceable to the newly minted socialist nation. What logic and principle, then, should govern the life of the heart for the socialist subject? In the remainder of this chapter, I read two representative texts about the Mao period and seek to understand the socialist grammar of emotion as an important link between early twentieth-century and post-Mao cultural politics (to which I turn in the Conclusion).

The socialist period (1950s–1970s) was the first time in Chinese history that the intimate realm came directly under the supervision and regulation of the state. The kingpin of the socialist grammar of emotion is the collective definition of sentiment in which love is shorn of all particularistic or personalistic valence and is to be exclusively aligned with a new universal category: class. A socialist subject "loves" another socialist subject for his or her class belonging, not for his or her moral qualities, intellectual prowess, economic standing, social status, or sexual appeal. Love ceases to be an affair of unique persons and singular hearts. Writers learn to wean themselves off the "revolution + romance" formula and turn to socialist realism whereby the only legitimate expression of love assumes the form of class passion. Redeploying the language of feeling, the practitioners of socialist realism presume to speak not as a critical observer, the "I" versus "them," but as one of "them," as "we." As Marston Anderson points out, the insistent voice of the collective "we," eager to "promulgate a new ideological vision of the world," signals the demise of critical realism (1990, 202).

Ironically, what makes the quantum leap from "I" to "we" possible is precisely the enlightenment paradigm of the layered self, of the self divided between the greater, dominant, or essential self and the smaller, lower, or empirical self. Or, when couched in the language of feeling as is often the case, it is the self poised between the centrifugal force of human love and centripetal force of romantic love. Intellectuals, after all, are most adept at self-fashioning, and it seems to require but an act of will to shed the latter and identify exclusively with the former. We have seen in *A New Tale of Heroic Sons and Daughters* how peasant characters emerge as the embodiments of the collective self and how they effortlessly subordinate love to heroism in their guerrilla warfare against Japan. But it would be a mistake to assume that the socialist grammar of emotion is a simple valorization of the peasant mode that Sulamith Potter theorizes for us, in spite of a half century's effervescence of emotion talk.

Rather, the socialist grammar is a synthesis of the Confucian, enlightenment, and revolutionary structures of feeling that have pervaded urban elite discourses in the first half of the twentieth century while incorporating elements of the peasant mode. As a result, it is a peculiar amalgamation of the regime of authenticity and the regime of theatricality. The regime of authenticity relies on a cultural theory that grounds social and political truths in the heart and is enacted through the representation of feeling. It underscores all three structures of feeling discussed in this book, so much so that if we have to choose one word to encapsulate the half century of emotion talk, it would be *authenticity*. The regime of theatricality, which characterizes the peasant mode, deemphasizes the social significance of emotion while valorizing the virtuosity of performance, or the presentation of feeling. As I intend to show in the discussion below, the socialist grammar of emotion, insofar as it is operable at the phenomenological level, requires the activation of both regimes.

The rustification imperative of the Mao years makes it advantageous for intellectuals to approximate and valorize the peasant mode of rendering emotion an inconsequential force in social life. Under their pen, peasant characters are uniformly extroverted, unlibidinal, and unsentimental, except that class enemies are still endowed with predatory sexuality which, rather than constituting their essence, is an expression of their reactionary class nature. With gender and sexuality no longer structuring dramatic conflicts, femininity or feminine desire becomes the telltale sign of either unregenerate "feudal" mentality or international class conspiracy (in which case female spies would wear their sexuality on their sleeves as a cheap and mostly futile ploy).

A typically positive female character in socialist realism is thus a desexed woman who comports an austere exterior, but who must not be a woman without feeling. Again, it is Ding Ling who gives us the supreme portraiture of the passionate socialist subject in her short story "Du Wanxiang," set in the Great Northern Wilderness, the place of her long exile during the Mao years.

The titular heroine follows her husband here and finds her true socialist self after enduring domestic isolation and spousal inattentiveness. Wanxiang's impeccable political credentials are grounded in her formulaically narrated sufferings in the Old Society (pre-1949 China) and are abundantly demonstrated through her superhuman feats of strength, perseverance, and sacrifice (gleaning grains in the field and turning every kernel over to the state while she and her family go hungry; carrying students one by one across an icy creek in deep winter). Tani Barlow calls Wanxiang the "modern everywoman of People's China," a papier-mâché figure shaped by layer after layer of party lines (in IMW, 329). Wanxiang is also an "ungendered, politically redemptive woman" whose source of power is not her feminine virtues, but "Communist aphorisms and ethical practices" (in IMW, 329, 330). One can hardly expect such a figure to be brimming with emotions, especially when the text denies us access to what we deem to be the mainstay of a passionate life: how she fell in love with her husband, how she felt during his long years of absence, and other such stock-in-trade elements of tales of the heart. And yet in the climax of the story, Wanxiang, now a model worker, moves the multitudes with a speech that is said to have flown straight from her heart.

The text describes the preparation of her speech this way:

> Du Wanxiang was going to give another talk about her personal experience. Her comrades at work launched into a frenzy of preparation. They were inspired to help her make this speech better and even more moving than usual. After talking with her for some time, they flipped through stacks of reports, magazines and directives, rifled the collected works of Marx, Lenin, and Chairman Mao, searching for quotations, and in the end, they produced a draft that was mellifluous yet to the point. But as Du Wanxiang studied the text, finding it an adequate speech in every respect, an old feeling of bitterness assailed her once again. She would not endure it again. Many times before she had read her speech aloud from the platform under the gaze of an audience of thousands, she'd felt anxious and bogus when the people applauded her. . . . Mouthing the words of others is cheating. . . . She still could not write a proper essay, but she could—no, she absolutely had to—speak her own truth. (IMW, 351–52)

Although the party deems adequate the *presentational* mode in which she reads from a collectively composed speech predicated on the universal Truth, Wanxiang insists on a *representational* mode that meets the party halfway with her own homespun truth spoken in her own plain voice. Her humble truth, it turns out, is fully structured by the socialist grammar of "speaking bitterness" (*suku*), and her plain voice is as conventionalized as any full-throated Maospeak text ubiquitous in that era. And yet she electrifies her audience: "[The audience] embraced all of this in their hearts, and each was intoxicated, overwhelmed with good fortune, feeling that it would be possible to ride out a tempest, sit astride great ocean waves, and fly over hill and dale to vanquish every sweated task. . . . an enormous wave of emotion welled from the hearts of those listening to Du Wanxiang" (IMW, 353).

Here, Ding Ling brings into play a hermeneutics of feeling that demands the alignment of the inner state and outer expression. Words must connect heart to heart, or else they risk becoming "bogus." Barlow speaks of the "emotional surgery" that Ding Ling effects in inserting her psychological portraits of female subjects into the communist characterology of typicality (2004, 225, 230–31). Only with Du Wanxiang is Ding Ling able to erase the tension that troubles her Yan'an-era stories, the tension generated when a female subject with a psychosexual interior seeks integration into the normative narration of the nation. With Wanxiang, a fully interiorized female subject who is seamlessly sutured to the official scriptural economy, the revolution of the heart is at last complete.[12]

Ding Ling was perhaps the last writer to maintain an unwavering faith in the socialist grammar of emotion. For many more intellectuals who have similarly engaged in voluntary or involuntary class transvestitism for decades, the socialist grammar was decidedly associated with the Other—the party and the peasantry. As soon as the political climate made it safe for them to write as "I" instead of "we," they resurrected love and sexuality and the enlightenment structure of feeling with a vengeance. Beginning with Zhang Jie's (b. 1937) "Love Cannot Be Forgotten," pensive, plaintive, and soul-searching narratives of love and desire flooded discursive and visual spaces (Brownell and Wasserstrom 2002; Chow 1995; Farquhar 2002; Farrer 2002; Larson 1999; Liu 2003; Lu 1993, 1995; Sang 2003; Zhang 2002; Zhong 2000). Once again, foreign romantic classics (for example, Charlotte Brontë's *Jane Eyre*) and Freud were feverishly consumed. Most of the 1980s narratives of suffering and awakening, or the so-called Scar Literature (*shanghen wenxue*), adopt the male perspective and follow the May Fourth paradigm of denouncing the ancien régime for its inhumanity, for blurring gender differences and for suppressing sexual desires. Zhang Xianliang's (b. 1936) *Half a Man Is a Woman* is perhaps its best-known specimen. In this novel, the Cultural Revolution is morally indicted not so much for its destruction of the rule of law, human solidarities, and personal liberties as for its emasculation of the male protagonist, as if the latter is the worst possible crime a regime could commit against its people.

But writers in the 1980s did not just write about themselves and their love/sex life, or the lack thereof. Some of those associated with the Root-Searching School (*xungen pai*) sought to find out whether the peasants too had been robbed of their fullness of being through emotional and sexual deprivation. In contrast to the presumed certainty of autobiographical truth that undergirds many Scar and Root-Searching narratives, the answer to this question seems lost in an epistemological fog because the peasants never seemed to have subscribed to the enlightenment structure of feeling in the first place. If emotion did not play a central role in their social life, how, then, to represent *their* suffering and degradation during those bleak years? Han Shaogong (b. 1953), the foremost practitioner of and spokesman for the Root-Searching School, chooses the death of Mao as the backdrop to a story about how the socialist grammar profoundly distorts the humanity of a peasant character named Changke. In "Lingxiu zhi si" (The leader's demise, 1992) Changke goes from an anonymous villager to a national hero, thanks to his suddenly discovered talent of weeping on demand. When the story opens with Mao's death, Changke is seized with fear and panic over his inability to feel and show genuine grief—a failure that can carry serious political consequences for him and his family. In the space of a few sentences, the author outlines the basic terms of the socialist grammar of emotion: although private, personal emotions do not have formal social consequences, politically sanctioned emotions—love of Mao, that is—are obligatory, and their expression carries life-and-death significance.

Because love of Mao is a sign of political belonging, it is not a democratic concept in the way that weeping is for Liu Tieyun. Class passion is finely calibrated according to a shifting calculus of class lineage, past sufferings, and revolutionary credentials. Changke's motive for grieving, therefore, is suspect because "his old man had never been in the Red Army or the Peasants' Association, and no aunt or sister-in-law of his had ever been violated by the Jap devils" (in Lau and Goldblatt 1995, 387, hereafter cited as LD). It is all the more crucial that he feels and is seen to feel unbounded sorrow over Mao's death to compensate for his insufficiently endowed class passion. In other words, he must mobilize the presentation of feeling to supplement his shortfall in its representation. Richard Sennett makes the following distinction between the two modes of expression:

Expression in the public world was presentation of feeling states and tones with a meaning of their own no matter who was making the presentation; representation of feeling states in the intimate society makes the substance of an emotion dependent on who is projecting it. The presentation of feeling is impersonal, in the sense that death has a meaning no matter who is dying. The representation to another of what is happening to oneself is idiosyncratic; in telling another person about a death in the family, the more he sees of what the death made you feel, the more powerful does the event itself become to him. . . . The differences between presentation and representation of feeling are not between the expressive and the inexpressive, per se. They are rather between the kind of emotional transaction in which people can call upon the powers of a particular art and emotional transactions in which they cannot. (1992, 314)

On the one hand, mourning for Mao is supposed to activate the representation of a feeling state whereby the substance of grief depends on who is projecting it and for whose death; on the other hand, the imperative to mourn— on pain of punishment—gives the whole affair an impersonal, theatrical color usually associated with the presentation of feeling. This double bind first makes Changke a victim and then a victor. When his wife's life was in danger during childbirth, or when his nephew accidentally drowned, Changke wept heartily. But now, exasperatingly, his tears refuse to oblige: "his damn eyeballs . . . would not squeeze out any tears" (LD, 391). He thinks with envy (which likely has replaced scorn) of his neighbor Benshan's daughter-in-law "who could dampen both sleeves with tears if so much as a chicken died" (LD, 387). The said daughter-in-law is much in demand in the village as a professional mourner whose "ability to weep at the drop of a hat in her captivating, undulating, sustained musical tones" (LD, 388) properly complements every funerary rite and gives much satisfaction to the bereaved family. With her, we are brought back to the social life of the peasantry whereby an emotional community is enacted through theatrical performance, or codified gestures and utterances, without reference to the interior emotional reality of the performer. The Maoist regime of emotion both relies on this mode of expression and demands more: it wants the peasants to align their inner feeling states with politically orchestrated theatrical performance. But, as Han's exceedingly ironic story shows, the peasant mode malfunctions as soon as the state attempts to hoist the regime of authenticity upon it for political purposes.

The intersection of the peasant mode and the party imperative is first dramatized as a comedy of errors starring the above-mentioned daughter-in-law.

Upon hearing that someone has killed himself, and without ascertaining that the suicide is a landlord (the default class enemy), she "undid the front flap of her jacket" and "started mopping up tears and snivel by the handful" until she is slapped in the face by Mingxi, the brigade party branch secretary (LD, 388). In this case, the regime of theatricality has gotten ahead of itself and become perilously unhitched from the regime of authenticity: the death of a class enemy has no intrinsic meaning and must not be mourned. Now, with the death of Mao, the village is preparing a mass commemorative rally that will be filmed by a state television crew on account of the fact that Mao once graced the village with his presence during the revolution. Mingxi lets it be known that he is counting especially on three families to meet the state's expectations of spontaneous grief: "They all came from dirt-poor backgrounds. Under the puppet regime they had no padded pants to wear in the cold weather and didn't even know whether money was round or square. They had plenty to cry about" (LD, 390). But for all, failure to demonstrate grief is not an option. Changke has indeed worked himself into such a nervous state that when he is asked to write a few elegiac couplets (he is among the few educated villagers) for the mourning hall, he inadvertently utters "celebration" instead of "memorial." This slip of the tongue only accelerates his nervous breakdown. As he awaits his downfall in a daze, the idea of his wife and children being left alone in this world stabs his heart deeply. At the memorial service, he is so utterly absorbed in his private misery—"since he could not cry, then he should either go to prison or take a bullet" (LD, 392)—that a flood of tears rushes forth unbidden.

It turns out that Changke's tears have saved the day. Because of the presence of the television crew with their "weird machinery," the villagers are either too frightened or too distracted to cry: "[Those] listed in the plan as principal mourners started to behave like criminals as soon as they got to the ceremony. They all looked at one another in panic. Everyone who got in front of the camera immediately looked somehow sneaky. It was as if the unfamiliar camera lenses were actually gun barrels; whoever they pointed at moved to one side or ducked behind somebody else" (LD, 393). When the state attempts to make a televised spectacle of the villagers who supposedly are emotionally wrecked by Mao's death, the villagers let it down, seemingly out of an instinctive suspicion of the camera as an intrusive organ of state surveillance. They refuse to perform for some unknown audience hidden far away inside the mysterious and threatening camera lens. They refuse to enact a community of sentiment with an absent presence, an abstract entity, a disembodied gaze. There is no shared script between themselves and this evil eye whose predatory gaze they dodge and evade rather than reciprocate. The dry eyes and quiet vocal cords, after all the conscientious preparation to weep, gives the lie to the communist theory of class passion.

When Mingxi gives the keynote address, his bumbling style also high-lights the problematic nature of the socialist transformation of the emotional and moral economy of the peasantry. First, Mingxi wants to run the memorial service in the ritual mode that encodes the most sincere feeling to him and the villagers: wearing sackcloth hoods, burning incense, and setting off firecrack-ers. Dissuaded, he resigns himself to a speech that starts off in the standard routine of "remembering past bitterness and relishing present happiness" (*yiku sitian*). But he soon gets carried away and begins to boast of the good life that he enjoys as a party branch secretary:

> He counted all the blessings that the leader had brought to his impoverished people. "Just take my family. These days I've got two big cabinets, two beds with carved decorations, sixteen chairs, a sewing machine, and two cigarette lighters. I've got one and my boy Qingqiang has one!" He looked around to see who was as yet not cowed by his and his son's cigarette lighters. "And my political standing is a lot higher than before. I'm the Party branch secretary, no need to mention that, of course. Qingqiang and his wife are both state cadres, and my eldest daughter is . . . great-grandmother Shazhi." Minxi meant that his daughter had participated in an amateur theater group and had had the honor of playing the older female lead in the model opera, *Shajiabang*. Mingxi did not, of course, leave out the final member of the fam-ily: "My old lady is . . . " he paused before finally finding a word that could be used in the new society and that was both dignified and not too far from the facts, "a woman, uh-huh, a woman." (LD, 394)

Characteristically, the good life is not a life of emotional fulfillment, but a life of the family prospering together and enjoying respect and admiration from their peers. Familial happiness is in turn gauged by its tangible posses-sions and the social (and political) standing of its members, not by bonds of love. Tellingly, when it comes to his wife, Mingxi is at a loss for words. He seems aware that he cannot resort to the old way of defining the conjugal relationship as hierarchical and analogous to the parent-child and ruler-subject relationships. The enlightenment mode of the conjugal relationship as egalitarian, free, and contractual is apparently not available to him either.

Indeed, the socialist grammar of emotion accentuates the peasant mode in discouraging the grounding of social relationships in emotion. As a result, Mingxi is unable to take pride in his wife whose emotional companionship would, in other cultural or historical contexts, be the first thing invoked, acknowledged, and profusely thanked.

Meanwhile, Changke's life is forever changed by his tearful eruption. Addressed as "Comrade Changke," he is invited to go up to the podium, and his hands are shaken by important personages. He weeps even louder, but now out of sheer joy: "He was pleasantly surprised and actually did feel like crying over the happy turn of events. . . . instead of going to prison, he could eat, sleep, feed his pigs, and read the papers with his mind at ease. . . . now his heart was full of warmth" (LD, 395). Honored and promoted as an exemplary mourner, Changke is paraded around the region to speak and cry at political meetings. Fortunately for him, the socialist grammar of emotion places as much emphasis on the public performance of feeling as on its hermeneutics. He is thus able to transform an embodied experience into a political sign. Michel de Certeau calls such a transformation an "act of suffering oneself to be written by the group's law," which is "oddly accompanied by a pleasure" because in the process one becomes "an identifiable and legible word in a social language" (1984, 140). We may very well take Changke's tears as an acknowledgment of the pleasure of inscription in a symbolic order.

But for the author, there is something profoundly grotesque about Changke's new role as a quasi-professional political mourner. Although no one would bother to question Benshan's daughter-in-law's emotional authenticity because her infectious wailing at funerals is part of the social script, there is something intolerably phony about Changke's on-command tears from a view grounded in the enlightenment structure of feeling. What the daughter-in-law does at funeral rites is the presentation of feeling for which death itself has meaning, regardless of who is dead, while Changke's new calling is also premised on the regime of authenticity—his grief is supposed to spring from a deep reservoir of class passion—and enacts the representation of feeling.

What is grotesque is the fact that the socialist grammar is a monstrous marriage of the regime of theatricality and the regime of authenticity. In its demand for the repeated and instantaneous show of "feeling states and tones," it calls for the presentation of feeling whereby what is stressed is the virtuosity of performance according to beloved conventions and what is mobilized are the powers of an art familiar to the peasants. Yet it also maintains a cultural theory of emotion that values authenticity and tolerates no hypocrisy; and it distributes symbolic capital according to this theory. Whereas Benshan's daughter-in-law is paid money or goods by fellow villagers in return for her expert performance, Changke is promoted by the party for his reservoir of seemingly spontaneous and ideologically correct emotion. Moreover, it absolutely matters who is dead and who is mourning. Thus mourning for a dead landlord is impolitic and mourning for Mao is mandatory; and the poorest peasants are expected to shed the most tears—not because they are the best mourners, but because their past sufferings have endowed them with the deepest fount of authenticity. In other words, the substance of their emotion—grief for Mao's death—depends on who they are, not how they present it. To *represent* one's feeling, one must therefore hold an inquest on one's inner self and one's political fitness. Whereas Benshan's daughter-in-law would feel no compulsion to align her life with her mourner's role, Changke works hard at the acrobatics of bringing his inner self in line with his public persona. In his public speeches, Changke tinkers with his memory and begins to reminisce about the past sufferings he never endured and about the heroic thoughts that he never entertained. Inserting himself into the official scriptural economy that constitutes the extent of public discourse and that supplies the narrative grammar for all personal testimonies, Changke is able to turn himself into an emotional jukebox:

> Every time he got to this point [how he studied Mao's writings by a lantern deep into the night] in his talk Changke got a lump in his throat. . . . Ever since the state funeral, for reasons Changke didn't understand, he could pump out tears more quickly than Benshan's daughter-in-law. As soon as somebody mentioned the leader, or as soon as he heard the national anthem or something like that, Changke would be overcome by emotion and his nose would tingle. He was completely unable to keep his nose under control and he could not calm the solemn emotions that welled up in his chest. (LD, 397)

Like Du Wanxiang, Changke has reached a state where it is no longer possible to distinguish private feelings and public expressions, inner impulses and outer necessities, the personal and the political. In other words, Changke has become a poster child of the socialist grammar of emotion as well as its most ludicrous parody. Writing in the early 1990s, when emotion again is claiming foundational status in social and cultural life, Han Shaogong finds the subversion of the enlightenment structure of feeling by the state profoundly disturbing. In contrast to Ding Ling, who apparently intended no irony in publishing "Du Wanxiang" (a story she initially wrote in the mid-1960s) after returning from her apocalyptic exile in the late 1970s,[13] Han Shaogong wrote his story precisely to debunk socialist paragons like Du Wanxiang and to expose the revolution of the heart as a monumental travesty. Changke is his Ah Q, the antihero of a national-historical tragicomedy. At the end the story, Changke pays a visit to Mingxi on his deathbed. "When he was on his last breath, Mingxi grasped Changke's hand and stared into his eyes for a long time, as if he had something to say. But phlegm stopped up his throat and he never did say anything" (LD, 398). Perhaps Mingxi, a peasant at heart whatever his official rank, means to ask Changke to cast off his dubiously magnified new self and return to his old, plain self.

• • •

As early as 1921, there were already calls for writers to look beyond themselves and yield the subjectivity of *qing* to the working classes. In a short commentary titled "Aiqing xiaoshuo de cailiao dao nali qu zhao?" (Where to find the material for sentimental fiction?), Weinan declares that the "my love" (*wo ai*) type of sentimental fiction (note that he uses the Butterfly generic term *ai qing xiaoshuo*) is full of saccharine clichés that make one laugh rather than cry. He believes that the stuff of sentimental fiction should not be limited to the "disappointment in love" (*qingchang shiyi*) of the playboys and playgirls of the upper and middle classes. The sufferings of the "fourth estate" (*di si jieji*) stemming from economic hardships are equally saddening. He gives the example of Maxim Gorky's "An Autumn Night" about two paupers searching for bread on a broken ship anchored in a frozen harbor and hugging each other for warmth. "How very sad!" writes Weinan. "I advise sentimental fiction writers to toss off the cloying tune of 'my love' and look for raw material among the fourth estate" (1921). The author is essentially calling for a regime of pity that is abundantly exploited by both Butterfly and May Fourth writers. The characters in the Butterfly–turned–May Fourth writer Ye Shengtao's (1894–1988) early stories, for example, are likened by Marston Anderson to "an affective sponge, steeped in the authorial emotion of *tongqing* [sympathy]" (1990, 98). But in the 1930s, writers have become discontented with futile "emotional almsgiving" (Lu Xun, in Wu Fuhui 1997, 167) and sought to transmute authorial sympathy into a utopian faith in the masses as self-activating and self-assertive historical agents.

The representation of the masses—in the figure of the crowd—has undergone dramatic transformation since the May Fourth era. As Anderson astutely observes, the "vengeful, persecutory crowds" made famous by Lu Xun have been replaced by "unified, purposeful political aggregations" in the hand of leftist writers such as Ding Ling (1990, 201). These writers frequently resort to metaphors of nature—fire, water, winds, or animal packs—to convey "a sense of the crowd's restless movement, of its growth by expansion, and of its potential destructiveness" (185). They also find themselves straining, often with little success, to stretch a mode of writing accustomed to plumbing psychic depths for the task of representing an externalized and physically imposing entity struggling for basic survival.

To shun the sterility of the crowd genre, the "local color" writers, inspired by Shen Congwen's (1902–1988) native soil fiction, turn to their native regions to mine rural or small-town life for subaltern authenticity. Nie Gannu, for example, peppers his narratives with saucy Hunan dialect. But the need to cast working-class characters as the unwitting agents of history reduces them to flat figures endowed with a few basic emotions but devoid of a rich inner life. They do not conceive of themselves apart from the sociohistorical roles they play; nor do they contemplate the fate of individual liberty when the individual is thrust onto the historical stage. In many of the local color stories, peasant characters are either embroiled in petty inter- or intrafamilial squabbles or immersed in a tranquil, primitive life until some calamity (such as war) strikes from the outside. Their suffering is a stamp of authenticity and a catalyst of historical agency, not an occasion for contemplation or sympathy. The challenge is therefore how to theorize a new kind of subjectivity that does not turn on the dialectic of sentiment and the attendant notions of individual autonomy and freedom. Ding Ling takes up this challenge tentatively in "Shanghai, Spring 1930" when she makes Mary's feminine charms fall on unresponsive eyes, suggesting that the revolutionaries do not locate their personal/collective truth in dyadic sexuality, but in something else—something altogether new. That something else, as the authors of *A New Tale of Heroic Sons and Daughters* as well as Ding Ling herself (as the author of "Du Wanxiang") tell us, is class passion. But if Changke's emotional metamorphosis proves troubling even to a fellow peasant, it is a downright abomination from the perspective of post-Mao writers. The cultural politics of the late twentieth century therefore begins with the dismantling of the revolutionary structure of feeling and the reclaiming of emotional life for the individual in the enlightenment mode.

The Intimate Conflicts of Modernity

"THE HEART'S NATIVE LANGUAGE"

In *The Scarlet Letter*, Nathaniel Hawthorne calls love "the heart's native language" (1997, 149). I invoke this phrase to commence this concluding chapter for two purposes: first, to acknowledge the power of the commonsensical understanding of love that this study has sought to contextualize and historicize; and second, to use the quotation marks to remind my readers that love is anything but the "native" language of the heart, and that whether it whispers or wails, the heart always already speaks in borrowed tongues. This book aspires to be a genealogy that records, interprets, and rescues the many utterances of studious and mimetic hearts in the literary, intellectual, and social discourses of the first half of the twentieth century. In working with the textual artifacts of the past, I use the structure of feeling to encompass not only the losses and dispersions in the transmission of history, but also emergent values and meanings "in solution" before they are "precipitated" and given fixed forms. Following Raymond Williams, I refuse to treat qualitative changes in social consciousness and lived experience as epiphenomenal of changed institutions or as merely secondary evidence of changed social and economic relations. As an all-pervasive discursive motif, love played an undeniable role in the modern transformations of identity and sociality. Few literate residents of China's urban centers could avow that the quality of their social experiences and relationships was not in some way tied up with the vicissitudes of love in the discursive arena.

The structure of feeling allows me to render into the paralanguage of intellectual inquiry the assumed, the articulate, the metaphorical, the polemical, and the allegorical dimensions of the experience of modernity. Throughout this book, I approached sentiment as an articulatory practice, rejecting the essentialist assumption of a natural, spontaneous, and timeless dimension of human life that all social systems seek to control by means of repression, channeling, or sublimation. This assumption has hampered students of Chinese literature from problematizing affective categories that appear to be rooted in some elemental reality and that have an indisputable basis in embodied experience. To write a genealogy of love is both to deny it essence, facticity, and universality, and to examine how discourses of sentiment produce precisely these effects and for what purposes.

This study does not pretend to be also a social history armed with verifiable data on actual patterns of courtship, marriage, and family life (which is altogether a different project). I must also distinguish my project from a neurobiological exploration of the problems of emotion and consciousness. If I may be allowed to adopt the neuroscientist's terminology for the moment, then I must state clearly that I am not concerned with the primary, secondary, or ambient emotions (and their neurological representations, or feelings) that are associated with either "core consciousness" or "extended consciousness" and that may or may not be dependent on language (see Damasio 1999). Rather, I am interested in the question of emotion only insofar as it is problematized in language, stabilized (though not fixed) as a concept, and employed in competing "games of truth." Thus, although emotion as a neurobiological phenomenon has an extralinguistic facticity, specific conceptualizations of emotion (such as romantic love) do not exist prior to their deployment in historically determined fields of utilizations.

My book does not take up many familiar everyday emotions such as anger, hate, shame, or fear. Rather, I have focused on what might be called the euphoric emotions clustering under the umbrella rubric of love. As I have shown, love comes in many different "guises": filiality, romance, eros, sympathy, patriotism; and the semantic fields of these love categories are in constant flux. They are not merely different, sublimated manifestations of the same essential somatic reality. The fact they exhibit a degree of linguistic kinship or stability should not blind us to the discontinuity that can be "dissimulated under the veil of a lexical permanence" (Mino Bergamo, quoted in Davidson 2001, 186). They are rather the "descriptions" under which intentional human actions and purposeful human identities have emerged in tandem (Hacking 1992, 80–81).

Ian Hacking invokes the philosophical dictum that all intentional human actions must be actions under a description to support his social constructionist thesis that our "descriptions," or our conceptual language of classification and identification, can "make up people," or call categories of people into being. He calls this approach "dynamic nominalism," the application of which is restricted to the realm of human actions. For after all, what things are "doing" decidedly does not depend on how we describe them. But when new modes of description are introduced, new possibilities for human action and identity also come into being (1992, 80–81, 87). In this spirit, I have sought to understand how new modes of being (such as the "man/woman of feeling," the "romantic lover," and the "patriot") and new possibilities for action (such as dying for love or for the country) were enabled by a new language or new inflections of an existing language. Arnold I. Davidson calls this approach "historical epistemology," or the "history of the emergence of games of truth" (2001, 181). In this book, we have been concerned with the games of truth about love: the origins and procedures for the production of truth discourses about love and other euphoric emotions. These "truths" are the product of the will to knowledge under conditions of global modernity, not universal or transcendental Truth that can be read back into earlier forms of knowledge in which, for example, romantic love was simply a conceptual impossibility. I therefore insist on taking literally the maxim that the past is a foreign country and concur with Harry Harootunian who calls for a "re-exoticization" of the past, "which emphasizes its difference from, not its identity with, the present and reminds us of how narrative seduces us into believing that the past leads to the present" (1988, 20).

I have employed a threefold scheme to narrate the genealogy of love: the Confucian, enlightenment, and revolutionary structures of feeling. The three structures overlap a good deal, but they each capture important qualitative

changes in the ways in which identities, values, and solidarities are negoti-
ated. They all testify to the centrality of sentiment but espouse different visions about how to resolve the fundamental predicament of modernity: to wit,
how to affirm the value and dignity of ordinary life without abandoning a
sense of the heroic, without giving up the quest for a higher life? What
should be the moral source of modern life: the inner self and its feelings and
desires, the emotionally close-knit family, the nation as a community of sympathy, or revolutionary activism with its poetics of sublimation and sacrifice?
The vast cast of historical actors in this book pondered and debated these
questions passionately. They disagreed often, and the differential power relations among them adjusted and readjusted to keep apace with the shifting
pattern of discursive hegemony. But they also agreed with and borrowed from
one another more than they realized or were willing to acknowledge. In the
late twentieth century, these questions would be pondered and debated again,
after three decades of party-legislated life of the heart. In what follows, I
briefly consider the late twentieth-century developments as a coda to the
present genealogy of love focused primarily on the first half of the century.

CIVILITY AND AUTHENTICITY

I mentioned in Chapter 7 that post-Mao writers took up the subjects of love
and desire as potent weapons of exposé, encoding emotional and bodily
experiences as symbolic of human resilience. They tended to portray the socialist era as a barren time when spontaneous personal feelings were driven
underground, as it were, by the ghoulish pantomimes of the Maoist political
theater. In contrast, the reform era was a time of liberalization and liberation, when forbidden feelings sprang right back to life as soon as the repressive lid was lifted. This is the central premise of Zhang Jie's story "Love
Cannot Be Forgotten." Judith Farquhar notes that the story's appeal has to
do with "the way in which love in the form of a personal passion that has
nothing to do with Maoist politics [is] centered and revalorized" (2002,
189). Whereas socialist writers like Ding Ling sought to eliminate the mess-
iness of romance in order to shore up the hegemony of revolution, post-Mao
writers denounced the latter in the name of the former. In the 1990s in particular, many came to believe that the Maoist nightmare could only be permanently dispelled along with the utopian dream of forging a perfect union

between feeling and expression, between the personal and the political, and between the everyday and the heroic.

Looking back at the genealogy of love in China's modern century, we may say that revolution and love have alternately sought to inhabit the space of the sublime and to demote their rival to the realm of the quotidian. Because the sublime is a state of "communitas," or an antistructure in which time freezes (see Turner 1982), it cannot sustain a narrative plot and must be deferred to the denouement. More often than not, love is the term relegated to the debased realm of the quotidian, where, paradoxically, it tends to receive far greater narrative attention, even if it must be overcome by its antithesis in the climax. This was, as we may recall, the case with the "revolution + romance" genre that flourished in the 1930s and 1940s. The typical "revolution + romance" story is fond of regaling its readers with the myriad flavors of romantic joy and agony, but it invariably abruptly stops at the moment of political awakening or the inauguration of political activism. If revolution must become the mainstay of everyday life rather than a deferred utopia, it also runs the risk of becoming banalized and subordinated to an alternative conception of the sublime. Republican-era progressive writers as well as early socialist realist writers wrestled with this challenge in their chronicles of the conflict between a romantic love that had come to structure quotidian experience since the 1920s, and the revolution that was now demanding to be the organizing principle as well as substance of everyday life. Jianmei Liu discusses some of the latter writers in her study of the "revolution + romance" genre. She shows that, contrary to conventional critical wisdom, writers in the first seventeen years of the People's Republic boldly dramatized the dilemma between personal liberty (borne in romantic/marital relationships) and political commitment. Some even went so far as to question the party's attempt to manage personal emotional life (Liu 2003, chapter 5). Not surprisingly, most of these writers were denounced during the Cultural Revolution for daring to posit a genuine rival to the imperious claims of politics. The inevitable consequence was the disappearance of realist narratives altogether; in their place were stylized and airbrushed "revolutionary model plays" that banished lived experience in order to revel in communist ecstasy.

When they reinstated love and desire as the privileged subjects of representation, post-Mao writers also brought back or reimported realism and modernism as proper narrative methods. While the realists tended to substitute love for revolution as the locus of the sublime and to signify the erotic as the last fortress of humanity, the modernists (and postmodernists) shied away from the heroic discourse altogether. Instead, they turned their literary gaze inward (the psyche) and outward (peasants, ethnic minorities, children, and idiots) and backward (history and mythology), seeking redemption not in the realm of the collective and the sublime, but in the personalistic, spontaneous, primitive, and libidinal. Once delinked from revolutionary romanticism and no longer a metaphor, love becomes a subject of phenomenological interest. Although some writers and commentators are wont to lament love's corruption in the age of rampant commercialization, others are fascinated by the human dramas and their narrative possibilities engendered by love's fungibility.[1]

What is encouraging about this trend is the new dignity of the smaller self and the suspicion of any claims made on behalf of the greater self. Try as it may, the party-state finds it increasingly difficult to demand that individuals give up their irrational impulses, selfish desires, and the pursuit of immediate pleasures for some larger, distant goals. Intellectuals are leery of assuming the role of zealous social reformers who browbeat people in the name of their "real" selves. Grand narratives no longer create the kind of groundswell of popular emotion that we are accustomed to witnessing in narrative and cinematic accounts of the Cultural Revolution. More often than not, such narratives are the object of nostalgia, exploited casually or even ironically for their entertainment and commercial values. The 1990s cult of Mao, for example, had to compete with the cults of a plethora of popular cultural icons ranging from Madonna and Michael Jordan to Lee Iacocca and Lee Kwan Yew. In this we see the popular, commercial expression of the fundamental condition of modernity: the fractured moral horizon on which no single moral source claims the allegiance of all.

Writing on the emergence of the cityscape as a privileged chronotope in the literature and film of the 1980s and 1990s, Xiaobing Tang speaks of a genuine "cultural revolution" in late twentieth-century China: "To all appearances, everyday urban life as normalcy now seems successfully instituted" (2000, 277). The normalization of the everyday is what is revolutionary when contrasted to its impoverishment in the revolutionary period when life was "nothing but ritualized content" full of "pious passion and longings" but little else (277). Tang's examples of the new affirmation of ordinary life include a novel with the declarative title *Shenghuo wuzui* (Life is not a crime, by He Dun, 1993) in which the author delights in describing the state-of-the-art living quarters of a character who is the manager of a department store (285). Projected onto the material world—with its plenteous comforts and delights—are the newly discovered dignity and value of everyday life. Material culture, in its sheer multiplicity and heterogeneity, also indexes human diversity. In puncturing the fantasy of homogeneity, the late twentieth-century "cultural revolution" celebrates the plurality of human personalities, sentiments, desires, values, hopes, dreams, and capabilities.

Tang points out that the affirmation of ordinary life is also accompanied by a sense of anxiety that is engendered by the continued need to "negotiate with the utopian impulse to reject everyday life" (284). I would argue, following Charles Taylor, that the anxiety stems from deeper and more diverse sources and that it is part of the global condition. As I have shown in this book, the modern affirmation of ordinary life, which entails the negation of a higher life, has had its most blistering detractors among the revolutionary generation— the generation most responsible for keeping the utopian impulse alive. In the 1990s and the new millennium, as the globalizing processes deepen, the critique of the everyday has become pluralized, and we can read anxiety into a range of social criticisms. First, in reaction to the single-minded pursuit of pleasures and profits, the romantic critic bemoans the loss of idealism. This is perhaps the most enduring criticism leveled against modern secular societies that profess "a utilitarian value outlook [that] is entrenched in the institutions of a commercial, capitalist, and . . . a bureaucratic mode of existence" (Taylor 1989, 500). For the romantic critic, this is an existence marked by mediocrity, banality, and ennui in which nothing commands unwavering loyalty and nothing is worth dying for. Lost are passion, meaning, heroism, and higher purposes in life. Marxist critics, for example, are saddened by the eagerness of the "new-new generation" (*xin xin renlei*) to bid farewell to the utopian ideals of the Mao era. The so-called New Left critics have been especially concerned about the rejection, along with zealotry, of an ethical commitment to such liberal values as justice, benevolence, and equity (see Davies 2001).

A related critique comes from the faithful, who lament the loss of spirituality and the abandonment of the quest for transcendence in the age of crass materialism and quick-fix therapeutic culture. The communitarian critic, in turn, accuses the consumer society of dissolving traditional ties and of thrusting individuals into "a series of mobile, changing, revocable associations" so that they "end up relating to each other through a series of partial roles" (Taylor 1989, 502). Instead of loyalty to political and moral communities, the consumer knows only brand loyalty and views all social relationships through the lens of capitalist exchange. The culture of expressive fulfillment, aided and abetted by commercial capitalism, creates "a society of self-fulfillers" (508) reluctant to acknowledge the web of obligations and dependencies they live in, who are incapable of sustaining communities beyond their immediate needs, and who paradoxically also grow steadily dependent on the helping professions. Last, the environmental critic charges that modern disenchantment has brought an end to less instrumental or exploitative ways of living with nature. Capitalism promotes what Albert Borgman calls "the device paradigm," whereby we rely on gadgets and devices designed to address specific problems and deliver some circumscribed benefit while withdrawing from "manifold engagement" with our environment (501). At its worst, our instrumental approach to nature has led to ecological irresponsibility and the destruction of our common habitat.

Although the romantic and communitarian critiques have had a steady presence in the discursive arena of reform China, the ecological and religious strands have acquired considerable traction among segments of the population beyond intellectual circles (consider, for example, the Falungong movement). At some level, these critiques all attempt to address the anxieties of everyday life, and some are more forthcoming in offering remedies or nostrums than others. In addition, they all gesture toward the possibility of recovering the heroic and the sublime. However, what Taylor largely leaves out in his delineation of the fractured horizons of modernity is the hegemonic discourse of nationalism, a chief protagonist (as well as antagonist) in this genealogy. Indeed, we may attribute the phenomenal rise of popular nationalism in the last two decades to the powerful yearning for a grand narrative that is not a rehash of communist clichés and yet is able to fill the void left by the passing of the heroic age.[2] Many romantic and communitarian critics have eagerly jumped on the bandwagon of nationalism, convinced that they have found a different and compelling "secular religion of the heart" (Hegel's definition of love) that will supply the common purpose, noble ideal, and hypergood that the disenchanted generation sorely lacks and needs. This has alarmed some observers, who see the collective swing to nationalism as the early stirrings of a militarist or ultranationalist empire that is prone to seek external means to resolve worsening domestic crises brought on by fission, corruption, inequity, and injustice.

The specter of nationalism also produces worrying domestic implications. At a time when the state is engaged in the governmental project of rebuilding "civility" (*wenming*) and producing high-quality (*gao suzhi*) citizens, the hegemony of nationalism threatens to foreshorten the (re)emergence of a "civilized" public sphere in which people relate to one another through the codes of civility rather than the hermeneutics of feeling. Already, the post-Mao revalorization of gender and sexuality inaugurated a totalistic rejection of the socialist grammar of emotion, particularly its ritualized and politicized mode of expression that forcefully melds the peasant nonvaluation of emotion and the collective reorientation of emotional life toward the holy trinity of party/state/nation. Much like their May Fourth predecessors, the post-Mao cultural critics approach Maoist constructs as the supreme achievement of hypocrisy. They mobilize the tactics of protest and unmasking to expose the fraudulence of the socialist subject who speaks the party's Truth from the depths of his or her heart. One of their favorite targets is a real-life People's Liberation Army soldier who was inducted into the national political pantheon in recognition of his success in reinventing himself according to the socialist grammar of emotion.

He is of course Lei Feng (1939–1962), a model soldier who not only led a perfectly scripted and thoroughly public life, but also kept a diary that gave testimony to the degree to which his life truly approximated communist aphorisms and to which his smaller self was merged with the greater self. How else, then, to debunk a selfless and sexless socialist subject if not by "revealing" that he was a vainglorious young man and that he had a robust, if low-key or hushed-up, love life? Since the 1990s, reportage and commentary that give the lowdown on Lei Feng have appeared in magazines, newspapers, and Internet forums. One commentator, for example, remarks sardonically that Lei Feng must have been incredibly busy before he died at the age of twenty-two to have won twenty-nine regional and national awards and distinctions. The same commentator also recalls how, as a grade school student, he was forced to pad his compositions with hokey lies because his teacher routinely required the students to recount their Lei Feng–style "good deeds" of the week. He concludes: "However benign his original intentions might have been, official incitements obliged Lei Feng to assume the role of a hypocrite" (Wang Boqing 2004).

If Lei Feng was the patron saint of the socialist service ethic, then his demystification signals a profound disaffection toward the all-pervading official public domain in which strangers were putatively united by class solidarity and moved by role models to serve one another with love and alacrity—in blank denial of the multiple forms of belonging, the entrenched system of bureaucratic hierarchy, the unequal distribution of opportunities and re-sources, and the privation and persecution of the politically disenfranchised. The post-Mao reaction to this schizophrenic social world has been the with-drawal to the private and the elevation of personal fulfillment above public service. The refusal to participate in an oppressively politicized public world is certainly a potent form of resistance, but it also has the consequence of ren-dering everyone "worldless" (Hannah Arendt's term), that is, without a civic arena in which to affirm one's public political existence. The normalization of privatized everyday life, for Rebecca Karl, is the obverse of the impossibility of politics in fin-de-siècle China, owing in large part to cultural producers' tendency to reinscribe their Mao-era experiences as "the universalized nega-tive definition of politics in general" (2005).

If public life has declined in western societies during the past two centuries according to Arendt, Habermas, Sennett, and others, it was positively in shambles in the wake of the Maoist revolution. The fallout of this destruction has yet to be fully contemplated. Yunxiang Yan's longitudinal study of pri-vate life in rural China reveals "a surge of egotism and the rise of the uncivil individual" that have accompanied the state-mediated process in which, *pace* Sulamith Potter, "romantic love, intimacy, and conjugality have become irre-placeable in the villagers' moral experiences" (Yan 2003, 217, 223). The un-civil individual, paradoxically, is both a "freak" creature coauthored by the state (226) and the target of the latter's crusading project of *suzhi* education. The postsocialist individual may have been liberated from the state and its stifling institutions, but he or she has not been liberated, in Foucault's words, "from the type of individualization which is linked to the state" (1982, 216), or the governmental project of civility

Ann Anagnost has shown how the discourse of civility is integral to the modernization project of the state, particularly the drive to become inte-grated into global capitalism (1997). It is also a top-down effort to dress up the realm of public authority as a voluntary but compliant public sphere. It still appeals to the socialist service ethic, as evidenced in the periodic cam-paigns to revive the "spirit of Lei Feng" (*Lei Feng jingshen*). But its rhetoric often pales in the face of multitudinous discourses of the private—love, sexu-ality, health, marriage, domesticity, friendship, leisure, career, and flexible accumulation—made ever more formidable by a roaring commercial econ-omy. With the retreat of the state, capitalism efficiently turns consumer de-sires into the ligaments of a new public sphere. Ironically, just as the socialist political economy used Lei Feng to camouflage the entrenchment of a caste system, capitalism summoned him back, both to sell nostalgia and to cloak the profit motive. In a study of food and sex in post-Mao China, Judith Farquhar offers a close reading of a street commercial poster that features an amiable Lei Feng summoning passers-by to visit a drug company's Web site. Farquhar asks pointedly: "for how long will Lei Feng be able to model the healthy, responsible, Chinese body? How much longer will a very local form of pleasure be available in the text of his portrait?" (2002, 289)

These days, Lei Feng–themed Web sites offer a wide range of services, from matchmaking to house hunting—precisely the kind of mundane preoccupations that Lei Feng sought to rise above. But the signifier of Lei Feng still carries a "local form of pleasure" that helps convey the message that the advertiser cares about the needs and concerns of consumers, reassuring them that someone has taken over the mantle of the altruistic individual and will take care of the myriad worries of daily life—something that the socialist state, even in its most paternalistic phase, largely failed to deliver. And even more reassuring is the knowledge that while the availability of the altruistic individual is unpredictable and unreliable, the profit-seeking provider of services can almost always be counted on, so long as one is willing to participate in the capitalist ritual of exchange. One pays for service rendered and is no longer obligated to the provider, whereas as the beneficiary of an altruistic deed, one is enjoined to reciprocate and emulate it on an ever-expanding scale and to do so for love of country. Whatever the pitfalls of the market, consumers are freed of the crushing sense of indebtedness, inadequacy, and bad faith foisted upon them by an onerous service ethic yoked to a regime of authenticity.

The regime of authenticity undermines the project of civility by locating the source of political virtues in the heart. While the state discourse of civility seeks to construct a new public composed of cultured, hygienic, decorous, disciplined, law-abiding, productive, and cosmopolitan citizens (against the prevailing stereotype of the illiterate, unsanitary, rude, disorderly, unproductive, and xenophobic Chinese), the regime of authenticity demands that they be first and foremost red-blooded Chinese whose structure of feeling is circumscribed by national sympathy. In a recent news story, Chinese soccer fans reportedly engaged in semi-riot activities at a Chinese-Japanese soccer match beneath a message on the scoreboard that read: "Be civilized spectators! Show a civilized manner!" (Yardley 2004). We might rephrase Judith Farquhar's questions this way: How much longer will it be before individual identity ceases to be inexorably bound up with the imperatives of national sympathy that not only incite bad manners, but also trump the larger goals of civility— peace, benevolence, sociability, rights, liberty, and justice—all in the name of love?

A central objective of this book has been to demonstrate the crucial role played by the discourse of love in the nationalist-oriented political and social imaginaries of twentieth-century China. Critics seeking to understand the nationalist "turn" in the late twentieth century have oftentimes attributed it to communist propaganda, which has the predictable effect of incensing many Chinese for whom patriotic love is felt in the pit of their stomachs and who chafe at being reduced to propaganda dupes. As Etienne Balibar has pointed out, the nationalization of society, or the making of the *Homo nationalis*, is never a matter of mere political indoctrination. Rather, the process of inculcation has to be integrated into a more elementary process of fixing the affects of love and hate and the representation of the self (Balibar and Wallerstein, 1991, 94).

I hope I have shown in this study that the confluence of history, politics, and culture has been such that love has lent far greater force to the regime of national sympathy and authenticity, with its ability to shape affective life and self-identity, than to a civility-oriented public sphere. Moreover, the socialist transmogrification of the structure of feeling was so bound up with the horrors of the Mao years that the post-Mao critique invariably took the form of debunking politicized emotions and reembracing the the sanctity of private emotions and ordinary life. As with the 1930s, the turn to the interior and private has also been fueled by a booming commodity and leisure industry; but the market, apparently, has not been a natural ally of civility, even if it seems to have helped revive the traditional arts of theatricality.[3] The politically and commercially driven privatizing trend is worrisome only because when all experiences, with the world as well as with other human beings, have been reduced to the all-consuming activity of the care of self, what is lost is what Hannah Arendt calls "the enjoyment of the world." As she puts it forcefully: "World alienation, and not self-alienation, as Marx thought, has been the hallmark of the modern age" (1958, 254). It remains to be seen whether the post-Mao rush to reconnect with the heart will give rise to a public sphere in which the political is not personal, in which biology or nationality is not destiny, and in which self-expressions animate the art of civility and the ideal of worldliness.

Notes

1. A school of popular fiction writers who flourished in the 1910s and continued to claim substantial mass readership throughout the 1920s and 1930s.

2. This does not mean that there was no division of the interior and exterior in premodern thought. The crucial difference is the way in which the modern interior is defined in affective (or sexual) terms and endowed with authorizing authenticity.

3. This point has profound implications for the question of homosexuality in nonwestern societies, historically as well as in the present.

4. I do not intend to participate in the debate among anthropologists on whether romantic love is specific to the modern West or universally shared. Charles Lindholm surveys the existing, albeit sparse, ethnographic evidence and concludes that romantic love does not necessarily require the following conditions derived from western history: a leisure class, complex social formation, normative heterosexuality, companionate marriage, nuclear family, sexual oppression, a cult of motherhood, or a quest for identity (1998, 257–58). Contrary to expectations, it is experienced in both modern western societies and "primitive" hunting and gathering societies, for both are societies in which "risk and danger are pervasive, and where the nuclear family and the reciprocal affection of husband and wife are the only source of solace and refuge" (254). In centralized and highly stratified societies, romantic love is experienced outside of marriage and family life—with paramours, courtesans, and prostitutes. Lindholm admits that of the 248 cases (of ethnic groups) surveyed, only 21 entertain the belief in romantic love (257). In the end, he is more decisive in refuting the sociobiologists who assert that love is hard-wired in *Homo sapiens* to facilitate evolution than he is in drawing conclusions about love's universality. What he does not take up is the dissemination and localization of the *discourse* of romantic love in colonial and postcolonial societies.

5. Anthony Giddens criticizes Foucault for focusing excessively on sexuality at the expense of gender, which leads to a virtual silence on the connections of sexuality with love. Giddens believes that the questions of gender, intimacy, and intersubjectivity can be better addressed in terms of love (1992, 24).

CHAPTER I

1. After citing the sixth-century author Liu Xie's famous dictum—"Emotion is the warp of literary pattern, linguistic form the woof of principle"—Anderson brilliantly points out that Chinese thinkers take it for granted that poetry will stir the emotions of its audience, but without fearing the subversive potential of such emotive resonance, as did Plato, or feeling the need to subject poetry to the supervision of a higher reason or banish it from civilization altogether. On the contrary, poetry is one of the highest forms of letters and was believed by none other than Confucius himself to have a salutary effect on both personal cultivation and governance (1990, 18). This goes to show that the dualism of reason and sentiment is a much later invention.

2. The Peach Garden oath is the oath of brotherhood taken by Liu Bei, Guan Yu, and Zhang Fei, who would go on to take up leadership of one of the tripartite powers of the Three Kingdom period. The bond among the three sworn brothers, immortalized in the *Romance of the Three Kingdoms*, is the archetype of male bonding in popular fiction and drama.

3. The most telling example is the story of the hunter Liu An, who, failing to obtain game for dinner, slaughters his wife and serves her flesh to Liu Bei and his entourage. Upon learning the gruesome truth, Liu is "deeply affected at this proof of his host's regard and the tears rain down as he mount[s] his steed at the gate" (Luo Guanzhong 1959, 1:194). The *Romance*, along with *The Water Margin*, is known for its extravagant celebration of male bonding. Here, women and marriages only become part of the plot if they are deployed strategically in political intrigues. Otherwise, wives and children trail behind the heroes in a narrative preoccupied with manly exploits and emotions. See Song (2004) for an in-depth analysis of the exclusion and denigration of women/heterosexuality in the homosocial worlds of the *Romance* and *The Water Margin*.

4. The gender distribution of the human versus the subhuman rarely varies. As Judith Zeitlin points out, insofar as the ghost is a shorthand for all yin elements and forces, it is always to human as female is to male. Thus the phrase *female ghost* is "something of a tautology" (1997, 243).

5. Mayfair Yang borrows these terms from Deleuze and Guattari to conceptualize the phenomenon of *guanxi* networks in contemporary People's Republic of China. For Deleuze and Guattari, the "rhizomatic" (decentered and meandering) growth of practical kinship extends beneath and crisscrosses the centripetal, arborescent structures of the state and is therefore potentially subversive (Yang 1994, 305–11).

6. For major studies of the courtesan genre and ghost/spirit genre, see Huntington (2003); Widmer and Chang (1997, part 1); Zeitlin (1993).

7. Despite its mythic frame, many of the novel's narratological features resemble the familiar techniques of modern realism: the presentation of the text as a document *trouvé*, the claim of pure referentiality, the assertion of fundamental novelty, and the denunciation of traditional literary models as artificial and injurious to morals (Anderson 1990, 8–10). For this and other reasons, *Dream* has been hailed as the first modern Chinese novel.

8. In addition to *Ernü yingxiong zhuan*, the following novels are also considered

pioneers in combining the chivalric and sentimental genres to create the *ernü ying-xiong* convention: *Haoqiu zhuan* (seventeenth century), *Shou gongsha* (eighteenth century), *Yesou puyan* (ca. 1780), and *Lingnan yishi* (ca. 1800) (see Chen Jie 1998; Luo Liqun 1990). I have chosen to examine *Ernü yingxiong zhuan* in detail because it is most self-conscious of its synthesizing effort. Kang-i Sun Chang believes that the convention goes back to the late Ming and extends to poetry as well. She quotes the late Ming scholar Zhou Quan as saying: "I think that what makes heroes heroes is that they love in greater measure than others. . . . Only those who can make great sacrifices can love truly" (1991, 10). Chen Zilong's (Ch'en Tzu-lung) poetry, according to Chang, owes much of its artistic force to the unity of romantic love and patriotism/loyalism. My focus on Wen Kang by no means gainsays such earlier articulations of the all-important credo of the cult of *qing*: the unity of all virtues.

9. The title of the novel is usually rendered as "A tale of heroic lovers," although it can very well be "A tale of heroic sons and daughters," "A tale of loving/filial heroes," or "A tale of love/filiality and heroism." The translation of this passage is adapted from Liu (1967, 125). James Liu translates *ernü* into "lovers" without much regard for Wen Kang's express desire to wrest the term away from its association with erotic love (rouge, powder, and catamites) and attach it instead to filial piety. I have kept the key terms *ernü* and *yingxiong* untranslated wherever possible to retain a measure of their indeterminacy. Subsequent citations in the text will use the abbreviation EYZ.

10. Cyril Birch, "*Ku-chin hsiao-shuo*, a critical examination," thesis (London, 1954), 295; cited in Ruhlmann (1960, 168). See also Cui Fengyuan (1986); Liu (1967); Luo Liqun (1990). Popular belief has it that a man's vitality is of a limited reserve, so he must guard against concupiscence and frivolous expenditures. Legends of such circumspect heroes are legion. For example, the founder of the Song dynasty, Zhao Kuangyin, is fondly remembered in popular narratives for his cool composure in the face of his escortee Jingniang's amorous overtures. See Song (2004, 175–79) for more examples of men proving their true heroic quality by keeping women at arm's length, sometimes by violent means.

11. In *The Water Margin*, Song Jiang, the captain of the outlaws on Mount Liang, joins their ranks only after he has ruthlessly murdered his adulterous wife. And Song is by no means the only rebel in the novel who, having slain a woman, is forced to flee to Mount Liang. See Chapter 5 for an extended discussion of this violent trope.

12. There is an important forerunner to this alternative tradition: Kong Shangren's *Taohua shan* (The peach-blossom fan, 1699). In this play, the lovers who were torn asunder by political turmoil reunite after three years of separation but voluntarily part again with the religiously inflected recognition of the futility of *qing*. As in *Dream*, the refusal of a comic resolution is a defiant statement that the play's vision of a sentimental existence cannot be accommodated by the existing social order. Before the idea that marriage was the telos of all romantic liaisons took root, an ending that brought the long-suffering lovers into wedlock would paradoxically diminish the sublimity of love as an extrainstitutional experience. The religious resolution accentuates both the impasse of *qing* and its uncompromising critique of the dominant order.

CHAPTER 2

1. Contemporary scholarship on Butterfly literature has been growing steadily since Perry Link's (1981) pioneering work. See also Chow (1991); Fan Boqun (1989); Gimpel (2001); Lee (2001); Yuan Jin (1994).

2. *Qin hai shi* (Stones in the sea, by Fu Lin, 1906), was also translated by Hanan and is included in the same volume with *The Sea of Regret*. Hanan believes that the two novels ought to be read back to back because they both deal, with varying degrees of boldness and virtuosity, with the problem of passion. Also, both were set against the background of the Boxer Uprising and were published in the same year. *Stones in the Sea* tells the story of puppy love between a young boy (the narrator) and a girl named Aren, their engagement with the consent of his affectionate father, and their separation during the chaos caused by the Boxers. When the lovers finally reunite in Shanghai, Aren is on the verge of death, having been sold into prostitution and endured boundless sufferings. Stricken by grief, the narrator too falls ill and struggles to write down the story of their tragic love. The first-person story is told with passion and candor, winning considerable admiration from Hanan, who calls it the first "I-novel" in Chinese literature, even though it is by no means the first autobiographical novel.

3. Although few scholars are drawn to the novel for its moral message, some do admire it on stylistic grounds. Michael Egan, for example, praises its unitary plot structure, a small and stable cast of characters, and dynamic and psychological characterization—characteristics that mark its affinity with nineteenth-century European realism and therefore set it apart from contemporary Chinese fiction (1980). Hanan concedes that Wu shows a degree of sophistication when it comes to describing the mental and emotional processes of the female protagonist, Zhang Dihua (1995, 13). Xiaobing Tang thinks highly of the novel for its nuanced treatment of the psychic experience of anxiety and fear, calling it an "intricate study of war trauma and human resilience" (2000, 32, 2).

4. Wu Jianren (1960, 30); Wu Jianren and Fu Lin (1995, 129). Subsequent citations from the English edition will use the abbreviation SR.

5. Already, we hear echoes of Mao Dun, who asks writers to treat love as an everyday routine without attaching too much significance to it and without undermining the primacy of revolution (see Chapter 7).

6. In the same year (1897), Tan Sitong (1865–1898) published his philosophical treatise *Renxue* (On benevolence), in which he proposed a similarly mechanical vision of the heterosexual relationship. For Tan, sex has nothing to do with morality or even pleasure because it is merely the contact of two fitted sides of a machine, like the movement of a piston driven by steam (Ono 1989, 37). Once this fact is comprehended, people will no longer obsess about "lust"; research centers will probably be set up everywhere for the study of "licentiousness," and experts will publish works explaining theories of sex. Though Tan seems to be describing the rise of the sexual sciences in Europe, Ono Kazuko finds Tan's vision thoroughly prescient: "had anyone ever proclaimed such a bold theory of sexual liberation?" (1989, 37).

7. James Townsend (1996), for example, questions the received wisdom in Chinese studies that the history of modern China is a long and painful transition from "culturalism" to "nationalism." He argues that this thesis overstates the prominence of culturalism in premodern China and fails to take into account class divisions as well as alternative currents such as statecraft. Moreover, it overlooks the slippage between culturalism and Han ethnocentrism and chauvinism (i.e., the fact that the culture of "culturalism" was never anything other than *Han Chinese* culture) and hence culturalism's easy alliance with either state or ethnic nationalism. The rise of modern nationalism, therefore, not only did not require the dissipation of culturalism, but actually drew much strength from its legacy. Prasenjit Duara (1995) makes a similar point concerning culturalism's complicity with modern nationalism. He takes issue with the prevalent view that nationalism is an unprecedented mode of collective consciousness made possible by the spread of print capitalism. He argues that premodern societies were fully capable of imagining abstract communities beyond the immediate ties of kinship and locality. In addition to forms of protonationalism like culturalism and ethnic chauvinism, there were networks of trade, pilgrimage, migration, and sojourning that linked villagers to wider communities and political structures (one might also add to this list the quasi-mythical space of *jianghu*). I find their theses entirely convincing, though the challenge is still how to theorize epistemic breaks in full cognition of the continuities.

8. One is tempted to see this in light of what C. H. Wang calls the "ellipsis of battle" convention in ancient Chinese poetry, a convention that is grounded in the cultural preference for ritual decorum (*wen*) over martial skills (*wu*). Wang uses this to explain the scantiness of combat description in, say, *The Book of Songs* or the "Ballad of Mulan" (1975). See Louie (2002) for an analysis of Chinese masculinity as ideally combining *wen* and *wu* attributes. For more comprehensive accounts of the history of Chinese chivalric fiction, see Hamm (2005, chap. 1); Luo Liqun (1990).

9. Sakai writes, "In order to say 'one dies *for* the country,' the fact of one's death must be substituted for the concept of death. At the same time, an individual who dies must be turned into a subject whose identity is constituted within the system of collective representations. . . . This statement ['dying for the country'] idealizes death and turns it into an end in itself. For this very reason, we always find some romanticism about death in any patriotism. Before being a matter of politics in the narrow sense of the term, patriotism is, first and foremost, a matter of collective representations. . . . Death always lies outside collectivity—it always constitutes the exterior. And patriotism pertains to the very device of displacement in terms of which the radical Otherness, the absolute exterior, of death is concealed and forgotten" (1997, 190).

CHAPTER 3

1. The kingdom of *qing* is also a world apart linguistically. In *Yu li hun*, for example, there are more than 50 *qing* compounds used recurrently throughout the novel. Besides a few common words such as *ganqing* (passion), *tongqing* (compassion), and *wuqing* (heartless), most of these idiosyncratic compounds are coined by Butterfly

sentimental writers but are no longer in use in standard modern Chinese. These compounds make up a rather specialized vocabulary and may well be called the "sentimental jargon." By strewing their texts with these at times awkward words, the writers seem to insist on an alternative ontology and epistemology on which the ideal world of sentiment should be built.

2. For Emmanuel Levinas, the risk or contingency of erotic love is what makes ethics possible because love privileges heteronomy over autonomy and disavows self-sufficiency (see Mitchell 2005).

3. Dooling and Torgeson (1998, 105); Feng Yuanjun (1997, 1). Subsequent citations from the English version will use the abbreviation S.

4. Lingzhen Wang contrasts Feng's story of "platonic love" to *The Peony Pavilion* with its "explicit references to sexual intercourse" and concludes that the former stays well within the normative boundary (2004, 76). The underlying assumption is that a text is not transgressive enough if it does not go "all the way," so to speak, with respect to sex. My point here is that romantic love was the nom de guerre of the rebellious May Fourth generation because what was pursued in its name was far more threatening to the Confucian order than the act of sexual intercourse could ever be.

5. Feng's agony over the conflict of filial love and romantic love falls squarely within the problematics of the enlightenment structure of feeling whereby the supremacy of romantic love renders other attachments peripheral, uncertain, and in need of justification. Lingzhen Wang reads Feng's stories as an attempt to "undermine the exclusivist heterosexual love model propagated during the May Fourth era" (2004, 77) and to affirm the eminently "traditional" relationship between a mother and daughter. She also suggests that the protagonist dies for love of mother and that this is "unheard of" in Chinese literary tradition (76). In my view, an ascriptive relation is never categorically traditional or modern; rather, as Foucault maintains, it is a codified norm that can cover a plethora of changing ethical practices (1990b). How one enacts the mother-daughter relationship and where it is situated in the ethical scheme of things can reveal a rich and dynamic field of historicity in the determination of ethical substance. Already, a daughter's filiopietism toward her mother receives relatively little elaboration in Confucian sentimentality. To give her life for the sake of *love* for her mother is indeed a modern gesture of affective agency (hence "unheard of"). On the other hand, it seems precipitous to claim that Junhua dies a filial daughter's death only or even primarily, while ignoring the question of transvaluation engendered by the adoption of love as a new hypergood.

6. Citations from the English anthology of Lu Xun's short stories will use the abbreviation LX.

7. This conflict is still very much with us today. Peter Berkowitz, for example, attributes antiromantic tendencies in contemporary American society to the uncontested primacy commanded by freedom: "The more we grow to love our freedom and embrace it as our defining feature, the more we learn to view ourselves as under no

overarching or enduring authority, connected to no community that commands our permanent allegiance, bound by no promise, principle, or duty that is not retractable or revisable" (2000, 132).

8. Lu subtitles the story "After the style of Xu Qinwen" and acknowledges elsewhere that he has modeled it on Xu's satirical piece "Lixiang de banlü" (An ideal companion, 1923). In Xu's story, a man describes to a friend his ideal of a wife in a language that barely conceals its mocking tone. The notion of companionate marriage that often accompanies the discourse of free love is here revealed to be worse than a castle in the air: it has been turned into a beguiling instrument of male narcissism and fortune hunting (Xu Qinwen 1984, 31–34). Written just months after Zhang Jingsheng published his controversial article "Aiqing dingze yu B nüshi de yanjiu" (The rules of love and a discussion of the affair of Miss B) in the same newspaper supplement (*Chenbao fukan*, 29 April 1923), Xu Qinwen's story could well have been a satirical rejoinder to Zhang's unconventional views that love is conditional and mutable. In this capacity, Xu joined many others who challenged Zhang in the heated debate that ensued. See Chapter 4 for a detailed discussion of this debate.

9. Godelier's work is more centrally concerned with things that are not exchanged but kept, to wit, the sacra, which includes divine favors that humans can never repay and solemn objects/institutions such as individuals (as persons) and the U.S. Constitution (1999).

10. Tani Barlow suggests that Sophia's friends as well as the narrator just know "how corrupt Ling really is" (2004, 146). My point here is that Ling's "corruption" is not an objective fact. He becomes so only through the prism of Sophia's radicalizing self-awakening. At a different point, Barlow seems to be making a similar point. She writes: "'Sophia's Diary' is an example of Ding Ling's characteristic bad faith in new women. As Sophia successively ignores her health, deceives her friends, embarrasses herself in front of strangers, she never doubts the truth that Ling is her own desire's creation" (147). Sophia's vehement denunciation of Ling evidently has more to do with her own disillusionment than with Ling's intrinsic qualities.

11. Shi Zhecun studied French literature at Zhendan University in Shanghai. An accomplished fiction writer and translator, he was also the editor in chief of the celebrated modernist journal *Xiandai* (*Les Contemporains*).

12. See McGrath (2001) for an interesting psychoanalytic reading of this story.

13. Flaubert's *Madame Bovary* was first translated into Chinese by Li Jieren (Shanghai: Zhonghua shuju, 1925). It went through many editions and reprints before 1949. Ding Ling reportedly read it a dozen times and borrowed extensively from it in her own writing (Barlow 1989, 27).

14. *Pinghu tongche* was first serialized in a travel magazine in 1935 and published in book form in 1941 (Shanghai, Baixin shudian). It is translated into English by William Lyell as *Shanghai Express*.

15. See Shih (2001) for a sustained study of the Beijing and Shanghai School of literature.

CHAPTER 4

1. Her other sister, Chen Bijun, was the fiancée of Wang Jingwei (1883–1944) at the time.

2. Zhang Jingsheng's article, entitled "Aiqing dingze yu B nüshi de yanjiu" (The rules of love and a discussion of the affair of Miss B), appeared in *Chenbao fukan* on 29 April 1923. It was reprinted, along with twenty-three responses from readers, eleven metacommentaries on these readerly contributions, and two replies from Zhang, in *Aiqing dingze taolun ji* (A discussion of the rules of love), published by Zhang's own Mei de shudian (Shanghai, 1928) (Zhang Jingsheng 1928). Citations from this collection will use the abbreviation ADT.

3. See Huang (2005, chap. 5) for a discussion of the ways in which women writers of the 1940s revived and amplified Zhang's theory of love and sexuality in their creative works.

4. As Tani Barlow notes, given the centrality of love in defining the new woman in progressive feminism of the 1920s, the fact that "the modern women are handling their own eroticism badly" greatly worried writers like Ding Ling (2004, 142). Women's poor handling of their sexuality is also a trope that registers the bankruptcy of *nüxing*, or the sexualized female subject.

5. According to Tze-lan Sang's study, female same-sex desire became a source of public anxiety and fear in China as women's autonomous sexuality began to emerge in such places as all-female schools. The prevalent views of female homosexuality as sexual inversion or a temporary stage of adolescence were derived mostly from the works of Havelock Ellis (Sang 2003, 23–25).

6. See Tsu (2005, 148–49) for another account of the trial and Pan Guangdan's commentary on the affair.

7. In European history, female perpetrators of "crimes of passion" were often acquitted on the assumption that their (sexual) passion tended to cloud their rational judgment (Lean 2001). This was not the case in China. Eugenia Lean's case study of Shi Jianqiao shows that only the moral sentiment of filial piety could serve an exculpatory function. Shi plotted the public assassination of the warlord Sun Chuanfang (to avenge her dead father) with a sense of impunity that could be accounted for not only by the general disrepute of warlords, but also by the social sanction of the filial avenger. That she won instant public sympathy and eventual judicial leniency bore this out. Public reactions differed sharply in love murder cases whereby only contempt and condemnation were reserved for "love-crazed" women who let their passions get the better of themselves.

8. A more accurate title would be, "The View of Love that Chinese Women Should Have, According to the Author." Wang Pingling is the author of over sixty volumes of fiction, essays, poetry, plays, and criticism. He published his first story, "Leifengta xia" (Beneath the Thunder Peak Pagoda), in *Shishi xinbao*'s "Xuedeng" supplement in 1920 and later became its editor. In the early 1930s, he founded, with Fan Zhengbo and others, *Qianfeng zhoubao* (The vanguard weekly) to promote

"nationalist literature" (*minzu zhuyi wenxue*) and engaged in debates with left-wing writers. In 1938, he chaired the All China Association of Writers and Artists Against Foreign Invasion (Zhonghua quanguo wenyi kangdi xiehui).

9. In an autobiographical narrative, Zhang Xichen recounts the fortuitous circumstances under which he came to edit the journal. When he assumed the post of editorship on recommendation from friends, he had absolutely no understanding of women's issues; so he went to the library and plowed through several Japanese books on the subject with only a smattering of self-taught Japanese (1931). An autodidact whose formal education consisted only of one year of middle school, Zhang emerged as one of the foremost advocates of women's liberation in the post–May Fourth era. After his dismissal from the Commercial Press in 1926, he founded *Xin nüxing* (The new woman, 1926–1929) and then Kaiming shudian (Kaiming Books). In the late 1920s, he engaged in a series of debates with both conservatives and radical anarchists, establishing himself as a vocal spokesman for the moderate liberal contingent of the cultural spectrum (see the next section).

10. Beginning in 1924, the journal ran a new column called "The Forum" (*taolun hui*), which featured readers' responses to questions posed by the editors such as "is it appropriate to seek marriage partner through advertisement?" (10:7), "can a man who respects women divorce his old-style, unsatisfactory wife?" (10:10), and "does a wedding ceremony need to be lavishly conducted?" (10:12). Many readers—anywhere from eight to fourteen per forum—took part in these discussions. After Du Jiutian took over, he switched to the essay contest (*zhengwen*) format on more conventional topics.

11. Ariès questions the pervading notion that modernity is characterized by the triumph of individualism over family-based social constraints. He asks, "where is the individualism in these modern lives, in which all the energy of the couple is directed to serving the interests of a deliberately restricted posterity? Was there not greater individualism in the gay indifference of the prolific fathers of the ancien regime?" (1962, 406). Although I object to Ariès's application of individualism to the libertarian (or libertine) lifestyle of premodern patriarchs, I second his call to pay greater attention to the nuclear family as a key context in which individualism should be understood. The study of the May Fourth denunciation of the patriarchal family should not be separated from the study of how the May Fourth generation and beyond sought to locate the modern individual in the nuclear family—in the contentious discursive space of nationalism and women's liberation. See also Glosser (1995) and Yeh (1992).

12. See Jones (2002) for a discussion of the "discovery of childhood" in Republican China and its ideological and commercial ramifications.

13. The phrase refers to Zhang Jingsheng's article, "Di sanzhong shui yu luanqiu ji shengji de dian he youzhong de guanxi" (The third kind of fluid and the egg in their relationship to the current of vitality and eugenics), which appeared in *Xinwenhua* 1:2, 1927, 23–48. Zhang formulated this provocative theory of female ejaculation to explain the congenital weakness of the Chinese racial stock: because Chinese women fail to release the third kind of fluid during intercourse—the result of igno-

rance and carelessness—the fetuses they carry tend to acquire a "moronic and retarded shape" (Dikötter 1995, 76–77). "The third kind of fluid" entered popular lexicon as the butt of risqué jokes. Zhang recalled customers coming into his bookstore and addressing the female clerks with the double entendre question, "Is 'The Third Kind of Fluid' out yet?" (1998, 24).

14. I discuss the question of hypocrisy at greater length in Chapter 6.

15. *Lingrou yizhi*, or the unity of body and soul, seems to be a poetic rendition of what the sociologist Niklas Luhmann calls "the unity of love, marriage and sexual relations" (1986, 126), the cornerstone of bourgeois domestic ideology. First given expression in eighteenth-century novels of feeling (such as Samuel Richardson's *Pamela*, 1740), it effected a revolution in the conception of love from something inherently extra-marital to "that curious excitement which one experienced on noticing that one had decided to marry" (127).

16. Chen is attuned to the class and racial complications of the eugenic movement. On the one hand, he notes with elitist alarm that birth control is mostly practiced by the upper classes, while the lower classes go on breeding inferior offspring en masse. On the other hand (and apparently without any self-consciousness), he rejects birth control in a gesture of defiance against the imperialist West. His reasoning goes like this: The white race controls nine-tenths of the world's territory with only a fraction of the world's population. No wonder they are concerned with their slow population growth and their ability to maintain this unnatural distribution of resources. We colored peoples ought to overturn the status quo and restore the natural state of affair (*ziran zhuangtai*). Why should we, then, trifle with birth control when we should be expanding our numbers and taking advantage of the decline of the white race to regain our rightful share of natural resources? We support birth control only on their part (Chen Jianshan 1924).

17. Zhang Xichen collected the initial exchange between himself, Zhou Jianren, and Chen Bainian, as well as all subsequent discussions on this topic in a book under the title *Xin xing daode taolun ji* (A discussion of new sexual morality). It was published by his own Kaiming shudian in 1926 as part of the series *Funü wenti congshu* (Series on the woman question). Zhang Xichen initiated the debate during his tenure as the editor of *Funü zazhi,* and the debate cost him the editorship (Link 1981, 251). His successor at *Funü zazhi* refused to publish his reply (as well as Zhou Jianren's) to Chen Bainian's attack; nor would *Xiandai pinglun,* which carried Chen's essay. Zhang and Zhou turned to Lu Xun for help, and Lu Xun obligingly published their essays in his *Mangyuan* magazine. Lu Xun attached an "Editor's Afterword" (Bian wan xieqi) lamenting that Zhang and Zhou were too far ahead of their time for the Chinese audience (*Mangyuan* 4, May 1925, in Zhang Xichen 1926b, 98–99).

18. The author seems oblivious to the contradiction between total sexual freedom and the implicit sexual norms that allow one to discriminate against "deviancies."

19. Author of *Quxiao rensheng zhexue* (The philosophy of antilife) (Yijiu'erba chubanbu, 1930).

20. See Lee (2006b) for a discussion of conservative efforts to restore love as a

moral sentiment in response to three translated texts: *Love and Duty* by S. Horose, *The Education of Love* (aka *Heart*) by Edmondo de Amicis, and "Three Generations" by Alexandra Kollontai.

CHAPTER 5

1. Davidson's (1987) parallel oppositions of sex/sexuality and anatomy/psychology in his writing on the emergence of sexuality seem overly schematic and largely leave out the social category of gender. Nonetheless, he is highly persuasive in establishing the linkage between sex and anatomy with the example of Christ's "sex" in Renaissance paintings that deliberately emphasize his genitalia to show that the incarnate Christ is a man in every sense of the word. In the context of discussing perversion, he reminds us how modern the notion is that a gay man may be a "woman" trapped in a man's body. This would have been utterly incomprehensible to the ancients because sex, as evidenced in pre-nineteenth-century iconography, proceeded from the body, particularly the sexual organs. It therefore makes no sense to suggest that an anatomical man may really be a psychological woman.

2. In asserting the modernity of sexuality, Davidson is of course following in the footsteps of Foucault. But Foucault's contemporaries have also made similar, even if less systematic and provocative, observations. For example, Richard Sennett notes in his classic chronicle of the decline of the public the degree to which sexuality has come to define who we are: "Whatever we experience must in some way touch on our sexuality, but sexuality *is*" (1992, 7). Davidson's "historical epistemology" is also close in spirit to Ian Hacking's "dynamic nominalism," or the idea that "numerous kinds of human beings and human acts come into being hand in hand with our invention of the categories labeling them" (1992, 87). More in the Conclusion.

3. The best work on indigenous Chinese approaches to sex/gender/reproduction has remained that of Charlotte Furth (1986, 1987, 1988, 1994, 1999).

4. I am aware that the question of Foucault's relation to psychoanalysis is far from settled. For my present purpose, suffice it to note that I use psychoanalysis and Freudianism interchangeably, and that I do not make a rigorous distinction between psychoanalysis and the other sexual sciences of the nineteenth and twentieth centuries— mainly in view of the fact that such a distinction was scarcely maintained by the Chinese intellectuals under study here.

5. According to Jingyuan Zhang's survey, the introduction of Freudian psychoanalysis, along with social psychology and sexology, began in the early 1920s and reached its height in the mid-1930s. Between 1930 and 1934, about twenty articles were published every month on Freudian theory (1992, 24). For the most part, however, interests in Freud were drawn to its implications for critiquing the Chinese tradition and reorganizing individual identity and social relationships.

6. Strictly speaking, *ars erotica* is an Orientalist invention that collapses a wide array of traditional ideas and practices concerning such matters as sexual intercourse, conception, pregnancy, childbirth, health, longevity, male empowerment, gynecology,

and even pediatrics. The May Fourth generation seems to have had little exposure to the indigenous *ars erotica* tradition. According to Judith Farquhar, before the 1980s, it was European and Japanese sinologists who showed deep interest in ancient Chinese sex lore. Authors like Robert van Gulik, Henri Maspero, and Joseph Needham are still authorities in this field (2002, 257). The sexual histories of China that they have produced are deeply embedded in twentieth-century Euro-American assumptions about sexuality. For an incisive critique of the locus classicus of this genre, Van Gulik's *Sexual Life in Ancient China* (1961), see Furth (1994). The thrust of Furth's critique is that Van Gulik imposes on the heterogeneous (medical, religious, literary) materials he surveys the assumption that there is a discrete, self-conscious, and transhistorical domain of the erotic for the experience of sexual pleasure in and of itself. The kernel of wisdom that he teases out of the bedchamber manuals of "a sexually enlightened Orient" conveniently echoes the norms of mid-twentieth-century western societies: the goal of marriage is "sexual fulfillment defined as mutual orgasm in a heterosexual lovers' bed" (129). Furth's own reading concludes that pleasure is almost always a means to other ends, and that it is bound up with a multiplicity of concerns encompassing individual life, sex roles, family continuity, governance, and spirituality. She writes: "orthodox Chinese medical discourse did not understand [sexual] pleasures as constituting an independent domain of 'sexuality,' but rather positioned the erotic at the fulcrum of body experiences implicating human longevity and even spiritual regeneration on one side and generativity and reproduction on the other" (145).

7. Pan Guangdan was educated at Qinghua University, Dartmouth College, and Columbia University, where he studied evolutionary biology and eugenics in the 1920s. In his long career as an intellectual and educator, he wrote extensively in the areas of eugenics, psychology, sociology, and ethnology. The initial draft of the Xiaoqing essay was written as a term paper for Liang Qichao's history survey course at Qinghua University (Huang 2005, 181). Pan published it under the title "Feng Xiaoqing kao" (Investigating Feng Xiaoqing) in *Funü zazhi* (The ladies' journal) while he was studying in the United States, though he was unhappy with the fact that the magazine left out all the poems under analysis. In 1927, he revised this article by "delving deeper into Xiaoqing's sexual pathologies" and published it as a monograph entitled *Xiaoqing zhi fenxi* (An analysis of Xiaoqing; Shanghai: Xinyue shudian). This edition also features several appendices, a drawing of Xiaoqing by Wen Yiduo, and seven photographs of Xiaoqing's tomb by a certain Zhang Xinyi from Hangzhou. In 1929, he reissued the book as *Feng Xiaoqing: Yi jian yinglian zhi yanjiu* (Feng Xiaoqing: A study of narcissism), adding a facsimile of Liang Qichao's laudatory remarks about the study (Pan Guangdan 1993, 1:3). Pan later translated Havelock Ellis's *Studies in the Psychology of Sex* into Chinese (*Xing xinlixue*, Shanghai: Shangwu, 1936, reprinted 1949). Included in this edition is his essay "Zhongguo wenxian zhong tongxinglian juli" (Enumerating instances of homosexual behavior in the Chinese archives).

8. For detailed studies of the Xiaoqing legend in the context of the late imperial cult of *qing*, see Ko (1994, 92–112); Widmer (1992).

9. Pan Guangdan (1993, 23); translation adapted from Widmer (1992, 152–53). Citations from Pan's text will use the abbreviation FXQ.

10. In an appendix entitled "Nüzi zuopin yu jingshen yujie" (Women's writing and melancholia), Pan gives a statistical analysis of a women's poetry anthology from the Qing dynasty (1644–1911). He notes that of a total of 234 poems with an average length of 60 to 70 words, there are 349 words connoting dejection and over 1,600 words carrying a negative valence. He rules out the several possible explanations for the preponderance of sadness and depression in women's poetry and reasserts his thesis that the etiology of female neurosis can only be sought in abnormal sexual development and unsatisfactory sex life (FXQ, 59–63).

11. See Tsu (2005, 149–53) for another account of Pan's study of Xiaoqing with a slightly different emphasis.

12. Wen Yiduo was a well-known May Fourth poet and friend of Pan Guangdan. He studied painting in the United States in the early 1920s.

13. An English translation of this ballad can be found in Birrell (1982, 53–62).

14. Yuan Changying held a master's degree in English drama from Edinburgh University and also studied French literature at the University of Paris. She published "Southeast Flies the Peacock" while teaching at Wuhan University. When university faculty and students staged this play in 1935, it was reviewed harshly by leftist critics, who considered its subject matter divorced from political reality. For a discussion of leftist criticism of women writers in the 1930s, see Larson (1998, chap. 5).

15. Likewise, Braester finds Pan Jinlian's confession evocative of "a distinctly modern ethics of passion" and "twentieth-century sensibilities," which in a way violates Ouyang Yuqian's own standards of historical realism (2003, 62, 71). My point here is that the authors did not necessarily see their rewritings as deliberate acts of anachronism, but as acts of revelation or exposition, of bringing the hidden truths of the psyche and body to the surface. I return to this point in the next section.

16. Whereas roaming bands of outlaws have traditionally been celebrated in popular literature for their righteousness (*yi*) and chivalry (*yingxiong*), monks are more often than not regarded with ambivalence and mistrust. Their ascetic order, though modeled on patriarchy and sharing many structural characteristics with secret brotherhoods, is seen as a mere cover for sordid dealings in money and lust. The popular anticlerical sentiment may be partly accounted for by the economic and social power that monastic establishments have exerted on lay life. But the popular critique invariably resorts to the tactic of moral unmasking, which revels in exposing some monks' inability to abide by the code of asceticism and in condemning them to the most violent and disgraceful form of death—naked corpses abandoned in the street, stumbled upon by strangers, disposed of by law, and devoured by wild beasts. The novel cites a ditty to drive home the condemnation: "Bestial unbridled shaven-pate/With a beauty in secret disported./His crimes besmirched all monks' names./In a lane his body lay/Naked in a pool of blood./Cast it off a cliff/In deep snow/To feed the tigers!/He forgot the scriptures the abbot taught him./Mulien rescued his mother/And went to Heaven,/But this thieving baldy/Disgraced his mother in death!" (WM, 741)

17. Sedgwick uses the term "male homosocial desire" on the basis of the assumption that the sexual drive, or libido, is the ultimate source of all human contact and feeling—an assumption that she critiques in a later work (2003, 17–18). Kam Louie borrows Sedgwick's "male homosocial desire" to challenge the conventional wisdom that the Chinese *wu* (martial) hero is an asexual he-man motivated entirely by worthy causes instead of sexual passions (2002, 23). Although I am sympathetic to his effort to expose the heterosexual assumption underlying this misperception, I am, for the reasons I am laying out in this chapter, uneasy with his insistence on sexualizing the *wu* hero by teasing out the erotic dimensions of his character, a process in which contemporary normative assumptions about sexuality often slip back. Even the term *bisexuality* (which Louie seems to prefer over homo- or heterosexuality) is problematic because it still subscribes to the truth discourse centering on sexuality.

18. See Sanday (1990). Peggy Sanday argues that fraternity gang rape is the means by which men disavow the homoeroticism that so patently underlies fraternal bonding. By committing the "pulling train," whose victim is often an unconscious woman, "the brothers vent their interest in one another through the [inert] body of a woman"; men who shy away from this ritual are derided as "gays" or "faggots" (11–12). Sanday concludes that both homophobia and compulsory heterosexuality are "strategies of knowledge and power centering on sex that support the social stratification of men according to sexual preference" (12).

19. Pondering the vastly different attitudes toward homoeroticism in ancient Greece and the contemporary United States, Sedgwick remarks that the "explanation will require a more exact mode of historical categorization than 'patriarchy' . . . since patriarchal power structures characterize both Athenian and American societies" (1985, 5). What is required, it seems to me, is none other than a Foucauldian history of sexuality that demonstrates how sexuality was essentialized as a fundamental and defining aspect of human experience in modern western societies.

20. For instance, when he is first brought to the Yang residence, Shi Xiu (and the reader) hears, before her person even appears on the scene, Qiaoyun's glib retort to her husband's summons to come forth and greet her "brother-in-law."

21. The bare foot (apparently not bound) is another telltale sign of the modernity of Shi's rendition. In traditional iconography, bound feet are never depicted without their lotus shoes, not even in pornographic prints (Wang 2000, 24). Other body parts, on the other hand, are invoked primarily for narrative purposes. According to John Hay, in traditional woodblock illustrations for pornographic novels such as the *Golden Lotus*, when a sexual act is the point of the plot at a given moment, bodies may become naked or partially naked to reveal some narratively essential detail such as the male or female genitals. But the nakedness is always integrated into the narrative context and is rarely a matter of secluded individual bodies disconnected from their surroundings (1994, 55–56).

22. Shu-mei Shih's argument that Shi Zhecun's turn to psychoanalysis is a quest for aesthetic autonomy proceeds from a narrow understanding of politics (2001, 354–66). For her, Shi's explorations of "psychoanalytic interiority" and "erotic-grotesque

fantasies" are essentially escapist (in her words, "nonideological and apolitical") because his fiction is usually set either in "a remote past of no immediate consequence to the present" or in the vertiginously cosmopolitan spaces of Shanghai where organized politics yields to the lures of the modern. True, psychoanalysis may not be immediately serviceable to the politics of the left or the right. But the self-conscious espousal of psychoanalysis is as political as is its rejection. Indeed, the purpose of this chapter is precisely to show how the use of psychoanalysis in the May Fourth and post–May Fourth context was both subversive and normative.

23. That Shi Zhecun's modernism is crucially hinged on whether he subscribes to what is known as May Fourth representationalism or the supreme faith in the powers of representation to usher in a new world, is the principal point of contention between Andrew Jones and William Schaefer (1998, 61, n69). Although I agree with Schaefer (and Shu-mei Shih to some extent) that Shi Zhecun is a modernist insofar as he self-consciously departs from familiar May Fourth themes and aligns himself with European and Japanese modernists, I also find persuasive Jones's argument that Shi betrays a faith in the power of representation to plumb the depths of the human psyche and to arrive at some ultimate truth. Shi Zhecun's unproblematic adoption of the totalizing framework of psychoanalysis leads him to believe that this truth always pertains to desire. Hence he structures the dramatic conflict of his fiction invariably between desire and the various forces that seek to contain, regulate, or suppress it, including religious asceticism, racial/national loyalty, and the code of fictive brotherhood.

24. The tattooing of skin in traditional China marks a "barbarian" from the "civilized" Chinese (Hay 1994, 62).

25. Andrew Jones argues that, at the level of text, the psychoanalytic rewriting of classical texts operates on an invasive logic of depth that extracts "confessions" from the source texts and grants the reader the pleasure of knowledge and mastery. When one reads Shi Zhecun's "Shi Xiu," for example, "one cannot help but note the underlying consonance between the voyeuristic pleasure Shi Xiu derives from the violent revelation of what lies inside [Qiaoyun's] body, the invasive ways in which Shi Zhicun [*sic*] extracts from Shi Xiu a confession of what goes on inside his head, and finally, the pleasure we take in these revelations of a truth that lies underneath the surface of things" (1994, 590). The "truth" that the text is forced to yield is the "sadistic violence" at the foundation of heroic brotherhood. The violence of the text, suggests Jones, is thus harnessed to the larger May Fourth project of cultural critique (589, 588).

26. Jean Baudrillard accuses the psychoanalytic investigator of perpetuating an "incredible" form of racism, "the racism of truth, the evangelical racism of psychoanalysis," because it refuses to allow for the possibility that the sexual act does not always have finality in itself, and sexuality does not always have "the deadly seriousness of an energy to be freed" (1987, 23, 28–29).

CHAPTER 6

1. *Fūdo* was translated into English in the 1960s as *Climate and Culture: A Philosophical Study.* It does not seem to have been translated into Chinese, though many Chinese intellectuals in the May Fourth and post–May Fourth eras could and did read a great deal of Japanese texts in that language. For an extended analysis of this text in the context of Japanese intellectual history in the interwar period, see Harootunian (2000, 269–82).

2. Such indeed was the charge leveled at the Manchu state of its attitude toward and treatment of overseas Chinese by revolutionary nationalists in their early days of activism overseas (see Duara 1997).

3. Lydia Liu points out that in fact there had been a Chinese translation of which Lu Xun did not seem aware: in 1903, Zuoxinshe in Shanghai published *Zhinaren zhi qizhi,* which is "a close rendering of [Tamotsu] Shibue's 1896 version of Smith's book in classical Chinese including the Japanese translator's notes and commentaries" (1995, 53). Theodore Huters disputes Liu's claim that Lu Xun read Smith before 1926 and directly injected the missionary theory of Chinese character into his literary creations, particularly the figure of Ah Q (1998, 575–79). It is no doubt more plausible to emphasize the larger discursive milieu spanning several decades and linguistic spheres than to pinpoint a single text as the source of a literary practice renowned for its complexity and reflexivity. But Smith's impact on Chinese intellectual discourses cannot be underestimated: *Chinese Characteristics* is still enjoying wide circulation and readership in reform-era China (Liu 2002, i)

4. Recent scholarship on Lu Xun has questioned this experience as the causa sine qua non of Lu Xun's conversion to literature (see Pollard 2002). For my purpose here, it is important to bear in mind that although the decision itself may well have been overdetermined, Lu Xun's retrospective account symptomatically points to a singular event. It is his reconstruction of the event, not what really happened, that has come to constitute the originary moment of modern Chinese literature.

5. In a nuanced analysis of Lu Xun's conflicted attitude toward women in public, Eileen J. Cheng (2004) attributes Lu Xun's distaste for cross-dressing actors and revolutionaries alike to his distrust of theatricality in general. Cheng seeks the reason for this in his fear that people are prone to confusing the stage with real life as well as in his paternalistic impulse to shield women from men's salacious gaze and media exploitation. One can also argue that Lu Xun is operating in the modern regime of authenticity whereby theatrical utterances and actions in the public space are inherently deficient in sincerity and moral integrity. Thus in refusing to present female spectacles in his writings, Lu Xun is not so much erasing women's agency, as Cheng suggests, as affirming the enlightenment hierarchy of public and private. Indeed, it is difficult to claim that he is "reinscribing the public as a distinctly male terrain" (29) when he comes down even harder on men whose public roles entail patent playacting—think of opera singer Mei Lanfang, Siming in "Soap," and all the "pseudo-moralists" who are the habitual butt of Lu Xun's barbed satiricism.

6. A parallel may be drawn between radical May Fourth pronouncements and the views expressed in an 1892 essay by the Japanese romanticist Kitamura Tōkoku: "Ensei shika to josei" (World-weary poets and women, originally published in *The Women's Magazine*). In it, Tōkoku makes a declaration that sounded as thunderous as a canon shot to his contemporaries: Love (*ren'ai*) is the secret key of life and the foundation of humanity (1977). The novelist Kinoshita Naoe explains his own reaction: "These words, so earnestly consecrated to love, were, I believe, the first such ever uttered in our country. Until then, love—the relationship between men and women—had seemed somehow sordid. No one had even spoken out against that attitude so explicitly" (quoted in Brownstein 1981, 100–101). For Tōkoku, the Japanese had never known true love—only sex—before his time. He thus disqualifies the entire pre-Meiji erotic literature from the category of "love" and blames the "pseudo-novelists" for debasing life with sordid fantasies and for failing to explore love's true nature. As in May Fourth discourse, "love" is very much a code word for individual autonomy and freedom.

7. This point, more or less, has been made by every scholar who has ever commented on the story, including Denton (1992); Lee (1973); Liu (1995); Tsu (2005); Zhang (1992)

CHAPTER 7

1. *Geming*, like *aiqing* and *lian'ai*, is a loanword neologism from modern Japanese. Jianhua Chen's (1999) study of the modern origins of *geming* takes us to the cross-linguistic translations and borrowings at the turn of the twentieth century involving such major thinkers as Liang Qichao and Sun Yat-sen.

2. Published by Sun Yat-sen's Minzhi shuju (Popular wisdom press) in Shanghai. For a brief history of the press as a Nationalist propaganda organ, see Fitzgerald (1996, 195).

3. David Wang notes that although it is unclear whether Jiang Guangci et al. were aware of Hong Ruizhao's pamphlet, "the leftists would have agreed with Hong that romantic love . . . works both as an impetus for and an impediment to revolution." Again, "change the label Hong cited from Nationalist to Communist, and one discerns an almost identical set of syndromes befalling revolutionary youth" (2004, 91).

4. In her book-length study of the "revolution + love" theme in twentieth-century Chinese literature, Jianmei Liu alternatively characterizes the theme as a "literary fashion" driven by the logic of the market and as a mode of expression for the revolutionary masses. The masses, according to her, favor a "combustible mode of expression" and find this formula "a perfect space to release their anxiety" (2003, 56). She points to festival-like scenes such as "revolutionary gatherings, demonstrations, and public lectures" to support her latter point (56). However, a page later, Liu concedes that the typical "revolution plus love" story tends to be wrapped up in an "atmosphere of gloom" and steeped in "the Wertherian type of passive sentimentality" (57). This is closer to what I am arguing here: that "revolution + romance" is an

intensely private genre; and that once the masses take center stage, the genre has run its course.

5. Xiaobing Tang considers this novella "a less than refined sample of the then-popular 'revolution and love' fiction churned out by the nascent literary left" (2000, 96). As we will see in this chapter, the Nationalist right was equally concerned with patrolling the intersection of revolution and love and produced their own, and no less insipid, samples.

6. Xiaobing Tang argues that Ding Ling's portrayal of Mary is fraught with ambiguity, wavering between sympathy and denunciation, intimacy and criticism. Tang attributes this ambiguity to the author's own situation as a housebound pregnant wife who was kept out of the "exciting and secretive world" of her husband, a fledgling writer and a member of the Communist Party. Thus Ding Ling is able to depict the "nonrevolutionary life" of the housewife in its "concrete pleasures" while branding it as the "opposite of a socially meaningful life" (2000, 107–9). And Mary certainly receives a great deal of narrative attention—far more than a negative character usually does in her later stories. Tang suggests that a sociologically oriented analysis would see Mary's problem as one that plagued many educated women who still had little access to the workplace and few opportunities for socialization (119–21). This line of analysis, I argue, is precisely what Ding Ling refuses to pursue.

7. This refers to the Nationalist Revolution launched by Chiang Kai-shek and the National Revolutionary Army made up of allied KMT and CCP forces (also known as the Northern Expedition) against divisive and destructive warlordism in 1926–1928. It brought China under the unified rule of the Nationalist Party.

8. Chen studied philosophy and literature in the United States and Germany between 1928 and 1933. In 1940, he formed the School of the Warring States (Zhanguoce pai) with Lin Tongji et al. and launched the coterie journal *Zhanguoce,* which promoted the fascist "philosophy of might" (*shangli zhengzhi*). He served in several cultural posts in the KMT government, including the director of Zhongguo qingnian jutuan (Chinese youth theater) and editor in chief of Zhengzhong Bookstore.

9. As much as Mao Dun disdains this formula, it signals his rejection of an even less desirable type exemplified in his trilogy *Shi* (Eclipse) written in the aftermath of the 1927 coup. Here young people disillusioned with the revolution retreat to the private life of romantic relationships, or, as Mao Dun himself did, to the equally private world of creative writing. Mao Dun adopted his pen name (which means "contradiction") at this point. Marston Anderson observes: "Shen's [Mao Dun's surname] failure in politics and his resulting apprehension of the complex forces (or contradictions) that governed political reality had somehow liberated his literary imagination. As he was later to say in an interview, 'I became an author because I was unsuccessful at practical revolutionary work'" (1990, 121). See also Liu (2003, chap. 2) for a discussion of Mao Dun as an exemplary practitioner of "revolution + romance"; and Wang (2004, chap. 3) for an account of the intersection of romance and politics in Mao Dun's personal life.

10. The novel is translated into English by Sidney Shapiro as *Daughters and Sons*

(New York: Liberty Press, 1952; Beijing: Foreign Languages Press, 1958). Citations from the English version will use the abbreviation DS. I have changed the Wade-Giles spelling of names to Pinyin.

11. This plot pattern is redeployed in what is perhaps the best-known and also the last specimen of the "revolution + romance" genre: *Song of Youth*. Meng Yue argues that the marriage plot symbolically figures the ideological struggle over the fate of the nation: men who have posed a sexual threat to the female protagonist Lin Daojing invariably turn out to be traitors (just like Zhang Jinlong), and Lin's marital choice is ultimately merged with "the question of which political force will legitimately dominate the nation's future" (1993, 128). Lin, in other words, must desire and eventually marry a communist cadre. It is significant that this genre structures women's participation in public, political life mostly in private, domestic terms (through romantic relationships) and closes off the possibility of a public "other than the one offered by the Communist Party" (129). The later repudiation of this genre goes even a step further: not only must the party and its political ideology be the sole bridge between a woman and the public, she must also relate to the party/public in a nonerotic mode—as a daughter, rather than as a lover. Once again, we see resonance with Wen Kang's ideals of heroic sons and daughters.

12. Judith Farquhar also takes note of the total, seamless convergence of the political and the personal in this story. She writes: "Much of [the story's nationalist language] takes the form of paeans to China and the Communist Party that are either transcriptions of Du Wanxiang's 'private' thoughts or outbursts by others who are inspired by her simple and undemanding service. . . . From the point of view of this kind of Maoist writing, loyalty and labor alone were not enough; service to the people was also expected to produce a 'lofty, solemn, and virginal glow' in citizens whose patriotism suffused their whole bodies" (2002, 169–70). The heart, in this scheme, is the epicenter of the radiant glow that in other contexts is simply called "love."

13. Tani Barlow argues that Ding Ling broke with her longtime stance of distancing herself from her heroines and identified emphatically with Du Wanxiang, who was an actual model worker whom she met on the state farm where she had lived during her exile: "So close was this identification that when Ding Ling recovered her political right to self-expression she wrote about herself through the subjectivity of Du, the ren'ge [character, social standing] of a fully realized, proletarianized, daughter of China" (2004, 196). Barlow also makes the point that Wanxiang's moral authority derives from "her ordinary goodness" (197). It is a Maoist cliché to characterize an exemplary socialist subject as "ordinary and yet extraordinary" (*pingfan er weida*). But such exemplars are anything but ordinary. Their normativity is rather the effect of their having become what Alasdair MacIntyre calls "characters" (see Chapter 1), persons who embody society's highest moral ideals—here the political, utopian ideals of socialism. The insistence on ordinariness has to do with the specifically communist politics of subalternity, or the idea that in the communist moral universe, the ordinary becomes great while the "great" (the lords of the past) are swept out of the proletarianized pantheon. The phrase "ordinary and yet extraordinary" is one of

those deliberate paradoxes of Maospeak coined to accentuate the totalistic remaking of Chinese society.

CONCLUSION

1. See Farrer (2002) for a study of late twentieth-century urban narratives in which irony and play jostle moral seriousness over matters of sexual motive and choice.

2. Communist ideology has always doubled as official nationalism in China, which functioned as the internal supplement to the more loudly trumpeted communist internationalism. This helps explain both the CCP's swift metamorphosis into a nationalist party and its tacit endorsement of popular nationalism. See Gries (2004) for a study of particularly virulent strands of popular nationalism in the late 1990s.

3. It has been reported here and there that professional mourners are not only back in business but are also in high demand. These new professionals and their patrons are not necessarily left over from an earlier era or episteme either. One music college graduate, for example, targets his "wailing services" (*peiku fuwu*) to an educated clientele. His Internet advertisement boasts of "a sonorous voice suffused with genuine feeling," guaranteed to stir up emotions and heighten the funereal atmosphere. He charges his clients according to a gradation of affectivity that is not shy of swaggering rhetoric: 100 yuan per hour for full-throated wailing (*fangsheng gaoge*); 200 yuan for wailing that disturbs neighbors in all four directions (*silin bu an*); 300 yuan for wailing that lingers for three days (*raoliang sanri*); 400 yuan for a torrential downpour (*qinpen dayu*); and 500 yuan for wailing that shatters mountains and cracks open the earth (*shanbeng dilie*). See news clips on http://cn.news.yahoo.com/050818/808/2eh8f.html or http://edu.yesky.com/edunews/371/2079371.shtml.

Character List

ai 愛
aidagara あいだがら
ai de chuxian 愛的初現
aiguo 愛國
aiqing 哀情
aiqing 愛情
aiqing de xingshi 愛情的形式
aiqing dingze 愛情定則
An Ji 安驥

Bai Liusu 白流蘇
Bai Liying (Liniang)
　白梨影（梨娘）
Bao Tianxiao 包天笑
beifen 輩分
Bi Hen 碧痕
bizhan 筆戰

Caitiao 采苕
caizi jiaren 才子佳人
canqing 慘情
Changke 長科
Chen Bainian 陳百年
Chen Bohe 陳伯和
Chen Diexian 陳蝶仙
cheng 誠
Chen Jianshan 陳兼善

Chen Jixia 陳季俠
Chen Linghua 陳淩華
Chen Quan 陳銓
Chen Que 陳碻
Chen Shujun 陳淑君
Chen Zhong'ai 陳仲藹
chulian 初戀
ci 慈
cong xin suo yu bu yu ju
　從心所欲不逾矩
cong yi er zhong 從一而終

datong 大同
dawo 大我
Du Jiutian 杜久田
Du Liniang 杜麗娘
duoqing ren 多情人
Du Wanxiang 杜晚香
Du Yaquan 杜亞泉

en 恩
erchong renge 二重人格
ernü 兒女
ernü siqing 兒女私情
ernü yingxiong 兒女英雄
Ernü yingxiong zhuan
　兒女英雄傳

331

fa hu qing, zhi yu liyi
　發乎情，止於禮儀
Fangxin Nüshi　芳心女士
Fan Liuyuan　范柳原
fanxing zhuyi　泛性主義
fei lian'ai lun　非戀愛論
fengjian　封建
Feng Xiaoqing　馮小青
Feng Yuanjun　馮沅君
Fūdo　風土
Funü zazhi　婦女雜誌

ganqing　感情
ganqing dingxiang　感情定向
gao suzhi　高素質
"Gebi meng"　割臂盟
"Gejue"　隔絕
geming　革命
Geming de qian yimu　革命的前一幕
geming jia lian'ai　革命加戀愛
gemingxing　革命性
Geming yu lian'ai　革命與戀愛
"Geming yu lian'ai de gongshi"
　革命與戀愛的公式
Gong Pengcheng　龔鵬程
Guangtao　光燾
Gu Chengwu　顧誠吾
Guifang　桂芳

haohan　好漢
heimu xiaoshuo　黑幕小說
He Mengxia　何夢霞
Henhai　恨海
He Yufeng　何玉鳳
Hong Ruizhao　洪瑞釗
hongyan boming　紅顏薄命
Huang Changdian　黃長典
Huangjin sui　黃金祟
Huanqing　歡情

huayu zhuyi　化欲主義
Huayue hen　花月痕
Hu Chunbing　胡春冰
Hu Ziyun　胡子雲

Jia Baoyu　賈寶玉
jia daoxue　假道學
Jiang Guangci　蔣光慈
jianghu　江湖
Jiaomu　焦母
Jiao Zhongqing　焦仲卿
jiepi　潔癖
jiewen　接吻
jieyu zhuyi　節欲主義
"Jinqian xuelei"　襟前血淚
jing　景
Jingying Nüshi　靜英女士
"Jiuhou"　酒後
jixing de xing shenghuo
　畸形的性生活
Juansheng　涓生
Junhua　雋華

Kindai no ren'ai kan
　近代の恋愛観
Kong Jue　孔厥
Kongque dongnan fei　孔雀東南飛
Kong Rong　孔融
kuqing　苦情
Kuriyagawa Hakuson　厨川白村

langman pai　浪漫派
Laocan youji　老殘遊記
Lei Feng　雷鋒
li　禮
lian'ai　戀愛
lian'ai bing　戀愛病
lian'ai geyan　戀愛格言
lian'ai kuada kuang　戀愛誇大狂

"Lian'ai shang wei chenggong, tongzhi
    bu xu nuli"　戀愛尙未成功，同志
    不須努力
Lian'ai shu　戀愛術
"Lian'ai yu xingjiao"　戀愛與性交
Lian'ai yu yule　戀愛與娛樂
lian'ai zhi shang　戀愛至上
Liang Guochang　梁國常
liangzhi　良知
lianmin de qinggan　憐憫的情感
Libailiu　禮拜六
lie　烈
lieqing　烈情
lijiao　禮教
lijiao de zhengteng
    禮教的蒸騰
"Lijiao yu siyu"　禮教與私欲
Lin Daiyu　林黛玉
Lin Shu　林紓
Ling Jishi　凌吉士
lingrou yizhi　靈肉一致
Ling Shuhua　凌叔華
"Lingxiu zhi si"　領袖之死
Liu Jichun　柳系春
Liu Lanzhi　劉蘭芝
Liu Mengmei　柳夢梅
Liu Mengying　劉夢瑩
Liu Tieyun (Liu E)　劉鐵雲 （劉鄂）
lixing　理性
Li Zhi　李贄
lizhi　理智
"Liushengji pian"　留聲機片
Lu Jianbo　盧劍波
lulin　綠林
"Lüxing"　旅行

Mao Yibo　毛一波
Meilin　美琳
Meisheng　梅生

meiwo　沒我
"Meiyu zhi xi"　梅雨之夕
mingfeng zhuyi　名分主義
"Ming hong"　冥鴻
Mingxi　明希

Nahan　吶喊
Nanshe　南社
Nie Gannu　聶紺弩
Niu Dashui　牛大水

Ouyang Yuqian　歐陽予倩

Pan Guangdan　潘光旦
Pan Jinlian　潘金蓮
Pan Qiaoyun　潘巧雲
Pingdengge　平等閣
Pinghu tongche　平滬通車
Puluo wenxue　普羅文學

qi　氣
Qiandi　謙弟
Qian Xingcun (A Ying)
    錢杏村 （阿英）
qianze xiaoshuo　譴責小說
qing　情
qingchang shiyiren　情場失意人
Qingcheng zhi lian　傾城之戀
qinggan　情感
qingjiao　情教
Qing Jiesheng　情劫生
qingjing　情景
qinglou　青樓
Qingshi　情史
qingwan　情玩
qingyu　情欲
qingzhen　情真
qingzhong　情種
qin qin zhi ai　親親之愛

qinzui　親嘴
qunxing　群性

ren　仁
Ren'ai no kachi　恋愛の価値
renge　人格
renlei ai　人類愛
renyu　人欲
Ruoquan　若泉

sangang　三綱
Sanzi jing　三字經
se　色
"Shafei nüshi de riji"
　　莎菲女士的日記
shanghen wenxue　傷痕文學
shangjian zhe shizhong de shengju
　　賞鑒這示眾的盛舉
"Shangshi"　傷逝
shangxin ren　傷心人
shehui qinhe　社會親和
shen　神
shenjing shuairuo　神經衰弱
Shen Yuanpei　沈原培
shilian　失戀
"Shimang ge"　十忙歌
Shinajin　支那人
Shisan mei　十三妹
Shi Xiu　石秀
shi yan qing　詩言情
shi yan zhi　詩言志
Shi Zhecun　施蟄存
Shizhen　士軫
shouxing　獸性
Shujue　樹玨
shu zhong zi you yan ru yu
　　書中自有顏如玉
Siming　四銘
siyu　私欲

suku　訴苦

tanci　彈詞
tan lian'ai　談戀愛
Tan Xihong　譚熙鴻
Tanying　曇影
Tao Sijin　陶思瑾
Tayama Katai　田山花袋
ti　悌
Tian Han　田漢
tianli　天理
Tian Yamei　田亞梅
tongqing　同情

Wang Dungen　王鈍根
Wang Juanjuan　王娟娟
Wang Pingling　王平陵
Wang Wei　望微
Wang Yangming　王陽明
Wang Yunzhang　王蘊章
Watsuji Tetsurō　和辻哲郎
Wei'ai congshu　唯愛叢書
wei daoxue　僞道學
weifa　未發
weili de daode　唯理的道德
Weinan　蔚南
weixin de daode　唯心的道德
Wei Zi'an　魏子安
Wen Kai　文鎧
Wen Kang　文康
wenming　文明
Wen Yiduo　聞一多
wuchang　五常
Wu Jianren (Wu Woyao)　吳趼人
　　（吳沃堯）
wulun　五倫
Wu Menghui　鄔孟暉
Wuqi zhi lei　無妻之累
wuqing de wanwu　無情的玩物

xia　俠
Xia Mianzun　夏丏尊
"Xiange yougan"　閑歌有感
xianqi liangmu　賢妻良母
xiao　孝
Xiaojing　孝經
xiaowo　小我
Xiaren　俠人
xiaxie xiaoshuo　狹邪小說
Xia Zengyou　夏曾佑
xieqing xiaoshuo　寫情小說
Xin ernü yingxiong zhuan
　　新兒女英雄傳
xing　性
xing　形
Xingshi　性史
xing xinli biantai　性心理變態
xingyu　性欲
"Xing zai xiangjian"　行再相見
"Xin liaozhai—Tang Sheng"
　　新聊齋－唐生
Xin nüxing　新女性
xin xing daode　新性道德
"Xin xu"　心許
xisu zhuyi　習俗主義
Xiugu　朽骨
Xu Hengshan　許衡山
Xun'ai de shiming　殉愛的使命
xungen pai　尋根派
Xu Qinwen　許欽文
xuwei　虛偽
Xu Zhenya　徐枕亞

yang er fang lao　養兒防老
Yang Sao　楊騷
Yang Shen　揚慎
Yang Xianjiang　楊賢江
Yang Xiaomei　楊小梅
Yang Xiong　楊雄

yanqing xiaoshuo　言情小說
"Yao"　藥
"Ye ji"　野祭
yi　義
yifa　已發
Yi Jiayue　易家鉞
yingxiong　英雄
yiqi　義氣
yin　淫
yiwu ganqing　義務感情
yiyin　意淫
Yoneda Shōtarō　米田庄太郎
Yongzhang　永璋
youfen wuqing　有分無情
youguozhe　憂國者
youqing ren　有情人
yu　欲
Yuan Changying　袁昌英
Yuan Jing　袁靜
yuanqing　冤情
Yuanyang hudie pai　鴛鴦蝴蝶派
Yu li hun　玉梨魂
yunming zhuyi　運命主義

"Zai Bali daxiyuan"　在巴黎大戲院
zajiao　雜交
Zhang Bichi　張璧池
Zhang Biyue　張璧月
Zhang Dihua　張棣華
Zhang Dongsun　張東蓀
Zhang Henshui　張恨水
Zhang Jingsheng　張競生
Zhang Jinlong　張金龍
Zhang Mengpin　張夢頻
Zhang Shujun　章淑君
Zhang Xichen　章錫琛
Zhang Ziping　張資平
Zhao Dongchen　趙棟臣
zhencao　貞操

Zhendan Nüshi　震旦女士

Zheng Yuxian　鄭玉弦

zhiguai　志怪

zhiqingren　至情人

Zhixin Zhuren　知新主人

zhong　忠

"Zhongshen dashi"　終身大事

Zhongshu　仲叔

zhongzu xingfu　種族幸福

Zhou Jianren　周建人

Zhou Shoujuan　周瘦鵑

Zhou Zuoren　周作人

Zhu Guangqian　朱光潛

Zhu Ziqing　朱自清

Zibin　子彬

ziji shixian　自己實現

Zijun　子君

zisi　自私

Ziyou jiehun　自由結婚

zizhi　自制

References

Abu-Lughod, Lila. 1986. *Veiled sentiments: Honor and poetry in a Bedouin society.* Berkeley: University of California Press.

———. 1990. Shifting politics in Bedouin love poetry. In *Language and the politics of emotion*, edited by Catherine Lutz and Lila Abu-Lughod. Cambridge: Cambridge University Press.

Allen, Joseph R. 1996. Dressing and undressing the Chinese woman warrior. *Positions: East Asia Cultures Critique* 4:343–79.

Anagnost, Ann. 1997. *National past-times: Narrative, representation, and power in modern China.* Durham, NC: Duke University Press.

Anderson, Marston. 1990. *The limits of realism: Chinese fiction in the revolutionary period.* Berkeley: University of California Press.

Appadurai, Arjun. 1990. Topographies of the self: Praise and emotion in Hindu India. In *Language and the politics of emotion*, edited by Catherine Lutz and Lila Abu-Lughod. Cambridge: Cambridge University Press.

Arendt, Hannah. 1958. *The human condition.* Chicago: University of Chicago Press.

———. 1963. *On revolution.* London: Penguin Books.

Ariès, Philippe. 1962. *Centuries of childhood: A social history of family life.* Translated by Robert Baldick. New York: Alfred A. Knopf.

Armstrong, Nancy. 1987. *Desire and domestic fiction: A political history of the novel.* New York: Oxford University Press.

Balibar, Etienne, and Immanuel Wallerstein. 1991. *Race, nation, class: Ambiguous identities.* Translated by Chris Turner. London: Verso.

Bao Sun. 1926. Ai de jiejing (The crystallization of love). *Funü zazhi (The ladies' journal)* 12:87–89.

Barlow, Tani E. 1991. Zhishifenzi [Chinese intellectuals] and power. *Dialectical Anthropology* 16:209–32.

———. 1994. Theorizing woman: Funü, guojia, jiating. In *Body, subject and power in China*, edited by Angela Zito and Tani E. Barlow. Chicago: University of Chicago Press.

————. 1989. Introduction. In *I myself am a woman: Selected writings of Ding Ling,* edited by Tani E. Barlow with Gary J. Bjorge. Boston: Beacon Press.

————. 2004. *The question of women in Chinese feminism.* Durham, NC: Duke University Press.

Baudrillard, Jean. 1987. *Forget Foucault.* New York: Semiotext(e) Foreign Agents Series, Columbia University.

Berkowitz, Peter. 1999. *Virtue and the making of modern liberalism.* Princeton, NJ: Princeton University Press.

————. 2000. Wooed by freedom? Why the young distrust love and fear commitment. *Atlantic Monthly,* 128–33.

Berlin, Isaiah. 1999. *The roots of romanticism.* Princeton, NJ: Princeton University Press.

Birrell, Anne. 1982. *New songs from a jade terrace: An anthology of early Chinese love poetry.* Translated by Anne Birrell. London: Allen & Unwin.

Block, Maurice, and Jonathan Parry, eds. 1982. *Death and the regeneration of life.* Cambridge: Cambridge University Press.

Braester, Yomi. 2003. *Witness against history: Literature, film, and public discourse in twentieth-century China.* Stanford, CA: Stanford University Press.

Brownell, Susan, and Jeffrey N. Wasserstrom, eds. 2002. *Chinese femininities, Chinese masculinities: A reader.* Berkeley: University of California Press.

Brownstein, Michael. 1981. Prophet of the inner life: Kitamura Tōkoku and the beginnings of romanticism in modern Japanese literature. PhD diss., Columbia University.

Butler, Judith. 1997. *The psychic life of power: Theories in subjection.* Stanford, CA: Stanford University Press.

Cao Xueqin. 1973. *The story of the stone.* Translated by David Hawkes and John Minford. 5 vols. London: Penguin Books.

Cass, Victoria. 1999. *Dangerous women: Warriors, grannies and geishas of the Ming.* Lanham: Rowman and Littlefield.

Chang, Kang-i Sun. 1991. *The late-Ming poet Ch'en Tzu-lung: Crises of love and loyalism.* New Haven, CT: Yale University Press.

Chatterjee, Partha. 1993. *The nation and its fragments: Colonial and postcolonial histories.* Princeton, NJ: Princeton University Press.

Chen Bainian. 1925. Yifu duoqi de xin hufu (A new talisman of polygamy). *Xiandai pinglun (The modern review)* 1, no. 14.

Chen Diexian. 1999. *The money demon (Huangjin sui).* Translated by Patrick Hanan. Honolulu: University of Hawaii Press.

Chen, Jianhua. 1999. Chinese "revolution" in the syntax of world revolution. In *Tokens of exchange: The problem of translation in global circulations,* edited by Lydia H. Liu. Durham, NC: Duke University Press.

Chen Jianshan. 1924. Youshengxue he jige xing de wenti (Eugenics and some questions about sex). *Minduo (People's bell)* 5, no. 4.

Chen Jie. 1998. *Zhongguo renqing xiaoshuo tongshi (A comprehensive history of the fiction of manners in China).* Nanjing: Jiangsu jiaoyu chubanshe.

Chen Pingyuan. 1989. *Ershi shiji Zhongguo xiaoshuoshi: Diyijuan: 1897–1916 (A history of twentieth-century Chinese fiction, volume 1, 1897–1916)*. Beijing: Beijing daxue chubanshe.

Chen Pingyuan and Xia Xiaohong, eds. 1997. *Ershi shiji zhongguo xiaoshuo lilun ziliao (di yi juan) 1897–1916 (Twentieth-century Chinese literary thought: A source book—Volume 1, 1897–1916)*. Beijing: Beijing daxue chubanshe.

Chen Quan. 1990. Geming de qian yimu (On the eve of the revolution). In *Zhongguo xiandai wenxue buyi shuxi (A supplementary compendium of modern Chinese literature)*, edited by Kong Fanjin. Vol. 5. Jinan: Mintian chubanshe.

Chen Weibo. 1927. Lian'ai yu xingjiao (Love and sex). *Xin nüxing (The new woman)* 1:567–74.

Cheng, Eileen J. 2004. Gendered spectacles: Lu Xun on gazing at women and other pleasures. *Modern Chinese Literature and Culture* 16:1–36.

Chow, Rey. 1991. *Woman and Chinese modernity: The politics of reading between West and East*. Minneapolis: University of Minnesota Press.

———. 1993. Virtuous transactions: A reading of three short stories by Ling Shuhua. In *Gender politics in modern China: Writing and feminism*, edited by Tani E. Barlow. Durham, NC: Duke University Press.

———. 1995. *Primitive passions: Visuality, sexuality, ethnography, and contemporary Chinese cinema*. New York: Columbia University Press.

Cui Fengyuan. 1986. *Zhongguo gudian duanpian xiayi xiaoshuo yanjiu (A study of classical Chinese chivalric short stories)*. Taipei: Lianjing chuban shiye gongsi.

Damasio, Antonio R. 1999. *The feeling of what happens: Body and emotion in the making of consciousness*. New York: Harcourt Brace.

Davidson, Arnold I. 1987. Sex and the emergence of sexuality. *Critical Inquiry* 14:16–48.

———. 2001. *The emergence of sexuality: Historical epistemology and the formation of concepts*. Cambridge: Harvard University Press.

Davies, Gloria, ed. 2001. *Voicing concerns: Contemporary Chinese critical inquiry*. Lanham: Rowman and Littlefield.

De Certeau, Michel. 1984. *The practice of everyday life*. Translated by Steven Rendall. Berkeley: University of California Press.

DeJean, Joan. 1991. *Tender geographies: Women and the origins of the novel in France*. New York: Columbia University Press.

Denby, David. 1994. *Sentimental narrative and the social order in France, 1760–1820*. Cambridge: Cambridge University Press.

Denton, Kirk A. 1992. The distant shore: Nationalism in Yu Dafu's 'Sinking.' *Chinese literature: Essays, articles, reviews* 14:107–23.

———, ed. 1996. *Modern Chinese literary thought: Writings on literature, 1893–1945*. Stanford, CA: Stanford University Press.

Dikötter, Frank. 1995. *Sex, culture, and modernity in China: Medical science and the construction of sexual identities in the Republican period*. Honolulu: University of Hawaii Press.

Ding Ling. 1989. *I myself am a woman: Selected writings of Ding Ling*, edited by Tani E. Barlow with Gary Bjorge. Boston: Beacon Press.

Doleželová-Velingerová, Milena, ed. 1980. *The Chinese novel at the turn of the century.* Toronto: University of Toronto Press.

Dooling, Amy D., and Kristina M. Torgeson, eds. 1998. *Writing women in modern China: An anthology of women's literature from the early twentieth century.* New York: Columbia University Press.

Du Yaquan. 1928. Guanyu qing yu li de bianlun (The debate on sentiment and reason). *Yiban (The ordinary)* 3:458–63.

Duara, Prasenjit. 1995. *Rescuing history from the nation-state: Questioning narratives of modern China.* Chicago: University of Chicago Press.

———. 1997. Nationalists among transnationals: Overseas Chinese and the idea of China, 1900–1911. In *Ungrounded empires: The cultural politics of modern Chinese transnationalism*, edited by Aihwa Ong and Donald Nonini. New York: Routledge.

———. 1998. The regime of authenticity: Timelessness, gender and national history in modern China. *History and Theory* 37:287–308.

———. 2003. *Sovereignty and authenticity: Manchukuo and the East Asian modern.* Lanham: Rowman and Littlefield.

Dumas *fils*, Alexandre. 1986. *La dame aux camélias*. Translated by David Coward. Oxford: Oxford University Press.

Edwards, Louise. 2001. *Men and women in Qing China: Gender in the Red chamber dream.* Honolulu: University of Hawaii Press.

Egan, Michael. 1980. Characterization in *Sea of Woe*. In *The Chinese novel at the turn of the century*, edited by Milena Doleželová-Velingerová. Toronto: University of Toronto Press.

Eide, Elisabeth. 1985. Optimistic and disillusioned Noras on the Chinese literary scene, 1919–1940. In *Women and literature in China*, edited by Anna Gertslacher, et al. Bochum: Studienverlag Brockmeyer.

———. 1989. The ballad 'Kongque dongnan fei' as Freudian feminist drama during the May Fourth period. *Republican China* 15:65–71.

Ellis, Havelock (E-er-li-si). 1926. Shanzhongxue yu lian'ai (Eugenics and love). *Funü zazhi (The ladies' journal)* 12:134–39.

Fan Boqun. 1989. *Libailiu de hudie meng (The romantic dreams of the Saturday School).* Beijing: Remin wenxue chubanshe.

Fangxin Nüshi. 1929. Zhang Biyue qiangsha Huang Changdian shijian zhi pipan (A commentary on the attempted murder of Huang Changdian by Zhang Biyue). *Xin nüxing (The new woman)* 4:349–58.

Farquhar, Judith. 2002. *Appetites: Food and sex in post-socialist China.* Durham, NC: Duke University Press.

Farrer, James. 2002. *Opening up: Youth sex culture and market reform in Shanghai.* Chicago: University of Chicago Press.

Featherstone, Mike. 1995. *Undoing culture: Globalization, postmodernism and identity.* London: Sage Publications.

Fei Xiaotong. 1991. *Xiangtu Zhongguo (Rural Chinese society)*. Hong Kong: Sanlian shudian.

Feng Menglong. 1986. *Qingshi (The anatomy of love)*. 2 vols. Shenyang: Chunfeng wenyi chubanshe.

Feng Yuanjun. 1997. *Feng Yuanjun xiaoshuo: Chunhen (The fiction of Feng Yuanjun: Spring traces)*. Shanghai: Shanghai guji chubanshe.

Fitzgerald, John. 1996. *Awakening China: Politics, culture, and class in the nationalist revolution*. Stanford, CA: Stanford University Press.

Flaubert, Gustave. 1965. *Madame Bovary: Backgrounds and sources and essays in criticism*. Translated by Paul de Man. New York: W. W. Norton.

Foucault, Michel. 1972. *The archaeology of knowledge and the discourse on language*. Translated by A. M. Sheridan Smith. New York: Pantheon Books.

———. 1982. The subject and power. In *Michel Foucault: Beyond structuralism and hermeneutics*, edited by Hubert L. Dreyfus and Paul Rabinow. Chicago: University of Chicago Press.

———. 1990a. *The history of sexuality: An introduction*. Translated by Robert Hurley. New York: Vintage Books.

———. 1990b. *The use of pleasure*. Translated by Robert Hurley. New York: Vintage Books.

———. 1994. *The order of things: An archaeology of the human sciences*. Reprint. New York: Vintage Books.

———. 1997. *Ethics: Subjectivity and truth*. Edited by Paul Rabinow. New York: New Press.

Furth, Charlotte. 1986. Blood, body and gender: Medical images of the female condition in China, 1600–1850. *Chinese Science*, no. 7.

———. 1987. Concepts of pregnancy, childbirth, and infancy in Ch'ing dynasty China. *Journal of Asian Studies* 46:7–35.

———. 1988. Androgynous males and deficient females: Biology and gender boundaries in sixteenth- and seventeenth-century China. *Late Imperial China* 9, no. 2.

———. 1994. Rethinking Van Gulik: Sexuality and reproduction in traditional Chinese medicine. In *Engendering China: Women, culture, and the state*, edited by Christina K. Gilmartin et al. Cambridge: Harvard University Press.

———. 1999. *A flourishing Yin: Gender in China's medical history, 960–1665*. Berkeley: University of California Press.

Gao Shan. 1926. Jinyu zhuyi he lian'ai ziyou (Puritanism and free love). *Xin nüxing (The new woman)* 1, no. 4.

Giddens, Anthony. 1992. *The transformation of intimacy: Sexuality, love and eroticism in modern societies*. Stanford, CA: Stanford University Press.

Gimpel, Denise. 2001. *Lost voices of modernity: A Chinese popular fiction magazine in context*. Honolulu: University of Hawaii Press.

Glosser, Susan. 1995. The business of family: You Huaigao and the commercialization of a May Fourth ideal. *Republican China* 20:80–116.

Godelier, Maurice. 1999. *The enigma of the gift.* Translated by Nora Scott. Chicago: University of Chicago Press.

Goethe, Johann Wolfgang von. 1962. *The sorrows of young Werther and selected writings.* Translated by Catherine Hutter. New York: New American Library of World Literature.

Gong Pengcheng. 1987. Yuanyang hudie yu wuxia xiaoshuo (The mandarin duck and butterfly school and knight-errantry fiction). In *Daxia (The great knight-errant).* Taipei: Jinguan chubanshe.

Gries, Peter Hays. 2004. *China's new nationalism: Pride, politics, and diplomacy.* Berkeley: University of California Press.

Gu Chengwu. 1919. Duiyu jiu jiating de ganxiang (Thoughts on the old family). *Xinchao (The Renaissance)* 1:157–69.

Guangtao. 1926. Aiyu—Xu Xia Mianzun yi *Mianbei* (Love and desire—Preface to Xia Mianzun's translation of *Futon*). *Yiban (The ordinary)* 1:377–81.

Gunn, Edward, ed. 1983. *Twentieth-century Chinese drama: An anthology.* Bloomington: Indiana University Press.

Habermas, Jürgen. 1991. *The structural transformation of the public sphere: An inquiry into a category of bourgeois society.* Translated by Thomas Burger. Cambridge, MA: MIT Press.

Hacking, Ian. 1992. Making up people. In *Forms of desire: Sexual orientation and the social constructionist controversy,* edited by Edward Stein. New York: Routledge.

Hamm, John Christopher. 1998. Reading the swordswoman's tale: Shisanmei and Ernü yingxiong zhuan. *T'oung pao* 84:328–55.

———. 2005. *Paper swordsmen: Jin Yong and the modern Chinese martial arts novel.* Honolulu: University of Hawaii Press.

Hanan, Patrick. 1995. Introduction. In *The Sea of regret: Two turn-of-the-century Chinese romantic novels.* Honolulu: University of Hawaii Press.

Harootunian, Harry. 1988. *Things seen and unseen: Discourse and ideology in Tokugawa nativism.* Chicago: University of Chicago Press.

———. 2000. *Overcome by modernity: History, culture, and community in interwar Japan.* Princeton, NJ: Princeton University Press.

Hawthorne, Nathaniel. 1997. *The scarlet letter: A romance.* Cambridge: Cambridge University Press.

Hay, John. 1994. The body invisible in Chinese art? In *Body, subject and power in China,* edited by Angela Zito and Tani E. Barlow. Chicago: University of Chicago Press.

Hegel, G. W. F. 1975. *Aesthetics: Lectures on fine art.* Translated by T. M. Knox. 2 vols. Oxford: Oxford University Press.

Hegel, Robert E. 1984. Making the past serve the present in fiction and drama: From the Yan'an forum to the Cultural Revolution. In *Popular Chinese literature and performing arts in the People's Republic of China 1949–1979,* edited by Bonnie S. McDougall. Berkeley: University of California Press.

Hembree, James M. 1997. *Subjectivity and the signs of love: Discourse, desire, and the emergence of modernity in Honoré d'Urfé's L'Astrée.* New York: Peter Lang.

Hoffman, Elizabeth Cobbs, and Jon Gjerde, eds. 2002. *Major problems in American history, Volume 2—Since 1865*. Boston: Houghton Mifflin.

Hong Jun. 1928. Hunzhan sheng zhong (In the cross-fire). *Xin nüxing (The new woman)* 3:1262–69.

Hong Ruizhao. 1928. *Geming yu lian'ai (Revolution and love)*. Shanghai: Minzhi shuju.

Hsia, C. T. 1968. *The classic Chinese novel: A critical introduction*. New York: Columbia University Press.

Hu Chunbing. 1931. *Ai de geming (The revolution of love)*. Shanghai: Xiandai shuju.

Hu, Ying. 1995. The translator transfigured: Lin Shu and the cultural logic of writing in the late Qing. *Positions: East Asia Cultures Critique* 3:69–96.

Huang, Martin W. 1998. Sentiments of desire: Thoughts on the cult of *qing* in Ming-Qing literature. *CLEAR (Chinese Literature: Essays, Articles, Reviews)* 20:153–84.

Huang, Nicole. 2005. *Women, war, domesticity: Shanghai literature and popular culture of the 1940s*. Leiden: Brill.

Huntington, Rania. 2003. *Alien kind: Foxes and late imperial Chinese narrative*. Cambridge: Harvard University Asia Center.

Huters, Theodore. 1998. Review of *Translingual practice. Harvard Journal of Asiatic Studies* 58:568–80.

———. 2005. *Bringing the world home: Appropriating the West in late Qing and early Republican China*. Honolulu: University of Hawaii Press.

Illouz, Eva. 1997. *Consuming the romantic utopia: Love and the cultural contradictions of capitalism*. Berkeley: University of California Press.

———. 1998. The lost innocence of love: Romance as a postmodern condition. *Theory, Culture and Society* 15:161–86.

Jay, Nancy. 1992. *Throughout your generations forever: Sacrifice, religion, and paternity*. Chicago: University of Chicago Press.

Jones, Andrew F. 1994. The violence of the text: Reading Yu Hua and Shi Zhicun. *Positions: East Asia Cultures Critique* 2:570–602.

———. 2002. The child as history in Republican China: A discourse on development. *Positions: East Asia Cultures Critique* 10:695–727.

Karl, Rebecca E. 2005. "Joining tracks with the world": The impossibility of politics in China. *Radical Philosophy*, May–June. Available at: http://www.radicalphilosophy.com/default.asp?channel_id=2188&editorial_id=17650. Accessed 16 September 2005.

Kitamura Tōkoku. 1977. Ensei shika to josei (World-weary poets and women). In *Tsubouchi Shōyō, Futabatei Shimei, Kitmura Tōkoku shū*. Tokyo: Chikuba shobo.

Ko, Dorothy. 1994. *Teachers of the inner chambers: Women and culture in seventeenth-century China*. Stanford, CA: Stanford University Press.

Kuriyagawa, Hakuson. 1928. *Jindai de lian'ai guan (Kindai no ren'aikan, Modern love)*. Translated by Xia Mianzun. Shanghai: Kaiming shudian.

Kutcher, Norman. 2000. The fifth relationship: Dangerous relationships in the Confucian context. *American Historical Review* 105:1615–29.

Lan, Hua R., and Vanessa L. Fong, eds. 1999. *Women in Republican China: A sourcebook*. Armonk, NY: M. E. Sharpe.

Larson, Wendy. 1998. *Women and writing in modern China*. Stanford, CA: Stanford University Press.

———. 1999. Never this wild: Sexing the Cultural Revolution. *Modern China* 25:423–50.

Lau, Joseph S. M., and Howard Goldblatt, eds. 1995. *The Columbia anthology of modern Chinese literature*. New York: Columbia University Press.

———, C. T. Hsia, and Leo Ou-fan Lee, eds. 1981. *Modern Chinese stories and novellas, 1919–1949*. New York: Columbia University Press.

Lean, Eugenia Y. 2001. Politics of passion: The trial of Shi Jianqiao and the rise of public sympathy in nineteen-thirties China. PhD diss., UCLA.

Leary, Charles L. 1994. Sexual modernism in China: Zhang Jingsheng and 1920s urban culture. PhD diss., Cornell University.

Lee, Haiyan. 1997. Love or lust? The sentimental self in *Honglou meng* [Dream of the red chamber]. *CLEAR (Chinese Literature: Essays, Articles, Reviews)* 19:85–111.

———. 2001. All the feelings that are fit to print: The community of sentiment and the literary public sphere in China, 1900–1918. *Modern China* 27:291–327.

———. 2005. Tears that crumbled the Great Wall: The archaeology of feeling in the May Fourth folklore movement. *Journal of Asian Studies* 64:35–65.

———. 2006a. Governmentality and the aesthetic state: A Chinese fantasia. *Positions: East Asia Cultures Critique* 14: 99–130.

———. 2006b. From abroad, with love: Transnational texts, local critiques. *Tamkang Review* 36: 189–225.

Lee, Leo Ou-fan. 1973. *The romantic generation of modern Chinese writers*. Cambridge, MA: Harvard University Press.

———. 1999. *Shanghai modern: The flowering of a new urban culture in China, 1930–1945*. Cambridge, MA: Harvard University Press.

Li, Wai-yee. 1993. *Enchantment and disenchantment: Love and illusion in Chinese literature*. Princeton, NJ: Princeton University Press.

Lindholm, Charles. 1998. Love and structure. *Theory, Culture and Society* 15:243–63.

Ling Shuhua. 1984. *Ling Shuhua xiaoshuo ji (The fiction of Ling Shuhua)*. Taipei: Hongfan shudian.

Link, Perry. 1981. *Mandarin ducks and butterflies: Popular fiction in early twentieth-century Chinese cities*. Berkeley: University of California Press.

Liu, James. 1967. *The Chinese knight-errant*. Chicago: University of Chicago Press.

Liu, Jianmei. 2003. *Revolution plus love: Literary history, women's bodies, and thematic repetition in twentieth-century Chinese fiction*. Honolulu: University of Hawaii Press.

Liu, Kwang-ching, ed. 1990. *Orthodoxy in late imperial China*. Berkeley: University of California Press.

Liu, Lydia H. 1995. *Translingual practice: Literature, national culture, and translated modernity—China, 1900–1937*. Stanford, CA: Stanford University Press.

————. 2002. Introduction to the 2003 edition. In *Chinese characteristics*. Norwalk, CT: EastBridge.

Liu T'ieh-yün. 1990. *The travels of Lao Ts'an*. Translated by Harold Shadick. Morningside ed. New York: Columbia University Press.

Louie, Kam. 2002. *Theorising Chinese masculinity: Society and gender in China*. Cambridge: Cambridge University Press.

Lu Jianbo. 1926. Tan xing'ai (On sexual love). *Huanzhou (The mirage)* 1, no. 7.

————. 1928. Tan xing (On sex). *Xin nüxing (The new woman)* 3:868–78.

Lu, Tonglin. 1993. *Gender and sexuality in twentieth-century Chinese literature and society*. Albany: State University of New York Press.

————. 1995. *Misogyny, cultural nihilism and oppositional politics: Contemporary Chinese experimental fiction*. Stanford, CA: Stanford University Press.

Lu Xun. 1964. *A brief history of Chinese fiction*. Translated by Yang Hsien-yi and Gladys Yang. Beijing: Foreign Languages Press.

————. 1977. *Lu Hsün: Selected stories*. Translated by Yang Hsien-yi and Gladys Yang. New York: Norton.

————. 1980. *Lu Xun: Selected works*. Translated by Yang Xianyi and Gladys Yang. 4 vols. Beijing: Foreign Languages Press.

————. 1981. *Lu Xun quanji (Complete Works of Lu Xun)*. 16 vols. Beijing: Renmin wenxue chubanshe.

————. 1998. *Fen (Graves)*. Beijing: Renmin wenxue chubanshe.

Luhmann, Niklas. 1986. *Love as passion: The codification of intimacy*. Translated by Jeremy Gaines and Doris L. Jones. Cambridge: Harvard University Press.

Lull, James, and Stephen Hinerman, eds. 1997. *Media scandals: Morality and desire in the popular culture marketplace*. New York: Columbia University Press.

Luo Guanzhong. 1959. *Romance of the three kingdoms*. Translated by C. H. Brewitt-Taylor. 2 vols. Rutland, VT: Charles E. Tuttle.

Luo Liqun. 1990. *Zhongguo wuxia xiaoshuo shi (A history of Chinese martial arts fiction)*. Shenyang: Liaoning renmin chubanshe.

Lutz, Catherine. 1986. Emotion, thought, and estrangement: Emotion as a cultural category. *Cultural Anthropology* 1:405–36.

————, and Lila Abu-Lughod, eds. 1990. *Language and the politics of emotion*. Cambridge: Cambridge University Press.

Lynch, Owen M. 1990. The social construction of emotion in India. In *Divine Passions: The social construction of emotion in India*, edited by Owen M. Lynch. Berkeley: University of California Press.

MacIntyre, Alasdair. 1984. *After virtue*. 2nd ed. Notre Dame: University of Notre Dame Press.

Mann, Susan. 2000. The male bond in Chinese history and culture. *American Historical Review* 105:1600–1614.

Mao Dun. 1935. "Geming" yu "lian'ai" de gongshi (The formula of revolution and romance). *Wenxue (Literature)* 4:181–90.

———. 1992. *Rainbow (Hong)*. Translated by Madeleine Zelin. Berkeley: University of California Press.

Mao Yibo. 1926. Wo de lian'ai guan (My view on love). *Xin nüxing (The new woman)* 2, no. 7.

McDougall, Bonnie S. 2002. *Love-letters and privacy in modern China: The intimate lives of Lu Xun and Xu Guangping*. Oxford: Oxford University Press.

McGrath, Jason. 2001. Patching the void: Subjectivity and anamorphic bewitchment in Shi Zhecun's fiction. *Journal of Modern Literature in Chinese* 4:1–30.

Meltzer, Francoise. 1987. Editor's introduction: Partitive plays, pipe dreams. *Critical Inquiry* 13:215–21.

Meng, Yue. 1993. Female images and national myth. In *Gender politics in modern China*, edited by Tani E. Barlow. Durham, NC: Duke University Press.

Mitchell, J. Allan. 2005. Romancing ethics in Boethius, Chaucer, and Levinas: Fortune, moral luck, and erotic adventure. *Comparative Literature* 57:101–16.

Mowry, Hua-yuan Li. 1983. *Chinese love stories from Ch'ing-shih*. Hamden, CT: Archon Books.

Nancy, Jean-Luc. 1991. *The inoperative community*. Minneapolis: University of Minnesota Press.

Nie Gannu. 1980. *Gannu xiaoshuo ji (The fiction of Nie Gannu)*. Changsha: Hunan renmin chubanshe.

Nivard, Jacqueline. 1984. Women and the women's press: The case of the "Ladies' Journal" (Funü zazhi) 1915–1931. *Republican China* 10, no. 1b:37–56.

Nussbaum, Martha. 2001. *Upheavals of thought: The intelligence of emotions*. Cambridge: Cambridge University Press.

Ono, Kazuko. 1989. *Chinese women in a century of revolution*. Translated by Joshua A. Fogel et al. Stanford, CA: Stanford University Press.

Pan Guangdan. 1993. *Pan Guangdan wenji (Collected works of Pan Guangdan)*. Beijing: Beijing daxue chubanshe.

Pateman, Carole. 1988. *The sexual contract*. Stanford, CA: Stanford University Press.

Peng Zhaoliang. 1926. Lian'ai de xinli (The psychology of love). *Xin nüxing (The new woman)* 1:29–32.

Plaks, Andrew H. 1977. Towards a critical theory of Chinese narrative. In *Chinese narrative: Critical and theoretical essays*, edited by Andrew H. Plaks. Princeton, NJ: Princeton University Press.

Pollard, David. 2002. *The true story of Lu Xun*. Hong Kong: Chinese University Press.

Potter, Sulamith Heins. 1988. The cultural construction of emotion in rural Chinese social life. *Ethos* 16:181–208.

Qian Xingcun. 1996. *Wanqing xiaoshuo shi (A history of late Qing fiction)*. Reprint ed. Taipei: Taiwan shangwu yinshuguan.

Qiandi. 1927. Lian'ai zhencao xin lun (A fresh view on love and chastity). *Xin nüxing (The new woman)* 2:525–31.

———. 1928. Fei lian'ai yu lian'ai (Anti-love and love). *Xin nüxing (The new woman)* 3:501–25.

Qu Shiying. 1920. Hunyin wenti (The problems of marriage). *Xin Shehui (New society)* 12:2–4.

Ren Chang. 1926. Rushi wo jie de lingrou wenti (My view on the question of body vs. soul). *Huanzhou (The mirage)* 1, no. 7.

Rorty, Richard. 1989. *Contingency, irony, and solidarity.* Cambridge: Cambridge University Press.

Rousseau, Jean-Jacques. 1998. *Essay on the origin of languages and writings related to music.* Translated by John T. Scott. Hanover: University Press of New England.

Ruhlmann, Robert. 1960. Traditional heroes in Chinese popular fiction. In *The Confucian persuasion,* edited by Arthur F. Wright. Stanford, CA: Stanford University Press.

Sakai, Naoki. 1997. *Translation and subjectivity: On Japan and cultural nationalism.* Minneapolis: University of Minnesota Press.

Sanday, Peggy Reeves. 1990. *Fraternity gang rape: Sex, brotherhood, and privilege on campus.* New York: New York University Press.

Sang, Tze-lan D. 2003. *The emerging lesbian: Female same-sex desire in modern China.* Chicago: University of Chicago Press.

Schaefer, William. 1998. Kumarajiva's foreign tongue: Shi Zhecun's modernist historical fiction. *Modern Chinese Literature* 10:25–70.

Sedgwick, Eve Kosofsky. 1985. *Between men: English literature and male homosocial desire.* New York: Columbia University Press.

———. 2003. *Touching feeling: Affect, pedagogy, performativity.* Durham, NC: Duke University Press.

Sennett, Richard. 1992. *The fall of public man.* New York: W. W. Norton.

Shi Nai'an. 1993. *Outlaws of the marsh.* Translated by Sidney Shapiro. 3 vols. Beijing: Foreign Language Press.

Shi Zhecun. 1991. *Shi Xiu zhi lian (The love of Shi Xiu).* Beijing: Renmin wenxue chubanshe.

Shih, Shu-mei. 2001. *The lure of the modern: Writing modernism in semicolonial China, 1917–1937.* Berkeley: University of California Press.

Singer, Irving. 1984. *Courtly and romantic.* Vol. 2 of *The nature of love.* Chicago: University of Chicago Press.

Smith, Arthur. 1894. *Chinese characteristics.* Fleming H. Revell.

Solomon, Robert C. 1991. The virtue of (erotic) love. In *The philosophy of (erotic) love,* edited by Robert C. Solomon and Kathleen M. Higgins. Lawrence: University Press of Kansas.

Sommer, Matthew Harvey. 2000. *Sex, law, and society in late imperial China.* Stanford, Calif.: Stanford University Press.

Song, Geng. 2004. *The fragile scholar: Power and masculinity in Chinese culture.* Hong Kong: Hong Kong University Press.

Sontag, Susan. 1977. *On photography.* London: Penguin Books.

———. 2003. *Regarding the pain of others.* New York: Picador.

Strand, David. 1997. Community, society, and history in Sun Yat-sen's *sanmin zhuyi.* In *Culture and state in Chinese history: Conventions, accommodations, and critiques,* edited by Theodore Huters, R. Bin Wong, and Pauline Yu. Stanford, CA: Stanford University Press.

Su Xuelin. 1983. *Zhongguo ersanshi niandai zuojia (Chinese writers of the 1920s and 1930s)*. Taipei: Chun wenxue chubanshe.

Sun, Lung-kee. 2002. *The Chinese national character: From nationhood to individuality.* Armonk, NY: M. E. Sharpe.

Sun Naixiu. 1995. *Fu-luo-yi-de yu Zhongguo xiandai zuojia (Freud and modern Chinese writers)*. Taipei: Yeqiang chubanshe.

Sun Zhongtian. 1996. Yu Dafu xiaoshuo yu Zhongguo xiandai wenxue (Yu Dafu's fiction and modern Chinese literature). In *Yu Dafu xiaoshuo quanji*. Changchun: Shidai wenyi chubanshe.

Tang, Xiaobing. 2000. *Chinese modern: The heroic and the quotidian.* Durham, NC: Duke University Press.

Tang Xianzu. 1980. *The peony pavilion.* Translated by Cyril Birch. Bloomington: Indiana University Press.

Taylor, Charles. 1989. *Sources of the self: The making of the modern identity.* Cambridge: Harvard University Press.

Terada, Rei. 2001. *Feeling in theory: Emotion after the death of the subject.* Cambridge: Harvard University Press.

Tian Han. 1919. Mimi lian'ai yu gongkai lian'ai (Secretive love vs. open love). *Shaonian Zhongguo (The Young China)* 1:33–35.

Townsend, James. 1996. Chinese nationalism. In *Chinese nationalism*, edited by Jonathan Unger. Armonk, NY: M. E. Sharpe.

Trilling, Lionel. 1971. *Sincerity and authenticity.* Cambridge: Harvard University Press.

Tsau, Shu-ying. 1980. The rise of the "new fiction." In *The Chinese novel at the turn of the century,* edited by Milena Doleželová-Velingerová. Toronto: University of Toronto Press.

Tsin, Michael. 1997. Imagining "society" in early twentieth-century China. In *Imagining the people: Chinese intellectuals and the concept of citizenship, 1890–1920,* edited by Joshua A. Fogel and Peter G. Zarrow. Armonk, NY: M. E. Sharpe.

Tsu, Jing. 2005. *Failure, nationalism, and literature: The making of modern Chinese identity, 1895–1937.* Stanford, CA: Stanford University Press.

Turner, Victor. 1982. *From ritual to theatre: The human seriousness of play.* New York: PAJ Publications.

Waley, Arthur, trans. 1987. *The book of songs: The ancient Chinese classic of poetry.* New York: Grove Weidenfeld.

Wang, Ban. 1997. *The sublime figure of history: Aesthetics and politics in twentieth-century China.* Stanford, CA: Stanford University Press.

———. 2003. Revolutionary realism and revolutionary romanticism: *The Song of Youth.* In *The Columbia Companion to Modern East Asian Literature,* edited by Joshua S. Mostow. New York: Columbia University Press.

Wang Boqing. 2004. Daochu he xu shuo Lei Feng (Speak no more of Lei Feng). Available at: http://members.aol.com/boqingw/yansha29.html. Accessed 6 August 2004.

Wang, C. H. 1975. Towards defining a Chinese heroism. *Journal of the American Oriental Society* 95:25–35.

Wang, David. 1992. *Fictional realism in 20th-century China*. New York: Columbia University Press.

———. 1997. *Fin-de-siècle splendor: Repressed modernities of late Qing fiction, 1849–1911*. Stanford, CA: Stanford University Press.

———. 2004. *The monster that is history: History, violence, and fictional writing in twentieth-century China*. Berkeley: University of California Press.

Wang, Gang. 1999. *Langman qinggan yu zongjiao jingshen: Wanming wenxue yu wenhua sichao (Romanticism and spirituality: Late Ming literary and cultural trends)*. Hong Kong: Tiandi tushu youxian gongsi.

Wang, Lingzhen. 2004. *Personal matters: Women's autobiographical practice in twentieth-century China*. Stanford, CA: Stanford University Press.

Wang, Ping. 2000. *Aching for beauty: Footbinding in China*. Minneapolis: University of Minnesota Press.

Wang Pingling. 1926. *Zhongguo funü de lian'ai guan (Chinese women's view of love)*. Shanghai: Guanghua shuju.

Wang Yunzhi. 1926. Shi ernü shenghuo de yuanquan (The wellspring of children's life). *Funü zazhi (The ladies' journal)* 12:44–46.

Watsuji, Tetsurō. 1971. *Climate and culture: A philosophical study*. Translated by Geoffrey Bownas: Hokuseido Press.

Weinan. 1921. Aiqing xiaoshuo de cailiao dao nali qu zhao? (Where to find the material for sentimental fiction). *Minguo ribao—Juewu*, 7 June.

Wen Kai. 1926. Ping *Funü zazhi* "ai zhi zhuanhao" (On The Ladies' Journal's special issue on love). *Yiban (The ordinary)* 1:298–301.

Wen Kang. 1976. *Ernü yingxiong zhuan (A tale of heroic sons and daughters)*. Taipei: Sanmin shuju.

Widmer, Ellen. 1992. Xiaoqing's literary legacy and the place of the woman writer in late imperial China. *Late Imperial China* 13:111–55.

———, and Kang-i Sun Chang, eds. 1997. *Writing women in late imperial China*. Stanford, CA: Stanford University Press.

Williams, Raymond. 1977. *Marxism and literature*. Oxford: Oxford University Press.

Wolf, Margery. 1972. *Women and the family in rural Taiwan*. Stanford, CA: Stanford University Press.

Wu Fuhui, ed. 1997. *Ershi shiji Zhongguo xiaoshuo lilun ziliao (di san juan) 1928–1937 (Twentieth-century Chinese literary thought: A source book—Volume 3, 1928–1937)*. Beijing: Beijing daxue chubanshe.

Wu Jianren. 1960. *Henhai (Sea of regret)*. Hong Kong: Guangzhi shuju.

———, and Fu Lin. 1995. *The sea of regret: Two turn-of-the-century Chinese romantic novels*. Translated by Patrick Hanan. Honolulu: University of Hawaii Press.

Wu Menghui. 1927. Lian'ai yu geming (Love and revolution). *Taidong* 1, no. 4:29–30.

Xia Mianzun. 1927. Xiange you gan (Thoughts on a folk ballad). *Xin nüxing* 1:475–81.

Xinwenhua xuehui. 1929. Preface to the *All about love series*. Shanghai: Wei'ai cong-shu she.

Xiugu. 1928. Lian'ai shang wei chenggong, tongzhi bu xu nuli (Love has yet to suc-ceed; my fellow comrades, you needn't exert yourselves). *Taidong* 1:193–95.

Xu Qinwen. 1937. *Wu qi zhi lei (The guilt of bachelorhood)*. Shanghai: Yuzhoufeng she.

————. 1984. *Xu Qinwen xiaoshuo ji (Selected works of Xu Qinwen)*. Hangzhou: Zhe-jiang wenyi chubanshe.

Xu Zhenya. 1994. *Yu li hun; xue hong lei shi (Jade pear spirit; chronicles of bygone tears)*. Beijing: Yanshan chubanshe.

Yan, Yunxiang. 2003. *Private life under socialism: Love, intimacy, and family change in a Chinese village, 1949–1999*. Stanford, CA: Stanford University Press.

Yang, Mayfair. 1994. *Gifts, favors, and banquets: The art of social relationships in China*. Ithaca: Cornell University Press.

Yang Sao. 1930. A-er-zhi-ba-sui-fu de jiehun lun (Arcibashev's [?] theory of marriage). *Beixin*, no. 4.

Yang Xianjiang. 1925. Zhongguo qingnian de lian'ai wenti (The problem of love among Chinese youth). *Minduo (People's bell)* 6, no. 5.

Yang Yi. 1998. *Zhongguo xiandai xiaoshuo shi (A history of modern Chinese fiction)*. 3 vols. Beijing: Renmin wenxue chubanshe.

Yardley, Jim. 2004. In soccer loss, a glimpse of China's rising ire at Japan. Available at: http://www.nytimes.com/2004/08/09/international/asia/09china.html. Accessed 9 August 2004.

Yeh, Wen-hsin. 1992. Progressive journalism and Shanghai's petty urbanites: Zou Taofen and the Shenghuo enterprise, 1926–1945. In *Shanghai sojourners*, edited by Wen-hsin Yeh and Frederic Wakeman. Berkeley: University of California Press.

Yi Jiayue. 1919. Jiehun zhi zhen yiyi (The true meaning of marriage). *Guomin (Citi-zens)* 1, no. 4:1–5.

Yoneda, Shōtarō. 1927. *Lian'ai zhi jiazhi (The value of love)*. Translated by Wei Huilin. Shanghai: Minzhi shuju.

Yu Dafu. 1996. *Yu Dafu xiaoshuo quanji (The complete works of Yu Dafu)*. 2 vols. Changchun: Shidai wenyi chubanshe.

Yu Jing. 1926. Shi wo ganji bujin de (My boundless gratitude). *Funü zazhi (The ladies' journal)* 12:65–68.

Yu Qiuyu. 1985. *Zhongguo xiju wenhua shi shu (A history of Chinese drama)*. Changsha: Hunan renmin chubanshe.

Yu Runqi, ed. 1997a. *Qingmo minchu xiaoshuo shuxi: Lunli juan (Compendium of late Qing and early Republican fiction: Ethics)*. Beijing: Zhongguo wenlian chuban gongsi.

————. 1997b. *Qingmo minchu xiaoshuo shuxi: Yanqing juan (Compendium of late Qing and early Republican fiction: Romantic love)*. 2 vols. Beijing: Zhongguo wenlian chu-ban gongsi.

Yuan Changying. 1985. *Yuan Changying zuopin xuan (Selected works of Yuan Chang-ying)*. Changsha: Hunan renmin chubanshe.

Yuan Jin. 1992. *Zhongguo xiaoshuo de jindai biange (The modern transformations of Chinese fiction)*. Beijing: Zhongguo shehui kexue chubanshe.

———. 1994. *Yuanyang hudie pai (The Mandarin Duck and Butterfly School)*. Shanghai: Shanghai shudian.

Yuan Jing (Yuan Ching) and Kong Jue (Kung Chueh). 1958. *Daughters and sons*. Translated by Sidney Shapiro. Peking: Foreign Languages Press.

———. 1956. *Xin ernü yingxiong zhuan (A new tale of heroic sons and daughters)*. Beijing: Renmin wenxue chubanshe.

Yue, Gang. 1999. *The mouth that begs: Hunger, cannibalism, and the politics of eating in modern China*. Durham, NC: Duke University Press.

Zeitlin, Judith. 1993. *Historian of the strange: Pu Songling and the Chinese classical tale*. Stanford, CA: Stanford University Press.

———. 1997. Embodying the disembodied: Representations of ghosts and the feminine. In *Writing women in late imperial China*, edited by Ellen Widmer and Kang-i Sun Chang. Stanford, CA: Stanford University Press.

Zhang Ailing. 1989. *Zhang Ailing xiaoshuo ji (The fiction of Zhang Ailing)*.Taipei: Huangguan chubanshe.

Zhang Dongsun. 1926. You zili de wo dao zizhi de wo (From the egotistic self to the rational self). *Dongfang zazhi (Eastern miscellany)* 23:5–13.

Zhang Henshui. 1993. *Zhang Henshui quanji (Complete works of Zhang Henshui)*. 62 vols. Taiyuan: Beiyue wenyi chubanshe.

Zhang, Jingyuan. 1992. *Psychoanalysis in China: Literary transformations, 1919–1949*. Ithaca: Cornell East Asia Program.

Zhang Jingsheng, ed. 1928. *Aiqing dingze taolun ji (The rules of love debate)*. Shanghai: Mei de shudian.

———. 1998. *Zhang Jingsheng wenji (Collected works of Zhang Jingsheng)*. 2 vols. Guangzhou: Guangzhou chubanshe.

Zhang Xichen. 1925. Du Chen Jianshan "Youshengxue he jige xing de wenti" (On reading Chen Jianshan's "Eugenics and some questions about sex"). *Minduo (People's bell)* 6, no. 2.

———. 1926a. Lijiao yu siyu (Confucianism and selfish desire). *Xin nüxing (The new woman)* 1:309–18.

———. 1928. Weiba yiwai zhi xu—Fei fei lian'ai lun bing jiujiao yu zhuzhang zajiao zhu jun (An addition to the tail—On anti–anti-love and seeking instruction from the advocates of promiscuity). *Xin nüxing (The new woman)* 3:886–92.

———. 1931. Cong shangren dao shangren (From a merchant to a merchant). *Zhong Xuesheng (Middle-school students)* 11:51–64.

———, ed. 1926b. *Xin xing daode taolun ji (A debate on new sexual morality)*. Shanghai: Kaiming shudian.

Zhang, Yingjin. 2002. *Screening China: Critical interventions, cinematic reconfigurations, and the transnational imaginary in contemporary Chinese cinema*. Ann Arbor: Center for Chinese Studies University of Michigan.

Zhao Dongchen. 1926. Fu'ai zhi jinxi guan (Fatherly love in old and new perspectives). *Funü zazhi (The ladies' journal)* 12:55–62.

Zheng Ying. 1930. *Lian'ai jiaoyu zhi yanjiu (A study on the education of love)*. Shanghai: Shangwu yinshuguan.

Zhong Huanye. 1926. Buyuan meiyou ta er huozhe (Will not live without it). *Funü zazhi (The ladies' journal)* 12:13–17.

Zhong Mi. 1919. Zhongguo xiaoshuo li de nannü wenti (Gender relations in Chinese fiction). *Meizhou pinglun (Weekly review)*, no. 7.

Zhong, Xueping. 2000. *Masculinity besieged? Issues of modernity and male subjectivity in Chinese literature of the late twentieth century*. Durham, NC: Duke University Press.

Zhou Shoujuan. 1994. *Aiqing juzi Zhou Shoujuan (The sentimental master Zhou Shoujuan: Selected stories)*. Taipei: Yeqiang chubanshe.

Zhu Guangqian. 1928. Tan qing yu li—Gei yige zhong xuesheng de shi'er feng xin zhi jiu (On emotion and reason—The ninth of twelve letters to a middle school student). *Yiban (The ordinary)* 3:185–91.

Index